The

Boundaries

of the

Canadian Confederation

The

Boundaries

of the

Canadian Confederation

Norman L. Nicholson

The Carleton Library No. 115
Published by Macmillan of Canada
in association with The Institute of Canadian Studies,
Carleton University

Canadian Cataloguing in Publication Data

Nicholson, Norman L., 1919-
   Boundaries of the Canadian Confederation

(The Carleton library; no. 115)

Revision and enlargement of the author's The boundaries of Canada, its provinces and territories, published by the government of Canada in 1954.

Bibliography: p.
Includes index.
ISBN 0-7705-1742-0 pa.

1. Canada — Boundaries. I. Carleton University. Institute of Canadian Studies. II. Title. III. Series .

FC179.N52 1979   911'.71   C79-094162-7
F1027.5.N52 1979

Printed in Canada for
The Macmillan Company of Canada Limited
70 Bond Street, Toronto
Ontario M5B 1X3

To
Edward G. Pleva

TABLE OF CONTENTS

LIST OF FIGURES

PREFACE

The origins of this book go back to the research which I carried out for a doctoral dissertation at the University of Ottawa. That dissertation was revised and partly rewritten and published by the government of Canada as *The Boundaries of Canada, Its Provinces and Territories* in 1954. It was reissued with no substantial changes ten years later. The present book is a revision and enlargement of the earlier work largely to bring it up-to-date and to add new material which has come to my attention in the last 25 years.

I am grateful to the federal government for permission to use my earlier published material in this way. I am also grateful for this opportunity to reiterate my thanks to the many people who contributed to this book by correspondence or by personal comment. In particular I owe much to Professor R.H. Shevenell of the University of Ottawa and to Dr. B. Zaborski, Dr. T. Jost, Dr. J.W. Watson and Dr. C. Whebell who are, or were, professors of geography at McGill University, the University of Ottawa, the University of Edinburgh, and The University of Western Ontario respectively. In the preparation of the present manuscript I am deeply indebted to Valentina Czyzewski who typed it with meticulous care and to F.W. (Derry) Graves for redesigning some of the maps which appeared earlier, compiling new ones and drafting all of them.

N.L. Nicholson,
London, Ontario.
January, 1979.

CHAPTER I

INTRODUCTION[1]

Boundaries have always been of particular interest to geographers, for geography is the study of the spatial distributions that go to make the surface of the earth what it is. Early geographers measured the bounds of land and sea. Later they plotted the boundaries of the great climatic zones. Much later they concerned themselves with the boundaries between races and religions. In modern times they have become interested in every kind of boundary, physical, economic, social, or political, that may have an effect upon the geography of the land, or may derive from it.

To some, physical boundaries are much more real than human ones and are, therefore, more geographical or, at any rate, more rewarding of study by geographers. Much has been made of the influence of physiographic boundaries upon the development of Canada and it is true that the Appalachian front, the edge of the Canadian Shield, and the Cordilleran front have played a significant role in Canadian affairs. It is also true that climatic boundaries have had a great effect on Canadian population. For example, the climatic limit of the growth of wheat did much to determine the settlement of the Prairies.

Yet although the influence of physiographic, climatic, edaphic, and biotic boundaries is considerable, it is by no means the whole of geography. Human boundaries are often more important than physical ones in changing the landscape and frequently transcend and supersede them. Quite immaterial things like cultural, legal and political systems can have a profound material effect upon the development and condition of the land and the boundaries which separate such systems have a special importance.

The study of such boundaries is one aspect of the field of political geography, which is concerned with the relationships between the earth and political areas. If a political area is regarded as any piece of the earth's surface possessing governmental unity, then boundaries may be regarded as one of the basic elements of such an area. Boundaries in this sense are man-made. They are much more than lines on a map; they are functional, cultural features planted on a physical landscape, vitally related to their bordering regions.[2]

As the modern state evolved, and the demand for the establishment of clearcut boundaries arose, it became more and more necessary to know where the territory of one state ended and that of another began. Parallel with this development, however, came the problem of the increasing complexity of administration within the state. Members of a central government could not be expected to be sufficiently familiar with all the requirements of different parts of the state, hence the growth of the practice of delegating power to local authorities, whose areas of administration also called for boundaries. The necessity of boundary lines has, therefore, come with the growth of organized society, the pressure of population on resources, and the lifting and widening of the material standards of living,[3] and thus the frontier became reduced, legally, to a line.

A further development was the growth of federal states, essentially combinations of states already organized and having their own external and internal boundaries. Although federation inevitably diminished the autonomy of the participating states, it did not eliminate them, and their boundaries usually remained unchanged. A federal system implies, by its very definition, an aggregation of local governing units, each exercising certain separate powers but conceding others to the federal government.[4] Canada is such a federated state and hence its political map presents a web of boundary lines, each of which marks the limit of territory within which an administrative unit exercises authority. The fact that several federal states (e.g., the United States of America) are states composed of former sovereign states makes it necessary to distinguish the completely sovereign state by capitalizing the word. When reference is made to a component part this is not done.

"By sovereignty is meant the authority of the State to have control of, or rule over, the territory and persons and objects present there. Within the territory the State exercises its legislative power, its administration of justice and its administrative authority".[5] Canada, being a federal State, has divided some aspects of sovereignty between the federal government and the provincial governments. The provincial boundaries determine for millions of people the ideas their children shall be taught in school and the language in which they shall be taught. In Canada, education is a provincial matter, and every province has a different school system and a different syllabus of subjects. Boundaries can also determine the books, newspapers, and magazines that people shall be able to buy and read; the kind of money they shall use; the markets in which they must buy and sell; and the kinds of food they eat. For example, the sale of margarine was prohibited in the province of Quebec but permitted in the province of Ontario. To at least some extent, boundaries may restrict the movements of people, the exchange of goods, of money, even of ideas. There is no sharp line of division between the functions of international and internal boundaries,[6] but the magnitude of the effect of boundaries on persons and things must vary with the degree of authority of the political unit and the extent of the administrative powers exercised within it. As such authority decreases, so the effects of boundaries decreases, and thus, even from this point of view, there must be different types of boundaries, depending on the degree of their effects or functions.

In Canada, each administrative authority has its territorial limits defined by boundaries. A piece of land owned by an individual has its boundaries, within which that individual may exercise certain authority. His land, however, is subject to the local governing body, and this in turn is responsible to a provincial authority, which is itself, in the last analysis, responsible to the authority of the State.

Thus the State "Canada" is first delimited by boundaries. Some of these are boundaries with other States or major political units. These boundaries are usually referred to as international boundaries. International boundaries may be coextensive with the boundaries of federally controlled land, such as the Yukon Territory. The 141st Meridian separates not only Canada and the U.S.A., but also Yukon Territory and Alaska. Usually, however, the International Boundary is coextensive with provincial boundaries. The 49th Parallel separates Canada and the United States as well as British Columbia, Alberta, Saskatchewan, and most of Manitoba from the United States. The remaining boundaries of Canada are the seaward boundaries of the territorial waters and are usually referred to as "national boundaries".

Canada is, however, made up of ten provinces and two territories, each of which has its own boundaries. Not all of these boundaries separate areas with similar administrative functions. Some are true interprovincial boundaries, such as the boundary between Alberta and Saskatchewan. Sometimes, however, a boundary separates a province from a territory or from Canadian territorial waters. As the last two are under the direct jurisdiction of the federal government, such boundaries might be termed "federal-provincial". Although, as has been pointed out, provincial boundaries may coincide with international boundaries, a provincial boundary can never be coextensive with a purely national boundary because all navigable waters are under the control of the federal government. Another type of boundary separates two adjacent territories, such as the boundary between Yukon and the Northwest Territories. As both areas are under federal control, the boundary between them might be described as inter-territorial. Finally, there are boundaries within the territories, such as that between Mackenzie and Keewatin, that can be called "intra-territorial" boundaries. Figure 1 illustrates a classification along these lines.

Then each province is further subdivided into municipalities, which vary from province to province. In Nova Scotia, Ontario, and Quebec the first order of municipalities is made up of counties, which are further subdivided into cities, towns, villages, and townships, although there are minor variations even here. In the other provinces the two orders of municipalities are lacking. Instead, the municipalities are either rural or urban, the latter being made up of cities, towns, and villages, but again with variations.

But no matter how the municipalities are arranged, the smallest of them includes a multitude of further boundaries that mark the limits of private property held either by individuals or corporations. Even these may have boundaries within them that represent the limits of the smallest economic units, such as fields or city lots.

Previous Work

Studies of international boundaries are much more common than those of the internal boundaries of states. This is particularly true of Canada, and the reports of the International Boundary Commission are authoritative, comprehensive, well documented, and well illustrated.

The first comprehensive approach to the major internal boundaries of a federal State seems to have been made by the United States Geological Survey. A bulletin on this subject was published as long ago as 1885. This has been enlarged and revised six times since then, the latest edition appearing in 1964.[7]

The appearance of this pioneer work did much to focus attention on the geographical problems associated with boundary location and since then professional geographers have advanced the geographical study of boundaries very con-

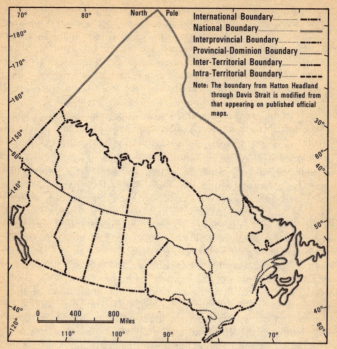

Figure 1. The major political boundaries of Canada. The
eastern part of the Arctic sector boundary from
Cape Chidley to 60 degrees east is only approx.

siderably. Prescott, in addition to general boundary studies,[8]
has long concerned himself with the boundaries of Nigeria
which culminated in the only other comprehensive book on
the major internal boundaries of a federal State.[9]

Literature on particular aspects of Canadian boundaries,
both international and internal is by no means lacking.
White[10] dealt most intensively with the international boundaries of Canada and there have been several notable studies
of the boundaries of individual provinces and regions.
Ganong's monograph on the boundaries of New Brunswick,
which was published in 1901,[11] will long remain a classic in
its field. Ireland[12] dealt with the boundaries of British Columbia, and Beriault[13] with problems that directly relate to
political boundaries in the Canadian Arctic. But demarcation
and the geographical setting of boundaries have generally
been ignored, Jones,[14] Dagenais[15] and Minghi[16] being among

the few to have published geographical studies of any parts of Canada's present boundaries until 1963 when Dorion's exhaustive treatment of all the aspects of the Quebec-Newfoundland boundary appeared.[17]

The Present Study

In studying boundaries, four basic questions arise, namely: where does the boundary occur; when and under what circumstances did it take shape; what influenced its location; how does it affect the land? A fifth question would be, has it changed, and if so where, when, and how? It is relatively easy to indicate, where existing boundaries are, but in a survey of past boundaries difficulties are experienced, either because the boundaries were not too clearly defined, and sometimes not mapped, or because the maps were not accurate. An attempt has been made in this book to show the boundaries as they actually existed.

In a growing country like Canada, boundaries have frequently changed in accordance with new situations and needs. Therefore, their development is an indication of the development of the country. Indeed, they are, in a way, the summation of the development that has gone on and that has called for final definition and recognition on the ground. The book traces the main changes in this light.

Thus the main purpose of the book is to describe the evolution and location of the boundaries, to analyze the associated problems, and to classify the types of boundaries that have arisen in Canada. It is essentially a geographical appraisal. Historical, political, and economic factors are necessarily analyzed and considered, but the emphasis has been upon the geographical reasons for, descriptions of, and results of, boundary location.

As Canada's international boundaries have an extensive literature, and as municipal and local boundaries are of strictly local importance, emphasis has been directed chiefly towards the various provincial and territorial boundaries. During the course of this work every interprovincial boundary has been crossed at least once and the geographical situation on either side examined. In addition, the International Boundary has been crossed and surveyed in a similar way at several points, and the Keewatin-Franklin boundary area has been visited. But it was neither possible nor desirable to deal fully with every detail of certain boundary controversies; a selection only has been made in order to show

how boundary problems have been dealt with in Canada in varying circumstances. Thus, the Ontario-Manitoba boundary is taken as an example of an interprovincial problem; the Canada-Newfoundland boundary as one concerning primarily two members of the Commonwealth. The solution to the New Brunswick-Quebec boundary dispute rested partly on on international agreement as well as an interprovincial one, and the boundaries between Alberta, Saskatchewan, and Manitoba exemplify modern boundary establishment in very recently developed areas. With this somewhat restricted objective, no attempt has been made to present a full statement of events that were concerned with boundaries in which is now Canada, but only those that appear to be significant in understanding the pattern of evolution of these boundaries and in determining the relationship between the evolution and geographical principles.

It is also on this basis that the selection and method of presentation of the maps is made. The maps on discovery and exploration, for example, are not intended to portray every detail or to show every voyage and journey made. The intention is rather to show the extent of the first most important expeditions and the parts of present-day Canada that were covered or touched upon. The same principle applies to boundary descriptions. The exact description is not always quoted. It appears in full if it is needed to show the inadequacy of its accuracy, or, with some of the more recent ones, the precision of the description. Some have been included in order to give the reader something of the "flavour" of the geographical language as it was used in different periods of Canada's history.

CHAPTER II

THE DEVELOPMENT OF MAJOR POLITICAL BOUNDARIES PRIOR TO 1782

Pre-European Period

Canada was, of course, populated to some extent before its existence was known to Western Europeans. These aboriginal inhabitants had their own political organizations, and although the details are not known in every respect, there is little doubt that boundaries of a sort did exist between some of the tribes. Such boundaries probably arose from the association of a group with a habitat whose food supply was regarded as exclusively its own. Hunting territory divisions were characteristic of the northern Indian tribes of Algonkian stock. These divisions constituted the main bond of union and interest in the families that composed the bands, and all male members shared the right of hunting and fishing within a particular territory. These hunting lands or territories were more or less fixed tracts of country, the boundaries of which were determined by certain rivers, ridges, lakes, or other natural landmarks such as swamps and clumps of trees.[1]

In southeastern Canada, the boundaries between Indian tribes were principally watersheds. They seem to have been continued seaward to prominent coastal features, along general lines continuing the watersheds. Thus, in what is now New Brunswick, Martins Head on the Bay of Fundy probably separated the Micmacs and Malecites, and Point Lepreau the St. John River Indians from the Passamaquoddies.[2]

On the northwest coast of British Columbia, the Indians were less migratory and had more sharply defined territorial boundaries. The Haida, Tlinkit, and Tsimshian Indians portioned out all the land on their seaboard villages among the separate families as hunting, fishing, and burying grounds.[3] These were regarded as private property and were handed on from generation to generation. If they were used by anyone other than the owner, the privilege had to be paid for.

Every salmon stream had its proprietor, whose summer camp would be set up where the run of the fish was greatest. With the Iroquois tribes, tribal property included agricultural land, on which the Indians grew corn, beans, squash, sunflowers, and tobacco, and this agricultural land they divided among the various families.

To the Eskimos, the frozen sea off some promontory often constituted a tribal sealing ground within which poachers would be killed. Even today, boundaries exist between various Eskimo families. By tacit agreement certain areas are regarded as the hunting preserve of one group to the exclusion of all others.

Thus, although boundaries between various population groups did exist, they were generally ill-defined, and varied from time to time, because the lands were not usually held in permanent occupancy and cultivation, as the people relied mainly on hunting and fishing. The pre-European boundaries had little or no effect on the evolution of the major boundary pattern of Canada as it is known today.

Proclamations of Sovereignty, 1450-1600

The visits to and possible settlements in North America by the Norsemen around 1000 A.D. had even less to do with boundary evolution in Canada than the activities of the aboriginal inhabitants. The first political boundary in North America was established in 1494 by the Treaty of Tordesillas, which delimited the "spheres of influence" of Spain and Portugal. The line agreed upon by the two countries corresponded approximately with the sixtieth meridian west, but it soon fell into desuetude, and left no trace in the present boundary pattern.[4] Canada began its development with a later period of discovery and exploration that can be characterized as a prelude to successful European settlement. This period began with the "opening" of the Newfoundland fisheries and the voyages of Cabot, Cartier, and Frobisher, and saw the first attempts at colonization.

John Cabot's voyage in 1497 was made under charter from Henry VII of England. This Royal Charter was the first political instrument specifically referring to part of what is now Canada, and resulted, in 1498, in the first formal act of possession relating to the northern part of this continent made by any European power. In that year Cabot claimed all the coast as far south as latitude 34 degrees in the name of the King of England. Similar procedures were probably

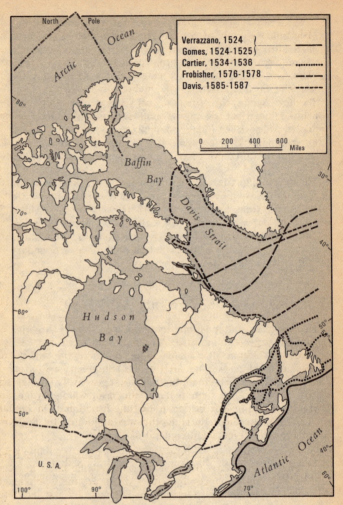

Figure 2. Major voyages of discovery and exploration in eastern Canada before 1600.

followed by such men as Fernandes, 1499, the Corte-Reals, 1500-1502 and Fagundes, 1520, for Portugal, Verrazzano, 1524, for France, and Gomez, 1524-25, for Spain. Although the voyages resulted in certain claims to general regions, these claims are not perpetuated in any boundary existent today.

The next significant step was taken by Jacques Cartier in

1534. His traditional "first voyage" through the Strait of Belle Isle and the Gulf of St. Lawrence ultimately resulted in his arrival at Gaspé Peninsula, where he set up a wooden cross as a token of his claim to that area for the King of France. His second voyage (1536) extended his discoveries to the sites of the present cities of Quebec and Montreal, and thus to the "land and province" of Canada. His third voyage (1541) made no substantial addition to geographical knowledge.

After Cartier's voyages, the "Canada" that he had discovered and named was the object of no further interest until 1542-53, when the Sieur de Roberval attempted unsuccessfully to form a settlement on the St. Lawrence. Martin Frobisher's voyages in 1576, 1577, and 1578 extended knowledge as far as Baffin Island and Hudson Strait. After Frobisher, Davis made three voyages in 1585, 1586, and 1587, during which he reached the strait named after him and explored its western shore southward from 66 degrees 40 minutes north.

Meanwhile, Sir Humphrey Gilbert, who had been given a charter in 1578 by Queen Elizabeth I, sailed with five ships and two hundred and sixty men to the island of Newfoundland. He established a colony there and proclaimed the sovereignty of his Queen over the island in 1583, but the colony came to a premature end. These were not the first people to live on the island, however, for every part of the east coast was familiar to English fishermen, who were in virtual control at the time of Gilbert's arrival. Gilbert and part of his fleet were lost on the homeward voyage and such men as he left behind joined the fishermen. On January 12, 1598, the Sieur de la Roche was appointed by the King of France as Lieutenant-General of

Canada, Hochelaga, Newfoundland, Labrador, the River of the Great Bay, of Novembegue, and the lands adjacent to the said provinces and rivers which are the whole length and depth of the country provided they are not inhabited by the subjects of any other Christian Prince.[5]

But the settlements he intended to establish met fates similar to those of Roberval and Gilbert.

A few years before this, in 1592, the Greek explorer Juan de Fuca, discovered the strait now named for him, on the Pacific coast; the discovery was not significant to Canada's boundary development until a very much later date.

Thus, in 1601, with the beginning of a new century, Canada still awaited settlement. Most of the early activities

in the New World were based on the search for a passage
to the "Far East", or on the desire for precious metals, and
were not fundamentally concerned with settlement. However,
"sovereignty" had been proclaimed over large areas of eastern
Canada, names had been added to the political map of North
America, and the stage had been set for later boundary
evolution.

The Beginnings of Settlement, 1600-1763

In 1603, Champlain followed in Cartier's footsteps up the
St. Lawrence and beyond to Lachine. The next year, with
the Sieur de Monts, he sailed to Acadia under commission
from the King of France. The commission sets forth the
first precise boundaries assigned by France in the New World
as follows:

> . . . . pour representer nôtre persone aux païs, territoires,
> côtes et confins de la Cadie, à commencer dés le quaran-
> tiéme degré jusques au quarante-sixiéme; Et en icelle
> étendue ou partie d'icelle. . . .[6]

This would appear to be the first occasion on which
parallels of latitude were used officially to describe boundaries
in Canada, limits, 40 to 46 degrees, which were intended to
include the region between Cape Cod and Cape Breton.
De Monts and his expedition explored the Bay of Fundy and
the harbour at the mouth of St. John River and then went
on to the present St. Croix River, near the mouth of which
they spent the winter of 1604-05. In a new voyage in 1608,
Champlain founded and named Quebec – the first settlement
in Canada that has had an uninterrupted existence to the
present day, although long before the founding of Quebec
there was a permanent trading post at the mouth of the
Saguenay that was probably established by Basque fishermen
early in the 16th century. During the following years Champlain explored the country in various directions. Among
other things, he discovered the lake that bears his name,
ascended the Ottawa River, and crossed to Georgian Bay.
At his death in 1634, however, New France was little more
than an outpost in the wilderness.

Meanwhile, the English had been settling Virginia, the
boundaries of which had been fixed by charter of King
James I in 1606, allowing the London Company to form
settlements between 34 degrees north and 38 degrees north:
the Plymouth Company also was allowed to form settlements

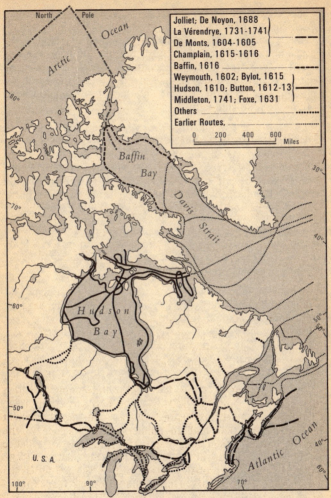

Figure 3. Major voyages of discovery and exploration in eastern Canada between 1600 and 1763.

between 41 degrees and 45 degrees of latitude. It has been suggested that the southern limit of these claims can be traced back to the fact that Cabot reached 34 degrees north in 1497.[7] It is also worth noting that it was in the Plymouth Company charter of 1606 that the 45th parallel was mentioned for the first time as a political boundary, although the true genesis of its present use as a political boundary may stem from a Dutch charter of 1614.[8]

The boundaries of these British colonies overlapped the French claims, and conflict ensued. But in 1620 King James I gave a new patent to the Plymouth Company that extended their northern boundary to 48 degrees, and included not only the coast region but the interior of the continent as well, in the following terms:

> . . . . all that Circuit, Continent, Precincts, and Limitts, in America, lying and being in Breadth from Fourty Degrees of Northerly Latitude, from the Equnoctiall Line, to Fourty-eight Degrees of the said Northerly Latitude, and in Length by all the Breadth aforesaid, throughout the Maine Land, from Sea to Sea . . . shall be the Limitts, and Bounds and Precincts of the said second Collony. . . .[9]

The extension was probably made in order to establish a British claim to Acadia, but it did not remain in force long, for the next year James I made a grant of Nova Scotia to Sir William Alexander in the following terms:

> . . . . all and single, the lands of the Continent and islands situated and lying in America, within the head or promontory commonly called Cape of Sable, lying near the forty-third degree of north latitude, or thereabouts; from this Cape, stretching along the shores of the Sea, westward to the roadstead of St. Mary, commonly called St. Mary's Bay, and thence northward by a straight line, crossing the entrance, or mouth, of that great roadstead Bay of Fundy which runs toward the eastern part of the land between the countries of the Suriqui and Etchimine, commonly called Suriquois and Etchimines, to the river generally known by the name St. Croix, and to the remotest springs, or source, from the western side of the same, which empty into the first mentioned river; thence by an imaginary straight line which is conceived to extend through the land, or run northward to the nearest bay, river, or stream emptying into the great river of Canada; and going from that eastward along the low shores of the same river of Canada to the river, harbour, port, or shore, commonly known and called by the name Gathepe or Gaspie, and thence south-southeast to the isles called Bacalos or Cape Breton, leaving the said isles on the right, and the mouth of the said great river of Canada, or large bay, and the territory of Newfoundland, with the islands belonging to the same lands on the left; thence to the headland, or point

of Cape Breton aforesaid, lying near latitude forty-five degrees or thereabouts; and from the said point of Cape Breton toward the south and west to the above mentioned Cape Sable, where the boundary began; including and containing within the said coasts and their circumference, from sea to sea, all lands of the continent with the rivers, falls, bays, shores, islands, or seas, lying near or within six leagues on any side of the same on the west, north or east sides of the same coasts and bounds and on the south-southeast (where Cape Breton lies) and on the south side of the same (where Cape Sable is) all seas and islands south-ward within forty leagues of said seashore, thereby includ-ing the large island commonly called Isle de Sable or Sablon, lying towards Carban, in common speech south-southeast about thirty leagues from the said Cape Breton seaward and being in latitude forty-four Degrees or there-abouts. . . .[10]

This delimitation was remarkable in that it was the first national patent that ever was clearly bounded within America by particular and specific geographical features. There were, however, two inconsistencies in these boundaries. First of all they overlapped those of the grants to the Plymouth Com-pany, but this difficulty was easily solved when the Plymouth Company relinquished its claim to the area common with the Alexander grant. Secondly, they, like their other British predecessors, overlapped the boundaries of the area claimed by France. This was particularly important, because in 1627, the King of France granted a charter to the Company of One Hundred Associates for the development and govern-ment of New France, the boundaries of which were defined as extending from Florida to the Arctic Circle, and from Newfoundland on the east to the "great fresh water sea" on the west, including all the "lands in the watershed of the St. Lawrence and its tributaries, and of the other rivers of Canada which flow into the sea, as well as any other lands over which the company may extend the French authority". In 1627 war broke out between the two countries. This temporarily terminated with the Treaty of St. Germain-en-Laye in 1632, which restored all places in Acadia to France but in the meantime, the first Scottish settlement in Nova Scotia had been made in 1629, when colonies were planted on the eastern coast of Cape Breton Island and at Port Royal.[11]

In 1635 the Council for New England granted Lord William Alexander, son of Sir William Alexander, a tract of land adjacent to that granted to his father in 1621. Despite these events, however, Cromwell, Lord Protector of Great Britain, in 1656, granted most of the present Nova Scotia, New Brunswick, and Prince Edward Island to Thomas Temple and two associates. But a further outbreak of war with France, which terminated with the Treaty of Breda in 1667, also restored to France all Acadia, which had a local Governor responsible to the Governor of Quebec. Intermittent disputes over the interpretation of these treaties occurred between France and Britain, which in 1686 resulted in an agreement between the monarchs of the two countries. This agreement recognized the need for drawing a boundary line between the respective possessions of the two countries in the New World and provided for the settlement of this boundary by a joint commission.[12] But it was never put into effect. Open warfare between the two countries broke out again in 1689. It concluded in 1697 with the Treaty of Ryswick, which again restored the British conquests to France, but the war of 1702-1713, which terminated with the Treaty of Utrecht (1713), resulted in the French surrender of her interests in Nova Scotia (Acadia, but not including Cape Breton Island) and Newfoundland (except for certain fishing rights) to the British. During the negotiations regarding the treaty, reference was made to the boundaries between the French and English areas, but the language of the treaty with regard to them remained vague.

In the meantime, the voyages of Frobisher and Davis in the Hudson Bay area had been followed up. A series of expeditions started by Henry Hudson in 1610 was continued by Sir Thomas Button in 1612 and 1613. Button erected a cross at the mouth of Nelson River and took possession of those parts in the name of Great Britain. Robert Bylot and William Baffin followed in 1615 and 1616, and Captains Foxe and James in 1631, each taking formal possession of the places where he landed. But further political development in this area had to wait for 40 years until 1670, when Prince Rupert and seventeen associates obtained from King Charles II a charter as the Governor and Company of Adventurers of England trading into Hudson's Bay. The boundaries of the territory over which the Company were to be "true and absolute lords" were defined as follows:

> . . . . all these seas, straits, bays, rivers, lakes, creeks and sounds in whatsoever latitude they shall be, that lie within the entrance of the straits, commonly called Hudson's Straits, together with all the lands and territories upon the

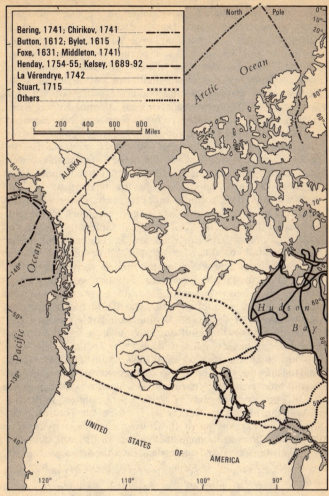

Figure 4. Major voyages of discovery and exploration in western Canada before 1763.

countries, coasts, and confines of the seas, bays, lakes, rivers, creeks and sounds aforesaid, that are not already actually possessed by or granted to any of our subjects, or possessed by the subjects of any other Christian Prince or State, . . . and that the said lands be . . . called "Rupert's Land".[13]

This area has generally been taken to be the entire area draining into Hudson Bay. But the charter went even beyond "Rupert's land". Where their own government ended, the Company were to have the sole right of trade in all the "havens, bays, creeks, rivers, lakes and seas", into which they could find passage from their own area. Their first step was to place trading posts around the shores of Hudson's Bay, and by 1682 these had been established at Rupert River, Albany River, Hayes Island, Port Nelson, and New Severn.[14]

France disputed the Hudson's Bay Company's claim from the start, particularly because the French missionaries and traders had extended and consolidated Champlain's discoveries, and it was not until the Treaty of Utrecht that France relinquished her claims, although the final treaty did not establish any definite limits between the territory of France and that of the Hudson's Bay Company. Thus at the conclusion of the war of 1702 to 1713, Canada, Cape Breton Island, Labrador, Anticosti Island, and the present Prince Edward Island remained French, but the boundaries between these territories and those of the British to the north and south of them were not precisely delimited and remained a matter of dispute. However, the treaty provided for the appointment of commissioners to settle such disputes, and of the efforts of these commissioners, those concerned with the boundary of the Hudson's Bay Company lands are of greatest significance here. Indeed, the Treaty of Ryswick provided that the question of the ownership of the posts on Hudson's Bay should be left to the decision of a joint Anglo-French commission, but although a commission appointed for this purpose did meet in 1699, it accomplished nothing.

Again, prior to the Treaty of Utrecht, the Hudson's Bay Company stated the terms it wished to have incorporated in the treaty about to be concluded, although this was not done. In 1714, the Company again described its limits as follows:

. . . . and from the said Lake (Mistassini) a Line to Run Southwestward Into 49 Degree North Latitude . . . and that the Latitude be the Limitt. . . .[15]

This is significant if only for the fact that it is the first official mention of the 49th Parallel in connection with a boundary line. A further proposal followed in 1719, and the British Government instructed the commissioners to obtain the boundary as follows:

That the same begin from the Island called Grimington's Island or Cape Perdrix in the Latitude of 58½ North . . .

further, That a Line be drawn from the South Westward of the Island of Grimington or Cape Perdrix (so as to include the same within the limits of the Bay) to the Great Lake Misconsinke alias Mistosseny, dividing the said Lake into two Parts . . . and that where the said Line shall cut the 49th Degree of Northern Latitude, another Line shall begin and be extended Westward from the said Lake, upon the 49th Degree of Northern Latitude . . . .[16]

However, the commissioners accomplished nothing, but various historians and cartographers confused these attempts to settle boundaries with actual settlement, a situation that became significant at a later date.

Between 1713 and 1763, France made a determined effort to secure a firm foothold on the interior of North America. Her missionaries and traders pushed west of the Great Lakes into parts of what is now western Canada. This phase of development was most marked by the work of Daniel de Greysolon, Sieur du Lhut, which began in 1678. It was extended by Jacques de Noyon, who arrived at Lake of the Woods in 1688, and the work of both culminated in the voyages of the Sieur de la Vérendrye and his sons. Between them they crossed what is now southern Manitoba (1731), certainly reached the edge of the Rocky Mountains (1742), and may have penetrated much farther to the westward.

In 1741, war again broke out between France and Britain. It concluded in 1748 with statesmen on both sides realizing that the old boundary question had to be definitely and finally settled. For the next 15 years, three distinct methods were used to bring about a decision. The first two – an International Joint Commission and direct diplomacy – failed. The third – open warfare – succeeded, and the years 1756 to 1763 saw the final struggle between France and Britain in North America that was finally resolved by Wolfe's conquest of Quebec.

The Treaty of Paris and its Results

The Treaty of Paris produced the greatest rearrangement of boundaries in North America that had hitherto occurred. It is for this reason that the war that immediately preceded it is sometimes called the "War of the Boundary Lines". France now definitely withdrew from the mainland of North America. She ceded to Britain, Canada, Cape Breton Island, most of the islands in the Gulf of St. Lawrence, all of the then Nova Scotia, and all her former territories east of Mississippi River, except New Orleans, which went to Spain. She also ceded to Spain all her former territory west of Mississippi River from the Gulf of Mexico northwards to the sources of Missouri River, known as Louisiana. Britain gained the Spanish possessions east and southeast of Mississippi River, which included Florida, and thus, at this date, the entire eastern half of the North American continent was British territory. All boundary questions in this area now became questions between provinces, all under one crown. All that remained to France were the islands of St. Pierre and Miquelon off the coast of Newfoundland. The islands had been captured by the British in 1702 but were returned to France in 1763 "to serve as a shelter for the French fishermen . . . not to fortify the said islands, to erect no buildings upon them but merely for the convenience of the fishery."[17]

Having acquired so much new territory, it then became necessary for Britain to provide the machinery by which it could be governed. In that part of the territory that now forms part of Canada, three political areas had existed prior to 1763 – Quebec, Newfoundland, and Nova Scotia. These were retained, but the boundaries were more precisely delimited. In the case of Quebec, the precise boundaries presented some problems, for, as early as 1762, the British military governors in Quebec and Montreal had stated that it was impossible to ascertain exactly what part of North America the French styled Canada, although from the trade they carried on it appeared that Canada included all the Great Lakes and the Mississippi basin above the junction of that river with the Illinois. But to place all this area under one colonial jurisdiction at the close of the war was considered unwise by the British Board of Trade and Plantations. First of all, formal inclusion within Canada might imply that the British title to these lands was the result of the Treaty of Utrecht, whereas it was considered to rest on antecedent rights, an impression the British wished particularly to convey to the Indians. Secondly, if the Indian territory were annexed to one particular province and subjected to its laws, that province would have an unfair advantage over the other provinces with respect to the Indian trade. Thirdly, the laws of the province could not be enforced without establishing military garrisons throughout the area, which, even if it were feasible, might possibly cause friction between the civil and military governors. Finally, it was suggested that the boundaries of Canada should be restricted in order to prevent settlement from spreading too far from established government, trade, and communication.[18]

Therefore, in 1763, a Royal Proclamation was issued describing the boundaries of Quebec as follows:

> . . . . bounded on the Labrador coast by the River St. John and from thence by a Line drawn from the Head of that River, through the Lake St. John, to the South end of the Lake Nipissim; from whence the said Line, crossing the River St. Lawrence, and the Lake Champlain, in 45 Degrees of North Latitude, passes along the High Lands which divide the Rivers that empty themselves into the said River St. Lawrence from those which fall into the Sea; and also along the North Coast of the Baye des Chaleurs and the Coast of the Gulph of St. Lawrence to Cape Rosieres, and from thence crossing the mouth of the River St. Lawrence by the West End of the Island of Anticosti, terminates at the aforesaid River of St. John.[19]

Lake St. John is the source of Saguenay River, whereas Lake Nipissing is connected by French River to Georgian Bay and Lake Huron. From Lake Nipissing the boundary ran to the west of, and parallel with, the Ottawa River until it met the St. Lawrence at the Long Sault Rapids. Thus the "core area" of French settlement was enclosed within the province. Its internal communications were maintained, yet from its borders easy access to the Indian territory and the other British provinces for trading purposes was preserved.

The same Royal Proclamation assigned to the Government of Newfoundland the "coast" of North America from "the River St. John's to Hudson's streights, together with the Islands of Anticosti and Madelaine, and all other smaller islands lying upon the said Coast".[20] The purpose of this award to Newfoundland was to allow its fishermen to extend their codfishing operations to the coast of Labrador and the adjacent islands, and the western boundary had been fixed at River St. John's (the present Rivière St. Jean) in the belief that the French Canadians had no settlements east of it.

All other parts of the mainland north of the St. Lawrence, not included in Quebec, Newfoundland, or the territory granted to the Hudson's Bay Company, were assigned to the Crown.

The islands of St. John and Cape Breton, or Isle Royale, with the lesser islands adjacent thereto, were annexed to the Government of Nova Scotia.

The boundaries of Nova Scotia were set forth in greater

detail in the commission to Montague Wilmot, as Governor of the Province, under date of November 21, 1763, as follows:

> . . . To the northward our said province shall be bounded by the southern boundary of our Province of Quebec, as far as the western extremity of the Baye des Chaleurs, to the eastward by the said Bay and the gulf of St. Lawrence to the Cape or Promontory called Cape Breton in the Island of that name including that Island, the Island of St. John's and all other Islands within six leagues of the coast, to the southward by the Atlantic Ocean from the said Cape to Cape Sable including all other islands, within forty leagues of the coast, with all the rights, members and appurtenances whatever thereunto belonging and to the westward, although our said province hath anciently extended and doth of right extend as far as the River Pentagoet or Penobscot, it shall be bounded by a line drawn from Cape Sable across the entrance of the Bay of Fundy to the mouth of the River St. Croix, by the said river to its source and by a line drawn due north from thence to the southern boundary of our Colony of Quebec.[21]

The reasons for this unification of the Maritimes were chiefly to consolidate Great Britain's claims to the area. The part that was later to become New Brunswick had been claimed by Britain as a legal and integral part of Nova Scotia for half a century, although civil government was not established. But with the withdrawal of the French forces, the government of Nova Scotia was able, for the first time, to exercise effective authority. St. John's Island and Cape Breton Island, which had been expressly granted to France in 1713, now had to be provided with new government. Thus the annexation of these three areas to Nova Scotia was not only the best, but almost the only solution. It was not a union of colonies, but merely an extension of territorial jurisdiction.[22]

British North America Before the Revolution, 1763-1782

From 1763, the territorial expansion of Canada was purely British, and it was from this date that definite political boundaries began to emerge. The emergence of these boundaries was, for the greater part of the period, connected with political developments in the colonies south of Quebec and Nova Scotia.

The Quebec Act 1774 stemmed from such developments, as well as from the need to make some further provision for administration of the country outside the limits of the Quebec of 1763. Eleven years had passed since it had been decided to leave the area west of Quebec as an Indian reserve. It was maintained that the area had become "the theatre of disorder and confusion"[23] and the time had now arrived for some recognized law and government to be extended to it. More was now known about the area; such permanent settlers as it had were French rather than British, and it was obviously better for them to be included with Quebec rather than with any of the purely British colonies. It was also thought that the Indians would be better cared for under the government of Quebec. Furthermore, the waterways made communication to the west easier from Canada than from the southern colonies. Thus the new southern and western boundaries of Quebec remained as they had been since 1763, as far as the intersection of the 45th parallel with the river. From this point they followed the St. Lawrence and the Great Lakes up to the point on the south shore of Lake Erie where the old French route to the Ohio left it. From this point the boundary ran across country to the Ohio and thence to the Mississippi.

The act also restored Labrador, Anticosti, and the Magdalen Islands to Quebec, and the boundaries of the old province were further defined as extending north to the Hudson's Bay Company's territories. The interval between 1774 and the Royal Proclamation of 1763 had also shown that the French Canadians had a variety of claims upon the coast of Labrador between St. John River and the Strait of Belle Isle. It was discovered that a cod fishery was impracticable off the greater part of the coast and that it could be used only "for that species of sedentary Seal Fishery which is in its nature inconsistent with the Regulations of the Fishery at Newfoundland".[24] Consequently, when the Governor of Newfoundland issued a regulation in 1765 forbidding the sedentary fishermen of Quebec to fish on the coast of Labrador, they protested, and the Lord of Trade in London proposed, in 1772, that the southwestern section of the Labrador coast between the River St. John and the Anse des Espagnols should be restored to Quebec. Ultimately, however, it was decided that this partition would be inadequate to protect the interests of the Quebec fishermen, and the whole of Labrador was transferred to their province.

The boundary clause of the Quebec Act of 1774 was as follows:

> bounded on the South by a Line from the Bay of Chaleurs, along the High Lands which divide the Rivers that empty themselves into the River Saint Lawrence from those which fall into the Sea, to a Point in Forty-five Degrees of Northern Latitude, on the Eastern Bank of the River Connecticut, keeping the same Latitude directly West, through the Lake Champlain, until, in the same Latitude, it meets the River Saint Lawrence; from thence up the Eastern Bank of the said River to the Lake Ontario; thence through the Lake Ontario, and the River commonly called Niagara; and thence along by the Eastern and South-eastern Bank of Lake Erie, following the said Bank, until the same shall be intersected by the Northern Boundary, granted by the Charter of the Province of Pennsylvania, in case the same shall be so intersected; and from thence along the said Northern and Western Boundaries of the said Province, until the said Western Boundary strike the Ohio; But in case the said Bank of the said Lake shall not be found to be so intersected, then following the said Bank until it shall arrive at that Point of the said Bank which shall be nearest to the North-western Angle of the said Province of Pennsylvania, and thence, by a right Line, to the said North-western Angle of the said Province; and thence along the Western Boundary of the said Province, until it strike the River Ohio; and along the Bank of the said River, Westward, to the Banks of the Mississippi, and Northward to the Southern Boundary of the Territory granted to the Merchants Adventurers of England, trading to Hudson's Bay; and also such Territories, Islands, and Countries, which have, since the Tenth of February, One Thousand seven hundred and sixty-three been made Part of the Government of Newfoundland, be, and they are hereby, during His Majesty's Pleasure, annexed to, and made Part and Parcel of, the Province of Quebec.[25]

Thus was the contention met that the trade and prosperity of Quebec had suffered from the separation of the upper Indian trading posts and the coast of Labrador from Canada. Thus, too, were all the Illinois country and all the western lands for which Britain and France had fought confirmed to Canada.

But it must also be mentioned that a far from minor reason for the westward extension of Quebec was the fact that the southern colonies were on the verge of revolution and that

Britain was, therefore, loth to trust them with the Indian territory. Unfortunately, the passage of the Quebec Act was taken as a further provocation by the southern colonies, as they objected to the great extension southward of the boundaries of Quebec, which would interfere with the westward expansion of all the colonies lying north of the 37th parallel (the latitude of the mouth of the Ohio). In 1776, they revolted and declared their independence.

Meanwhile, the expulsion of the Acadians from St. John's Island in 1758, and the withdrawal of the French military forces, had left the island almost deserted. In order to begin to recolonize this territory, the British Government sent a surveyor to the island in 1764. At that time only thirty families were living on the island, in an extremely poor condition. After the survey, the land was granted to absentee proprietors in England, and by 1767 the whole of the island had been disposed of in this manner. However, no sooner had the landlords received their grants from the Governor of Nova Scotia than they felt the necessity for a capital seat within their own territory.[26] They petitioned the king for the complete separation of their island from the mainland, stressing the inconvenience of having to refer all judicial and legal matters to Halifax. At the best of times the journey to Halifax was tedious and expensive, and during the winter months it was impracticable because of ice. They also pointed out that the peninsula of Nova Scotia, with settlement projects of its own, could hardly be expected to give energetic support to immigration schemes for the island, and they could hardly have been unmindful of the risk of their own proprietary rights involved in prolonged control by the Halifax legislature with its New England traditions of liberalism.[27] The island was, therefore, separated from Nova Scotia in 1769; it was renamed Prince Edward Island in 1798.

Some of the Acadian expatriates had gone to St. Pierre and Miquelon, but in 1778, following upon France's declaration of war against Britain, the British Navy was instructed to take possession of the islands and remove the inhabitants.[28]

Thus, by 1782, settlement in parts of what is now southern Canada had become firmly established. Proclamations of sovereignty had been made in northern Canada and definite delimitations of territory had been made comprising six divisions – the provinces of Quebec, Nova Scotia, and St. John's Island (Ile St. Jean), the Hudson's Bay Company territories, Newfoundland, and certain lands belonging directly to the Crown. Although these delimitations contained what later proved to be inconsistencies, they had been settled according to the geographical lights of the time, but no attempt was made to demarcate these legal lines on the ground. The American revolution was drawing to a close, foreshadowing boundary changes of even more significance to Canada than those that had preceded it.

CHAPTER III

THE DEVELOPMENT OF MAJOR POLITICAL BOUNDARIES FROM 1782 TO 1866

After 6 years of warfare, negotiations for peace began between Great Britain and the American colonies. These were concluded in 1783 by the Treaty of Paris, following which the United States of America came officially into being. It is from this date that Canada's present southern international boundary began to take more definite shape. Indeed the American revolution had such a profound effect on Canada that it was almost refounded as a result of it.

International Consequences of the American Revolution

One effect of the American Revolution was to reverse Great Britain's relative position as it had existed at the time of the Treaty of Ryswick. So far as territorial claims and counter-claims were concerned, Great Britain, after the revolution, occupied France's former position, and the United States Great Britain's. It was natural then that the United States should press for the same boundaries between themselves and Canada as Britain had claimed against the French. The ultimate result was that Great Britain retained the Quebec, Nova Scotia, and Newfoundland of 1763; St. Pierre and Miquelon were restored to France and the inhabitants evacuated in 1778 enabled to return, and the Illinois Country and the lands south and west of the Great Lakes that had been included in Quebec by the Act of 1774 were lost to the U.S.A. The original limits between the United States and British territory were first definitely described in the provisional treaty of November 30, 1782, and the definitive treaty of peace, concluded September 3, 1783, defined them in similar terms as follows:

. . . from the North-west Angle of Nova Scotia, viz., that Angle which is formed by a line drawn due North, from the source of St. Croix River to the Highlands, along the said Highlands which divide those Rivers that empty themselves into the River St. Lawrence from those which fall into the Atlantic Ocean, to the North-western-most head of Connecticut River; thence down along the middle of that River to the 45th degree of North latitude; from whence by a line due West on said latitude until it strikes the River Iroquois or Cataraquy[1]; thence along the middle of the said River into Lake Ontario; through the middle of said Lake until strikes the communication by water between that Lake and Lake Erie; thence along the middle of said communication into Lake Erie; through the middle of said Lake until it arrives at the water-communication between that Lake and Lake Huron; thence along the middle of said water-communication into the Lake Huron; thence through the middle of said Lake to the water-communication between that Lake and Lake Superior; thence through Lake Superior, Northward of the Isles Royal and Phelipeaux, to the Long Lake[2]; thence through the middle of said Long Lake, and the water-communication between it and the Lake of the Woods, to the said Lake of the Woods; thence through the said Lake to the most North-western point thereof, and from thence on a due West course to the River Mississippi; thence by a line to be drawn along the middle of the said River Mississippi, until it shall intersect the Northmost part of the 31st degree of North Latitude; South by a line to be drawn due East from the determination of the line last mentioned, in the latitude of 31 degrees North of the Equator, to the middle of the River Apalachicola or Catahouche; thence along the middle thereof to its junc-tion with the Flint River; thence straight to the head of St. Mary's River, and thence down along the middle of St. Mary's River to the Atlantic Ocean: East by a line to be drawn along the middle of the River St. Croix, from its mouth in the Bay of Fundy to its source; and from its source directly North to the aforesaid Highlands, which divide the Rivers that fall into the Atlantic Ocean from those which fall into the River St. Lawrence: comprehend-ing all Islands within 20 leagues of any part of the shores of The United States, and lying between lines to be drawn due East from the points where the aforesaid Boundaries between Nova Scotia on the one part, and East Florida on the other, shall respectively touch the Bay of Fundy, and the Atlantic Ocean; excepting such Islands as now are, or heretofore have been, within the limits of the said Province of Nova Scotia.[3]

After the usual compromises between the two sides had been agreed upon, the precise location of the boundary was probably based on the application to the existing maps of the time of principles previously adopted. The idea of dividing each of the Great Lakes (except Michigan) into two parts had first appeared in the Quebec Act of 1774, and it must have appeared logical to extend the lake boundary to the western shore of Lake Superior. The boundary farther westward must also have appeared to be a logical extension of the river-lake line, particularly as the map the negotiators had before them was one made by John Mitchell in 1755 that showed Lake of the Woods and its water connection with Lake Superior. However, in deciding upon this section of the boundary, the British negotiators overlooked the fact that in agreeing that the United States should have Grand Portage they were dealing a severe blow to the Canadian fur trade. This portage route was of the greatest economic importance to Canada, for by it passed the goods of the Montreal fur merchants en route to the western territory and down it came furs worth £200,000 a year. The new boundary prevented the use of this route, as the topography of the country on the north or British bank of the river made a portage there impossible. The North West Company, therefore, employed two men to search for another route from Lake Superior to Lake Winnipeg entirely within British territory. They found a canoe route from Lake Superior by way of Lake Nipigon, Sturgeon Lake, and English River to Portage de l'Isle on Winnipeg River, but this route was so inconvenient and difficult that it was never adopted by the traders. Furthermore, owing to disputes between the British and United States governments regarding the implementation of some of the terms of the treaty in 1783, the Grand Portage route continued to be used by the Canadians for another 17 or 18 years. When finally compelled to abandon it, the traders used the Kaministiquia route, which had, fortunately, been "rediscovered" in 1798. Only a few miles north of the new international boundary, it had been used by the French traders before 1763 and then forgotten.

In any case, by this time, other controversial points about the boundary had come to a head. Mitchell's map was so inaccurate that at least nine distinct boundary problems arose.[4] The Treaty of London, 1794 (Jay's Treaty), began the process of clarifying these. Among other things, the treaty also provided for the protection of the fur trade and the security of the Grand Portage route by permitting the free passage of both traders and goods across the portage on both sides of the boundary.[5]

Under the fifth article of this treaty, commissioners were appointed to deal with another of these problems. They were asked to determine exactly what river was truly intended under the name of the River St. Croix in the Treaty of Peace in 1783. This had become an acute problem when Nova Scotia proceeded to grant land on the eastern bank of Schoodic River to Loyalist refugees from the United States, and Massachusetts requested the Governor of Nova Scotia to recall "those subjects of His Majesty" who had settled in what he considered to be Massachusetts. Excavations at the mouth of the Schoodic disclosed the remains of the Sieur de Mont's winter camp of 1604 and conclusively identified it as the St. Croix of Champlain;[6] the commissioners decided accordingly on October 25, 1798.

Internal Consequences of the American Revolution

The independence of the United States affected Canadian boundaries in other ways also. In all cases, however, the ultimate cause of the change was due to the fact that, at the close of the Revolutionary War, thousands of Loyalists moved into what remained of British North America. Naturally they took up lands in those areas that had hitherto been unsettled.

In Nova Scotia, these lands were mainly in the St. John Valley and along the north shore of the Bay of Fundy, and it was to these areas that most of the Loyalists went in eastern Canada. This sudden advent of thousands of immigrants, many of whom were destitute, created judicial and administrative problems with which the government of Halifax was unable to deal adequately, particularly as it had equally urgent problems nearer home owing to immigration to various parts of its peninsular territory. The apparent neglect by the authorities in Halifax and the delays in the issue of land patents only accentuated the inconvenience that had been felt before the Loyalists influx, owing to the fact that the remoter parts of the province lacked courts and land offices and also an adequate voice in the Assembly. Consequently, in 1784, New Brunswick was established as a separate colony, the division being made from Cumberland Arm of the Bay of Fundy across the Chignecto Isthmus to Baie Verte. However, as strong a motive for this decision was the "divide and rule" policy of the British authorities. With the experience of the American revolution fresh in their minds, they took the view that small, separate colonies would show less independence than large ones. "The object . . . was to govern by means of division, to break them down as much as possible into petty isolated communities, incapable of combination, and possessing no sufficient strength for individual resistance to the Empire".[7] Indeed, the British government must have been particularly satisfied at seeing a separate Loyalist government erected between the New England states and peninsular Nova Scotia, whose conduct during the revolution had been under considerable suspicion. This was hardly surprising, as on the eve of the Revolution more than half of the population was classified as American. The British Under Secretary of State for the Colonies had even suggested the creation of another province between New Brunswick and Maine.[8]

About 3,000 Loyalists went to Cape Breton Island – a relatively small number. After the peace of 1763, no grants of lands were made on the island, in order to prevent monopolies and encourage the fisheries, as the French had done. Licences to occupy fishing lots were issued, but no other legal title. This situation continued, at first, to apply to Loyalists after the American Revolution. They could obtain free grants and other allowances in the rest of Nova Scotia but not on Cape Breton Island. Consequently, most of them followed the majority of the older inhabitants in the exploitation of the fisheries. Owing to these unique conditions, as there were no absolute titles to land, the inhabitants were not freeholders and could not send representatives to a constitutional assembly. Consequently, special legislation had to be drafted for Cape Breton, and it was, therefore, separated from Nova Scotia in 1784.

In Quebec, most of the unsettled lands were southwest of the Ottawa River and along the north shores of Lakes Erie and Ontario. Before 1763, as has been pointed out, the French did considerable exploration, not only in what is now Canada but also in the whole of North America. Apart from long overland journeys such as those of the La Vérendryes, they explored intensively the area about the Great Lakes. But their areas of settlement never extended much farther west than Montreal. Indeed, it was not until after the signing of the peace treaty between the French and the Iroquois in 1700, which removed the threat of Indian aggression, that the land northwest and west of Montreal was cleared and settled. This area was first divided in 1702, when two seigniories were granted to Pierre Joybert de Soulanges and Philippe Rigaud de Vaudreuil; the seigniories of Rigaud and Nouvelle Longueuil were added in 1732 and 1734 respectively. Land clearance and settlement proceeded very slowly until 1763, however, when a more determined effort was made to find settlers at "the eleventh hour of the French dominion".[9]

In the Ottawa Valley, although a pioneer farmer had cleared land near Chats Falls in 1776, little other settlement occurred before 1796. Only one grant of land had been made during the French régime in what is today the Ontario part of the valley, when the seigniory of Pointe à l'Orignal was granted to François Provost in 1674. It extended along the south shore of Ottawa River for 6 miles, and inland for 6 miles, and with the grant went the right to fish, hunt, trade with the Indians, and exploit any minerals found within its limits. Today the area is occupied by the township of Longueuil, named after the family to which the seigniory eventually passed. It was their intention to colonize it, but the first concession was not granted until February 24, 1791, and by 1792 it had only four inhabitants.

In the extreme southwest of the province, settlement was associated with the post established after 1701 by the French at Detroit on the north bank of Detroit River. But as late as 1748, there was only one permanent white settler on the south shore of the river. During the following year 22 grants of land were made to immigrants from the District of Montreal all being long narrow strips fronting on the river in the typical river-front pattern of the French Canadians. In 1750 the only seigniory granted in this part of the present Ontario was made to Paul Joseph Le Moyne. He did not settle on his land but there is some evidence that he may have subgranted to it several habitant families.[10] A few British settlers came to the area after 1763, and there was a slight increase after 1783 owing to the development of the fur trade.

Thus the majority of the 10,000 Loyalists who had settled between the Detroit River and Montreal were west of the Cedars and Coteau rapids on the St. Lawrence below Lake St. Francis, and between the lands granted in seigniory and the small settlement near what is now Windsor. The French feudal system of land tenure was contrary to the ideas of these Loyalists, who held their land in free and common

socage and they also resented the absence of popular government to which they had been accustomed in the former
colonies that were now part of the United States. Some 1,300
Loyalists had settled around Cataraqui, on the site of the
present Kingston, and in 1785 a petition was presented on
behalf of the new settlers asking for the creation of a district
distinct from the province of Quebec whose capital should
be Cataraqui and that the "blessings of the British Laws . . .
and an exemption from the (French) tenures . . . be extended
to the settlement". It also drew attention to the delay in the
administration of justice while the area remained part of
Quebec "the distance from Detroit to Montreal being not
less than Six Hundred Miles, without any Road whatsoever,
and the water communication exceedingly tedious, precarious,
and during the winter season, absolutely impassable".[11] Many
similar petitions followed this and ultimately the British
government took definite steps to divide the province of
Quebec at the boundary of the seigniory granted to De
Longueuil. So far as the settlers near Detroit were concerned,
it was the opinion of Dorchester, the Governor of Quebec,
that they would not choose to migrate to the lower part of
the province even if good land was offered to them. If they
did move it would be "attended with much inconvenience,
as would their being left insulated and attached to the
district of Montreal". He, therefore, merely advised that care
should be taken to secure their property and civil rights. The
Constitutional Act of 1791 merely declared the Royal intention to divide the province of Quebec into two separate
provinces to be called Upper Canada and Lower Canada.
Precise boundaries were not mentioned because of the difficulty of describing the boundaries between the two provinces
and the United States, which depended upon the clarification
of certain matters arising from the Treaty of Paris of 1783.
The interprovincial boundary was ultimately described by an
Order in Council dated August 24, 1791, as follows:

> To commence at a stone boundary on the north bank of
> the Lake St. Francis, at the cove west of Pointe au Bodet,
> in the limit between the township of Lancaster, and the
> seigneurie of New Longueuil, running along the said limit
> in the direction of North, thirty-four degrees west, to the
> western-most angle of the said seigneurie of New Lon-
> gueuil, thence along the north western boundary of the
> seigneurie of Vaudreuil running north twenty five degrees
> east, until it strikes the Ottawas River, to ascend the said
> River into the lake Temiscaming, and from the head of the

said lake by a line drawn due north until it strikes the boundary line of Hudson's bay, including all the territory to the westward and southward of the said line to the utmost extent of the country commonly called or known by the name of Canada.[12]

A more detailed description had been included in the second draft of the Constitutional Bill as follows:

. . . a partition line of various courses running due South from a Stone boundary fixed on the north bank of the Lake Saint Francis in a cove of the River of Saint Lawrence, West of Point au Boudet in the limit between the Township of Lancaster and the seigniory of New Longueuil to the Southernmost extent of His Majesty's Dominions and running in a Northerly direction from the aforesaid stone boundary along the Western or inland bounds of the said Seigniory of New Longueuil and of the Seigniory of Vaudreuil, according to their various courses, until it strikes the Uttawas River, thence in a direct Line to the nearest point in the centre of the navigable channel of the said river, thence ascending the middle of the navigable Channel of the said river to the Lake Temiscaming, thence through the middle of the said Lake to the most Northerly extremity thereof, and thence running due North, to the boundary of the Territory granted to the Merchants Adventures of England trading to Hudson's Bay.[13]

The main difference between the provisional clause and the one ultimately adopted is that the former made some attempt to indicate that the boundary should divide the *navigable* channel of the Ottawa river between the two provinces. But the fur traders in Montreal had not been anxious for the division of the Old Province of Quebec and had hoped that the boundaries of Upper Canada would be delimited in such a way that at least the route by the Ottawa River would lie entirely within a region which they could control in the event of disputes arising out of misconduct or trespass on the part of their employees.[14]

The provisional clause also designated the boundary to run through the *middle* of Lake Temiscaming and indicated the need for the boundary to run south of Pointe au Bodet as well as north. Of course if this had been adopted and taken literally, the boundary would have extended right across Lake St. Francis, thence through Huntingdon county in Lower Canada to the International boundary at New York

State. Actually little concern seems to have been shown for the apportioning of Lake St. Francis. Much may have been taken for granted because the lake, especially the western half, whose shores were sparsely populated by people of Scottish origin, was looked upon as common property, a connecting highway and a means of intercourse rather than a dividing feature in much the same way as the Ottawa river and Lake Temiscaming were regarded by the people living on their opposite shores. The early unity of the two shores of the western portion of Lake St. Francis is evident in many of the geographical names of the maps of today. On the Quebec side there is Dundee Centre, Isle of Skye, Fraser Point and Fraser Creek while almost opposite, on the Ontario side is another Fraser Point and Fraser Creek in company with such places as Glen Donald and MacGillivray Bridge. The fact that these three water boundaries (through Lake Temiscaming, the Ottawa river and Lake St. Francis) were left vague is evidence which supports the contention that rivers unite the people on either side of the river rather than divide them. This was also exemplified by the boundaries between Indian tribes referred to in Chapter II.

. But the boundary descriptions in the 1791 Order in Council were later found faulty in other respects and a note to this effect appears on the plan of part of the Province of Lower Canada made by order of Lord Dorchester in 1794 and 1795. One error was due to the use of the name of "Seigneurie of Vaudreuil" instead of "Seigneurie of Rigaud". The latter had sometimes been referred to by the former name but it led to confusion as there was another Seigniory of Vaudreuil to the east of Rigaud. The northern part of this section of the boundary was obviously intended to follow the western limits of the Seigniory of Rigaud. Secondly, the directions that the boundary was to follow, according to the Royal Proclamation, were not precisely the directions the boundaries of the seigniories actually followed. The western limits of New Longueuil had an actual bearing of N.37°W., not N.34°W., and Rigaud N.19°30′E., not N.25°E.[15]

But by and large, the Canadians of French descent were set apart with their own government thus enabling them to preserve their own law and customs without conflict with the new Canadians of American and British descent who had settled in Upper Canada and established a different set of institutions. The "triangle" between the Ottawa and St. Lawrence Rivers was accordingly included in the Province of Lower Canada, but this area, from the point of view of regional geography, is properly part of the Montreal plain and the boundary, therefore, was not merely a line dividing people of different national origins. So far as the anomaly of the Seigniory of L'Orignal is concerned, De Longueuil advertised the property for sale in 1784, so that his decision to dispose of his rights may not have been a result of the impending boundary decision. However, by 1796, when he finally succeeded in finding a buyer, the boundary decision had been made, and undoubtedly strengthened his wish to leave a province that was essentially British.[16] His land went to an immigrant from the United States named Nathaniel Treadwell and in 1797 L'Orignal village was founded by English-speaking settlers.

Newfoundland and the fisheries in the Gulf of St. Lawrence were also affected by the American revolution, despite their apparent remoteness from the American-Canadian frontier. The people of New England regarded the North Atlantic fisheries as vital to their prosperity, and their fishermen had been accustomed, as British subjects, to conducting their operations off the coast of Labrador and the island of Newfoundland. By the treaty of 1783 they retained this right, but were forbidden to dry or cure fish on the island. Drying and curing was, however, permitted in "any of the unsettled Bays, Harbours and Creeks of Nova Scotia,[17] Magdalen Islands, and Labrador, so long as the same shall remain unsettled".[18] So far as Labrador and the coasts of the St. Lawrence estuary were concerned, this added to the problems of the government at Quebec. Indeed it was said that there was "no government on the coast" of Labrador, and in the Baie de Chaleur area there were "many inconveniences prejudicial to the due management of the said Fisheries . . . from the want of a regular and competent Government".[19] The latter was partly accounted for by the lack of a precisely described southern boundary for Quebec in the Quebec Act of 1774, and attention was given to it prior to the Constitutional Act of 1791. It was even suggested that the fishing settlements in Gaspé might, with advantage, be annexed to New Brunswick, particularly in view of their distance from Quebec city. But, in spite of the distance, Gaspé was easier to reach from Quebec than St. John's and its commercial ties with Quebec were also much stronger. This would also appear to have been true of the Magdalen Islands, for in 1809 they were confirmed by the Newfoundland Act as being under Quebec jurisdiction. This Act, however, transferred to Newfoundland the coast of Labrador from the River St. John to Hudson Strait, Anticosti Island, and all other smaller islands that had been annexed to it

by the Royal Proclamation of 1763. In the meantime, Newfoundland had gained and lost St. Pierre and Miquelon yet
again. Following the outbreak of war with France in 1793,
the islands had again been occupied by Britain and the
inhabitants once more evacuated. Those who expressed a
desire to go to the U.S.A. were permitted to do so, the
remainder were sent back to France. With the cessation of
"permanent settlements", the islands were annexed to Newfoundland. They were restored to France at the conclusion
of the war in 1802 but the war broke out again in 1803
before the inhabitants could return and the islands reverted
to British control.[20] They were returned to France by the
Treaty of Ghent in 1814, recolonised in 1816 and have
remained French ever since.

Developments in the West

Meanwhile, after a lapse of over 150 years following
Juan de Fuca's discoveries, exploration had been taking place
along the north Pacific coast of North America. The Russians,
Bering and Chirikov, had initiated the activity in 1741, and
were followed by a number of Spanish explorers working
from their post established in 1770 at Monterey. In 1778,
Captain Cook explored the Pacific coast from 43 degrees
north to 70 degrees north and claimed the northwest coast
of America for Great Britain. La Perouse, the French explorer, supplemented the work of the Russians, Spaniards,
and British along the coast in 1786. These discoveries led
to great interest in the area by many nations. Eventually,
the Spaniards clashed with the British and when they seized
the British post at Nootka Sound an expedition under Captain
George Vancouver was dispatched from England. Vancouver's
extensive voyages continued from 1792 to 1794. He took
formal possession of all the coast from 45 degrees north
to Cape Spencer and divided it into five parts – New Georgia,
from 45 degs. N. to 50 degs. 30 mins. N. (Desolation Sound);
New Hanover, northward to 53 degs. 30 mins. N. (Point
Staniforth); New Cornwall, north to 56 degs. 30 mins. N.
(Point Rothsay) and New Norfolk, north to 58 degs. N. (Cape
Spencer.) But he made no attempt to set an eastern limit
to the territories, and as they had little influence on later
boundary development their boundaries are mainly of historical importance.[21]

On land, the North West Company, which had been
formed in 1783, and the Hudson's Bay Company were explor-

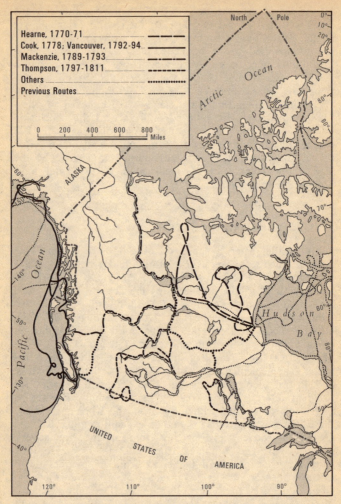

Figure 5. Major voyages of discovery and exploration in
western Canada between 1763 and 1814.

ing and exploiting the Pacific and Arctic regions north of
Columbia River. Although the Hudson's Bay Company had
been established primarily as a trading company, it was also
to promote discovery. Many of the exploratory journeys,
however, were almost accidental, arising as they did largely
from the fur trade. The earliest was that of Henry Kellsey,

1691-92. It is impossible to reconstruct the course of his journey accurately, but he was one of the first men, if not the first, to explore any part of the Canadian northwest. Henday, in 1754-55 may have reached 114 degrees west. Some of the most important of the early exploratory journeys were made by Samuel Hearne, particularly that of 1769-71, when he reached the Arctic Ocean at the mouth of Copper-mine River. In 1789, Alexander Mackenzie descended the river later named for him, and on another remarkable journey, in 1793, reached the Pacific Ocean. He thus showed that the Atlantic and Pacific coasts of Canada could be connected by overland routes, and showed the possibility of obtaining complete control of the fur trade of North America, from 48 degrees north to the Pole, with the exception of the Russian area. "To this", he said, "might be added the fishing in both seas and the markets of the four quarters of the globe".[22]

Thus the end of the century saw a controversial but none the less described boundary between the British territory that was to become Canada and the United States. It also saw the rearrangement of provincial boundaries in the eastern part of British North America, and the beginning of its political development in the West. Academic though Vancouver's boundaries are, one cannot help but notice, in his use of parallels of latitude, the similarity between them and the earliest boundaries on the east coast.

The first major change of the century relating to boundaries occurred in 1811, when Lord Selkirk was granted 116,000 square miles of territory by the Hudson's Bay Company (Figure 22). The area was intended for settlement, and comprised the Red River Valley, bounded as follows:

Beginning on the western shore of Lake Winnipic, at a point in fifty-two degrees and thirty minutes north latitude; and thence running due west to Lake Winipigashish, other-wise called Little Winnipic; then in a southerly direction through the said lake, so as to strike its western shore in latitude fifty-two degrees; then due west to the place where the parallel of fifty-two degrees north latitude inter-sects the western branch of the Red River, otherwise called Assiniboine; then due south from that point of intersection to the height of land which separates the waters running into Hudson's Bay from those of the Missouri and Mississippi Rivers; then in an easterly direc-tion along the height of land to the source of the River Winnipic (meaning by such last-named river the principal branch of the waters which unite in the Lake Saginagas); thence along the main stream of those waters and the middle of the several lakes through which they pass, to the mouth of the Winnipic River; and thence in a northerly direction through the middle of Lake Winnipic, to the place of beginning: which territory is called Assiniboia. . . .[23]

In spite of the confusion that still existed as to the exact location of the boundary between Lake Superior and Lake of the Woods it is clear that part of the area included within the boundaries of the Selkirk grant lay within United States territory, and the grant was, therefore, inoperative to that extent. A year later, however, war broke out between Great Britain and the United States, and our attention must once more turn to the international scene.

Further Development of International Boundaries

Louisiana, which had been ceded by France to Spain by the Treaty of Paris in 1763, had been returned to France in 1800. In 1803 France sold the territory to the United States of America, and this purchase raised the question of the precise boundary between the United States and British North America from Lake Superior to the Pacific Ocean.

It will be recalled that by the Treaty of Paris, 1763, the boundary between British North America and United States territory was from the northwest angle of Lake of the Woods westward to the sources of the Mississippi River. This, in itself, was geographically impossible because the Mississippi rises well to the south of the latitude of Lake of the Woods, a fact that appears to have been common knowledge among the fur traders of the time and was shown with reasonable accuracy on many maps drawn before 1782. The official negotiators, however, were ignorant of this. They relied upon the Mitchell map of 1755, the northwest corner of which was unfortunately taken up with an inset so that the sources of the Mississippi could not be shown; these, according to the legend, were not yet known but were "supposed to arise about the 50th degree of latitude and western bounds of this map".

This situation, and the vague northern and western boundaries of the Louisiana Territory, raised the subject of the whole south-western boundary of Canada, but before these two boundary matters were settled the disputants were involved in the War of 1812. Under the Treaty of Ghent (1814), which brought an end to hostilities, the opportunity was taken to provide for a final adjustment of all outstanding matters of dispute and controversy that had arisen from the boundaries as described in the treaty of 1783. As a result of the new treaty four commissions were set up, two of which reached definite conclusions, the other two leaving questions still in doubt. In 1818 this was followed by a convention between Great Britain and the United States that extended the International Boundary westward along the 49th Parallel to the "Stony" (Rocky) Mountains in the following terms:

> It is agreed that a Line drawn from the most North Western Point of the Lake of the Woods, along the forty ninth parallel of North Latitude, or, if the said point shall not be in the Forty ninth Parallel of North Latitude, then that a Line drawn from the said Point due North or South, as the Case may be, until the said Line shall intersect the said Parallel of North Latitude, and from the Point of such Intersection due West along and with the said Parallel shall be the Line of Demarkation between the Territories of the United States, and those of His Britannic Majesty, and that the said Line shall form the Northern Boundary of the said Territories of the United States, and the Southern Boundary of the Territories of His Britannic Majesty, from the Lake of the Woods to the Stony Mountains.[24]

The first part of this clause required a determination of the "most northwestern corner of the Lake of the Woods." This was carried out in 1826 and a monument raised to mark the location. As it was north of 49 degrees N., it resulted in an idiosyncracy in the boundary which cut off a wide peninsula from Manitoba allotting it to the U.S.A. even though it was not accessible by land from American territory.

The early use of the 49th Parallel as a boundary has already been mentioned. Claimed by the Hudson's Bay Company in 1714-19 as the southern limit of their territory, it had become so frequently marked on maps that when the United States purchased the Louisiana Territory from France, the 49th Parallel was assumed by them to be its northern boundary and was eventually accepted by the negotiators of the 1818 Convention. As both the Louisiana Territory and the Hudson's Bay Company's territory had been described according to drainage basins, no single parallel of latitude could satisfactorily separate them. However, there is a rough coincidence between the Hudson Bay-Gulf of Mexico divide and the 49th Parallel, and although the height of land between the two drainage basins is no mountain range, along much of its course it is marked by groups of low hills. If one parallel of latitude had to be selected there could have been worse choices than the forty-ninth.

Obviously this boundary crossed the southern part of the Selkirk grant, and the Selkirk Estate was, therefore, obliged to relinquish its claim to the area south of the 49th Parallel, which became absorbed into the Dakotas and Minnesota. In the 7 years between the time the grant was made to Selkirk and the extension of the International Boundary to the Rocky Mountains, settlement as far south of Fort Garry (Winnipeg) as 49 degrees north, was very sparse. However, in the very year that the International Boundary extension was agreed upon, a party of French Canadians from Lower Canada settled in the neighbourhood of Pembina with the intention of farming. There they were joined by half-breeds and hunters; houses were built and a church erected. This settlement was probably established under the impression that it was in British territory, but in 1822 doubts about this arose and most of the settlers were persuaded to move farther north and the Hudson's Bay Company's fort (Fort Daer) was abandoned. In the following year observations by American authorities showed that the whole of the settlement of Pembina with the exception of a single log house was within the United States. "About 350 people, two-thirds half-breeds, the rest Swiss and Scotch, preferred to remain at Pembina under the protection of the United States government".[25]

Thus, by 1822, the Selkirk settlement had been mainly confined to the area north of the 49th Parallel. Actually, one post north of Pembina remained on United States soil until 1876, connected by wagon road to Fort Garry; for the movement of local trade had always been influenced by regional rather than political forces and this long continued in the face of merely political considerations.[26]

The situation with regard to the area west of the Rocky Mountains was covered by Article III of the 1818 Convention. According to its terms, the area was to be "free and open" to the "vessels, citizens and subjects" of both Great Britain and the United States for a period of 10 years without prejudice to the claims of either side.[27] This Article was inserted simply because traders of both countries were active in the area. In fact, three countries were by now involved in the whole of the Pacific Northwest. Great Britain, by virtue of the activities of Cook, Vancouver, and the Hudson's Bay and North West Companies (which joined forces in 1821); the United States, especially after 1819 when, by the Treaty of Florida Blanca, Spain ceded to the United States all her rights and claims north of latitude 42 degrees north; and Russia.

The first Russian settlement in the area had been established in 1784 on Kodiak Island. This was followed by several others along the Pacific coast of North America, particularly after 1799, when Russia granted the Russian-American Company exclusive trading privileges north of the 65th parallel.

In 1821, Alexander I of Russia issued a Ukase granting rights of "commerce, whaling and fishing, and of all other industry" on the North American coast between Bering Strait and latitude 51 degrees north to Russian subjects exclusively and prohibiting foreigners from approaching the coast within 100 miles. The United States protested against this, denying in toto the Russian claim south of latitude 55 degrees north and asserting some claim to the coasts as far as 61 degrees north. Great Britain also objected, as she claimed the coast to approximately 58 degrees north, the northern boundary of Vancouver's "New Norfolk".

The conflicting interests of Russia, the United States and Great Britain in this area were partly resolved by treaty. In 1824, by a convention between Russia and the United States, the former renounced all claims to territory south of 54 degrees 40 minutes north, and in 1825 Russia and Great Britain reached an agreement on the boundary between their respective territories, which became known as the Alaska boundary.

In the negotiations over this boundary, the Russian Government was guided by the representations of the Russian-American Company and the British Government by those of the Hudson's Bay Company. The boundary the negotiators were seeking to define was thus very largely the boundary between the areas of operations of these companies.

The Russians were particularly interested in retaining control of the Pacific coast of North America north of 55 degrees north, which was the southern limit mentioned in the trading charter of 1799. Their most southern and easterly settlement in 1821 was at Sitka. Great Britain, however, was anxious that the territory that she claimed in the interior should not be shut in by a coastal strip controlled by another power. The Hudson's Bay and North West Companies certainly had no posts on the Pacific coast between the 51st and 60th parallels, but it was recognized by both parties that the Mackenzie River area was within their jurisdiction. In the first informal stages of the negotiations, Great Britain proposed Cross Sound and Lynn Canal, at approximately 58 degrees north, as the boundary on the coast, and a due north line from the head of Lynn Canal at approximately 135 degrees west, as the boundary on the mainland. The Russians proposed 54 degrees north as the coastal boundary and whatever longitude would leave Mackenzie River on the British side of the frontier.

The Russians insisted that the southeastern part of the boundary should be a line roughly paralleling the coast at some distance inland, but the farther south and east the Russian demands went, the farther westward did the British push the meridional boundary. At successive stages of the negotiations, the 139th, 140th, and 141st meridians were all mentioned. Ultimately, the 141st meridian was selected as the boundary, probably because it was the line running north from Mount St. Elias. This was one of the few outstanding and unmistakable features in a relatively unknown land, and so supplied a point of reference for both the northern part of the boundary and the southeastern part. Throughout the negotiations, however, the land boundary was really secondary to the question of the extent of Russia's maritime jurisdiction, and, therefore, the shifting of the land boundary a few miles in one direction or the other was not regarded as of great importance by either nation. It was not until later that the Russians moved far inland. In 1838, they built a small blockhouse at the present site of Nulato (long. 158 degs. W.) and in 1842 they established a trading post there which became the most inland, as well as the most northerly (lat. 64 degs. 45 mins. N.) of the Russian American Company's posts.[28] Exploration had extended up the Yukon some 240 miles beyond this point to the mouth of the Tanana river and this seems to have been the furthest point ever reached by Russian traders. Occasionally traders of the Hudson's Bay Company reached the same point from the east although their most westerly post was at Fort Yukon founded in 1847 presumably on the assumption that it was in British territory although eventually demonstrated to be in long. 145 degs. 18 mins. W. – well within Russian America.

Articles III and IV of the treaty of February 28, 1825, defined the line of delimitation between the Russian-British territory as follows:

III . . . . Commencing from the southernmost point of the island called Prince of Wales Island, which point lies in the parallel of 54 degrees 40 minutes, north latitude, and between the 131st and 133rd degree of west longitude (meridian of Greenwich), the said line shall ascend to the north along the channel called Portland Channel, as far as the point of the continent where it strikes the 56th degree of north latitude; from this last mentioned point, the line of demarcation shall follow the summit of the mountains situated parallel to the coast as far as the point of intersection of the 141st degree of west longitude (of the same meridian); and, finally, from the said point of intersection, the said meridian line of the 141st degree, in its prolongation as far as the Frozen Ocean, shall form the limit between the Russian and British possessions on the continent of America to the north west.

IV. With reference to the line of demarcation laid down in the preceding Article it is understood:

1st. That the island called Prince of Wales Island shall belong wholly to Russia.

2nd. That whenever the summit of the mountains which extend in a direction parallel to the coast, from the 56th degree of north latitude to the point of intersection of the 141st degree of west longitude, shall prove to be at the distance of more than 10 marine leagues from the ocean, the limit between the British possessions and the line of coast which is to belong to Russia, as above mentioned, shall be formed by a line parallel to the windings of the coast, and which shall never exceed the distance of 10 marine leagues therefrom.[29]

The boundary between British territory and the United States, however, remained unsettled until the Oregon Treaty in 1846. The arrangement made for joint occupation in 1818 had been extended in 1827 for an indefinite period. In this frontier region between 42 degs. N. and 54 degs. 40 mins. N. the boundary being sought was largely the boundary between the spheres of influence of the Hudson's Bay Company and the American Fur Company, just as the Alaska boundary had depended upon the spheres of influence of the Russian-American Company and the Hudson's Bay Company. The Columbia River seemed increasingly to become the *de facto* boundary separating the operations of the British and U.S. companies and as early as 1824 the British government had offered a boundary that followed the 49th Parallel westward to Columbia River and then followed that river to its mouth. The United States, however, insisted on an extension of the 49th Parallel to the Pacific Ocean. They repeated their proposal in 1826, contending that they needed the safe, commodious harbours of Puget Sound rather than the dangerous entrance to Columbia River, which the British proposal would have left them. The Americans also put forward the principle of contiguity, claiming that the acceptance of the 49th Parallel as a boundary east of the Rocky Mountains established their right to the prolongation of the boundary westward along that parallel.[30]

In the meantime, the Hudson's Bay Company had been exploring, exploiting, and consolidating the areas between Russian territory and the 49th Parallel, and in 1841 the Governor of the Company approved the choice of a new site for Fort Vancouver because he had come to the conclusions that when the International Boundary was fixed it should go through Juan de Fuca Strait.[31] But by 1846 American immigration into the Oregon area had increased to such an extent that there were 700 American settlers there as against 400 British, although there were only 8 American settlers north of Columbia River when the Oregon dispute entered its final stage.[32] In 1844, negotiations between Britain and America began again. The British repeated their offer of 1824 with a free port or ports. The United States declined and, despite President Polk's pre-election cry of "Fifty-four Forty or Fight" which was based on the 1824 convention with Russia, ultimately repeated their proposal of 1826, with a free port or ports on Vancouver Island. This the British rejected, but finally proposed the 49th Parallel, reserving the whole of Vancouver Island. The United States agreed to this and the boundary extension was described as follows:

> From the point on the forty-ninth parallel of north latitude where the boundary laid down in existing treaties and conventions between the United States and Great Britain terminates, the line of boundary between the territories of the United States and those of Her Britannic Majesty shall be continued westward along the said forty-ninth parallel of north latitude to the middle of the channel which separates the continent from Vancouver's Island; and thence southerly through the middle of the said channel, and of Fuca's Straits to the Pacific Ocean: provided, however, that the navigation of the whole of the said channel and Straits, south of the forty-ninth parallel of north latitude remain free and open to both Parties.

Thus, after rejecting the 49th Parallel four times, the British government proposed it in 1846! It has been suggested that the reasons for this apparent "about face" were that, by 1846, Columbia River was not so essential to the trade of the Hudson's Bay Company as it had previously insisted, and also that the British government was not especially interested in or concerned with Oregon, particularly if it was going to involve it in war.[33] In these circumstances, the parallel was probably chosen because it had been suggested by the United States in 1818, and also because it was a convenient extension of a boundary already agreed upon, and bisected the area in dispute. But although the forty-ninth parallel was the first *de jure* boundary in the region, the fact that the Columbia river had become a *de facto* boundary meant that there was a real shift in boundary location. As a result effective U.S. sovereignty in the area between the forty-ninth parallel and the Columbia river did not supersede that of the Hudson's Bay Company for some time after partition. Although the Hudson's Bay Company was permitted to retain possessory rights to its holdings on Puget Sound and the Columbia river, "Company traffic between Puget Sound and Victoria had to travel an extra 350 miles to pass United States customs at the mouth of the Columbia River."[34] Their operations were made more difficult as "foreigners" were not allowed to trade with the Indians and the posts were finally abandoned in 1871, twenty five years after the boundary treaty.

The boundary resulting from the treaty also cut off the southern part of the Point Roberts peninsula from British Columbia allocating it to the U.S.A. Like the Lake of the Woods peninsula it is not accessible by land from American territory. This was not a problem until the 1960's when there was a rapid increase in both vacation and permanent Canadian residents moving from the nearby Vancouver region to the U.S. territory.

> These taxed but unrepresented new residents, expecting all the normal suburban services, find that the border's function as an immigration and customs barrier complicates their day-to-day living.[35]

Further Adjustments in the East

Meanwhile, in the east, still further boundary adjustment had been taking place between the British colonies. In 1820, Cape Breton Island was re-annexed to Nova Scotia. It will be recalled that its separation in 1784 stemmed from the intention to reserve the island as a headquarters for the fisheries and for the working of the mines. But, in the meantime, a survey of the island for colonization purposes had been completed and grants of land had been authorized. Gradually, therefore, through immigration and settlement, the number of inhabitants entitled to vote increased, so that by 1820 the situation of 1783 no longer existed and there remained no reason why any special legislation should be needed for the island.

In Newfoundland, the territorial change of 1809 still did not satisfy the fishermen of Lower Canada, and their complaints were aggravated by such measures as the Judicature Act of 1824, which empowered the Governor of Newfoundland to institute courts that administered laws with which they were unfamiliar. Eventually a compromise was reached and the British North America (Seigniorial Rights) Act was passed in 1825. It enacted that

> . . . . so much of the said coast (Labrador) as lies to the westward of a line to be drawn due north and south from the bay or harbour of Ance Sablon, inclusive, as far as the fifty-second degree of north latitude, with the island of Anticosti, and all other islands adjacent to such part as last aforesaid of the coast of Labrador, shall be and the same are hereby re-annexed to and made a part of the said province of Lower Canada. . . .[36]

Discontent and friction arising out of the effects of the Constitutional Act of 1791 were also developing in the two Canadas. By 1806 this situation was becoming strongly vocal. In Lower Canada, as might have been foreseen prior to 1791, the English-speaking residents resented being in a minority in the House of Assembly and they feared the weakness of the disunited colonies of British North America in case of attack by a foreign power.[37] The French-speaking residents resented the immigration of English-speaking immigrants into the Eastern Townships.[38] Upper Canada was dissatisfied with the distribution of revenues, for, as a result of the division of Canada in 1791, she was compelled to import all seaborne articles through territory under the administration of another government, either through Lower Canada or through the United States. Thus, trade via the St. Lawrence River was commanded by Lower Canada, and in order to collect a customs revenue, it was necessary for Upper Canada either to establish custom houses on the boundary with Lower Canada, or to come to some arrangement whereby a certain proportion of the duties levied at Quebec, which was the port of entry of Lower Canada, would be paid to the government of Upper Canada. The latter course was taken, but "numerous circumstances concur[red] to render vain any attempt permanently to regulate to the satisfaction of both Provinces the division of the Revenue."[39] Some of the people of Montreal maintained that the revenue difficulties would force Upper Canada to trade increasingly with the United States, particularly in view of the canals that had been constructed in New York state, and that this might result in a movement for political union.

The solution to many of these problems appeared to lie in the union of the two provinces, and in 1822 a bill was introduced into the Imperial Parliament to this effect. But there was too much opposition to it, particularly from the French-speaking inhabitants of Lower Canada, and it was withdrawn. Those in favour of union immediately advocated a substitute for it, namely the annexation to Upper Canada of that portion of Lower Canada between the Ottawa and St. Lawrence rivers together with the island of Montreal. This would provide Upper Canada with its own port of entry.[40] Ultimately after petitions and counter-petitions, arguments and counter-arguments, committees and reports, the union of the provinces was decided on and by an Act of 1840, Upper Canada and Lower Canada were reunited to form the Province of Canada.

Disputes were still occurring between the British colonies and the United States over the interpretation of the United States boundary treaty of 1783, particularly with regard to the section of the boundary between New Brunswick and Maine. An attempt had been made to settle the matter peaceably in 1827, when it was referred to arbitration under a convention between Great Britain and the United States. The award of the arbitrator, the King of the Netherlands, was made in 1831 but was not accepted by either country. In the same year, some people attempting to hold an election under United States laws were arrested by New Brunswick authorities. In 1836 a Canadian justice of the peace was arrested by United States authorities for endeavouring to carry out his duties in what he believed to be British territory. Finally, an American official was arrested by New Brunswick authorities when he attempted to arrest British subjects who were cutting timber in the Aroostook region; this action resulted in something little short of actual war between New Brunswick and Maine – the so-called Aroostook War.[44]

In 1842, however, when Lord Ashburton, on behalf of Great Britain, paid a special visit to the United States to settle boundary problems, final agreement was reached on the remaining doubts that had sprung from the Treaty of 1783, and with the Oregon Treaty of 1846, the boundaries of British North America with the United States from the Bay of Fundy to the Gulf of Georgia were at last delimited satisfactorily, apart from minor details.

The West Coast

In spite of the Oregon Treaty of 1846, the British still considered it necessary to consolidate their territory on the Pacific coast north of the 49th Parallel. In 1849, a Crown Grant of Vancouver Island was made to the Hudson's Bay Company, provided it would establish a colony thereon, and Governor Blanshard was empowered by his commission to exercise jurisdiction not only over Vancouver Island, but also all adjacent islands between the 49th and 52nd degrees of north latitude.

The matter was accentuated by the discovery of gold in the area. As early as 1850, Governor Blanshard had reported the existence of gold on Queen Charlotte Islands, which in 1852 resulted in Governor Douglas being commissioned as Lieutenant-Governor of the islands. Although the commission was not intended to sanction the colonization of the islands, the act became important in 1858, when the remainder of what is now southern British Columbia became another crown colony. This step had been forced upon the British Government through the discovery of more gold on Fraser River and in the Cariboo district. This resulted in an influx of an estimated 30,000[42] miners into an area with a white population of about 750 only, of whom 300 were at Victoria. The Indian population was about 15,000, and one of the dangers of the gold rush was that it might produce difficulties between the natives and the whites and lead to disorder. But a far greater political danger was the fact that most of the incoming miners were Americans, and Governor Douglas was fearful they might try to establish an independent government that might become annexed to the United States. The British Government, therefore, on July 1, 1858, introduced a Bill "to provide for the government of New Caledonia". The boundaries then laid down were: on the south, the frontier of the United States; on the west, the Pacific Ocean; on the north, the 55th parallel; and on the east, the watershed between the streams that flowed into the Pacific and those that flowed into the Atlantic and Arctic Oceans.

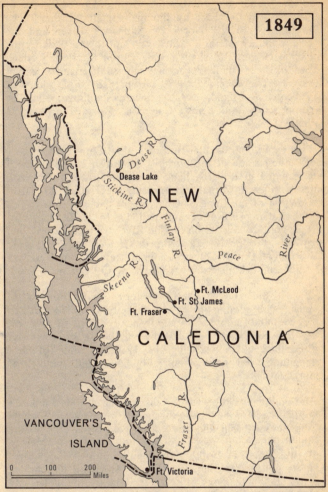

Figure 6. New Caledonia and Vancouver's Island, 1849.

However, an amendment was proposed extending these boundaries because it was thought that the gold found on Fraser River was only a trifling indication of that to be found at its headwaters, which rose north of the 55th parallel, and the final act "to provide for the Government of British Columbia" established the boundaries as follows:

to the South by the frontier of the United States of
America, to the East by the main chain of the Rocky
Mountains, to the North by Simpson's River and the
Finlay branch of the Peace River, and to the West by the
Pacific Ocean, and shall include Queen Charlotte's Island
and all other Islands adjacent to the said territories except
as hereafter excepted. . . . No part of the Colony of
Vancouver's Island, as at present established, shall be
comprised within British Columbia for the purposes of
this Act.[43]

The expiration of the Hudson's Bay Company's licence
in 1859 left some of the territory of British North America
not included in Rupert's Land or in the British Pacific colonies without a formal government, other than the direct
jurisdiction of the Imperial Government under the provisions
of the Indian Territories Act of 1859. In 1862, reports of
further gold discoveries on Stikine River were confirmed, and
eventually the British Government decided to declare the
Governor of British Columbia administrator of the Territory
of Stickeen, delimited by an Order in Council as follows:

. . . . the said Strickeen territories shall comprise so
much of the dominions of Her Majesty as are bounded to
the west and south-west by the frontier of Russian America,
to the south and south-east by the boundary of British
Columbia, to the east by the 125th meridian of west
longitude, and to the north by the 62nd parallel of
north latitude.[44]

The only explanation for the eastern and northern limits is
that they were to be extensive enough to include the whole
of the Stikine basin and any future gold discoveries to the
north.

By this time the British Government, in striking contrast
with its policy immediately after the American Revolution,
was encouraging unions of smaller administrative units, and
in 1863 the decision was reached to amalgamate the western
mainland possessions. In any case the Select Committee of
the House of Commons on the Hudson's Bay Company had
recommended, as early as 1857, that means should be provided "for the ultimate extension of the colony of Vancouver's Islands over any portion of the adjoining mainland
to the west of the Rocky mountains, on which permanent
settlement may be found practicable". The creation of two
separate colonies, therefore, appears to have been merely

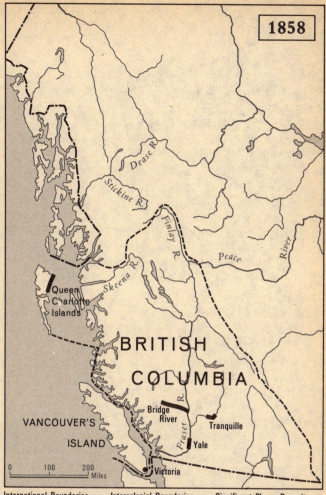

International Boundaries ━━━Intercolonial Boundaries ━ ━ ━ Significant Placer Deposits ▅▅▅

Figure 7. British Columbia and Vancouver's Island, 1858.

an interim step in the full implementation of this recommendation. British Columbia was, therefore, now to comprise

all such territories . . . . as are bounded to the South by the
territories of the United States of America, to the West by
the Pacific Ocean and the frontier of the Russian Ter-

Figure 8. Colonial boundaries on the Pacific coast, 1862.

ritories in North America, to the North by the sixtieth
parallel of north latitude, and to the East, from the
boundary of the United States northwards, by the Rocky
Mountains and the one hundred and twentieth meridian
of west longitude, and shall include Queen Charlotte
Island and all other Islands adjacent to the said Territories,

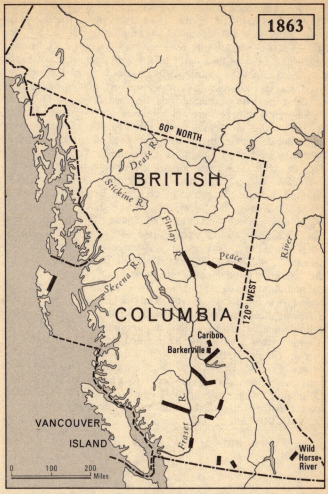

Figure 9. British Columbia and Vancouver Island, 1863.

except Vancouver Island and the Islands adjacent thereto.[45]

No explanation was offered for the withdrawal from the 62nd to the 60th parallel as the northern boundary, but the fact that the latter parallel is the nearest convenient one to the commencement of the boundary along the 141st Meridian, established in the 1825 treaty with Russia, may have influenced this decision. Moreover, gold mining on Stikine River was almost over in 1863. Access to Glenora, which had become the centre of the gold rush, was not easy, and the journey to it from Victoria took from 3 weeks to a month. Also the mining season was short, mining operations on the river being possible only between July and October. Consequently, "there were never more than 500 miners on the Stikine"[46] and the "rush" soon subsided. Thus it may have been decided that there was no need for the northern boundary of British Columbia to extend as far north as 62 degrees north. The extension of the eastern boundary from the 125th to the 120th meridian was made so as to include the gold districts discovered in the Peace River area in 1862. The chief mining camps were on Peace River itself and on Vital, Germansen, and Manson Creeks. British Columbia and Vancouver Island were united as one colony in 1866, when the latter expressed a willingness to unite with the mainland, and hence the boundaries of British Columbia as they are known today came into being.

Thus, immediately prior to Canadian Confederation, the boundaries of British North America between the United States of America and the Russian territory of Alaska were delimited, apart from a few minor sections. British North America itself was politically divided by the boundaries of British Columbia, Canada, New Brunswick, Nova Scotia, Prince Edward Island, and Newfoundland. The remaining area was either under the control of the Hudson's Bay Company, being made up of Rupert's Land and the Northwest Territory, or directly under the British Government.

CHAPTER IV

INTERNATIONAL AND NATIONAL BOUNDARIES

The year 1867 marks the beginning of the political development of Canada as a separate State, for by the terms of the British North America Act a federal union of the provinces of Canada, New Brunswick, and Nova Scotia came into being. These political units retained the boundaries that had already been established, with the exception that the former province of Canada was divided into the provinces of Ontario and Quebec, the line of division between them being identical with the line of division that had existed between Upper and Lower Canada from 1791 to 1840, following the Constitutional Act, and that had been modified during the period of their Union from 1840 to 1867.

In 1868, the Rupert's Land Act authorized the acquisition by the Dominion of Canada of "Rupert's Land and the North-Western Territory" although the full title to these territories was not transferred from the Hudson's Bay Company to Canada until 1870, and they were not actually transferred until 1871. A few days after this, British Columbia entered the federal union, and in 1873 Prince Edward Island followed. The boundaries of British Columbia remained exactly as previously defined and the boundaries of Prince Edward Island, of course, presented no difficulty.

The Northern Limits of Canada

An outstanding problem, however, was the limit of "Rupert's Land and the North-Western Territory", particularly on the north. This problem was brought into focus in 1874, when an American naval officer applied for a mining claim on the shores of Cumberland Sound, Baffin Island. As a result, the British Colonial Secretary asked the government of Canada if it wished to have the British territories adjacent to those of the Dominion on the North American

Figure 10. The extent of the territory of the Hudson's Bay
           Company according to a map by J. Arrowsmith,
           published in 1857.

continent formally annexed to Canada so as to exercise
"such surveillance . . . as may be necessary to prevent the
occurrence of lawless acts" in the area.

A second request was made, meantime, for a grant of land
on Baffin Island for fishing and mining, and eventually the
Canadian government informed the Colonial Office that it
was "desirous of including within the boundaries of the
Dominion, the territories referred to, with the islands adjacent" – a decision that was incorporated into a Canadian
Order in Council dated October 9, 1874. There followed an
interchange of correspondence between London and Ottawa
as to the precise manner in which the transfer should take
place and a Canadian Order in Council dated April 30, 1875,
suggested that an Imperial Act of Parliament should be
passed defining the eastern and northern boundaries of the
territory to be transferred and that the northern boundary should be "the utmost limit of the continent of
America, including the islands appertaining thereto" and the

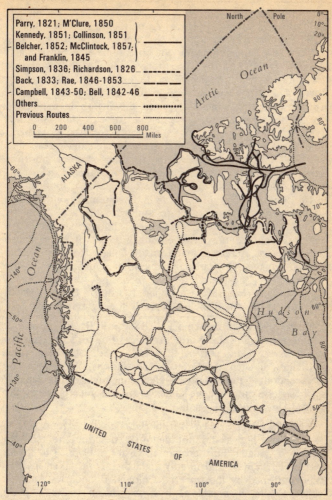

Figure 11. Major voyages of discovery and exploration in western Canada between 1814 and 1867.

eastern boundary should allow for the possible inclusion of "such portion of the North West coast of Greenland as may belong to Great Britain by right of discovery or otherwise".[1] Matters proceeded slowly, however. The British Colonial Secretary endeavoured to accelerate them by referring to the United States mining expedition to Baffin Island, which had taken place in the meantime, without official permission, and was said to have obtained graphite and mica worth over $100,000. He further pointed out that reports had appeared in the newspapers drawing the attention of United States citizens to the northern territories and to the American expeditions that had been sent to explore certain parts of them. This American activity in the north had begun in the 1850's when the Americans joined the British in the search for Sir John Franklin (Figure 11) but some of Hall's journeys (1860-62, 1864-69, and 1871-73) had occurred after Confederation. As a result, the Colonial Secretary felt that great difficulty would be experienced in including the far northern area in Canada unless steps were speedily taken to place the title of Canada "upon a clear and unmistakable footing".

Consequently, on May 3, 1878, resolutions were carried in the Canadian Parliament to authorize the acceptance by Canada of the northern territories, although at least one member opposed the move on the grounds of expense. An address, was, therefore, made to the Queen from the Senate and Commons of Canada requesting a definition of the northeasterly, northerly, and northwesterly boundaries of Canada. This resulted in an Imperial Order in Council, dated July 31, 1880, which included the following statement:

> From and after September 1, 1880, all British territories and possessions in North America, not already included within the Dominion of Canada, and all islands adjacent to any of such territories or possessions, shall (with the exception of the Colony of Newfoundland and its dependencies) become and be annexed to and form part of the said Dominion of Canada. . . .[2]

This, in effect, passed British rights to the Arctic islands to Canada, but it did not definitely describe the territory added to Canada. Furthermore an Order in Council is not an Act of Parliament and in July 1895 the action taken in 1880 was confirmed by the Imperial Colonial Boundaries Act.[3]

Meanwhile, a notable British expedition under Captain Sir G. S. Nares had explored the northern coasts of Ellesmere Island and Greenland in 1875-76 hoisting the British flag at a number of places in the area. Americans had also continued their activities in the far north. Schwatka explored King William Island in 1878-80 erecting a cairn and displaying the American flag at the northern extremity of the island. Greely (1881-84) erected a cairn and displayed the American flag in the central part of Ellesmere Island much of which he explored (Figure 12).

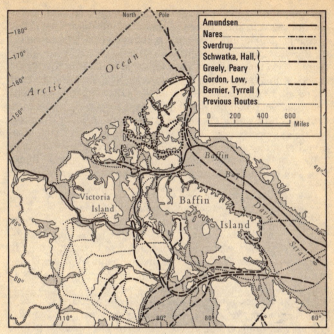

Figure 12. Major voyages of discovery and exploration in
northern Canada between 1867 and 1906.

In 1884, some 3½ years after the northern islands had
been transferred to Canada, the Canadian government sent
an expedition to the north in the D.G.S. *Neptune* under the
command of Lieutenant A. R. Gordon. Its main purpose
was to investigate the sea route to Churchill through Hudson
Bay. Scientific stations were established in Hudson Strait,
where observers spent the winter of 1884-85.[4] In 1885 and
1886 the work continued in the *Alert*, again under the
command of Lieutenant Gordon, and many of the islands in
Hudson Bay and Strait as well as settlements in what is
now northern Newfoundland, Quebec, Ontario, and Manitoba
were visited and reported on.[5] However, despite these expeditions, Canada appears to have given no documentary recognition to the fact that her boundaries had been extended
until October 1895, when an Order in Council constituting
certain provisional districts was passed.

The boundaries of the District of Franklin were described
as follows:

Beginning at cape Best, at the entrance to Hudson strait, from the Atlantic; thence westerly through said strait, Fox channel, gulf of Boothia, Franklin strait, Ross strait, Simpson strait, Victoria strait, Dease strait, Coronation gulf and Dolphin and Union strait, to a point in the Arctic sea, in longitude about 125°30′ west, and in latitude about 71° north; thence northerly including Baring Land, Prince Patrick island and the Polynea islands; thence northeasterly to the 'farthest of Commander Markham's and Lieutenant Parr's sledge journey in 1876, in longitude about 63½° west, and latitude about 83¼° north; thence southerly through Robeson channel, Kennedy channel, Smith sound, Baffin bay and Davis strait to the place of beginning.[6]

But the description in this Order in Council was defective, for although the districts of Yukon and Mackenzie were so delimited as to include the northern part of the continent with all the islands within 3 geographical miles, the description of Franklin was not so worded as to include all the islands more than 3 miles from the mainland. Yet the Order maintained that its effect was to divide into provisional districts all the unorganized and unnamed parts of Canada. Its actual effect, however, was virtually to declare that certain islands in the Arctic Ocean were not part of Canada, and an amending Order in Council dated December 18, 1897, corrected the former description of the districts of Yukon and Mackenzie so that they included the islands for 20 miles from the coast, and Franklin all the others, thus:

all those lands and islands comprised between the one hundred and forty-first meridian of longitude west of Greenwich on the west and Davis strait, Baffin bay, Smith sound, Kennedy channel and Robeson channel on the east which are not included in any other provisional district.[7]

By this time a fourth Canadian government expedition had sailed north, for in June 1897 the *Diana* left Halifax under Commander William Wakeham. Like the Gordon expeditions, this was concerned with the Hudson Bay route, but it sailed as far as a group of whaling stations in Cumberland Sound, eastern Baffin Island. Wakeham's farthest north was Kekerten Island (65° 42′ N.) where he

landed and hoisted the Union Jack in the presence of the agent, a number of our own officers and crew, and the Esquimaux, formally declaring in their presence that the flag was hoisted as an evidence that Baffin's Land with all the territories, islands and dependencies adjacent to it

were now, as they always had been since their first discovery and occupation, under the exclusive sovereignty of
Great Britain.[8]

Thus it is from 1897, from the Canadian point of view at
least, that the present land area definitely extended to the
Arctic Ocean, although at this time no specific mention
seems to have been made of any claim to undiscovered
islands or to a formal extension of Canada to the North Pole.
Any thought of claiming part of Greenland, however, appears
to have been given up.

This early period in Canada's growth is interesting in that
the pattern of expansion paralleled so closely that which
occurred when various parts of the country had been claimed
for Spain, Portugal, France, and England. The initial interest
in the trade route through Hudson Strait and Bay is reminiscent of the European powers' desire to find a Northwest
Passage and Wakeham's proclamation of sovereignty hardly
differed from those of the 16th century explorers. Canada
had quickly become a "colonial power". She had inherited
more than mere territory from her motherlands – she had
inherited their very motives and methods for consolidating
her territorial acquisitions.

The Alaskan Boundary

The year 1867 was important not only because confederation was then achieved. It was important also from the
point of view of Canada's boundary development, because
in that year the United States purchased Russia's North
American territorial possessions. The landward boundaries
of Alaska were those described in the convention of 1825
between Russia and Great Britain. The language of this
description is clear with regard to that part of the boundary
running along the 141st Meridian although the U.S.A. took
more than two years to officially inform the Hudson's Bay
Company at Fort Yukon that their establishment was within
Alaska and that its operations had to cease. This followed
upon an exact determination of the longitude of Fort Yukon
but no other efforts were made to carry out surveys in connection with the 141st Meridian boundary until 1887.

But disputes arose over the interpretation of the description
of the remainder of the Alaska boundary – the "panhandle"
portion. The original description was probably based on
Vancouver's chart, the information on which had been greatly

supplemented since 1794. In the light of this newer information, the description was defective, and the resulting disputes were accentuated when the value of the natural resources of the area were realized. One of the earliest problems resulted from the discovery of gold in the Cassiar district of British Columbia, the only practical access to which was via Stikine River, which involved passing through United States territory (see Figure 8). In 1872 and 1874, the government of British Columbia officially pressed for the demarcation of the boundary. The area was then sparsely populated, and the United States recognized that if no action was taken until more settlement occurred serious antagonism might result. But when they estimated the cost of the survey they were unwilling to proceed. They were not even willing to compromise by marking the points at which the boundary crossed the rivers falling into the Pacific Ocean.[9] Therefore, in the interests of working harmoniously together, the local American and Canadian customs officers on the Stikine decided quite unofficially, in 1875, that the boundary should be taken as crossing the river at a point some $2\frac{1}{2}$ miles below Buck's, a Canadian trading post. In the following year, the American collector of customs at Sitka was instructed to consider Buck's as being in United States territory. But in the meantime Canada, tired of waiting for an official survey, had sent an engineer to locate the boundary on Stikine River. He fixed upon a line some 19 miles from the coast "at right angles thereto"[10], which the United States agreed to accept *pro tem* without prejudice to the claims of either side that were still to be resolved.

As the importance of the Cassiar diggings diminished, the interest in the location of this part of the boundary lessened, but by the early 1880's gold mining was becoming important on the upper Yukon. The Chilkoot and White passes at the head of Lynn Canal were the principal routes to this area, and their possession was sought by both Canada and the United States in order to control the trade passing through them. Under a convention of 1892, the Chief Astronomer of Canada and the Superintendent of the U.S. Coast and Geodetic Survey made a reconnaissance survey of the coast region from Portland Canal northward. This showed that there was no distinct range of mountains parallel with the coast but a whole "sea of mountains".

In 1896 the rush to the gold fields of the Klondike began. Miners in tens of thousands were entering the gold fields, and as Canada claimed the territory at the head of the Lynn Canal, and United States revenue officers ruled that their regulations forbade the landing of British vessels anywhere on the shores of that inlet, friction ensued. Although Americans who entered the Yukon had to meet the demands of Canadian customs, these seem to have been less exacting than those of the United States. Ultimately, the importance of finally defining the boundary was recognized, and in 1899 a joint commission provisionally agreed that the summits of Chilkoot and White passes, on the Dyea and Skagway trails, and a point on Chilkoot River at its junction with Klehini River, on the Dalton trail, were points upon the boundary. A convention between Great Britain and the United States in 1904 created an Alaskan Boundary Tribunal to attempt further settlement. The crucial question facing it was whether the treaty of 1825 called for a boundary drawn around the heads of the inlets or parallel with the general trend of the coast. The United States contended that it meant an unbroken chain of mountains exactly parallel with the coast and that as no such chain existed, the boundary should be 10 marine leagues from the shore, including the heads of all bays and inlets. The Canadian contention was that there were mountains parallel with the coast and that, according to the treaty, the boundary should follow their summits and cut across all inlets and fiords. The boundary ultimately adopted was as follows:

> It commences at Cape Muzon. Thence it crosses in a straight line to the mouth of Portland Channel (Canal), this entrance being west of Wales Island, and passes up the channel to the north of Wales and Pearse Islands to the 56th parallel of latitude. Thence the line runs from one mountain summit to another, passing above the heads of all fiords. At the head of Lynn Canal it traverses White and Chilkoot Passes. Thence by a tortuous southwesterly course it reaches Mount Fairweather and thence follows the higher mountains around Yakutat Bay to Mount St. Elias.[11]

The mountains chosen served the same purpose as the 10 marine league strip proposed by the U.S.A., for they shut Canada off just as effectively from access to the sea. When Russia held Alaska, the treaty with Britain of 1825 had made it clear in Article VI.

> that the subjects of His Britannic Majesty, from whatever quarter they may arrive, whether from the ocean, or from the interior of the continent, shall forever enjoy the right of navigating freely, and without any hindrance whatever,

all the rivers and streams which, in their course towards the Pacific Ocean, may cross the line of demarcation upon the line of coast.[12]

But when Russia sold Alaska to the U.S.A., the treaty of 1867 declared the "cession of territory and dominion" to be "free and unincumbered by any reservations, privileges, franchises, grants or possessions".[13]

The American *lisière* still adds considerably to the difficulty of communication and shipment between British Columbia and the Yukon. A minor irritation concerns the 110 mile White Pass and Yukon railway built in 1898-99 to connect Whitehorse, Yukon with the port of Skagway, Alaska. On the northward run American crews man the trains for the 40 miles to Bennett, Yukon. Then a Canadian crew takes over for the remaining 70 miles to Whitehorse. On the southward journey the crew is "switched" in reverse order. Many proposals have been made to change the general boundary situation some of which are discussed in Chapter IX.

Arctic Boundaries

In the meantime exploration had been continued in the northern regions. Vast areas of new land had been discovered by an expedition under the command of Otto Sverdrup of Norway, which entered the Arctic archipelago in 1898 and began 4 years of exploratory journeys. They first passed through Smith Sound to Kane Basin and wintered at Havne-fiord, southern Ellesmere Island. Sledge journeys were carried out northward to 81°N. and westward to 98°W., a cairn being erected on the west coast of Ellesmere Island and the Norwegian flag hoisted above it. The party wintered at Goose Fiord (76°48'N.; 89°W.) and in the spring of 1901 further exploration extended to 79°30'N. and 106°W.[14] In the course of this work, the expedition discovered, explored, and named parts of Cornwallis, Finlay, King Christian, Devon, Axel Heiberg, Ellef Ringnes, and Amund Ringnes Islands – an approximate area of 100,000 square miles, possession of which was taken in the name of the King of Norway.[15] The Norwegian claim was not withdrawn until 1930, when it was abandoned on Canada's agreeing to pay the costs of the Sverdrup expedition.

In the spring of 1903, Canada decided to send a vessel to patrol the waters of Hudson Bay and the eastern Arctic

Main National and		Manitoba	M.
International Boundaries	—.—.—	New Brunswick	N.B.
Provincial Boundaries	—.—.—	Prince Edward Island	P.E.I.
Inter-Territorial Boundaries	—.—.—	Nova Scotia	N.S.

Figure 13. The major political boundaries of Canada, 1867-1869.

islands to aid in the establishment of permanent stations
for the collection of customs, the administration of justice,
and the enforcement of Canadian law.[16] It visited the western
part of Hudson Bay, Baffin Island, and Lancaster Sound,

Figure 14. The major political boundaries of Canada, 1873-1905.

Main National and		Manitoba	M.
International Boundaries	—·—·—	New Brunswick	N.B.
Provincial Boundaries	—··—··—	Prince Edward Island	P.E.I.
Inter-Territorial Boundaries	—···—···—	Nova Scotia	N.S.

raising the Canadian flag and taking formal possession of
Ellesmere Island, Devon Island, and Somerset Island. In
1906-07, Captain Bernier, in command of the *Arctic*, carried
out similar operations but on a much wider scale. Proceeding

to Albert Harbour, north Baffin Island, he informed the whalers there that they must take out licences under Canadian whaling regulations; he landed at no less than fifteen places, on different islands, and took formal possession of them in the name of Canada, usually by raising the flag, reading a formal document, erecting a cairn, and depositing in it the document of possession. Whenever natives were encountered they were informed that they were Canadians and were expected to conform to the laws of Canada. Customs duties were collected from whalers to the extent of several hundred dollars.[17]

While Bernier was still in the Arctic, Senator Pascal Poirier (possibly with the Order in Council of 1897 in mind), speaking in the Canadian Senate, on February 20, 1907, moved that the time had come for Canada to make a formal declaration of possession of the lands and islands situated in the north country, and extending to the North Pole. The senator based his proposal mainly on the fact that discovery of the Arctic islands had been made chiefly by the British whose rights Canada had inherited. But the fifteen or so expeditions to the north following Confederation had included those of the Norwegian, Sverdrup, and several Americans, and it was these more recent events that were focussing public attention on the far north.

In the course of his speech, Senator Poirier maintained that all the islands between 141 and 60 degrees west longitude up to the North Pole were Canadian territory. He suggested that the division of the Arctic area according to what has since become known as the "sector principle" would reduce international conflict in the area; that the Arctic islands might prove a valuable asset to Canada should minerals be discovered there or the climate get warmer; and, finally, he drew attention to the fact that Canada's east and west coasts were restricted by the southward extension of Alaska and the northern extension of Newfoundland's dependency, Labrador, which was not then part of Canada, and that it might eventually become necessary "to have the North Pole as a way out of the Dominion".

This proposal has assumed great significance in modern times, not only because it applies to Canadian claims over a particular part of the earth's surface but also because it propounded the "sector principle". Although, as a result of the senator's statements, Canada is generally credited as being the first country to lay claim to a sector of either of the Polar regions, it should be noted that the so-called sector principle is merely a variation of a theme quite common in the evolution of North American boundaries.

It has already been shown that in various areas of Canada proclamations of sovereignty had been made from early times, and that the areas included in such proclamations were often defined merely by parallels of latitude or longitude or both. The Treaty of Tordesillas began with a line of longitude, the early French boundary documents with lines of latitude. The sector claim merely used two lines of longitude as the east-west limits of a proclamation of sovereignty. The southern limit was an area which was known and over which sovereignty was established; the northern limit was the Pole. Thus the "sector principle" was merely a variation of a standard method used throughout the history of Canada to extend political sovereignty from a settled area to an unknown area. To claim unknown lands was not new. Jeffreys, in 1761, for example, maintained that Canada's limits to the west extended "over countries and nations hitherto undiscovered". The Duc de la Rochefoucauld (1795) went even further, and stated that Upper Canada comprised "all the known and unknown countries extending as far as the Pacific . . . and is bounded also northwards by unknown countries". Others maintained that "as to Canada, or New France, the French would scarce admit it had any bounds to the north on this side of the pole".[18] Hence, not even the idea of Canada extending to the Pole was new in Poirier's speech. What made the speech so notable was the fact that it was a quasi-official public utterance, whereas previous official records of the northern limits of Canada had been by Order in Council, and the fact that it was a statement of sovereignty made in the 20th century but in the manner of the 16th century. However, Senator Poirier's proposal was not adopted, and the Minister of the Interior dissociated himself from it.[19]

In the following year Captain Bernier again sailed north, and on Dominion Day, 1909, he and his crew "assembled around Parry's rock to witness the unveiling of a tablet placed on the rock, commemorating the annexing of the whole of the Arctic archipelago". The tablet reads, in part, as follows:

This Memorial is erected today to commemorate the taking possession for the Dominion of Canada of the whole Arctic Archipelago lying to the north of America from longitude 60 degrees west to 141 degrees west up to latitude 90 degrees north.[20]

The Polar claims do not appear to have been officially stated in public until June 1925, when the Minister of the

Interior stated, on several occasions, during debates in the House of Commons, that Canada claimed "right up to the Pole".[21] He also defined the longitudinal limits of the claim and tabled a map showing its extent. In December 1953, the Prime Minister of Canada reiterated the claim during House of Commons debate when he said:

> We must leave no doubt of our active occupation and exercise of our sovereignty in these northern lands right up to the pole.[22]

Lines delimiting the sector have subsequently appeared on political maps of Canada published by the federal Government. These it is presumed, however, should merely be regarded as lines of allocation, which are delimited through the high seas or unexplored areas for the purpose of allocating lands without conveying sovereignty over the high seas.

Territorial Waters

Senator Poirier's proposal might have raised a discussion on the whole question of territorial waters, for although his sector claim is presumed to apply only to land within the sector, the presence of the sector boundaries on official maps almost implies a claim to the "high seas" forming part of the Arctic Ocean, over which it has always been presumed that it is impossible for national sovereignty to exist.

The Fisheries Disputes
Territorial waters had been involved incidentally in disputes over the North Atlantic coast fishery since 1713 when, by the Treaty of Utrecht the French were allowed to fish and dry their catch along that part of the shore of the island of Newfoundland north from Cape Bonavista and around the northern point south to Point Riche. The Treaty of Versailles (1783) changed these limits to Cape St. John and south to Cape Ray. But there was constant trouble between the French and Newfoundlanders because the former regarded this portion of the shore as exclusively theirs while the latter claimed "concurrent rights" with the French. Other problems also arose and eventually France surrendered her right to land and dry fish in consideration of compensation to be paid to the owners of all existing French establishments on the Treaty Coast. This compensation of private claims was

disposed of in 1905 when award amounts totalling £55,000 were paid by the British government.[23]

It has already been pointed out that following the American revolution the inhabitants of the United States had been given equal rights with British subjects to fish in all British North American waters, except that the Americans were not permitted to dry and cure fish on the island of Newfoundland. At the conclusion of the War of 1812, the British claimed that the United States had forfeited these rights, and in 1818 a new treaty was agreed upon; this restricted the Americans to fishing on the south coast of Newfoundland from Cape Ray to Rameau Islands; on the western and northern coast from Cape Ray to the Quirpon Islands, on the shores of the Magdalen Islands, and on the coasts, bays, harbours, and creeks from Mount Joly on the south coast of Labrador to and through the Strait of Belle Isle and thence northward indefinitely along the coast.[24] At the same time, American fishermen were given the liberty to dry and cure fish in any of the unsettled parts of these sections of the coasts of Newfoundland and Labrador. Elsewhere, the United States renounced the right of fishing or drying or curing fish on, or within 3 marine miles of any of the coasts, bays, creeks, or harbours of British North America.

In this treaty no explanation or definition of the term "bays" was given, or any method of determining the line from which the 3 marine miles was to be measured. In interpreting the treaty, Great Britain contended that "bays" meant all those waters that, in 1818, every fisherman and mariner knew as bays, and claimed that the 3-mile limit should be measured from a line joining the headlands of such waters. The United States, on the other hand, maintained that the bays should be confined to small indentations and that the 3-mile limit should be measured from a line following the sinuosities of the coast.

In these circumstances, trouble resulted whenever the British authorities seized American vessels for alleged illegal fishing, and disputes of varying seriousness occurred. In 1854 the "Reciprocity Treaty" admitted American fishermen to all British coast fisheries in the Atlantic in exchange for the admission of British fishermen into certain U.S. coast fisheries but this was terminated in 1866 and the U.S. fishermen reverted to the treaty of 1818. Ultimately, Great Britain and the United States agreed to submit all points in controversy to arbitration by the Hague Tribunal, for settlement in accordance with International Law. Of the seven decisions the tribunal made, that concerning territorial waters was as follows:

> In the case of bays the three marine miles are to be measured from a straight line drawn across the body of water at the place where it ceases to have the configuration and characteristics of a bay. At all other places the three marine miles are to be measured following the sinuosities of the coast.[25]

They also recommended a series of lines drawn from headland to headland of the bays in dispute, marking out definitely the points beyond which American fishermen could not go.

In a treaty signed by Great Britain and the United States in 1912, it was agreed that so far as they were applicable to Canada, these recommendations would become effective, except that Hudson Bay and Newfoundland were specifically excluded from the agreement.

Water Boundaries With The United States

While the fisheries controversy had been going on, water boundaries with the United States had been creating difficulties. The first of these arose out of the interpretation of the language of a treaty, this time over the boundary through the Gulf of Georgia to the Pacific Ocean, which was described in the Oregon Treaty of 1846 as follows:

> to the middle of the channel which separates the continent from Vancouver's Island; and thence southerly through the middle of the said channel, and of Fuca's strait to the Pacific Ocean: Provided, however, that the navigation of the whole of the said channel and straits, south of the forty-ninth parallel of north latitude, remain free and open to both parties.[26]

There was no single obvious "channel", owing to the existence of islands in the southern part of the Gulf of Georgia. Two, however, were in common use, Rosario Strait, between the major islands and the continental mainland, and Canal de Haro, between the islands and Vancouver Island. The first of these routes had been more frequently used in the days of sailing vessels and the British claimed that the boundary should pass through it. It was the channel marked on Vancouver's chart, and presumably, therefore, that to which the negotiators of the Oregon treaty

must have referred. Canal de Haro, on the other hand, had
become more popular with the increasing use of steamships,
and the United States maintained that the boundary should
run through it. The problem really involved the sovereignty
of the islands between the mainland and Vancouver Island.
The largest of these was San Juan. It was used only by
Indians until 1850, apart from the fact that some cattle belonging to the Hudson's Bay Company were pastured there.[27]
But in 1850 the Hudson's Bay Company established a salmon
cannery on the island, and in 1851 a post. Various incidents
occurred between the British and Americans, each occupying
and administering the island when they could, and with the
end of the United States Civil War, official action was
taken to settle the matter. The main argument of the United
States was that the only reason that led the negotiators
of the Oregon treaty to take the boundary south of the
49th Parallel was to give all of Vancouver Island to Great
Britain. The problem was referred to arbitration by the
Emperor of Germany, who in 1872 rendered an award in
favour of the United States.

On the opposite side of the continent, there was still
some doubt as to the exact course of the boundary in
Passamaquoddy Bay. This was corrected by the treaty concluded between Great Britain and the United States on May
21, 1910.

which laid down the position of the line by courses and
distances, starting from a point between Treat Island and
Campobello Island – and running thence in a general
southerly direction to the middle of Grand Manan Channel.
Popes Folly Island and the lighthouse between Woodward
Point and Cranberry Point were left within United States
territory.[28]

The Limits of Canadian Territorial Waters

Territorial waters again became a significant factor in
October 1932, when the activities of the Royal Canadian
Mounted Police in dealing with smugglers made it necessary
to consider the question of the extent of Canadian territorial
waters. Officially "Canadian territorial waters" means any
water designated by any Act of the Parliament of Canada
or by the Governor-in-Council as the territorial waters of
Canada, or any waters not so designated being within three
marine miles of any of the coasts, bays, creeks, or harbours of

Canada, and includes the inland waters of Canada.[29] Using generally accepted terminology, territorial waters were the marginal seas within 3 marine miles of the coast of Canada or of base lines delimiting the national waters of Canada, as determined in accordance with international law and practice. National waters mean the waters that form part of the national territory of Canada. It will be recalled that, in 1910, the Hague Tribunal had made certain decisions and awards regarding the boundaries between national and territorial waters, where they were adjacent, in so far as they concerned the North Atlantic Fishing Limits under the Treaty of 1818 between Great Britain and the United States. The problem that faced the Canadian government in 1932 was that such boundaries needed to be defined for the areas not considered by the Hague Tribunal. In 1937, an Order in Council was passed that set forth the unanimous views and recommendations of a Committee of the Privy Council in relation to the delimitation of territorial waters in respect of the St. Lawrence estuary and of the bays, gulfs, and straits of Nova Scotia, New Brunswick, and Prince Edward Island, the Pacific coast, and Hudson Bay and Strait. It is noteworthy that in the case of the bays, gulfs, and straits in Nova Scotia, New Brunswick, and Prince Edward Island, the base lines were drawn in accordance with the recommendations of the Hague Tribunal. (These were modified after 1964 in accordance with the Geneva Convention of 1958 under which waters enclosed by headlands distant up to 24 miles are territorial waters.) It is also to be noted that in the St. Lawrence estuary the base line from which territorial waters were to be measured was "a line drawn from Cape Rosières on the Gaspé Peninsula to the west end of the Island of Anticosti to the mouth of the River St. John". Hudson Bay and Strait were regarded as national waters, as territorial waters were to be measured from a line "from Button Island to Hatton Headland on Resolution Island". This was presumably on the grounds that Hudson Bay and Strait together constitute an "historic bay", as although the entrance to them is about 32 miles wide, historically sovereignty was asserted over the area by Great Britain and France and was implied by the Hudson's Bay Company's charter. Furthermore, Hudson Bay and Strait had been specifically included in the districts of Ungava, Keewatin, and Franklin as defined by the Order in Council of 1897, were declared to be territorial waters of Canada by Act of Parliament in 1906[30], and are, at the present time, an integral part of the Northwest Territories.

Finally, it will be noted that no action was then to be taken with regard to Arctic waters. Senator Poirier's "sector", therefore, still remains in an indefinite official state, but it has recently come to take on added meaning with the possibility that large areas of sea ice may be used as airfields. If this becomes a reality, then the question of sovereignty over the ice in "Poirier's sector" will no doubt have to be examined, for it will have some of the aspects and uses of dry land. The use of the polar ice is a reality. In 1956-57, Russians made 30 landings on polar ice within 150 miles of Canadian land. The landing closest to the Canadian shore was 121 miles from Ellesmere Island, but there were other landings only 130 miles from Prince Patrick Island and 140 miles from Banks Island. This led to the contention that Canada should officially claim "the ice cap lest the Russians occupy it and build airfields and radar lines on it."[31] By 1962 there was some evidence that the Russian drift stations in the central Arctic basin had "acquired a perman- ent character."[32] However the federal Minister of Northern Affairs in 1956 felt that any claim by Canada could not be substantiated as "the polar ice cap in the Arctic Ocean was the high seas, whether liquid or frozen,"[33] a view that was shared by other international authorities.[34] Perhaps, as the Canadian secretary of State for External Affairs said in 1969 the general principles of international law may have to be applied in a special way in the case of frozen waters."[35]

The question of the claim to complete control of all the waters within the polar sector (as opposed to semi-permanent sea ice) is a slightly different one especially since 1954 when H.M.C.S. *Labrador* became the first deep-draft vessel to sail through the Northwest Passage. If pressed, the claim would probably not be accepted by either the U.S.S.R. or the U.S.A. For example, Commander Steele, USN describing a relatively recent voyage through Parry Channel said

We lay to at the edge of the anchorage in *international waters* . . . Barely discernible were the Quonset huts and installations ashore [at Resolute, on Cornwallis Island].[36]

However, the federal government considers that at least the channels between the islands are Canadian waters with some evidence of U.S. support. In 1957 the Prime Minister stated that they were consulted

about the usual movement of supply ships for United States requirements . . . Each year the United States navy has been required to apply for a waiver of the provisions of the Canada Shipping Act, since the cargo ships they charter operate in Canadian coastal waters . . . We make it a condition of the consent we have given to these arrangements that they apply for a waiver from the provisions that would otherwise apply in Canadian territorial waters.[37]

In addition, Canada endeavours to have some ships of her own attached to any U.S. expeditions for exploration and survey. The giant U.S. oil tanker, S.S. *Manhattan,* for example, was escorted by the Canadian Department of Transport icebreaker *John A. Macdonald* when it made the voyage through the arctic islands in 1969.

International Adjustments

Article V of the 1908 Treaty concerning the boundary between the United States and Canada provided for the survey and demarcation of the boundary. The survey showed the necessity for certain minor adjustments. These were made the basis of a further treaty, which was signed at Washington on February 24, 1925.

The first of these adjustments concerned Lake of the Woods. Surveys showed that the line drawn south from the northwestern point of the lake intersected the water boundary in Northwest Angle Inlet in five places "adjacent to and directly south of the said northwesternmost point, and that there are two small areas of United States waters in Lake of the Woods, comprising a total area of two and one-half acres, entirely surrounded by Canadian waters".[38] No permanent monuments were ever erected on the boundary lines north of the most southerly of these points of intersection, so that the southernmost of them was adopted in lieu of the previously established northwesternmost point. By this change Canada gained the $2\frac{1}{2}$ acres of water area.

The second adjustment concerned the lines between monuments established on the 49th Parallel east of the Rocky Mountains. They had been established as curved lines, following the parallel, in 1908 but were now changed to straight lines. By this change Canada lost about 30 acres of land.

The third adjustment was made to extend the boundary in Passamaquoddy Bay seaward to the limit of territorial waters of Canada and the United States. By this, Canada gained a water area of about 9 acres.

The Labrador Boundary

If one were to accept the "sector principle" as having settled Canada's northern boundaries, the only major outstanding boundary problem by 1927 concerned Labrador, a "dependency" of the island of Newfoundland. The original acquisition of this dependency dates from the Royal Proclamation of 1763, but it was transferred to Quebec in 1774 and back to Newfoundland in 1809, and changes were made in its extent in 1825. Thus Labrador was tossed back and forth like a shuttlecock but in these see-sawings it is significant that each time control was returned to Newfoundland the territory it regained was reduced by an area predominantly occupied by French Canadians, who undoubtedly objected to English law. That any territory ever passed back to Newfoundland was probably due to a similar dislike on the part of Newfoundland fishermen for Quebec law. By the Labrador Act of 1809, Newfoundland lost the Magdalen Islands, and by the Labrador Act of 1825, Anticosti and part of the north shore of the St. Lawrence, but a certain part of Labrador was repeatedly re-annexed to Newfoundland. Apart from the modification of 1825, this part must have had the same extent as it had in 1763. Whatever its area, it must have been sufficiently great for the administration of justice, so far as it affected the fishermen.

However, no attempt was made to define clearly the inland boundary of Labrador. The issue was first raised in 1888 by Robert Pinsent, a judge of the Supreme Court of Newfoundland, when he observed a discrepancy between the extent of Newfoundland's jurisdiction in Labrador as defined by the Newfoundland Letters Patent of 28th March, 1876, and as shown by a map of Labrador published in 1880 by the authority of the Canadian Minister of the Interior.

The 1876 Letters Patent appointed Sir Stephen Hill Governor of the

> Island of Newfoundland, and the islands adjacent, and all the coast of Labrador from the entrance of Hudson's Straits to a line to be drawn due north and south from Ance Sablon on the said coast to the fifty-second degree of north latitude, and all the islands adjacent to that part of the said coast of Labrador. . . .[39]

This appeared to Pinsent to allot a much smaller area of Labrador to Newfoundland than the map indicated, and he considered that the matter should be rectified so that there would be no doubt as to the jurisdiction of the courts of

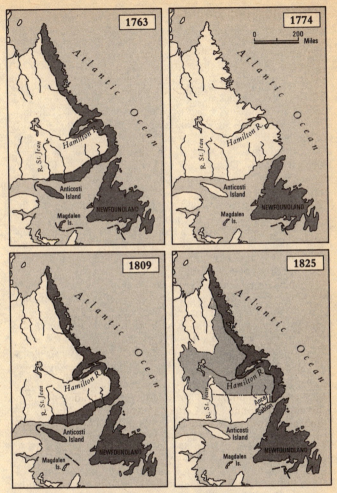

Approximate limits of Newfoundland and its dependencies, in diagrammatic form only ── ── ──
Approximate landward boundary between Canada and Newfoundland after 1927 ── ·── ·──

Figure 15. The evolution of the boundaries of Newfoundland.

Newfoundland. The Canadian Department of the Interior reported that the line was marked as a dotted line and described as "supposed" or "undefined".[40] There the matter rested, in effect, until the beginning of the twentieth century, when the existence in the interior of Labrador of timber that could be used for making paper was realized. For in 1902 the Grand River Pulp and Lumber Company obtained from the government of Newfoundland leases to cut timber on an area of 297 square miles on both the north and south sides of Hamilton River between Lake Melville and Grand Falls.

The government of Quebec, on hearing of this, maintained that the area concerned was under its jurisdiction, and warned the company that all the territory south of Hamilton River belonged to the province of Quebec, that the right to cut timber there could be acquired only from it, and that any cutting upon the territory in question without a licence from the Quebec Department of Lands, Mines, and Fisheries would be considered a violation of the law and would be dealt with accordingly.[41]

The Quebec government also referred the matter to the government of Canada which maintained that nothing could be included within Newfoundland Labrador but coasts and islands, and that "coast" could not possibly be so interpreted as to include the territory through which Hamilton River flows, hundreds of miles from the ocean.[42]

The Newfoundland government disagreed with this interpretation, but proceedings were nevertheless taken against some of the alleged "poachers" and ultimately the governments of Canada and Newfoundland agreed to submit the matter to the Judicial Committee of the Privy Council.

Newfoundland contended that the boundary should be the line drawn due north from Ance Sablon (now known as Blanc Sablon) as far as the 52nd degree of north latitude, thence northwards along the watershed of rivers flowing into the Atlantic Ocean, to Cape Chidley. Canada submitted that the boundary was a line delimiting the area of the coast accessible and useful to the fisheries and proposed that it should be located and defined as a line to be drawn from the eastern headland of the bay or harbour of Blanc Sablon, on the south, to Cape Chidley on the north, at a distance of 1 mile from high-water mark on the sea-coast of Labrador.

Both sides based their cases on the interpretation of various Orders in Council, proclamations, and statutes, but the Judicial Committee supported the "height of land" argument on several grounds. First of all, under international law, occupation of a sea-coast was said to carry with it a right to the whole territory drained by the rivers that empty their waters into it. Furthermore, in the absence of any specified boundary or of any special feature (such as a political frontier) that could be taken as a boundary, they recognized the difficulty of suggesting any point between the seashore and the watershed at which a line could be drawn. However, the line of the watershed running from Cape Chidley southward was for a considerable distance the eastern boundary of the Hudson's Bay Company's former territory, and so the watershed might for that distance form a "political" as well as a "natural" boundary for the "coast" of Labrador. Thirdly, in their opinion, the language of the Imperial Act of 1825 implied that the expression "coasts of Labrador" as used in 1763 and 1809 was understood by the British Parliament in 1825 to have comprised the country back to the watershed.

The Committee considered the Canadian contention that the boundary should be drawn 1 mile from high-water mark was unsound. A large part of this mile-wide strip lay at the summit of high cliffs, was inaccessible from the sea, and was, therefore, useless to the fishery, which, according to Canada's argument, had been the reason for allotting the coast of Labrador to Newfoundland. Secondly, access to wood for repairs was essential for the proper conduct of the fishery, and sufficient wood could be obtained for this purpose only if the fishermen were free to cut timber for an average distance of 3 miles and a maximum of 5 miles from high-water mark. This was confirmed by the practice invariably followed by the Newfoundland government, which, when granting timber concessions on the island of Newfoundland itself, always reserved a margin of at least 3, and sometimes 5, miles for the use of fishermen. Third, the 1-mile limit was impractical because

> there are places where a broad peninsula is joined to the mainland by a neck of not more than two miles in width, and in each of these instances the one-mile strip would meet in the neck of the peninsula and cut off by an interposed barrier of Newfoundland soil all access to the Canadian enclave on the broader part of the promontory.[43]

However, the Privy Council did not feel that the boundary claimed by Newfoundland in the south was warranted by the terms of the statute of 1825. For these and other reasons, their Lordships were of the opinion that

> the boundary between Canada and Newfoundland in the Labrador Peninsula is a line drawn due north from the eastern boundary of the bay or harbour of Ance Sablon as far as the fifty-second degree of north latitude, and from thence westward along that parallel until it reaches

the Romaine River, and then northward along the left or east bank of that river and its head waters to their source and from thence due north to the crest of the watershed or height or land there, and from thence westward and northward along the crest of the watershed of the rivers flowing into the Atlantic Ocean until it reaches Cape Chidley.[44]

As a result, Woody Island, a small island lying opposite Ance Sablon, and claimed by both Canada and Newfoundland, was awarded to Canada because it lies just west of the boundary line.

Thus, in 1927, Newfoundland's sovereignty was confirmed over an area of some 112,000 square miles of territory, and the eastern boundary of Canada was defined. The only question that seems to have arisen with regard to the actual description of the boundary (as opposed to other issues which are discussed later) concerned Port Burwell where a Hudson's Bay post and an R.C.M.P. post were situated. It was located on the western side of Killinek Island in Hudson Strait, and Cape Chidley, the northern terminus of the Labrador boundary, is the northeasternmost point of the island. The watershed boundary passes between them so that Port Burwell was judged to be in Canada and as the islands in Hudson Strait are not part of Quebec, the non-Labrador portion of Killinek island is within the Northwest Territories.[45]

From Sea to Sea

Not for long, however, was Canada to have a land boundary on the east, for in 1949 Newfoundland joined Confederation and became Canada's tenth province.

The boundaries of the new province remained essentially as they had been when Newfoundland was a separated political entity. Some changes in terminology resulted, however, for whereas it had been common to refer to the island of Newfoundland simply as "Newfoundland" and for the "Coast of Labrador" to be regarded as its dependency, both areas now had the same status, for together they formed one province. Furthermore, any Newfoundland "territorial waters" passed to the control of the government of Canada. Exactly what these territorial waters were may be a matter of doubt. It has been mentioned earlier that the agreement between Great Britain and the United States in 1912 did not cover Newfoundland waters, but they were covered by the recommendations of the Hague tribunal and it appears unlikely that these could be successfully challenged.[46]

But the entry of Newfoundland into Confederation also raised other problems with regard to Canada's territorial waters, which, in the east, had last been defined by the Order in Council in 1937. For example, should the Gulf of St. Lawrence now be declared a "mare clausum", as had been done with Hudson Bay in 1937? Canada had subscribed to the view that her territorial waters included the marginal sea within 3 marine miles of the base lines on the coast. But the configuration of Canada's coast was such that if this was strictly adhered to there was an international passage through such water bodies as Hudson Strait and Hudson Bay, the channels between many of the Arctic islands, and between Vancouver Island and the Queen Charlotte Islands and the mainland. In 1956 it was reported that the federal government intended to claim as Canadian territory the Gulf of St. Lawrence and Hecate Strait[47] and in 1960 the Canadian Secretary of State for External Affairs told a Commons committee that Canada asserts that the Gulf of St. Lawrence is Canadian territorial water, but other countries had not officially recognized this claim. For example, in 1963 a U.S. authority was quoted as saying that the United States considers the Gulf of St. Lawrence part of the high seas.[48] Nonetheless, jurisdiction over the marginal seas of Canada has been extended in recent years owing to the need to conserve the resources they contain and to explore systematically the resources below the sea bed. These extensions followed the International Conference on the Law of the Sea in 1959 when it was decided that the mineral resources of continental shelves – the sea bed out to where the water is 200 metres (approximately 100 fathoms, some 600 feet) deep – belong to adjacent countries. This gave Canada an increase of one-seventh its total land area, a potentially important region for mineral research. To a depth of 200 metres the right of the coastal state is exclusive; no other State can stake a claim within this limit. At greater depths, possession goes with ability to exploit. The convention applies only to land beneath the sea, not to the waters and not to the airspace above.

Concern over the proper utilization and conservation of the resources of the sea itself were dealt with by setting up "fishing zones"

those areas of the sea contiguous to the territorial sea of Canada and having as their inner limits, the outer limits of

the territorial sea and, as their outer limits, lines measured
seaward and equidistant from such inner limits so that each
point of the outer limit line of a fishing zone is distant
nine nautical miles from the nearest point of the inner
limit line.[49]

Although the Act of Parliament establishing these zones
was proclaimed in 1964, precise limits were not announced
until 1967 (for most of the Atlantic coast)[50] 1969 (for the
Pacific coast)[51] and 1971.[52] The latter designated the Gulf of
St. Lawrence, the Bay of Fundy and Queen Charlotte Sound,
Hecate Strait and Dixon Entrance as Fishing Zones 1, 2 and
3 respectively which is noteworthy in the light of the remarks
made earlier regarding the possibility of these areas being
regarded as territorial waters. No further action was taken
with regard to the Arctic. It should be noted that these
actions did not extend the territorial limits of Canada.
"Canadian waters" means the territorial sea of Canada and
all internal waters of Canada. "Canadian fisheries waters"
means all waters in the fishing zones of Canada, all waters
in the territorial sea of Canada and all internal waters of
Canada.[53]

However in 1976 it was announced that "in light of the
crisis situation pertaining in the fisheries off Canada's coasts,
the areas under fisheries jurisdiction on the Atlantic and
Pacific coasts would be extended to 200 miles as of January
1, 1977."[54] The details were promulgated in November
1976.[55]

The intention to extend the fisheries limits in the Arctic
to 200 miles by March 1, 1977 was also stated but no details
were given beyond the fact that the northern limit of the
Atlantic zone was 66 degs. 15 mins. N.

But if the entry of Newfoundland stimulated matters with
regard to territorial waters, it also refocused attention on
its boundary with Quebec, which in 1949 ceased to be an
international boundary and became an interprovincial one.
The maps published by the province of Quebec still do not
show this boundary "pour cause". Attention will, therefore,
now be turned to an examination of the ways in which the
other interprovincial boundaries of Canada evolved.

CHAPTER V

SETTLING THE OLDER PROVINCIAL BOUNDARIES

The boundary situations existing in Canada in 1873 are summarized in Table I. The limits of Prince Edward Island were known exactly; it had, of course, no interprovincial boundaries. The boundary between New Brunswick and Nova Scotia had been delimited and demarcated since 1858. The boundaries of British Columbia and Manitoba, and the New Brunswick-Quebec boundary, were precisely delimited, as was the boundary between Quebec and Ontario in the main. But the western and northern boundaries of Ontario and the northern and eastern boundaries of Quebec were only loosely defined, and it was this fact that led to the first problems Canada had to face with regard to her major internal boundaries. Although the interprovincial boundaries between Nova Scotia, New Brunswick, and Quebec were settled by 1873, their settlement had been by no means a simple matter, and an examination of the problems involved in these earlier interprovincial disputes provides a background for the remaining problems connected with Ontario and Quebec with which Canada was confronted virtually at the time of its creation.

The Nova Scotia-New Brunswick Boundary

The present boundary between New Brunswick and Nova Scotia was established in 1858-59, but there had been a division between these two parts of historic Acadia long before that. Such a division was first contemplated by Sir William Alexander in 1624, "the country of New Scotland, being dividit into twa Provinces".[1] Alexander's own map shows Alexandria, the present New Brunswick, and Caledonia, the present Nova Scotia.

During the period of French occupation, between 1632 and 1636, two grants were made in Acadia. In 1632, the Company

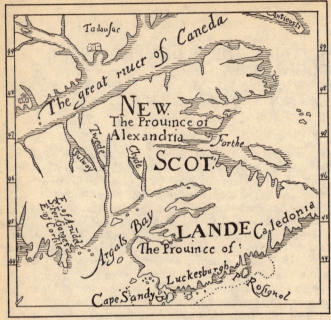

Figure 16. Sir William Alexander's map of New Scotland.

of New France granted the Bay of Fundy and the River
St. Croix to De Razilly, and in 1635 they granted the territory
at the mouth of St. John River to Charles La Tour. After
the death of De Razilly in 1636, his rights in Acadia devolved
upon his brother, who sold them to Charnisay, one of
De Razilly's lieutenants. Charnisay immediately insisted upon
these rights, which led to disputes with La Tour, as the
boundaries of their grants overlapped. The matter was referred to the King of France, who in 1638, established
boundaries between his two lieutenants in a letter to Charnisay
as follows:

> . . . . vous soyez mon Lieutenant général en la côte des
> Etchemins, à prendre depuis le milieu de la terre ferme de
> la Baie Françoise[2], en tirant verse les Virgines, et Gou-
> verneur de Pentagoet; et que le charge du sieur de La Tour
> mon Lieutenant général en la côte d'Acadie, soit depuis
> le milieu de la Baie Françoise jusqu'au détroit de Canseau.
> . . .[3]

These boundaries, although still not stated with absolute

TABLE I

Boundary Situation, 1873

Boundary	Status		
	Demarcated	Precisely delimited	Generally delimited
International –			
Canada-United States	x		
Canada-United States (Alaska)			x
Canada-Newfoundland			x
Intranational –			
Quebec-New Brunswick	x		
New Brunswick-Nova Scotia	x		
Prince Edward Island	x		
Ontario-Quebec		x	
Manitoba-Ontario		x	
British Columbia-Territories		x	
Manitoba-Territories		x	
Quebec-Territories			x
Ontario-Territories			x

precision, in effect awarded the peninsula to La Tour and the mainland to Charnisay.

Such a division was also tacitly recognized as existing between the territories of the English and French during the time when the limits of Acadia were under discussion prior to 1735, but its final adoption in 1784 was probably not influenced by the earlier use.

The causes leading up to the decision to constitute New Brunswick a separate province have been fully discussed in Chapter III. When the decision was taken, in 1784, three dividing lines were considered. The line finally adopted was described in the commission dated August 16, 1784, to Thomas Carleton as Captain-General and Governor-in-Chief of New Brunswick as

  . . . . to the south by a line in the centre of the Bay of Fundy, from the River St. Croix aforesaid to the mouth of the Musquat River, by the said river to its source and from thence by a due east line across the Isthmus into the Bay Verte. . . .[4]

This boundary appears to have been entirely satisfactory to New Brunswick, but it did not suit the authorities at Halifax at all. The boundary area, notably between Sackville and Amherst, had been settled between 1761 and 1765 by New Englanders, with later additions from Yorkshire, England. Large numbers of immigrants from the United States settled in other parts of what is now Nova Scotia at about the same time, while few went elsewhere in the New Brunswick part. Conversely, of the Loyalists who migrated to British North America in 1783, only a few went to the head of Chignecto Bay, the majority going to the St. John Valley. In Nova Scotia, where fewer Loyalists settled, the New Englanders had a proportionally greater share in the government and it was natural that these people should be regarded by Nova Scotia as "belonging" to them rather than to New Brunswick. The new boundary divided these "old" settlements between the two provinces, and Nova Scotia made most determined efforts to have it changed. The arguments put forward by the House of Assembly of Nova Scotia in 1792 stated that the division line was vague and indeterminate because of the many sources of Musquat River and that it inconvenienced the inhabitants of the counties of Cumberland and Westmorland by dividing their land so that some parts were subject to the government of New Brunswick and other parts to Nova Scotia. The limits of the jurisdiction of the courts in the border counties were also alleged to be difficult to determine and hence a further inconvenience. As a result, Nova Scotia was deprived of part of its revenue. No assessments could be levied and collected and the laws could be easily evaded.

These arguments aroused spirited rejoinders in New Brunswick. The legislature of that province not only maintained that there had been no complaints from the inhabitants concerning the boundary, but also that it was the most natural boundary that could be drawn between the two provinces. Its whole length was less than 17 miles and the part where any possible uncertainty could exist did not exceed one-fifth of the total distance and, moreover, passed through wilderness land. The controversy dragged on for several years, but no major changes were made in the boundary of 1784 and so the matter appears to have ended.

The definition of the boundary as ultimately accepted by Nova Scotia and New Brunswick and confirmed by the

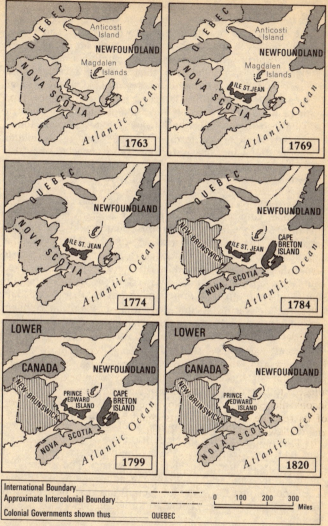

Figure 17. Boundary evolution in the Gulf of St. Lawrence region.

legislatures of both provinces, following enactment by the Imperial Government, was as follows:

> Commencing at the mouth of the Missiguash River in Cumberland Bay, and thence following the several courses

of the said river to a post near Black Island, thence north fifty-four degrees twenty-five minutes East, crossing the South end of Black Island two hundred and eighty-eight chains to the South angle of Trenholm Island, thence North thirty-seven degrees East eighty-five chains and eighty-two links to a post, thence North seventy-six degrees East, forty-six chains and twenty links to the portage, thence South sixty-five degrees forty-five minutes East, three hundred and ninety-four chains and forty links to Tidnish Bridge, thence following the several courses of said river along its northern upland bank to its mouth, thence following the northwesterly channel to the deep water of the Bay Verte, giving to Nova Scotia the control of the navigable waters on Tidnish River.[5]

This does not precisely follow the boundary described in Carleton's commission. The minor changes were probably made so as to effect a compromise that would benefit both provinces. In the upper reaches of the Missiguash the boundary runs in such a way as to give the entire river to Nova Scotia. It does not start from the source of the river, but some 2 miles to the southwest of it, thus leaving the entire highway from Cumberland Basin to Baie Verte, and the grants along it, to New Brunswick. Probably in compensation for the allotment of this territory to New Brunswick, the line does not continue to the sea but stops at Tidnish River, which went to Nova Scotia.

The New Brunswick-Quebec Boundary

In 1784, the northern boundary of Nova Scotia became the northern boundary of New Brunswick. As already stated, this had been defined, in 1763, as the watershed between the rivers that drained into the St. Lawrence and those that drained into the sea. In 1784, the commission to Thomas Carleton, as first Governor of New Brunswick, described the northern and western boundaries of the new province as follows:

. . . . bounded on the westward by the mouth of the River St. Croix, by the said river to its source, and by a line drawn due north from thence to the southern boundary of our Province of Quebec, to the northward, by the said boundary as far as the western extremity of the Bay des Chaleurs.[6]

Shortly after this a controversy broke out between the surveyors-general of Quebec and New Brunswick, mainly because the seigniory of Madawaska and part of Temiscouata were south of the watershed and, therefore, according to Carleton's commission, should have gone to New Brunswick. But Quebec had been exercising some jurisdiction over these areas for many years. It was under its authority that the seigniory of Madawaska had been granted in 1683; in 1763 Quebec had issued a proclamation prohibiting all Canadians from interfering with the Indian hunting grounds above the Great Falls of the River St. John, and in 1784 an Indian had been tried by the Quebec authorities for a murder committed at Madawaska.

But at this time the boundary between British and American territory was in dispute, and it was quite apparent to the authorities that if the northern watershed were fixed as the boundary between New Brunswick and Quebec then it would have to be accepted as the boundary between Canada and the United States in the area immediately west. In these circumstances, neither New Brunswick nor Quebec would gain Temiscouata and Madawaska: these areas would go to the United States. Quite apart from the loss of this territory *per se,* it would also have meant that the invaluable line of communication through it, connecting the Maritime Provinces with the other British colonies, would be lost. In those days, when the rivers were the principal highways, St. John and Madawaska Rivers afforded the only practical link between Quebec and Halifax. In summer it was shorter, safer, and cheaper than the sea route via the St. Lawrence, and in winter it was the only practical route.

An attempt at settlement occurred in 1787, but was fruitless, and New Brunswick assumed jurisdiction over the Madawaska district and granted licences of occupation to a number of Acadians. Shortly after this, however, Governor Carleton of New Brunswick suggested that the boundary might be described so as to run from the western extremity of the Baie de Chaleur, along the River Restigouche to its source, and thence by a straight line westward to the already established watershed boundary.

This suggestion of Carleton's with regard to the Restigouche was followed up by occupation, whether intentional or not. Quebec exercised jurisdiction north of its mouth and New Brunswick south of it, and as a result the river became recognized as the boundary by the people living in the area. But it was certainly never officially recognized, and the signing of the Ashburton Treaty with the United States in 1842 revived the problem, because that treaty effected a compromise with respect to the international boundary, and territory south of the highlands or watershed divide and west of the "due north line" remained in British hands. The main activities in this area were concerned with lumbering, in which not only individual citizens were interested, but also the provincial governments, as these derived a large part of their revenues from stumpage on timber cut on public lands. Some settlement had, by this time, occurred in the area, mainly under the authority of New Brunswick, whose laws were, therefore, more familiar to the new inhabitants than those of Quebec. Furthermore, the rivers were still the main means of transportation, and the southward flowing St. John and its tributaries the Madawaska and St. Francis formed the outlets for the timber and other products of the country. During the struggle with the United States over the International Boundary, New Brunswick had stoutly maintained jurisdiction over much of the area and had frustrated attempts at occupation from the state of Maine. Lower Canada (Quebec) on the other hand took no active part in these operations.[7]

But the two provinces could not agree on the disposition of the territory, so the British government appointed a commission to examine the situation. The commission, in 1848, recommended a division of the territory in dispute by prolonging the straight line of the treaty of 1842 to 47°50′ N. (it will be noted from their map (Figure 18) that this parallel was actually north of 47°50′N.), and continuing the boundary east along this parallel to Kedgewick River, which would then form the boundary with the Restigouche to the Baie de Chaleur. Part of Restigouche River was retained as the boundary because settlement had taken place in both provinces from some distance on each side of the river. The remaining part of the boundary placed most of the country in dispute in New Brunswick, to which province the commission considered it would be "beneficially and properly assigned".[8]

But although New Brunswick was prepared to agree to the recommendations of the report, the Province of Canada was not. The British government, therefore, in 1850, suggested that two arbitrators be appointed, one by each province, to decide the question, and in 1851 they rendered their decision, which became the foundation of the boundary as it exists today. In their final judgment the arbitrators made adjustments to the satisfaction of both sides and the

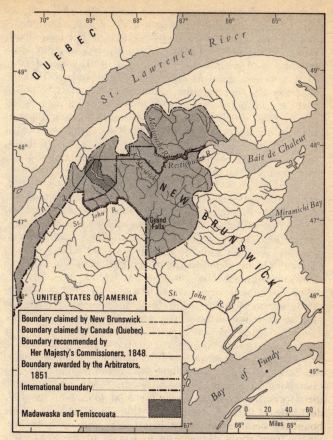

Figure 18. The Quebec-New Brunswick boundary (after a map
                accompanying the Report of Her Majesty's Boundary
                Commissioners, 1848).

disputed boundary was finally settled by Imperial Act of
Parliament in 1851, as follows:

> That New Brunswick shall be bounded on the West by
> the Boundary of the United States, as traced by the
> Commissioners of Boundary under the Treaty of Wash-
> ington dated August 1842, from the Source of the Saint
> Croix to a Point near the Outlet of Lake Pech-la-wee-kaa-
> co-nies or Lake Beau, marked A. in the accompanying

Copy of a Part of Plan 17 of the Survey of the Boundary
under the above Treaty; thence by a straight Line connecting that Point with another Point to be determined
at the Distance of One Mile due South from the Southernmost Point of Long Lake; thence by a straight Line drawn
to the Southernmost Point of the Fiefs Madawaska and
Temiscouata, and along the Southeastern Boundary of those
Fiefs to the South-east Angle of the same; thence by a
meridional Line Northwards till it meets a Line running
East and West, and tangent to the Height of Land dividing the Waters flowing into the River Rimouski from those
tributary to the Saint John; thence along this tangent Line
Eastward until it meets another meridional Line tangent
to the Height of Land dividing Waters flowing into the
River Rimouski from those flowing into the Restigouche
River; thence along this meridional Line to the 48th Parallel
of Latitude; thence along that Parallel to the Mistouche
River; and thence down the Centre of the Stream of that
River to the Restigouche; thence down the Centre of the
Stream of the Restigouche to its mouth in the Bay of
Chaleurs; and thence through the Middle of that Bay
to the Gulfs of the Saint Lawrence; the Islands in the
said Rivers Mistouche and Restigouche to the Mouth of
the latter River at Dalhousie being given to New Brunswick.[9]

By this Act, Temiscouata and the Seigniory of Madawaska
were assigned to Canada, and the upper reaches of St.
John River went to New Brunswick. As the southern
boundary of the seigniory was taken as the interprovincial
boundary, it was deemed reasonable to extend this line
westward to the International Boundary, and to award to
Canada the territory lying west of the Seigniory and north
of this line. The area involved was of little use to New
Brunswick, and would have presented very awkward administrative problems if left under her jurisdiction.

The next part of the boundary was the northern watershed
always claimed by New Brunswick, although it does not
follow the natural windings of the watershed, but lines that
were thought at the time to be tangential to its windings
and would, therefore, be easy to demarcate. The next part
of the line is the parallel of 48 degrees. This may have
been chosen not only because it was an even parallel but
because it was also thought to form almost another tangent
line to the highlands and, as a substitute for the 47°50′ N.
of the commission of 1848, it also gave some additional

territory to New Brunswick in compensation for the loss of part of the Madawaska area. Also as compensation to New Brunswick, the Mistouche (later identified as the Patapedia) was chosen as part of the river boundary, as it was the first large river east of the Kedgewick, which formed part of the boundary claimed by Canada.[10]

The Western and Northern Boundaries of Ontario

When the Province of Canada was divided into Upper and Lower Canada in 1791, Upper Canada had been defined as including "the utmost extent of the country commonly called or known by the name of Canada". A proclamation by Governor Simcoe in 1792 divided Upper Canada into electoral districts and defined Kent, the westernmost one, in similar phraseology. As a result, when the province of Ontario was created it claimed to extend to the Rocky Mountains on the west and the Arctic slope on the north and north-west.

But after the surrender to Canada in 1870 of all territorial rights and claims of the Hudson's Bay Company, the government of Ontario became interested in securing a more precise definition of its boundaries on the west and north. On November 3, 1869, the Lieutenant-Governor of Ontario, in his opening address to the Legislature, referred to the transfer to Canada of the Northwest Territory and suggested an early definition of the boundary line between that territory and his province.[11]

This boundary depended upon the definition of the southern limit of the Hudson's Bay Company's former territories. None of the boundaries of "Rupert's Land" and the "Northwestern Territory" had ever been authoritatively determined with precision. According to the Hudson's Bay Company, Rupert's Land extended to the watershed of all rivers flowing into Hudson Bay and was so depicted on the maps drawn by Arrowsmith, the company's geographer. This appears to be the greatest extent of Rupert's Land under any reasonable interpretation.

On the other hand, in 1700, after the Treaty of Ryswick, the Hudson's Bay Company had informed the Lords of Trade and Plantations that, if it became necessary, it was willing to accept 53 degrees north, or Albany River, as its southern boundary on the west coast of the bay. The company specifically stressed, however, that "the whole streights and Bay" belonged to it by right and, as events turned out, the suggested boundary never became operative. The government of Ontario, however, claimed this as the province's northern boundary. It maintained that the territory south of this line and north of the watershed of the Great Lakes, which was conceded by the treaties of Utrecht and Paris, reverted to the British Crown and not to the Hudson's Bay Company. The Hudson's Bay Company's employees who operated in this area after 1700 did so, Ontario maintained, as British subjects with merely the same rights and privileges as other traders.[12]

The government of Canada, however, took the view that the height of land between the St. Lawrence and Hudson Bay constituted the northern boundary of Ontario. This skirted the northern shores of Lakes Superior and Nipigon at distances of from 15 to 50 miles.

The western boundary depended upon the interpretation of various Acts of Parliament, Royal Proclamations, and Commissions since 1763. Ontario contended that the boundary was a due north line from the source of the Mississippi (approximately 95°14′ W.). This contention was based on Sir Guy Carleton's Commission as Governor of Quebec, issued a few months after the Quebec Act of 1774, which described his government as extending from the confluence of the Ohio and Mississippi northward along the eastern bank of the Mississippi to the southern boundary of the Hudson's Bay Company's territories. But the federal government defined this eastern boundary as the prolongation of a due north line from the confluence of the Ohio and the Mississippi. This interpretation was based on the phrase in the Quebec Act of 1774 that defined the boundary of Quebec as extending along the bank of the Ohio River "Westward, to the Banks of the Mississippi, and Northward to the Southern Boundary of the Territory granted to the Merchants Adventurers of England, trading to Hudson's Bay". By this interpretation the boundary would be in approximate longitude 89°9′ W. The country between this meridian and that claimed by Ontario, about 275 miles in width from east to west, became known as "The Disputed Territory".

The federal boundary would have divided the existing settlements on the shores of Thunder Bay and alienated from Ontario a large area over which it had for some time been exercising jurisdiction. Even by 1857, over 25,000 acres of land had been patented by the Province of Canada on the north shore of Lake Superior west of longitude 88°50′ W. By the time of Confederation an additional 10,000 acres had been patented in the same area, and included the village

of Prince Arthur's Landing, the settlement around Fort William (the site of the projected terminus of the Canadian
Pacific Railway), and the townships of Blake, Crooks, Pardee,
Paiponge, Oliver, Neeling, and McIntyre. If the "Disputed
Territory" were not awarded to Ontario, all of this rapidly
developing area would be excluded from that province,
leaving to it a narrow strip north of the Great Lakes and
south of the height of land.[13]

In 1872 the government of Ontario was called upon by the
federal Department of Public Works to pay for the maintenance of a police force at Thunder Bay and for construction
at Prince Arthur's Landing. The payments were made, but,
because the areas to which they referred were being claimed
by the federal government, Ontario asked under what authority the expenditures in question had been made.

This led to provisional boundaries being agreed on; these
were confirmed by Orders in Council of both governments,
in 1874, as follows:

> On the West: – the meridian line passing through the most
> easterly point of Hunter's Island, run south until it meets
> the Boundary Line between the United States and Canada,
> and north until it intersects the fifty-first parallel of latitude;
> and the said fifty-first parallel of latitude shall be the
> Conventional Boundary of the Province of Ontario on the
> North.[14]

The westerly provisional line thus agreed upon was at about
91 degrees west longitude.

In 1878, in an endeavour to settle the question, three
arbitrators were chosen and their conclusions became known
as "The Award". The terms, which were satisfactory to the
province of Ontario, were accepted by that province on
March 11, 1879, by 42 Vict. Cap. 2, but the legislation necessary to give them binding effect was not passed by the
federal government and the Award, therefore, remained
inoperative.

The problem was, however, brought sharply into focus in
December 1880, when the Manitoba Legislature passed an Act
extending the boundaries of that province. This Act was
confirmed by the federal parliament on March 21, 1881, by
44 Vict. Cap. 14. It was not, however, confirmed by the
province of Ontario, for the extension of Manitoba eastward
was to the "westerly limits of Ontario", which, in Canada's
view as well as Manitoba's, followed the meridian of the
confluence of the Ohio and the Mississippi. Had Ontario
agreed to the Manitoba Boundary Act, it might have been

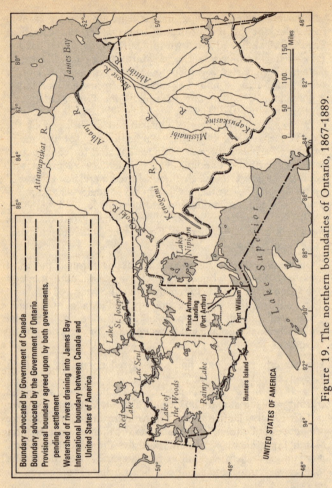

Figure 19. The northern boundaries of Ontario, 1867–1889.

interpreted as meaning that she relinquished all claim to the "Disputed Territory". Manitoba had very practical reasons for wanting her eastern boundary "to correspond with the line marked as the west boundary of Ontario, near the eighty-ninth meridian of west longitude". She wished to be able to supply the "prairie portions" of the province with the timber of the eastern portion and also to obtain a port on Lake Superior.[15] Practically the entire economy of the border region was dependent upon the vast stands of pine, spruce and tamarack to be found there. Meanwhile, uncertainty and confusion was reported from the area in dispute. Kenora, which was in the portion claimed by Ontario, was incorporated as a Manitoba town in 1882. In 1881, the stipendary magistrate appointed to exercise jurisdiction within the provisional boundaries said:

> You can have but little conception of the difficulties and disappointment [the explorers and miners] have met with here. They have expended all their money in exploring and in surveys, expecting an early return for their investment and toil, which they felt sure they would if the boundary question was settled, so that deeds could be procured for their locations. Without a title nothing can be done with mining capitalists, who require to have an undisputed title to the lands in which they risk their money. The delay . . . in settling the question of the boundary will ruin many, and they will be driven from the locality never to return, causing loss to the merchants and others who have made advances . . . There is no civil court to collect debts, no land agent to locate settlers, no registry office to record deeds, no timber agent to protect the forest. There are timber locations to be had, but there is no security for the expense of exploring and surveying them. . . .[16]

Clearly the matter had to be settled, and it was finally agreed to submit the case to the Judicial Committee of the Privy Council for a definite decision. In 1884, the Committee upheld the award made in 1878, which was described by the Canada (Ontario Boundary) Act, 1889, as follows:

> Commencing at the point where the international boundary between the United States of America and Canada strikes the western shores of Lake Superior, thence westerly along the said boundary to the north-west angle of the Lake of the Woods, thence along the line drawn due north until it strikes the middle line of the course of the river discharging the waters of the lake called Lake Seul or the Lonely Lake, whether above or below its confluence with the stream flowing from the Lake of the Woods towards Lake Winnipeg, and thence proceeding eastward from the point at which the before-mentioned line strikes the middle line of the course of the river last aforesaid, along the middle line of the course of the same river (whether called by the name of the English River or, as to the part below the confluence, by the name of the River Winnipeg) up to Lake Seul or the Lonely Lake, and thence along the middle line of Lake Seul or Lonely Lake to the head of that

lake, and thence by a straight line to the nearest point of
the middle line of the waters of Lake St. Joseph, and
thence along the middle line until it reaches the foot or
outlet of that lake, and thence along the middle line
of the river by which the waters of Lake St. Joseph dis-
charge themselves to the shore of the part of Hudson's
Bay commonly known as James Bay, and thence southeasterly following upon the said shore to a point where
a line drawn due north from the head of Lake Temiscamingue would strike it, and thence due south along the
said line to the head of the said lake, and thence through
the middle channel of the said lake into the Ottawa River,
and thence descending along the middle of the main channel
of the said river to the intersection by the prolongation
of the western limits of the Seigneurie of Rigaud, such
mid-channel being indicated on the map of the Ottawa
Ship Canal Survey made by Walter Shanly, C.E., and
approved by Order of the Governor General in Council,
dated the twenty-first July, one thousand eight hundred and
eighty six; and thence southerly, following the said westerly boundary of the Seigneurie Rigaud to the south-west
angle of the said Seigneurie, and then southerly along the
western boundary of the augmentation of the Township
of Newton to the north-west angle of the Seigneurie of
Longueuil, and thence south-easterly along the south-western
boundary of said Seigneurie of New Longueuil to the
stone boundary of the north bank of the Lake St. Francis,
at the cove west of Point au Baudet, such line from the
Ottawa River to Lake St. Francis being as indicated on
a plan of the line of boundary between Upper and Lower
Canada, made in accordance with the Act 23 Victoria,
chapter 21.[17]

The Ontario-Quebec Boundary

The description of the Ontario boundary in the Act of
1889 is noteworthy in that it amplifies and corrects the
description of the boundary between Upper and Lower
Canada made in 1791 – the boundary which automatically
became the Ontario-Quebec boundary upon Confederation.
The main clarification in the 1889 document is that the
boundary shall run through the *middle* channel of Lake
Timiskaming and the *middle* of the main channel of the
Ottawa River, points that were raised in the draft of the
Constitutional Bill of 1791 but dropped from the Order in

Council following the Constitutional Act. The correction concerns the boundary around the Seigniories of Rigaud and New Longueuil, to which attention was drawn in Chapter III.

However the Act did not clarify the situation with regard to the boundary between Ontario and Quebec in the St. Lawrence river. Between 1840 and 1867 settlement in this area had increased and as more details of the geography became known and mapped, so the need for more precision in local boundary descriptions manifested itself, as well as the necessity for considerable changes in county and township boundaries. The descriptions of such political units as lay on either side of the pre-1840 interprovincial boundary provided at the same time the detail lacking in the Order in Council that set out the boundary between Upper and Lower Canada. Thus the act "to make certain alterations in the Territorial Divisions of Upper Canada"[18] stated that the limits of the townships lying on the River Ottawa should extend to the middle of the main channel thereof, with the exception of certain islands that were specifically dealt with. Those described as "in front of" the Seigniory of La Petite Nation, and the Grand Calumet and Grand and Little Allumette Islands, for instance, remained part of Lower Canada, and the Upper Canada boundaries extended to the middle of the main channel between these islands and the south bank of the Ottawa River. Similarly the county of Glengarry was described as including the offshore islands and a parliamentary representation act of 1853[19] stated that the county of Huntingdon, on the opposite shore of Lake St. Francis but in Lower Canada, was to be partly bounded by the St. Lawrence river "including all islands nearest to the said county and . . . opposite to the same." In no case however was there any definition of a common line separating the two counties which has led to difficulties as some of the "offshore islands" are quite close to the centre of Lake St. Francis. The situation was further complicated by the fact that the limits of Glengarry were stated as extending to the middle of Lake St. Francis *and* the middle of the main channel of the St. Lawrence. These two lines are as much as a mile and a quarter apart in some cases. At the time that these pieces of legislation were enacted, it was of course not known that Canada would be divided again; however, such details as they contain are the only basis for this section of the Ontario-Quebec boundary.

By "gentlemen's agreement" fish and game authorities use

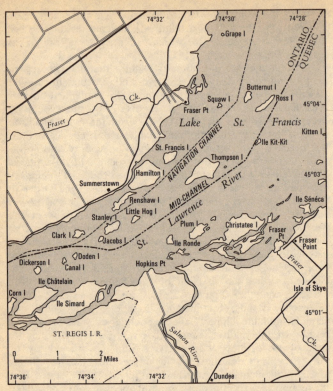

Figure 20. Part of the Ontario-Quebec boundary region in Lake St. Francis.

these two lines to define a sort of neutral zone or "no man's land" extending from three miles east of St. Anicet to Cornwall Island. It contains the principal islands, Ross, Butternut, Thompson and Stanley, as well as lesser ones. Residents of both provinces may fish within this zone, but not beyond its farther limit. For duck hunting, the unmarked "middle of the lake" – for this particular purpose accepted as the Ontario-Quebec boundary, – is the dividing line.[20]

But such an arrangement is not a satisfactory solution. As recently as March 1976 two men appeared in provincial court charged under Ontario's Game and Fish Act for hunting on Lake St. Francis without a valid licence. When asked by a conservation officer for their licences, they produced Quebec papers and maintained that they were still in Quebec because of their position in relation to the shipping channel. Although the two were convicted the judge suspended sentence because of the confusion in recognizing the provincial boundaries on the lake.[21] This is but one example of similar incidents which have occurred over the years.

The division of the Province of Canada into Ontario and Quebec produced some other results which could not have been foreseen in 1867. Late in 1857, Ottawa had been designated as the future seat of government of the Province of Canada and under the British North America Act, ten years later, it became the seat of government of the Confederation.[22] This changed the constitutional position of Ottawa. As the provincial capital it would have been under the direct control of the government located there and if government establishments had been situated across the river in Canada East they would have been under the jurisdiction of the same government. But with separation, Ottawa simply became another municipality in Ontario responsible to the provincial government in Toronto. Yet the "major tenant" in Ottawa was the federal government and, as was anticipated by some[23] it generated added municipal costs and responsibilities but had "no say in whether or how these were met."[24] As the needs of the federal government for space increased it spread its activities across the Ottawa river to Hull in Quebec thus producing the same situation there as it had in Ottawa. In 1913 a Federal Plan Commission was instructed to prepare a plan for "the future growth and development of the City of Ottawa and the City of Hull" and in 1927 a Federal District Commission was set up which included residents of both Ottawa and Hull. But not until 1945 were the boundaries of the District defined. When they were, they were described by Order in Council and were for planning purposes only. "In 1958 the National Capital Act was passed changing the Federal District Commission to the National Capital Commission, and extending the size of the National Capital Region to a rough square of 1800 square miles around Ottawa and Hull"[25] and describing its boundaries in meticulous detail.[26]

Quebec has argued that this is a threat to "its territorial integrity."[27] One other aspect of Quebec's integrity involves the preservation of an atmosphere where Francophones can freely use their own language and enjoy their own culture. In the National Capital region there is some fear that assimilation of the francophones into the anglophone culture is taking place – in other words that the boundary between Ontario and Quebec is not fulfilling the function intended for the boundary between Upper and Lower Canada in 1791 (even though until 1871 the French-speaking population of the District of Hull was in a decided minority). This led a former Chairman of the National Capital Commission to recommend that

> In moving departments or agencies to Hull, the federal government give priority to those which have a relatively high proportion of Francophones.[28]

The Northern Limits of Quebec

But the outstanding problems with regard to the boundaries of the province of Quebec in 1867 were somewhat similar to those of Ontario. The boundary on the west was reasonably clear, but the limits on the north and east were vague.

The government of Quebec appears to have taken these problems up at about the time that the Judicial Committee of the Imperial Privy Council upheld the 1878 "Award" to Ontario, when they appointed two select committees to consider the question of the northern and northwestern limits of the province. They concluded that although the 52nd degree of north latitude was the northern boundary it would be better to select a boundary that followed the physical features of the landscape in the neighbourhood of this parallel. As with Ontario, Quebec extended as far north as the Hudson's Bay Company's territories, whose limits had been established for Ontario in 1889, according to those that the company had itself been willing to accept in 1700. On the east coast of Hudson Bay, this had been Ruperts River, but the company was later asked to state whether it would consent to a reduction to latitude $52\frac{1}{2}$ degrees north, if the French refused to accept this, and the company, on January 29, 1701, agreed to accept Eastmain River (then called the Canuse), latitude 52°14′ N., as the boundary. Consequently, since 1867, Quebec had some claim to extend as far north as this line.

After the passing of the Canada (Ontario Boundary) Act of 1889, Quebec pressed the matter of the determination of its boundaries more vigorously. The Lieutenant-Governor of Quebec pointed out to the federal government that a boundary following 52 degrees north latitude would be entirely "artificial" and would run about 925 miles through almost inaccessible wilderness. It would be difficult to lay out, quite apart from the expense, which he estimated to be about

$1,000,000. Yet only a few miles to the north a "natural" boundary existed that could follow Eastmain River for 420 miles and Hamilton River to the limits of Labrador, leaving some 160 miles only between the headwaters of the Eastmain and Hamilton to follow an imaginary line. Furthermore, it was maintained that as Ontario had been awarded an additional 108,925 square miles of territory and a "natural" boundary, Quebec was entitled to a similar award, even if only in partial compensation for "that portion of New France annexed to Newfoundland". A boundary such as proposed would achieve this, whereas a boundary that followed the 52nd parallel would give Quebec 62,800 square miles only.

Whether it fully agreed with all Quebec's arguments or not, the government of Canada raised no objections with regard to the general location of the boundary, but was dubious about detail. It felt that neither government had enough information to deal definitely with the matter. Notwithstanding the 1889 award to Ontario, it appeared to be by no means certain that a line drawn due north from the head of Lake Timiskaming would intersect the shores of James Bay. Furthermore, the Deputy Minister of the Interior reported that "next to nothing is known about the Eastmain but, this much is certain, like every other river, it has several branches and before it could be adopted as a boundary it would be necessary to determine which of these branches is the Eastmain River". The same was true of Hamilton River, and it was feared that these rivers might prove to rise far to the north of latitude 52 degrees north and hence give Quebec far more territory than was intended. Exploratory surveys of the proposed boundary area were, therefore, made by the Department of the Interior, and in 1890 Ogilvie determined that the due north line from Lake Temiscaming would meet James Bay. As a result of A. P. Low's investigations from 1892 to 1894, he found that 20 miles from the coast the Eastmain branched, and he was at first unable to determine which was the main branch. Three hundred miles from the coast, the river divided again. However, by 1895 the Dominion Surveyor General was in a position to report that there was sufficient information to describe a well-defined line for the northern boundary of Quebec. It was found possible to follow rivers and lakes except for a distance of about 175 miles between Patamisk Lake and Ashuanipi River. Here, it was suggested, the boundary should follow the 53rd parallel of latitude. Some consideration was given to the use of a watershed line in its place, but although the watershed line was desirable from some points of view, it would be difficult to determine, particularly as it was known that several lakes in the area discharged in two directions. The advantage of having the boundary on an even parallel of latitude enabled any point on it to be easily and instrumentally fixed without the necessity of ascertaining the precise latitude of Patamisk Lake in the first place.

Ultimately the Quebec Legislature agreed to this boundary, and although this was regarded by some as going further than the legal limits, the Parliament of Canada concurred, and in 1898 the northern and eastern boundaries of the province of Quebec were defined as follows:

Commencing at the head of Lake Temiscamingue, thence along the eastern boundary of the province of Ontario due north to the shore of the part of Hudson Bay commonly known as James Bay, and thence north-easterly following up the said shore to the mouth of the East Main River, and thence easterly ascending along the middle of the said river up to the confluence of the branch thereof flowing from Patamisk Lake, and thence ascending along the middle of the said branch up to Patamisk Lake, and thence along the middle of the said lake to the most northerly point thereof, the said point being about fifteen miles south from the Hudson's Bay Company's post on Lake Nichigun, and approximately in latitude fifty-two degrees fifty-five minutes north, and longitude seventy degrees forty-two minutes west of Greenwich; thence due east along the parallel of latitude of the said point to the intersection of the river discharging the waters of Lake Ashuanipi, which river is known under the names of Hamilton or Ashuanipi or Great Esquimaux River, and thence descending along the middle of the said river through Menihek, Marble, Astray and Dyke Lakes to the most southerly outlet of Dyke Lake, and thence along the middle of the said outlet to Birch Lake, and thence along the middle of Birch and Sandgirt Lakes to the most southerly outlet of Sandgirt Lake, and thence along the middle of the southern channel of the Hamilton River to Flour Lake, and thence along the middle of Flour Lake to its outlet, and thence along the middle of the Hamilton River to the Bay du Rigolet or Hamilton Inlet, and thence easterly along the middle of the said bay or inlet until it strikes the westerly boundary of the territory under the jurisdiction of Newfoundland, and thence southerly along the said boundary to the point where it strikes the north shore of the Ance Sablon, in the Gulf of St. Lawrence.[29]

In a draft suggestion made by the Geological Survey of Canada on the location of the northern boundary of Quebec the concluding phrase read ". . . along the main channel of Hamilton River to its mouth". Recognizing that this ignored Newfoundland's possible claims along the coast, this phrase was modified, but it was still without precision as far as Quebec's boundary with Labrador was concerned.

However, long before this was considered, there were other boundary problems to be faced by the government of Canada, which concerned the areas not included in any of the provinces.

CHAPTER VI

THE "UNORGANIZED" NORTHWEST

Apart from the problems with regard to the precise limits of the provinces of Ontario and Quebec, that Canada as a whole had inherited, she also inherited the problem of the creation of administrative units within the territory formerly controlled by the Hudson's Bay Company, when she acquired Rupert's Land and the Northwest Territories in 1870. The problems related to the creation of the administrative units were of a different nature from those mentioned in the previous chapter, owing to the fact that the establishment of the boundaries was not primarily based on historical documents and treaties.

The British Government's decision with regard to the future of the Hudson's Bay Company's territory was based on the recommendation of the Select Committee of its House of Commons of 1857 and on the reports of Captain John Palliser's western explorations of 1857-60. But in 1870, when the government of Canada acquired the title to thousands of square miles of territory, the area contained a population of only 48,000, the information on its topography, soil, and climatic conditions was very vague, and there were practically no reliable data or statistics on record. Palliser's report had not been strikingly optimistic. Parts of the west he considered to be by no means suited to settlement[1] and, in his opinion, the time had forever gone by for securing a line of communication from Canada to the Pacific exclusively in British territory. "The unfortunate choice of an astronomical boundary" he said, "has completely isolated the Central American possessions of Great Britain from Canada in the east, and has also almost debarred them from any eligible access from the Pacific Coast on the west"[2], a conclusion that is reminiscent of the fears that the United States-New Brunswick boundary would sever easy communication between the Maritimes and the St. Lawrence in 1784. So that in spite of Sir John A. Macdonald's words that the government had one great country before them to do with as they liked[3], its southern boundary was the

first fact of its political geography that had to be faced. This
had only been established on paper. In 1871, it was reported
that

> law and order are wholly unknown in the region of the
> Saskatchewan in so much as the country is without any
> executive organisation and destitute of any means of en-
> forcing the authority of the law . . . Bands of outlaws and
> desperadoes from Montana and the neighbouring Territories
> had established trading posts or 'forts' on British soil,
> whence they supplied poisoned 'fire water', arms and am-
> munition to the Blackfeet and other Indians, in exchange
> for buffalo robes and other peltries . . . They had in fact
> organised a traffic which effectively impoverished the
> Country and demoralized the Indian while supplying him
> with the means of making himself dangerous.[4]

Early Boundary Problems in the Territories

How did the Hudson's Bay Company administer this huge
territory? The truth is that it was not primarily concerned
with administration *per se,* but with the development of the
fur trade. However, this in itself demanded organization and
the company, therefore, divided British North America into
four great departments. The Northern Department embraced
the area between the United States boundary to the south,
the unknown Arctic on the north, Hudson Bay on the east,
and the Rocky Mountains on the west. The Southern Department extended "from James Bay southward to the provinces of Upper and Lower Canada and east to include East
Main, the eastern coast of Hudson Bay". The Montreal
Department covered "the Company's business in Upper and
Lower Canada, the King's Posts and, later, Labrador"; and
the Columbia Department covered the valley of the Columbia
River, and, after 1825, the Canadian Pacific slope called
New Caledonia.[5]

These departments were subdivided into districts, the
boundaries of which usually approximated to watersheds, as
the waterways were the arteries of communication and trade
in the fur trade period. But it was not the general practice
to set exact geographic limits for fur-trade districts. Even the
fur-traders themselves did not agree on the boundaries of
such districts, or even their numbers, with the result that
their limits had little direct influence on official boundary
descriptions.

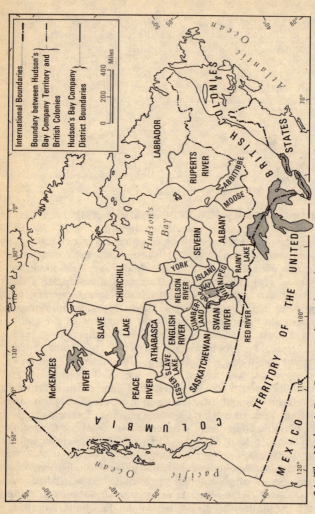

Figure 21. The Hudson's Bay Company's district boundaries according to a map by J. Arrowsmith, published in 1832.

The government and the company, of course, occupied diametrically opposite positions. The company was not interested in settlement – it was in fact, if anything, opposed to it. To the government, on the other hand, settlement was vital to the building of a nation, and settlement meant surveys. Its primary consideration, therefore, was to devise a system under which the country could be rapidly and accurately subdivided into land holdings and which would forestall the confusion that would follow large-scale immigration into unsurveyed territory. As a result, a system of surveys was approved by Order in Council more than a year before the transfer of the territories.[6]

The lines resulting from these surveys were the first formal boundaries in the "unorganized" Northwest Territories, but they did not constitute boundaries with the functions under discussion here. But with rapid immigration and land settlement new governments were necessitated. There were several ways in which "unorganized territory" could be "organized". Separate provinces could be created out of "unorganized territory" or parts of the "unorganized territory" could be included in an adjacent province, merely by extending the boundaries of the province. Alternatively the "unorganized territory" could be divided into tracts and each tract could then be given limited jurisdiction over its own affairs under the over-all jurisdiction of an administrative centre in a neighbouring province or under administration controlled completely from Ottawa.

The Creation of Manitoba

The creation of the province of Manitoba arose out of the settlements established in the Red River Valley by Lord Selkirk. The area that Selkirk selected for settlement in 1811 and subsequently established as Assiniboia included the bed of glacial Lake Agassiz. In 1834, however, the settlement reverted to the Hudson's Bay Company and "the boundaries were changed from the meticulous details of Selkirk's grant to a circular tract with a radius of fifty miles from Fort Garry".[7] As created by the Dominion Act of 1870[8], the province of Manitoba did not quite double this area, as its boundaries were the parallels of north latitude 49° to 50°30′ and the meridians of west longitude 96° to 99°, and hence covered about 14,340 square miles. But the boundaries so defined did not correspond with the Dominion Lands System of surveys, and, consequently, in 1877, in order to

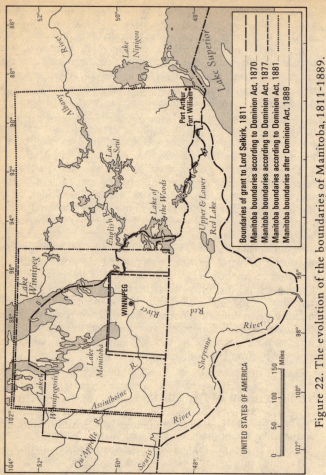

Figure 22. The evolution of the boundaries of Manitoba, 1811–1889.

facilitate the correct registration of land titles in Manitoba and the adjoining parts of Keewatin and the Northwest Territories, the provincial boundaries were redescribed according to the Dominion Lands System.[9] This procedure did not alter the total area of Manitoba, but did cause the eastern and western boundaries to be moved westward about 5 miles.

A Lieutenant-Governor was appointed for the remainder of the unorganized territory and, as settlement increased, his powers were extended and his advisory body enlarged. But it was soon clear that even this did not provide adequate machinery for the proper administration of the area. In 1876 a plan for the creation of four provinces between Manitoba and British Columbia was prepared at the request of the Minister of the Interior, but was not proceeded with, probably because it was considered premature. The greatest inconvenience was felt where settlement was heaviest – immediately west and east of the boundaries of Manitoba; the eastern area was dealt with first.

The Creation of Keewatin

It has already been pointed out that the western and northern boundaries of Ontario were in dispute almost as soon as the Dominion of Canada was created. In order to provide for government in the general area west of Ontario, a large portion of the Northwest Territories, covering about 395,000 square miles, was detached and set apart as a separate district under the name of the District of Keewatin on October 7, 1876, by virtue of the proclamation of the Keewatin Act. The act was intended to be temporary in character, being merely intended to give good government to the area north and east of Manitoba and west of Ontario, and read as follows:

Whereas it is expedient, pending the settlement of the western boundary of Ontario, to create a separate Territory of the Eastern part of the Northwest Territories: Therefore, Her Majesty, by and with the advice and consent of the Senate and House of Commons of Canada, enacts as follows:

1. All that portion of the Northwest Territories, bounded as follows, that is to say:

Beginning at the westerly boundary of the Province of Ontario, on the international boundary line dividing Canada from the United States of America; then westerly, following upon the said international boundary line, to the easterly boundary of the Province of Manitoba; thence due north, along the said easterly boundary of Manitoba, to the north-east angle of the said province; thence due west, on the north boundary of said Province, to the intersection by the said boundary of the westerly shore of Lake Manitoba; thence northerly, following the westerly shore of the said lake, to the easterly terminus thereon of the

Portage connecting the southerly end of Lake Winnipeg-osis with the said Lake Manitoba, known as "The Meadow Portage"; thence westerly, following upon the trail of the said portage, to the westerly terminus of the same, being on the easterly shore of the said Lake Winnipegosis; thence northerly, following the line of the said easterly shore of the said lake to the southerly end of the portage leading from the head of the said lake into "Cedar Lake", known as the "Cedar" or "Mossy Portage"; thence northerly, following the trail of the said portage, to the north end of the same on the shore of Cedar Lake; thence due north, to the northerly limits of Canada; thence easterly following upon the said northerly limits of Canada, to the northerly extremity of Hudson's Bay; thence southerly, following upon the westerly shore of the said Hudson's Bay, to the point where it would be intersected by a line drawn due north from the place of beginning, and thence due south, on the said line last mentioned, to the said place of beginning; shall be, and is hereby set apart as a separate district of the said Northwest Territories by the name of the District of Keewatin.[10]

It will be recalled (see Chapter V) that in 1874 the longitude of the most easterly point of Hunter's Island (long. 90°58′ W. approx.) had been agreed upon as the provisional western boundary of Ontario. This then must have been the eastern boundary of Keewatin at the time of its creation, although its permanent position was always in doubt until the question of the boundary between Ontario and Manitoba was settled in 1889.

The Lieutenant-Governor of Manitoba became Lieutenant-Governor of the new District of Keewatin, with a council of six persons to aid in the administration of the affairs of Keewatin. Their services were soon called upon when it was discovered, shortly before the district was officially pro-claimed, that an epidemic of smallpox had been in existence for some months on the west side of Lake Winnipeg among the Icelanders who had settled there during 1875 and the summer of 1876.[11] Before it was realized that the disease was smallpox, it had spread among the Indians in the vicinity. Consequently, on November 31, 1876, the six members of the Council of Keewatin were named as a Board of Health for the district. When this Board was organized, the spread of smallpox throughout Keewatin, Manitoba, and the North-west Territories seemed inevitable, and the fact that the disease was localized and confined to comparatively narrow limits was due to the energy of the Board of Health and its officers,[12] which at least demonstrated the need for organized government in the area.

Problems Farther West

At the same time as Keewatin was created, a Mounted Police post on Swan River, popularly known as Fort Livingstone, became the administrative centre for what remained of the Northwest Territories; in 1877, it was removed farther west to Battleford. All transactions in real property had to be recorded in the office of the Registrar for the Northwest Territories there, and the obvious inconveniences of such an arrangement ultimately caused complaints from the settlers, so in 1880 an Order in Council was passed erecting the Turtle Mountain, Little Saskatchewan, Touchwood Hills, and Prince Albert sections into registration districts. The influx of population into these areas also raised the question of the franchise, so in the same year three electoral districts were created – two adjoining Manitoba on the west, and one known as the Prince Albert Settlement. But the residents of the first two areas, at least, were not satisfied with these developments. They had, on various occasions, expressed a desire to be incorporated into the province of Manitoba, which they contended, was "too circumscribed",[13] and on July 1, 1881, by Dominion Act, the boundaries of Manitoba were extended so as to become

On the south the International boundary, on the west the centre of the road allowance between the twenty-ninth and thirtieth ranges west of the Principal meridian as surveyed in the Dominion Lands Survey System; on the north the centre of the road allowance along the twelfth base line of the Dominion Lands Survey System; on the east the easterly limit of the District of Keewatin . . . that is, the westerly boundary of the Province of Ontario.[14]

It thus included a considerable proportion of the then settled districts of the Territories and relieved the Territorial government of the supervision of the municipal and educational affairs of such centres of population as the Little Saskatchewan, Rapid City, Birtle, Birdtail Creek, and Turtle Mountain.[15]

But meantime, settlement continued to increase in the Northwest Territories. The rate of development was accelerated by the construction of the Canadian Pacific Railway, which was completed in 1885. In 1882, by an Order in Council, the area south of the thirty-second correction line of the Dominion Lands System; west of Athabasca and Slave Rivers and the line between the tenth and eleventh ranges of Dominion Lands townships west of the fourth initial meridian; and south of the eighteenth correction line of the Dominion Lands System[16] was divided into the provisional districts of Assiniboia, Saskatchewan, Athabaska, and Alberta, to be governed by a Lieutenant-Governor with his capital at Regina, Saskatchewan. These districts were created for federal, administrative, and postal purposes and were rarely referred to in the local legislature at Regina. Nevertheless, it is instructive to examine the geographical setting of the new boundaries. First of all, the northern boundary of the area divided into provisional districts was approximately 60°N., west of 111½°W., and 55° N. east of that meridian (Figure 26) and the position of this line interestingly reflects the fact that the pattern of settlement in the area was already being affected by the factors of the physical environment. These were the western limits of the Canadian Shield and what was thought, at that time, to be the position of the 60 deg. F. mean summer isotherm, which would have represented the northern limit of the climatic and soil conditions that are suitable for mid-latitude agriculture. Furthermore, it must be remembered that the early settlers in western Canada avoided the open grasslands and took up land in the wooded areas and river valleys. Each of the new provisional districts included a major river valley or part of one – the Assiniboine, Qu'Appelle, and South Saskatchewan in Assiniboia; the North Saskatchewan in Saskatchewan and Alberta; and the Athabasca and Peace in Athabaska. In addition, before the coming of the railway there were considerable settlements of half-breeds at Edmonton, Prince Albert, and Battleford.[17] The first of these was included in Alberta and the other two in Saskatchewan. The territorial capital had already migrated northwestward along the "park belt" and was now in the grasslands to the south at Regina. It was presumably because this area had different physical characteristics that it was set apart as Assiniboia. Even after the trans-Canada railway had been completed, the map of population distribution of 1886 shows clearly an east-west break between the districts of Saskatchewan and Assiniboia; the break roughly corresponds with the sparsely populated areas of the Bear, Allan, Touchwood, and Beaver Hills, a factor that was probably taken into account in locating the provisional boundary.

The boundaries of the District of Saskatchewan were described as follows:

. . . . to be bounded on the south by the districts of
Assiniboia and Manitoba; on the east by Lake Winnipeg
and the Nelson River flowing therefrom into Hudson Bay;
on the north by the eighteenth correction line of the
Dominion land survey system, and on the west by the line
of that system dividing the tenth and eleventh ranges of
townships numbered from the fourth initial meridian.[18]

This description is given in detail, not only to serve as
an example of how the provisional districts were described
but also to show that in the case of Saskatchewan the
boundaries overlapped those assigned to the District of Keewatin in 1876. The intention was probably to include the
settlements that had sprung up in the "overlapping portion"
in the provisional district of Saskatchewan, because it was felt
in Ottawa that they were economically and socially akin to
the other settlements in that district rather than to those in
Keewatin. By an Order in Council dated May 7, 1886, the
"overlapping portion" – that part of Keewatin lying between
Manitoba and the eighteenth correction line and west of
Nelson River – was re-annexed to the Northwest Territories
in order to become properly a part of Saskatchewan. The
Lieutenant Governor of Keewatin did not agree however and
constantly recommended that this action be reversed and that
the western boundary revert to the straight line "drawn due
north from the north end of the portage leading from the
north end of Lake Winnipegosis into Cedar Lake, known as
Cedar or Mossy Portage", (as described in the Keewatin Act
of 1876). He stated that the line

about long. 100 degs. W., is departed from with no apparent advantage to the district in which the departure
places it, while much inconvenience, trouble and added
expense is caused the District of Keewatin by the difference of the provisions which relate to intoxicants, and the
increased difficulties in the administration of justice in the
latter District.[19]

But he went further by saying that

what would cover the same ground and still further extend
the benefits of Keewatin administration, [would be] a
division of the immense region between Eastern Keewatin
and Athabaska, and above Athabaska to British Columbia
and Alaska, into several large territories, over which the

Keewatin Act, or some legislative enactment based upon its wise provisions, should obtain.[20]

He was here referring to the still unorganized and unnamed districts of the Northwest Territories north of those created in 1882, and in 1895 "for the further convenience of settlers and for postal purposes", the Minister of the Interior recommended that four such districts be established and named Ungava, Franklin, Mackenzie, and Yukon, and that changes be made in the boundaries of the districts of Athabaska and Keewatin so as to enlarge their areas.

The first five of these proposals took account of the increase in population of various parts of the Northwest Territories by extending Athabaska eastwards so as to include the area north of Saskatchewan, east of Keewatin, and south of the 60th parallel,[21] and by dividing all of the remainder of the territories into districts. But still the western boundary of Keewatin remained unchanged and in 1900 the Lieutenant-Governor of Manitoba and Keewatin wrote as follows:

> For years it has been reported time and again that the boundaries of Keewatin were about to be adjusted. Should this intention be carried out, I would suggest that the western boundary of Keewatin be the present western boundary of Manitoba produced. If this were done, the illicit liquor traffic by way of Grand Rapids could be controlled, and the portion of country involved could be more easily governed from Winnipeg than Regina.[22]

Keewatin itself had clearly always been something of a special problem.

The Reorganization of Keewatin

It will be recalled that, by 1889, the Ontario-Manitoba boundary dispute had been settled. The decision that gave to the province of Ontario the territory south of Albany River and as far west as Lake of the Woods limited the District of Keewatin to the territory lying directly north of the province of Manitoba, and fixed its eastern boundary at the longitude of a line running north from the western boundary of the province of Ontario. This left the status of the area between Keewatin and James Bay and north of Ontario in doubt, and when, prior to 1895, the creation of new districts in the territories was being contemplated, this area was something of a problem. There seemed to be little doubt that the area should be associated with Keewatin, but the problem was how to rearrange the boundaries of Keewatin so as to effect this.

The Lieutenant-Governor of Keewatin recommended the addition of this area to Keewatin.

It is . . . expedient that provision be made for the incorporation into Keewatin of that extensive district which has for its south-eastern boundary the English River, Lac Seul, the Albany River and the west coast of James Bay, left free for such incorporation by the acceptance by Ontario and Manitoba of the western and eastern boundaries respectively.[23]

In his view, it was accessible only through Hudson Straits or by the rivers that flow into Lake Winnipeg, and could, therefore, be effectively governed only in the manner in which the District of Keewatin was governed. To him, at least, this was "so obvious as to need no comment."[24]

Two other proposals were considered by the federal government in 1892. One was that the area proposed by the Lieutenant-Governor should be limited on the north and west by Lake Winnipeg and Churchill River. The reason given for this was that such boundaries would give a territory within the jurisdiction of the Lieutenant-Governor of Manitoba, who was also the Lieutenant-Governor of Keewatin, within which the greater part of the population then in Keewatin was to be found, and which could be administered with convenience from Winnipeg because of the comparative facility with which it could be reached by water from that point via Red River and Lake Winnipeg and its tributaries. However, the boundaries of Keewatin according to this proposal would have been rather irregular and would involve a lengthy description. Because of this, a third proposal suggested the 49th meridian west as the western boundary instead of the longitude of the Mossy Portage meridian.

However, it was by no means universally agreed that the area under consideration was not already part of Manitoba, for the boundaries of that province had, in 1881, been extended to "the westerly limits of Ontario". If, after the Canada (Ontario Boundary) Act of 1889, the word "westerly" was interpreted broadly so as to include the northwestern boundaries of Ontario, then it could be argued that the "doubtful area" was part of Manitoba.[25] In these circumstances, no immediate action was taken. Two more boundary proposals were then made. One was to the effect that the eastern limit of Keewatin should be the prolongation, due north, of the dividing line between Ontario and Quebec. The other was that the western boundary of Keewatin should be the 2nd meridian of the Dominion Lands System (102 degrees west longitude), which would have meant re-attaching part of the district of Saskatchewan to Manitoba. This was not recommended, as it was an "imaginary" line, and a "geographical" boundary like Lake Manitoba and Nelson River was preferable. Furthermore, it would not have "improved" the map, as it would have left in the District of Keewatin a narrow wedge of the Porcupine Hills country "jammed in between Saskatchewan and Manitoba".

The ultimate recommendation chose a western boundary between the 2nd meridian and 99 degrees west, namely, 100 degrees west, and included in Keewatin the area between Hudson Bay and the northerly boundary of Ontario.

These and the other changes in territorial boundaries suggested by the Minister were made by Order in Council in 1895; the Order also recommended that the Keewatin boundary changes be authorized by an Act of Parliament. This, however, was not done, as discrepancies were found to exist in the descriptions of the district boundaries, and in 1897 there was promulgated a further Order in Council cancelling the Order of 1895 and previous orders and approving the recommendations of the Minister of the Interior that the districts of Assiniboia, Saskatchewan, and Athabaska remain as they were established in 1895; it also provided that the boundaries of Ungava, Keewatin, Mackenzie, Yukon, and Franklin should be slightly changed[26] according to a given description and map. These changes in boundaries were made mainly to ensure that all the islands between 141 degrees west and Davis Strait were included in one or other of the provisional districts, which the Order in Council of 1895 had failed to do. Ungava, Franklin, and Keewatin were also so defined as to embrace the whole of Hudson Bay and Strait. But legislation regarding these changes was never introduced, and it would appear, therefore, that the districts, except in so far as they were authorized by the subsequently cancelled Order in Council of 1882 had no legal existence.[27]

Meanwhile an Act of 1887 had given representation at Ottawa to the territories, and an Act of 1888 had set up an elected territorial legislature at Regina. These developments clearly pointed toward provincial status for some, at least, of the territories, but before that stage was reached further developments occurred in the far northwest.

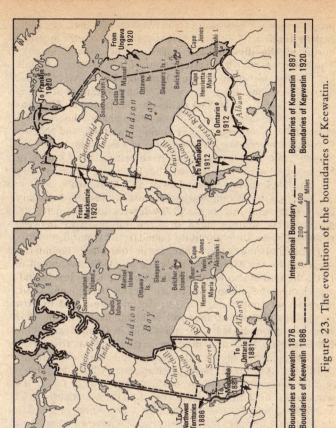

Figure 23. The evolution of the boundaries of Keewatin.

The Creation of Yukon Territory

Reports that that part of the Yukon Valley lying within Canada was of great economic value, particularly in regard to its mineral wealth, had been reaching Ottawa for several years prior to 1886. The mineral was, of course, gold, and the number of miners entering the area increased rapidly. About three hundred were estimated to be in the area in the summer of 1887, and in 1895 an Order in Council was passed creating the Provisional District of Yukon with the following boundaries:

Beginning at the intersection of the 141st meridian of west longitude from Greenwich with a point on the coast of the

Arctic sea, which is approximate north latitude, 69°39′, . . . thence due south, on the said meridian . . . for a distance of about 650 miles, to a point in latitude about 60°10′ north, at which it will intersect the disputed boundary between Canada and the United States on the North Pacific coast; thence in an easterly direction, along the said undetermined boundary . . . . to its intersection with the 60 parallel of north latitude; thence due east along the parallel of latitude . . . . for a distance of about 550 miles, to the Liard river, in approximate longitude 123°30′ west, thence northerly along the middle line of said river, for a distance of about 10 miles till opposite the highest part of the range of mountains which abuts upon the river near the mouth of Black river; thence to follow the summit of said range in a northwesterly direction to the southernmost source of the Peel river; thence to follow northward the summit of the main range of mountains which runs approximately parallel to Peel river; on the west, as far as the intersection of the said range with the 136th meridian; thereafter to run due north to the Arctic Ocean, or to the westernmost channel of the Mackenzie delta, and along that channel to the Arctic Ocean; thence northwesterly following the windings of the Arctic coast, ... including Herschel island, and all other islands which may be situated within three (3) geographical miles, to the place of beginning.

Provided, that in respect to that part of the line, between the Liard river and the southernmost source of the Peel river, the summit to be followed is the watershed summit separating streams entering the Liard river below Black river, or flowing directly into the Mackenzie further north, from streams flowing westward either to the Yukon or to upper branches of the Liard river.

Provided, that in respect to the part of the boundary described as following northward the main range of mountains on the west side of the Peel river, the line shall run along the watershed between streams flowing eastwardly to the Peel river, and those flowing westwardly to branches of the Yukon, Porcupine, etc., except where such watershed shall be more than 20 miles distant from the main stream of the Peel, when the highest range within that distance shall be the boundary.[28]

The number of miners increased to thousands after the famous Klondike strike on August 17, 1896. This influx, as has already been pointed out, caused an international boundary situation, but it also demanded an internal adjustment to allow for the proper administration of the area, and in 1897 the District of Yukon was proclaimed a judicial district, with the same boundaries. However, later the same year the Yukon Provisional District was redescribed as follows:

> On the south by the province of British Columbia and the United States territory of Alaska; on the west by the said United States territory of Alaska; on the north by that part of the Arctic ocean called Beaufort sea; on the east by a line beginning at the mouth of the most westerly channel of the delta of the Mackenzie river; thence southerly, following the line of the watershed separating the streams flowing into the Arctic ocean west of the place of beginning from those flowing into the Mackenzie river, to the line of watershed between the basins of the Mackenzie and Yukon rivers; thence following the said line of watershed to the line of the watershed separating the streams flowing into the Mackenzie river, or into the Liard river below the point where the said Liard river intersects the sixtieth parallel of latitude in approximate longitude 124 degrees and 20 minutes west of Greenwich, from those flowing into the upper waters of the Liard river; thence following the said line of watershed to the northerly boundary of British Columbia, the said district to include the islands within twenty miles from shore of the Beaufort sea as far east as the meridian of the most westerly channel of the delta of the Mackenzie river.[29]

The differences between the descriptions of 1895 and 1897 are significant. In 1895 the boundaries embraced all islands within three geographical miles of the coast; in 1897 they included the islands within twenty miles from the shore. Secondly the 1895 boundaries included the major western tributaries of Peel River in the Yukon (leaving the river itself in Mackenzie District); the 1897 boundaries excluded all the major western tributaries of the Peel from the Yukon and was clearly an attempt to make the eastern boundary of the Yukon follow a major watershed.

While these boundary changes had no effect upon the area of settlement in the southwest of the District, it became increasingly clear that it was necessary to make further provision for the maintenance of law and order because about ninety per cent of the people in the District were aliens and few of them intended to settle there permanently. Indeed, the intention of many of them was to "make a fortune" and return to their families in other parts of the world.[30] Conse-

quently, on June 13th, 1898 the District of Yukon was constituted a separate Territory by Act of Parliament and
assigned the same boundaries as it had when created a
Provisional District in 1895.[31] However, the Yukon Territory
Act was amended in 1901 and the boundary description extended the territory to twenty miles from the coast (as in
the Order in Council of 1897) and eastward so as to embrace
most of the watershed of Peel river as follows:

> On the south, by the province of British Columbia and the
> United States Territory of Alaska; on the west by the said
> United States Territory of Alaska; on the north, by that
> part of the Arctic Ocean called Beaufort sea; and on the
> east by a line beginning at the point of intersection of the
> left bank of the Liard river, by the northern boundary of
> the province of British Columbia in approximate longitude
> 124°16' west of Greenwich; thence northwesterly along the
> line of the watershed separating the streams flowing into
> the Liard river below the point of beginning or into the
> Mackenzie river, from those flowing into the Liard river
> above the point of beginning, or into the Yukon river, to
> the line of watershed of the basin of Peel river; thence
> northerly along the line of watershed between the Peel
> and Mackenzie rivers to the sixty-seventh degree of north
> latitude; thence westerly along the parallel of the sixty-
> seventh degree of north latitude to the line of watershed
> between the Peel and Yukon rivers; thence northerly along
> the said line of watershed to the trail across the portage
> in McDougall pass between Rat and Bell rivers; thence
> due north to the northern limit of the Yukon Territory;
> the said Territory to include the islands within twenty
> statute miles from the shores of the Beaufort sea as far
> as the aforesaid due north line from McDougall pass.[32]

These boundaries are different in character from those
assigned to the provisional districts farther south in that in
the east they attempt to follow topographical features rather
than parallels of latitude and longitude. The very vagueness
of their description, however, indicates how little was known
of the geography of the region. The intention was to make
them largely correspond with the watershed between the
Yukon and Mackenzie river systems.[33] The reason for this
was, presumably, because the gold being mined was alluvial
or "stream gold" and as the purpose of the creation of the
separate territory was to bring law and order to the mining
settlements and activities, the territory had to include all
the possible gold mining areas, i.e., Yukon River, its tribu-

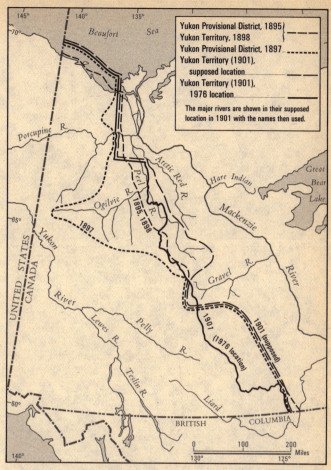

The major rivers are shown in their supposed
location in 1901 with the names then used.

Figure 24. The eastern and northern boundaries of Yukon, 1895-1901.

taries, and associated waterways. In this respect the boundaries
of the Yukon Territory were similar in purpose to the extension of the boundaries of British Columbia to the 120th
meridian west and the 60th parallel in 1863. In the case of
British Columbia, however, the delimitation was made purely
in terms of latitude and longitude, so as to include all the
possible potential alluvial gold areas that existed on both sides
of the Pacific Ocean-Arctic Ocean divide.

Figure 25. Territorial and intra-territorial boundaries, 1870-1876.

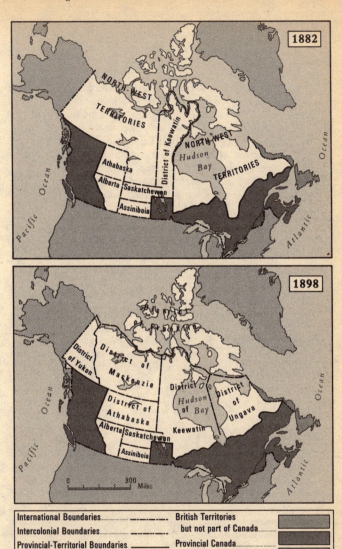

Figure 26. Territorial and intra-territorial boundaries, 1882-1898.

Boundary evolution in the Northwest Territories between 1870 and 1898, therefore, saw two different types of boundaries emerge. The first type was based on lines of the Dominion Lands System – the only type of boundary possible in an area that was being rapidly settled by agriculturalists in a region that lacked marked physical features. The idea of boundaries that approximately followed lines of latitude and longitude was then extended into those parts of the territories that were north of the area of likely agricultural development, partly, it appears now, to uphold Canadian sovereignty in the north. The second type of boundary was basically a watershed one, as exemplified in the Yukon Territory.

The boundaries of Keewatin showed a combination of both these features. This reflected the fact that Keewatin was a "bridge" between the two types of economy – that based on agriculture or exploitation of the plains and that based on the more primitive fur trade of the forest and tundra. The fact that the boundaries of Keewatin were changed and amended so many times and as the result of many different suggestions also reflects the "buffer-like" situation of the territory between the older settled areas of the east and the newly developed areas of the west.

The creation of the separate Yukon Territory in the extreme northwest of continental Canada resulted from a remarkable increase in population in that area. But even greater increases of population were occurring in the areas farther south, and emphasized the necessity for additional boundary changes.

CHAPTER VII

NEW PROVINCES AND RESULTING ADJUSTMENTS

During the period 1897 to 1905, the territories developed very rapidly. In the years immediately following Confederation, their small population had been scattered, and was concentrated chiefly in a few small communities that had grown up about the old trading posts and the new Northwest Mounted Police posts. With the active immigration policy that followed, Manitoba received most of the new Canadians until the Canadian Pacific Railway was constructed in the early 1880's, when population began to spread westward at an unprecedented rate. Immigration was under the control of the federal government, but the task of providing for the immigrants by the construction of local works and improvements was the responsibility of the territorial government. The problems (mainly financial) created as a result of this gradually became almost insurmountable, and, consequently, the territories began to look forward to provincial status.[1]

The various opinions and arguments advanced on this question are of concern here only in so far as they have a bearing on boundary evolution and significance. If the territories, or any parts of them, were to be erected into provinces, what should the boundaries of the latter be?

New Provinces

Several proposals were put forward regarding the possible boundaries for new provinces. The people of the territories themselves were by no means unanimous even with respect to the number of provinces, and in the Assembly proposals for one, two and three provinces all found supporters; there was also a small group that favoured the annexation of a part of the territories to Manitoba. The federal government had at times considered four provinces. Each of these proposals will now be examined briefly.

Annexation to Manitoba

During the controversy over her eastern boundary, Manitoba had contended that it should be extended westwards to the 2nd meridian of the Dominion Lands System (102 degrees west) and had made repeated requests to the federal government to have this brought about. In 1883 the Executive Council of the province of Manitoba expressed this desire officially, and so advised Ottawa in 1884. In 1884 a further Order in Council was passed by the Executive Council of Manitoba to the same effect, and this was followed 2 weeks later by a resolution passed by the Legislative Assembly of the province deputing the members of the Executive Council to proceed to Ottawa to procure from the federal government a settlement of what they maintained were their rights to have the boundaries of the province extended. In 1901, the Manitoba legislature passed a further resolution requesting the extension of the province into adjacent districts that possessed agricultural, commercial, and educational interests "in a great measure common" to its own, and including as much of the territory as might be consistent with economical and efficient government.[2] An even stronger and more lengthy resolution along similar lines was passed by the legislature in 1902. This resolution contended that it was "of the highest importance" to the province of Manitoba and the Northwest Territories that the former "should be increased by an extension of boundaries so as to embrace and include a portion of the districts of Assiniboia and Saskatchewan and northwards to Hudson Bay".[3] Still further resolutions in similar terms were adopted in 1905 and 1906.

Some support for a westward extension of Manitoba had come from Alberta. In 1897 the City Council of Calgary passed a resolution that:

> The material interest and prosperity of the districts would be best promoted and the multiplication of Governments avoided by adding that portion of Assiniboia lying between the Province of Manitoba and the Third meridian to Manitoba and erecting the remainder of Assiniboia, Alberta and Saskatchewan into one Governmental District with Provincial powers.

This was not an entirely disinterested view of Manitoba's case, however, for on March 16, 1901, the *Calgary Albertan* reported the same proposal with the suggestion that Calgary should become the capital of the new province to the west of Manitoba. The proposal reappeared from time to time, particularly when it was known that a final decision was

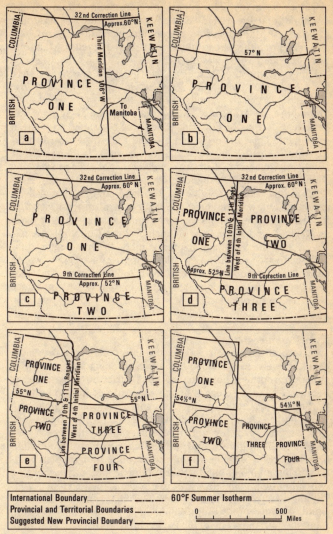

Figure 27. Suggested new provinces in Western Canada prior to 1905.

about to be made. The geographical reasoning followed the argument that the eastern part of the territories was naturally tributary to Manitoba, that the climatic conditions were alike, and the agricultural possibilities very similar, even if Manitoba were extended as far west as Regina.[4]

However, most of the inhabitants of the territories were opposed to any annexation. Premier Haultain maintained that the territorial laws were better suited to western conditions than those of Manitoba. Manitoba's municipal system was patterned on that of Ontario, which was not suited to western settlement. The territories had evolved their own local institutions in line with their particular needs, such as the system of local improvement districts, and had not introduced the "cumbersome" and "expensive" system in use in Ontario.[5]

Manitoba refused to give up, however, and in 1905 a delegation to Ottawa presented the request of a united legislature for an extension of the province's boundaries "as far west as Regina" and northward to include Fort Churchill, Nelson River, and the Territory tributary thereto. They argued that the westward extension would comprise a region whose agricultural conditions were similar to their own, and that they were entitled to an area equal in size to any province about to be formed.[6]

Two Provinces

A second suggestion was to the effect that two provinces should be erected, divided by a line running east and west along the southern boundary of the District of Saskatchewan, because of the differences in the physical geography between the north and the south. The south, it was maintained, was a flat, treeless prairie, adapted to large farming operations such as grain-growing and ranching, whereas the north was rolling, well watered, and possessing abundant wood and hay, making it suitable for mixed farming and smaller holdings. The dividing line between these conditions, would, it was submitted, coincide with the northern boundary of Assiniboia extended westward to the Rocky Mountains. Furthermore, the north and south would each possess transportation facilities, as the Canadian Pacific and Canadian Northern Railway Companies were each operating transcontinental lines running east and west.[7]

Other groups in the west[8] advocated two provinces divided by a boundary running north and south. They considered that legislation beneficial to the eastern and northern parts of the territories, where the raising of cereal crops was practically the sole activity, was injurious to the southwest portions, where cattle and horse ranching prevailed. If they could not have one single province with diversified interests they wanted "complete severance" of the "stock country" of Assiniboia and Alberta and the mixed farming country of northern Alberta from the farming country of Assiniboia and Saskatchewan. The suggestions for the exact location of the dividing line varied only in detail. In order not to divide the range lands, the 105th line of longitude was suggested, or that the line should run east of Swift Current, through Swift Current itself, through Moose Jaw, or "at the most" through Maple Creek.

But in addition to these arguments one must also consider the sectional ambitions of Calgary and Edmonton, both of which desired to be capitals.[9]

Three Provinces

A group in Prince Albert advocated three provinces – Assiniboia and the southern part of Alberta (by extending the northern boundary of Assiniboia to the Rockies), northern Alberta and the Peace River country (by extending the western boundary of Saskatchewan to the northern boundary of Athabaska), and Saskatchewan and eastern Athabaska. Such a division, they submitted, would meet the wishes and aspirations of the people, would simplify the question of rivalry over the location of the capital, and would maintain a balance among the various provinces.

One Province

The idea of a single political unit between the Great Lakes and British Columbia was current long before Confederation. As a result of his exploratory surveys, Captain Palliser "felt decidedly in favour" of a single British colony from British Columbia up to, and including, the Red River settlement. He suggested that its southern boundary should be the 49th Parallel from the "east shore of the Lake of the Woods, to where it meets the crest of the Rocky Mountains". The remaining boundaries should commence at the 49th Parallel on the western shore of Lake of the Woods, and follow the western margin of that lake "to the watercourse which unites with Lake Winnipeg, from thence extending around the eastern shore of Lake Winnipeg, and following the water course of that lake to the 54th parallel of N. lat. in long. 98° W."; thence along this parallel to its intersection with the crest of the Rocky Mountains.[10] He estimated that the area of such a unit would be 240,000 square miles, which in the light of the areas of the provinces of today was not unreasonable.

The Premier of the territories always favoured the erection of one strong united province, and believed that the desire for division was simply founded upon the ambition of certain cities to become provincial capitals. He held that there was no point in the territories, however remote, which, with the aid of telegraph, telephone, and railway, could not be administered by one western government. He could not recall a single occasion when there had been any conflict of interest upon any question raised in the legislature, and although admitting that geographical diversity existed, felt that the situation merely called for diversity of treatment. For "no one could map out a province, however small, which would not have diversity of interests".[11]

In a draft bill that placed the views of the executive council of the territories before the federal government "one province" was envisaged, to be made up of the Districts of Assiniboia, Saskatchewan, Alberta, and that part of the District of Athabaska lying to the south of the 57th parallel of north latitude.

Four Provinces

As has been mentioned, the federal government had at times considered the erection of the Northwest Territories into four provinces. The various proposals are worth presenting because of the light they shed on the principles of boundary-making that Ottawa considered important and also because they provide a better understanding of the decision ultimately reached.

In 1876 the Deputy Minister of the Interior had informally submitted a plan for the division of the Northwest Territories into provinces, which was based upon the projected route of the Canadian Pacific Railway (Figure 27). This route passed north of Fort Pelly and the Elbow of Saskatchewan River and continued westerly to the Rockies via Edmonton. The suggested arrangement of provinces would have enabled each to share equally the advantages of the railway.

The abandonment of this route in favour of one passing south of Fort Ellice and Qu'Appelle and towards the Rockies by the valley of the south branch of the Saskatchewan resulted in a second plan of division (Figure 27) in 1881. The suggestion was framed with the object in mind of reasonable areas for the different provinces, of the equalization of such areas as far as practicable, and of securing to each province, as nearly as possible, an equal share of the natural resources of the Territories, including all those advantages which could be foreseen.

The areas of two of these suggested provinces were estimated at 95,000 square miles each, and the areas of the other two at 100,000 square miles and 122,000 square miles respectively. It was recognized that provinces three and four were smaller than one and two, but it was felt that this was more than counterbalanced in province two by the existence of a very considerable amount of "unavailable" land, made up of mountains, and the swampy country said to exist around the headwaters of Athabasca River, and in province one by the large tract of swampy country said to exist north of Lesser Slave Lake, and between Athabasca and Peace Rivers.

The known natural resources of each of these areas were also examined and described, and the whole area was considered in relation to the position of the summer isotherm of 60°F., as it was known at that time, which was regarded as the northerly limit of the area climatically suited to the growing of cereals to advantage.

The Decision

In 1905, Sir Wilfrid Laurier introduced legislation providing for the creation of two provinces. Manitoba's request to be extended westward so as to include a strip of the Northwest Territories had been refused on the grounds that it would be against the wishes of those occupying the strip in question, which had become a settled area with defined and well-established institutions, occupied by people who had, in the main, resided there for a sufficient length of time to become the owners of the property they occupied.[12]

Ottawa[13] took the view that the Northwest Territories covered too large an area for a single province. It was also of the opinion that the area north of approximately 60 degrees north and west of Keewatin was "absolutely unfit for agriculture", and that although it possessed indications of mineral wealth, without agriculture there could be little hope of "thick and permanent settlement", and, consequently, stable provincial government. It was the intention, therefore, to give provincial autonomy to that part of the territories situated between the American boundary and the 60th parallel of north latitude, and between British Columbia and Keewatin. This area, comprising 550,345 square miles, was still, in the federal government's estimation, too large for a single province, when compared with the other members of Confederation, and, consequently, it was proposed to divide it into two of approximately equal size, by a line running north and south along the 4th meridian (110 degrees west), giving to each of the new provinces an area of about 275,000 square miles and a population of about 250,000.

The first of the new provinces was to be called Alberta and was to have the following boundaries:

> commencing at the intersection of the international boundary dividing Canada from the United States of America by the fourth meridian in the system of Dominion land surveys; thence westerly along the said international boundary to the eastern boundary of the province of British Columbia; thence northerly along the said eastern boundary of the province of British Columbia to the northeast corner of the said province; thence easterly along the parallel of the sixtieth degree of north latitude to the fourth meridian in the system of Dominion lands surveys as the same may be hereafter defined in accordance with the said system; thence southerly along the said fourth meridian to the point of commencement.[14]

The second was to be called Saskatchewan, with the following boundaries:

> commencing at the intersection of the international boundary dividing Canada from the United States of America by the west boundary of the province of Manitoba, thence northerly along the said west boundary of the province of Manitoba; to the northwest corner of the said province of Manitoba; thence continuing northerly along the centre of the road allowance between the twenty-ninth and thirtieth ranges west of the principal meridian in the system of Dominion lands surveys, as the said road allowance may hereafter be defined in accordance with the said system, to the second meridian in the said system of Dominion lands surveys, as the same may hereafter be defined in accordance with the said system; thence northerly along the said second meridian to the sixtieth degree of north latitude; thence westerly along the parallel of the sixtieth degree of north latitude to the fourth meridian in the said system of Dominion lands surveys, as the same may be hereafter defined in accordance with the said system; thence southerly along the said fourth meridian to the said international boundary dividing Canada from the United States of

America; thence easterly along the said international boundary to the point of commencement.[15]

There was criticism of the dividing line. Calgary, Medicine
Hat, and Macleod all objected to the division of the range
country. They maintained that the line should have been
farther east so as to take in all the grazing land south of
South Saskatchewan River even if north of the river it
swerved westward.[16] Both 105 degrees west and 107 degrees
west were suggested as suitable eastern limits of the range
country. 110 degrees west, it was contended, split those
interested in the livestock industry, would cause hardship by
increasing expenses owing to dealing with "two classes of
people", and would be very annoying to the stockmen if the
two new provinces adopted different sets of brand and stock
laws. While opposing the division of the territories into two
provinces, Premier Haultain likewise held the opinion that
the dividing line should be 75 miles farther east. The ranching
community of Maple Creek, which found itself within the
province of Saskatchewan, was, however, in favour of the
4th meridian perhaps because it had become a type of *de facto*
boundary since 1884. In that year the Minister of the Interior
had reported that

> Sheep raising is likely to become a valuable industry along
> the base of the Rocky Mountains within a very short
> time. The difficulties and disputes which have arisen in the
> United States in consequence of sheep and cattle grazing
> upon the same ranges, are not likely to be repeated on
> our side of the International Boundary; for a recent Order
> in Council provides for the exclusion of sheep from the
> territory bounded on the east by the Bow River and the
> 4th Meridian, and on the north by the northern branch
> of the High River, which is *par excellence* the cattle range
> of the North-West. There is much land within this territory
> which is well suited for sheep, and much outside of it
> equally well suited for cattle; but the dividing line, in addi-
> tion to being a distinct and well defined natural boundary
> for the largest half of its length, is probably the best that
> could have been devised; and the conflict it was intended
> to obviate, one which the public interest demands should be
> prevented at all hazards.[17]

It must be remembered that by 1901 settlement in the new
boundary area had not extended very far north of the 49th
Parallel, and the effect of the dividing line was, therefore,
felt chiefly in the southern parts of the new provinces. The

criticism that it divided the ranching country between Medicine Hat and Swift Current was not groundless. Even modern soil surveys have failed to reveal a better use for this land than extensive grazing, and, topographically, southwestern Saskatchewan differs markedly from southern Saskatchewan farther east. The only community of any size in the boundary region was further north at Lloydminster which had been incorporated as a town in the Northwest Territories in 1903. It was divided by the boundary and after 1905 there were separate incorporations of the parts in the two provinces until amalgamation in 1930. By the 1970's the city of Lloydminster, Alberta had a population of over 4,000 and the city of Lloydminster, Saskatchewan over 8,000. The differences in taxation and other financial benefits between the two provinces have seemed to favour the Alberta city and have led the Saskatchewan residents to "threaten" to secede.[18] It is doubtful, however, if the division has caused any permanent hardship.

The ultimate decision showed none of the concern for the geography of the country that had been in evidence since 1880, both with regard to the erection of provisional territorial districts and the suggestions for new provinces. As the *Calgary Herald* put it, "the dividing line . . . is wrong, placed there evidently in an arbitrary manner without consideration and without regard to the physical features of the country or its agricultural and grazing qualities".[19] But the federal government was well aware of these factors. Indeed, the Department of the Interior prepared a memorandum and a map that showed that the Province of Alberta was neither primarily semi-arid and hence suited only to ranching, nor the Province of Saskatchewan primarily suited only to growing grain.[20]

Boundary Extensions

The creation of the provinces of Alberta and Saskatchewan necessitated changes in the boundaries of the Northwest Territories, as the new provinces did not include those parts of the provisional districts of Saskatchewan and Athabaska lying north of the Manitoba boundary.

These either had to remain as separate provisional districts or be incorporated into the District of Keewatin, which was still under the Lieutenant-Governor of Manitoba. The necessary changes were accomplished in three stages. First of all, on the day that the two new provinces were proclaimed (July 20, 1905), an Act amending the Northwest Territories

Act was passed. This Act declared that the Northwest Territories should comprise Rupert's Land: all of the Northwest Territory except such portions thereof as comprised the provinces of Manitoba, Alberta, and Saskatchewan; the District of Keewatin; and the Yukon Territory. Secondly, four days later, an Order in Council was passed by the federal government whereby the whole of the territory comprised within the District of Keewatin was included in the Northwest Territories. Thirdly, by the Act of 1906, the boundaries of the Northwest Territories, as a whole, were redefined.

But the creation of the two "prairie provinces" also intensified the demands of Manitoba, Ontario, and Quebec for a northward extension, now that British Columbia, Alberta, and Saskatchewan all extended to the 60th parallel.

It has already been mentioned, incidentally, that Manitoba's earlier demands for an extension westward also included demands for an extension northward to Hudson Bay. The memorial to this effect, authorized by the Manitoba Legislature in 1905, resulted in a conference between Manitoba government officials and the Prime Minister of Canada, but the latter later stated that the northern extension would be held in abeyance until a conference with the representatives of Ontario, Quebec, Saskatchewan, and Manitoba could take place. At this conference the claims of each of the provinces could be examined.[21] Ultimately, however, a conference was held between the federal government and those of Saskatchewan, Manitoba, and Ontario only, in November 1906.

The Claims of Saskatchewan

Saskatchewan claimed an extension of her boundaries on two counts. In the first place she claimed that her boundaries should be extended eastward so as to include those parts of the Northwest Territories that were formerly part of the provisional districts of Saskatchewan and Athabaska. This claim was based on the fact that this territory was under the control of the administration of the Northwest Territories from its organization until the formation of the Province of Saskatchewan, when it was not included within the area of that province, and on evidence which showed that at least some of its inhabitants wished to be included within the Province of Saskatchewan.[22]

Secondly, Saskatchewan contended that her boundaries should be extended to the shores of Hudson Bay as a right so that the province could have direct water communication with the Atlantic Ocean by way of Hudson Bay and Hudson Strait. The province had already been given some encouragement to think of such an extension as a right by the Prime Minister of Canada,[23] and it contended that that part of the Northwest Territories bordering on Hudson Bay and lying between Nelson River and the 60th parallel of latitude should be awarded to it. It was maintained that a "natural" boundary line between the provinces of Saskatchewan and Manitoba would be found in Nelson River and that the awarding to Saskatchewan of the territory north of this river would not interfere with the granting of Manitoba's reasonable request to have her boundaries extended to Hudson Bay as "from the mouth of the Nelson river to where the province of Ontario touches James Bay" there was a coast of several hundred miles with which Manitoba's desire for an extension to the bay could be gratified.

> Further, it is submitted, that there is a vast expanse of territory lying south and east of the Nelson river, being part of the Northwest Territories and containing some 208,000 square miles which is available for the purpose of satisfying Manitoba's demand for increased area. . . . If this entire portion were given to Manitoba, that province would contain an area of over 280,000 square miles, a larger area than possessed by any other province of Canada, except the province of Quebec and the province of British Columbia. Even if the province of Ontario is considered to be entitled to recognition in the distribution of this territory, it is maintained, that there is sufficient area south and east of the Nelson river to satisfy all legitimate claims for an extension of boundaries both of the province of Manitoba and the province of Ontario.[24]

The Claims of Ontario

Ontario claimed a northward extension merely as a matter of right, although she supported Manitoba's request that her boundaries be extended to Hudson Bay. Ontario then suggested that this northward extension should be made by producing the existing eastern boundary of Manitoba northward until it struck Churchill River, and then following the middle of the channel of that river to its mouth, and that the territory of Manitoba be extended as far north, at least, as the 60th parallel of latitude. For "geographical and other reasons" the remainder of the territory of Keewatin lying east of the suggested eastern boundary of Manitoba, contiguous to

Ontario and bounded on the north and east by Hudson Bay and James Bay should be allotted to the province of Ontario. It was not stated what the geographical and other reasons were.

The Claims of Manitoba

The claims of Manitoba were much more forcefully presented and were supported by much more evidence than in either of the previous cases. The population of the province had increased from 62,260 in 1881 to an estimated 360,000 in 1906, a population in excess of either that of Alberta or Saskatchewan, which had each been given an area of approximately 175,000 square miles more than Manitoba, and it was felt that the province was entitled to increased area so as to enable it to occupy the independent position that was contemplated by the spirit of confederation. For these reasons an increase in area that would place it on a proportionate equality with the other provinces was requested. It was pointed out that in 1881 the federal government had been willing to increase Manitoba's area from 13,500 square miles to 154,000 square miles and that this increase would actually have taken place if it had not been for the later Privy Council decision. For this reason, the area lying west of the proposed Manitoba boundary of 1881, and not given to Ontario by the Privy Council decision, was claimed.

It was also maintained that it was the intention of the federal government, in 1876, at the time of the passage of the Keewatin Act, to ultimately extend the boundaries of Manitoba so as to include a large part of Keewatin, if not the whole of it. In support of this, it was pointed out that for centuries the only means of communication between the Red River settlements and the outside world was through this territory, by way of Hudson Bay. The powers of the Lieutenant-Governor of Manitoba as Lieutenant-Governor of Keewatin from 1876 to 1905, together with other evidence, were adduced to show that Manitoba had always been particularly identified with "Hudson Bay and the intervening territory", which was not true in the case of Ontario. It was further submitted that the development and administration of this intervening territory could best be secured by Manitoba, as the seat of government of Ontario was far removed from the area and, geographically, Manitoba was also in a much better position than the province of Saskatchewan. In any case, both these provinces, in Manitoba's opinion, had "limits and extent" abundantly sufficient to tax their energies and capabilities and it would be unwise further to increase their responsibilities.[25] With regard to those parts of the districts of Assiniboia, Saskatchewan, and Athabaska that were not included in the province of Saskatchewan when it was formed in 1905, Manitoba requested that they be given to her to preserve "geographical" symmetry and because they formed part of the territory in which Manitoba had asked an extension of boundaries for over 25 years. Manitoba also pointed out that, as the area was sparsely populated, the reasons given in 1905 for refusing her the strip of territory in the province of Saskatchewan immediately to the west of the boundary of Manitoba did not apply. But the strongest argument for Manitoba, in her own view, was that the legislature of the Northwest Territories, prior to the creation of the province of Saskatchewan, had stated that it had no pronounced views on the territory north of Lakes Winnipegosis and Manitoba and that it might be given to Manitoba.

The Claims of Quebec

The claim of the province of Quebec to a northern extension was made in a memorial from its Executive Council, dated November 9, 1907, which requested the government of Canada to annex to the province all the area between its northern boundary and Hudson Strait and between Hudson Bay, the Atlantic Ocean, and the "skirt of land" along the Atlantic Ocean that was "supposed to belong to Newfoundland", including the islands in Hudson Bay adjacent to the mainland. Specifically mentioned were the Ottawa, Sleepers, Bakers Dozen, Belcher, North Belcher, King George, Mansel, and Charles Islands, the islands of Ungava Bay, and the Button Islands.[26]

This claim was supported by a number of arguments. First of all, Quebec maintained that the area requested formed part of the province in a geographical sense, because it was wholly isolated from all other parts of Canada by a wide expanse of sea. Furthermore, it was maintained that this undeveloped region was necessary to Quebec, in order to protect the timber, fish, and game over much of the actual territory of the province, because the natives who occupied Ungava, in coming south to hunt in Quebec, were the cause of forest fires and the destruction of fish and wild life. Having caused this havoc they returned to their own "region", where they were beyond reach of the regulations made by the government of Quebec for the protection of its natural resources.

Quebec also took the view that, because of its geographical position, Ungava had everything to gain in becoming part of the province, as the government of Quebec was the most suitably situated to administer and develop Ungava's natural resources. Ungava offered to the other provinces neither advantage nor interest, and the federal government could not adequately administer the area without special and expensive organization.

Finally, the enlargement of its boundaries was claimed by Quebec as compensation for any advantages that Ontario, Manitoba, and Saskatchewan would gain if they were extended to the western shore of Hudson Bay.

The Decisions

It appears that the government of Canada gave consideration to the creation of entirely new provinces out of the areas lying north of Manitoba, Ontario, and Quebec but concluded that climatic conditions were such that new provinces could not be created. "If then, that territory cannot be turned into new provinces, does it not seem the best way to deal with it is to annex it to the existing provinces?" said the Prime Minister.[27] Having settled the policy, attention was then given to the details of implementing it. The claims of Saskatchewan were rejected because the weight of argument to have territory lying north of Manitoba and west of Saskatchewan allotted to either province was in favour of Manitoba.[28] The government of the day was also prepared to admit the claim of Manitoba to have its boundary extended northward to the 60th parallel, but the boundary on the east presented difficulties because the claims of Ontario and Manitoba overlapped.

Manitoba claimed an extension eastward to include the area between Albany River and Hudson Bay, to a meridian line drawn from the confluence of Mississippi and Ohio Rivers, this eastern meridian being based on Manitoba's earlier claims in 1881. Ontario claimed an extension westward to Churchill River.

The government did not think it advisable to agree to Manitoba's claimed eastward limit, because the boundary would have been brought into the vicinity of the longitude of Fort William, Port Arthur, and Lake Nipigon.[29] Neither could it agree to Ontario's claimed western boundary.

The Prime Minister of Canada pointed out that the new railway to Hudson Bay would probably have its terminus at Churchill, as Churchill had the best and perhaps the only, harbour on Hudson Bay. He then expressed the view that, in these circumstances, a town of some proportions would eventually grow up at the mouth, and on both sides, of Churchill River. If the river formed a provincial boundary then part of the town would be in Ontario and the other part in Manitoba. Then "complications would arise and the progress of the city might be materially retarded for the necessity of having legislation either from one province or the other. Therefore, it is far preferable, far more convenient and far more suitable in every possible way that the city be either in one province or the other."[30] One wonders if he had the situation of Lloydminster in Alberta and Saskatchewan in mind.

Ultimately the government decided to fix the northeastern boundary of Manitoba from the then northeast corner of the province over the height of land between Hayes River and Nelson River on one side and that between Hayes and Severn Rivers on the other. However, it was discovered that this definition might lead to complications because the height of land between the Hayes and the Severn did not extend all the way to the shore of Hudson Bay, but was met some distance from the shore by another height of land running east and west. Therefore, in order to follow the principles on which the definition was based and yet avoid a controversial description, the boundary had to be expressed differently, and it was determined that it should be a straight line from the northeast corner of the then boundary of Manitoba to the east end of Island Lake and thence on a straight line to the point where the 89th meridian of west longitude intersects the shore line of Hudson Bay. A resolution recommending this and the above northern and western boundaries was passed by the House of Commons in 1908.[31] No decision was made in 1908 regarding the extension of Quebec, beyond the proposal that, subject to the consent of the legislature of the province of Quebec, it would be expedient to extend the boundaries of that province so as to include all the territory to the north of it and extending to the waters of James Bay and Hudson Bay, and the entrance thereto from the sea.

Beyond the passing of these resolutions, however, no further action was taken on these extensions until February 1912, when Bills passed incorporating the proposed extensions, with the exception that Quebec was not enlarged so as to include the coastal islands, as the province had requested. In fact, no coastal islands were included in any of the three provincial extensions. One reason was the difficulty of giving a description of such islands that would be sufficiently definite. Another was that the islands might be necessary for federal purposes in connection with navigation and defence.[32] The boundary extensions were described as follows:

Ontario

Commencing at the most northerly point of the western boundary of the province of Ontario as determined by "The Canada (Ontario Boundary) Act, 1889", chapter 28 of the statutes of 1889 of the United Kingdom (the said westerly boundary being the easterly boundary of the province of Manitoba); thence continuing due north along the same meridian to the intersection thereof with the centre of the road allowance on the twelfth base line of the system of Dominion Land Surveys; thence northeasterly in a right line to the most eastern point of Island lake, as shown in approximate latitude 53°30′ and longitude 93°40′ on the railway map of Dominion of Canada, published, on the scale of thirty-five miles to one inch, in the year one thousand nine hundred and eight, by the authority of the Minister of the Interior; thence northeasterly in a right line to the point where the eighty-ninth meridian of west longitude intersects the southern shore of Hudson bay; thence easterly and southerly following the shore of the said bay to the point where the northerly boundary of the province of Ontario as established under the said Act intersects the shore of James bay; thence westward along the said boundary as established by the said Act to the place of commencement.[33]

Quebec

Commencing at the point at the mouth of East Main river where it empties into James bay, the said point being the western termination of the northern boundary of the province of Quebec as established by chapter 3 of the statutes of 1898, entitled An Act respecting the north-western, northern and north-eastern boundaries of the province of Quebec; thence northerly and easterly along the shores of Hudson bay and Hudson strait; thence southerly, easterly and northerly along the shore of Ungava bay and the shore of the said strait; thence easterly along the shore of the said strait to the boundary of the territory over which the island of Newfoundland has lawful jurisdiction; thence southeasterly along the westerly boundary of the said last mentioned territory to the middle of the Bay du Rigolet or Hamilton Inlet; thence westerly along the northern boundary of the province of Quebec as established by the said Act to the place of commencement.[34]

Manitoba

Commencing where the sixtieth parallel of north latitude intersects the western shore of Hudson Bay; thence westerly along the said parallel of latitude to the northeast corner of the province of Saskatchewan; thence southerly along the easterly boundary of the province of Saskatchewan to the international boundary dividing Canada from the United States; thence easterly along the said international boundary to the point where the said international boundary turns due north; thence north along the said international boundary to the most northerly point thereof at or near the northwest angle of the Lake of the Woods; thence continuing due north along the westerly boundary of the province of Ontario, by virtue of "The Canada (Ontario Boundary) Act, 1889", chapter 28 of the statutes of 1889 of the United Kingdom, (the said westerly boundary being the easterly boundary of the province of Manitoba) to the most northerly point of the said boundary common to the two provinces under the said Act; thence continuing due north along the same meridian to the intersection thereof with the centre of the road allowance on the twelfth base line of the system of Dominion Land Surveys; thence northeasterly in a right line to the most easterly point of Island Lake, as shown in approximate latitude 53°30′ and longitude 93°40′ on the railway map of the Dominion of Canada published, on the scale of thirty-five miles to one inch, in the year one thousand nine hundred and eight, by the authority of the Minister of the Interior; thence northeasterly in a right line to the point where the eighty-ninth meridian of west longitude intersects the southern shore of Hudson Bay; thence westerly and northerly following the shores of the said Bay to the place of commencement.[35]

The exclusion of the coastal islands in Hudson Bay and strait from Quebec was never entirely acceptable in that province, one official claiming "qu'il était ridicule de pretendre que ces îles ne sont pas partie du territoire du Québec"[36] and interest in them revived in 1962 when the mineral resources on some of them were anticipated to be of economic importance. It was the opinion of the federal Minister of Northern Affairs and National Resources at the time that if Quebec made an official claim it would be necessary to include Manitoba and Ontario in the discussions.[37]

There were no communities of any size along the Saskatchewan-Manitoba boundary as had been the case with the Alberta-Saskatchewan boundary. But extensive deposits of gold, copper, zinc and silver were discovered in 1915 in the Flin Flon area; mining began in 1927 and a community developed which straddled the boundary. As with Lloydminster, the division is at times, inconvenient and the differences in the taxation policies of the two provinces sometimes irksome so that amalgamation has been considered. "Should union become a reality a part of Saskatchewan will be included in the province of Manitoba, and problems in the adjoining community will be handled by the council of the town of Flin Flon."[38]

The Provisional Districts

To bring the Provisional Districts into conformity with the changes in boundaries effected in 1905 and 1912, their boundaries were further defined in 1918 by an Order in Council, which was to take effect in 1920.

Mackenzie was described as the area between the Yukon Territory, the 60th parallel of latitude, the continental shore of the Arctic Ocean, and the 2nd meridian in the Dominion Lands System.

Keewatin's boundaries were as follows:
Commencing at the point where the second meridian . . . . intersects the continental shore of the Arctic Ocean, thence easterly along the said shore to the most northerly point of Spence Bay, between Franklin Isthmus and Boothia Peninsula; thence northeasterly in a straight line across Boothia Isthmus to the most southwesterly point of Lord Mayor Bay in the Gulf of Boothia; thence southeasterly along the shore of the said Gulf to the most southerly point thereof; thence southerly in a straight line across Rae Isthmus to the most northwesterly point of Repulse Bay; thence southeasterly along the middle of Repulse Bay to Frozen straight; thence southerly along the middle line of Frozen straight to Fox Channel; thence southeasterly in a straight line to the most northerly point of Cape Wolstenholme in the Province of Quebec; thence

southerly following the eastern shore of Hudson Bay to
James Bay, thence southerly following the eastern shore of
James Bay to the point where it is intersected by the
boundary between the Provinces of Quebec and Ontario,
thence northerly following the western shore of James Bay
to Hudson Bay, thence westerly . . . . and northwesterly
following the southern shore of Hudson Bay to the point
where it is intersected by the parallel of the sixtieth degree
of north latitude, thence westerly along the said parallel
to the second meridian . . . . thence northerly along
the said meridian to the point of beginning.[39]

Franklin was described as consisting of that part of the
Northwest Territories not included in Mackenzie and Keewatin.

It will be noted that Franklin embraced the whole of
Hudson Strait and Keewatin the whole of Hudson Bay with
a westerly boundary along the 2nd meridian (102 degrees
west). The latter boundary was probably chosen as the
dividing line between Mackenzie and Keewatin, partly for its
convenience, as it was merely a continuation of the boundary
between Manitoba and Saskatchewan, and partly because it
roughly divides those areas of continental Canada north of
60 degrees north that are approached by the Hudson Bay-
Hudson Strait route from those approached via Mackenzie
River and its tributaries. In this sense, therefore, that part
of the 2nd meridian north of the 60th parallel may in 1918
have been considered as an approximation to a watershed
boundary. However, subsequent knowledge of the general
area through which it passes has shown that such approximation is not very close.

These inter-territorial boundaries were established before
there were any settlements in the boundary areas. Where
settlements have subsequently been set up, some rather odd
situations have developed. For example, the settlement of
Spence Bay on Boothia Isthmus, 100 miles removed from its
nearest neighbour, consisted, in 1950, of two small groups of
buildings, with a total white population of five. One group
formed the Hudson's Bay Company post, and the other the
R.C.M.P. post. Yet the boundary as delimited in 1918 places
the former in the District of Franklin and the latter in the
District of Keewatin. However, the nature of the inter-territorial boundaries is such that, in present circumstances, such
a situation is of academic interest only.

The Addition of Newfoundland

With the passage of the Order in Council of 1918, the political map of Canada as it existed prior to the Privy Council decision on the Newfoundland-Labrador boundary, came into being. But in 1949 Newfoundland was admitted to the Confederation as a province – the first "new province" since 1905. It was guaranteed the same territory as it had immediately prior to union and its western boundary was therefore no longer an international one but an inter-provincial one coinciding with Quebec's eastern boundary. The events concerned with its evolution prior to the Imperial Privy Council decision of 1927 were discussed in Chapter IV. There was some dissatisfaction in the province of Quebec over the decision, however, which became vocal almost as soon as Newfoundland joined Canada.[40]

By the 1950's the value of the natural resources distributed on either side of the boundary was becoming apparent.

The once-blank wilderness is now known to hold the world's largest unexploited iron ore deposits. The mighty Hamilton River has a harnessable potential of four million hp. (twice that of the Seaway) and at least 40 million cords of prime black spruce have already been mapped. Exploration continues for economic deposits of copper, titanium, lead, zinc, graphite, nickel and mica, with some production already underway.[41]

The iron ore deposits straddle the border region but the government of Quebec does not collect royalties on ore mined east of a line running through Knob Lake. Newfoundland provides police, education, welfare and other government services at Wabush and other points east of the Atlantic watershed. This, according to one premier of Quebec is *de facto* recognition of the border.[42] Nevertheless, maps published by the province of Quebec do not show the land boundary with the province of Newfoundland; it has, in fact, never been surveyed or demarcated. Nonetheless its existence delayed the developmnt of the Hamilton river (now called the Churchill) for more than two years. Churchill Falls, close to the Quebec-Labrador border, formed one of Canada's largest natural falls and the amount of power generated from them was sufficient to consider exporting some of the power to the U.S.A. But this involved policy decisions between Canada and the United States as well as political agreement between Newfoundland, within whose jurisdiction the falls were located and Quebec, through which the power would have to pass. When political agreement between the two provinces was finally reached in 1966, the first stage of power development was started.[43]

In the south of Labrador, that portion of the boundary which follows the 52nd parallel allocates the headwaters of the Romaine, Natashquan, Petit-Mecatina, St. Augustin and St. Paul rivers to Newfoundland on which Quebec would like to have a permanent water lease. During 1964, the premiers of the two provinces discussed exchanging about 11,000 square miles of territory containing these headwaters for 11,000 square miles of northern Quebec. But the idea was "no more than a thought"[44] and came to nothing.

In 1963, Dorion[45] published an exhaustive study of the boundary from an historical and geographical point of view and paid particular attention to the problems of demarcating and administering the boundary as presently delimited. He concluded with a number of alternative adjustments which might be made to the satisfaction of Quebec and in the following year a federal member of parliament from Quebec called for a committee to study the Newfoundland boundary. He contended that

> borders between these two provinces are vague and inde-
> finite . . . In many places . . . they are not defined clearly
> enough . . . they are against all logic, against all the
> principles of geography and anthropology, that is against
> all the laws of hydrography, mapping and demography.
> They also run counter to the laws of industrial develop-
> ment.[46]

While there may be some truth in this statement subsequent geographical and ethnographic[47] studies have shown that it is an exaggeration. In any event the proposal received no support from the Newfoundland members.

Thus the development of the major political boundaries from the point of view of delimitation has been dealt with. But a boundary can hardly be described as "fixed" until it has been demarcated in some way or other.

CHAPTER VIII

BOUNDARY DEMARCATION AND ADMINISTRATION

The place of boundary demarcation in the general process of boundary evolution has already been described in the introduction to this work. It means the marking of a boundary by some physical means. Boundary delimitation, as the foregoing chapters have shown, is a matter that may be decided upon quite rapidly or may occur after years of deliberation and negotiation, but the marking of a boundary upon the surface of the earth involves different problems.

The Process of Boundary Demarcation

The change from delimitation to demarcation is no easy one. It is easiest if the delimitation has been stated in such a manner that demarcation can begin as merely a matter of routine surveying. Such delimitation, however, has not always occurred in Canada.

Faulty delimitations have been attributed to inexact definition, unsuitable definition, contradictory definition, and unascertainable previous jurisdiction.[1] It has been shown that the earliest boundary delimitations in the northern part of North America were often arbitrary in their essential character and were usually vaguely worded and phrased, often having been drawn up by authorities far removed from the area involved. Even if the scene had been visited, detailed knowledge of it was usually scanty, and maps quite inadequate. In fact many of the early documents expressly included the right, if not the obligation, to explore a loosely defined area.

The development from delimitation to demarcation is particularly difficult, however, if a boundary is defined by natural features of the landscape, unless the definition includes a detailed account of the course of the boundary in relation to such features. Yet it was precisely these outstanding physical features that were seized upon in the relatively unknown parts of Canada in order to provide what were considered to be indisputable points of reference in boundary documents. The northern part of the Ontario-Quebec boundary was supposed to be the due north line from the "head" of Lake Timiskaming, but in 1872-73 the surveyors of the southern end of this line found no definite feature that they could agree upon as the "head" of the lake. They found two rivers flowing into the lake from the north, the two mouths being each broken up into five channels by four islands, with the two outside channels about $2\frac{1}{2}$ miles apart in longitude.[2] As a result, a decision acceptable to both governments had to be made.

The almost endless negotiations regarding the northern and western boundaries of New Brunswick resulted from another instance of faulty delimitation based on topographic features. In fact the only two inter-provincial boundaries still unsettled are of this nature – the Quebec-Newfoundland boundary and the Quebec-Ontario boundary between the 45th parallel and Lake St. Francis. The first of these boundaries is supposed to follow a watershed for the most part, but the location of the watershed is very difficult to establish on the ground. When it is recalled that the watershed between British Columbia and Alberta, long considered one of the most sharply defined in the world, was described by the surveyors as being "by no means so well defined on the ground as might be supposed",[3] the nature of the problem in Quebec-Newfoundland may be better appreciated.

Even when boundaries are delimited in terms of latitude and longitude, demarcation is not always a simple matter. The Canada-Alaska boundary along the 141st Meridian was completely defined, but the requirements for its demarcation could not be completely carried out owing to the physical nature of the terrain.[4]

However, as interest in the New World developed, and as its potential value came to be appreciated, more precise delimitation, and ultimately demarcation, became necessary. Parallel with these developments came closer and more effective administration, as well as new techniques in survey-ing and mapping, which made the task of demarcation much easier. Demarcation thus came to be regarded as an essential part of all boundary problems.

But because of the way in which it has evolved, boundary demarcation especially in Canada, is not even merely a matter of surveying and monumenting, for its ultimate objective must be the establishment of a true and unalterable boundary according to law, so that no possible dispute in regard to its position can arise in the future. It involves the following steps:

(a) The determination of the boundary line from documents of delimitation and field surveys.

(b) The marking of the boundary line on the ground, which involves the selection of sites for, as well as the erection of, monuments and markers.

(c) Plotting the location of the markers on large-scale maps.

(d) Drawing the boundary line on the map in accordance with the treaty of delimitation.

(e) Describing completely the boundary area from marker to marker, as well as the markers themselves.

(f) Preparing a comprehensive report for transmission to the governments concerned.

The Development of Boundary Demarcation in Canada

National Necessity

When the United States of America became independent and the boundary between it and territory remaining British was decided upon, it passed through some relatively thickly populated areas, and demarcation of the "dividing line", therefore, became an immediate necessity.

The present boundary between Quebec and New York and Vermont had been demarcated in 1771-74 as a boundary between British provinces. But the work was carried out in a rather crude manner, and accurate demarcation really dates from 1783. The delimitations included in the treaty of peace with the United States were, however, the subject of much dispute, as has already been pointed out, and the first monument under its provisions for demarcation was not erected until 1797, at the source of the "true River St. Croix".

The Treaty of Ghent, 1814, provided for two commissioners to ascertain the position of the boundary, as delimited in the treaty, from the source of St. Croix River to the St. Lawrence. Their "exploring line" between the source of St. Croix River and St. John River was marked and surveyed in 1817 and 1818. This work also included the erection of a monument on the south bank of the St. Lawrence to mark the western end of the 45th parallel section of the boundary. The commissioners, however, did not agree on the interpretation of the whole of the St. Croix-St. Lawrence boundary as delimited in the treaty, and no decision was reached until 1842, when the so-called "Webster-Ashburton" Treaty was negotiated.

This treaty not only delimited the boundary more precisely but also provided for surveying and marking it. This was carried out from 1843 to 1845. The section of this boundary between the source of St. Croix River and St. John River ("The North Line") followed the "exploring line" of 1817-18 and the 45th parallel ("The West Line") section followed the line surveyed in 1771-74. The resurvey of the latter disclosed that it diverged greatly, though not consistently, from the line it was supposed to follow, but it was nevertheless accepted as the "true boundary".[5]

The Treaty of Ghent, 1814, also provided for the fixing and determining of the part of the International Boundary from the most northwesterly point of Lake of the Woods to Lake Superior and empowered the commissioners to cause to be surveyed and marked such parts as required it. Comparatively little was known about the area involved, as the Mitchell map of 1755 indicated, and the survey made under the Treaty of Ghent was the first systematic one made in the area. It was carried out in 1824, and several places on the boundary were marked by means of monuments.[6]

The next part of the International Boundary to be determined and marked on the ground was the section west of the summit of the Rocky Mountains. This was carried out in 1857-61. At that time, however, the country adjacent to the boundary was sparsely inhabited and, in the high mountainous sections, settlement appeared unlikely at least for some time to come. Therefore, the boundary was demarcated through settled regions and at prominent stream crossings only, the intervals between marked sections being, in some cases, as much as 25 miles.[7]

The "plains section" of the 49th Parallel between the Rockies and Lake of the Woods was first surveyed and marked in 1872-75. The open character of the country rendered operations comparatively simple, and the line was marked at frequent intervals. But as transportation facilities were developed, and as the country on each side of the boundary became more populated, it became clear that this section of the boundary demanded a more definite demarcation, particularly at points where there were trails, or where grass and water were found in more than usual abundance and so caused cattle to cross into Canada from the United States. The R.C.M.P. were responsible for carrying out the quarantine regulations and were, at times, kept in the saddle almost day and night driving American cattle back across the border. Occasionally these cattle were seized under Canadian customs regulations, but the authorities were handicapped by not being able to locate the boundary for miles at a stretch. The nature of the geography of the prairies added to the difficulties of effectively administering the border area. Even in 1887 the federal Department of the Interior reported that

> In Dakota . . . the absence of a fair supply of wood for the purposes of fuel forms a serious drawback to successful settlement. For some years past the settlers of that Territory have been accustomed to supplement their inadequate fuel supply by systematically stealing from the public lands on the Canadian side of the boundary. The destruction of timber by Dakota settlers has been enormous, and in addition to which there was extensive smuggling and other evasion of our laws.[8]

Some of these difficulties arose from the fact that many of the original monuments in this section had been merely mounds of earth, which had deteriorated greatly since their construction.

In 1893, questions as to the adequacy of the demarcation of the 49th Parallel west of the Rockies began to arise, and in 1899 similar problems arose regarding the Quebec-New York line. In the same year difficulties arose with the boundary across Lake Erie. The federal Department of Marine and Fisheries requested

> such information as would enable their overseers to ascertain up to what point in the lake they might enforce the fisheries regulations of Canada; but on investigation it was found that no precise survey had been made of the north shore of the lake, and the definition of the middle line was in consequence impossible.[9]

The boundaries through the water channels to the Atlantic and Pacific Oceans also remained to be marked, although general maps of the boundaries in these areas had been prepared, and some range marks had been erected on the Atlantic part as early as 1893, following the seizure by Canada of seven American fishing vessels on the ground that they were operating in Canadian waters.

Finally, in 1908, a treaty was adopted by Canada and the United States of America providing for a more complete demarcation of the land and water parts of the whole International Boundary. It described the boundary in eight sections and provided for the appointment of a joint commission to locate or restore previously established marks and to place new marks in unmarked sections. The boundary through the St. Lawrence River and the Great Lakes was assigned to the International Waterways Commission, and the remainder of the boundary to the International Boundary Commission. The work under the treaty of 1908 was completed in the 1930's.

The treaty of 1908, however, did not include the boundary between Canada and Alaska. This boundary was surveyed and demarcated from 1904 to 1913, following an international convention signed in 1906.[10]

Provincial Expediency

Unlike Canada's international boundaries, at least those with the United States, her interprovincial boundaries were not demarcated until it became expedient to do so. This did not take place until settlement occurred, or was immediately anticipated in the boundary region, or until some administrative problem, usually connected with natural resources, arose. The only exception was the Quebec-New Brunswick boundary, which was demarcated in 1853-55. This was the first of Canada's interprovincial boundaries to be demarcated and it did not run through a densely populated area. But since its establishment depended on the settlement of the Quebec-United States boundary, this demarcation can be said to be more closely tied to international necessity than to provincial expediency.

The New Brunswick-Nova Scotia boundary was not demarcated until 1859, although the main course of the boundary became recognized by the people who lived near it by about 1800. The delay was partly due to the difficulty of demarcation at the source of the River Misseguash. It rises in an area of floating bogs, and the numerous small streams and lakes in the vicinity made it difficult to determine the true source of the river, and its various windings in the upper reaches. Ultimately the boundary did not attempt to follow these windings, but followed compass lines along the general direction of the river.[11] Apart from this, the only other interprovincial boundary that ran through settled country before 1867 was the southern part of the Quebec-Ontario boundary. As this happened to be mainly the Ottawa River, demarcation was unnecessary until settlement spread north of Lake Timiskaming. This began in 1872-74 when the "due north line" from Lake Timiskaming was surveyed to the height of land between Hudson Bay drainage and Great Lakes drainage, some 42 miles north of the zero point on the lake.[12]

Not until 1897 did further interprovincial demarcation occur. It was pointed out by the federal government in 1887 that "for judicial and other purposes it is very important that the portion of the Ontario-Manitoba boundary extending from the Northwest angle of Lake of the Woods to Winnipeg river be defined at once". In 1893, an Order in Council was passed pointing out that still no steps had been taken "to determine its position on the ground."

> As . . . berths were being licensed by the governments of both Canada and Ontario in comparatively close proximity to where this line would be found to lie, the opinion was expressed that the provinces of Ontario and Manitoba should join with the Dominion in appointing a commission for the purpose of effecting the necessary survey during the then ensuing season – that is to say, the season of 1894. The authorities of both provinces mentioned were communicated with accordingly. The government of Ontario agreed to the proposal, but the government of Manitoba took the view that, not being the owners of the timber, the minerals or the public lands,[13] they did not appear to be sufficiently interested in the immediate delimitation of the boundary to warrant the incurring of any expenditure at that time.[14]

Eventually, the need became so urgent[15] that the federal government and the government of Ontario each agreed to pay one half of the costs. Consequently, the survey was not completed until 1897.

Hardly had this survey been completed than the next began, but this time in a more remote area – northwestern British Columbia. For in 1898, owing to the discovery of gold in the Klondike and the consequent influx of people to the area, questions of jurisdiction arose between the British Columbia and federal governments. Following respresentations by British Columbia, the Minister of the Interior directed that the boundary between British Columbia and the newly formed Yukon Territory be demarcated. This work was carried on during the years 1899-1901 and again in 1907-1908. About 157 miles of boundary were surveyed and marked on the ground. Commencing on the west side of Teslin Lake, the line runs westward to Tatshenshini River, with a break of 9 miles in the mountainous country between Takhini and

Hudson Rivers. It was not considered necessary to survey the 65 miles of permanently snow-covered mountains from Tatshenshini River westward to the Alaska border.[16]

In the meantime, the southeastern part of British Columbia was being developed. Valuable coal deposits had been located at widely separated points in the region of the boundary, which was to follow the watershed of the Rocky Mountains. As a result, leases of coal lands had been issued by both the Dominion and the province. In some instances the descriptions of these leases were based on surveys that assumed a provisional boundary, as the watershed was very ill-defined in places. As a result, surveys made by federal and provincial surveyors were based on differing provisional boundaries, and often overlapped. This in turn led to problems of administration, such as the collection of royalties on coal and the control of mining operations under the respective statutes of the Dominion or the province. Administration of the extensive forest resources on either side of the watershed also stressed the necessity for demarcating the boundary so that surveyors in private practice, timber lessees, fire wardens, and game guardians could govern their activities accordingly.[17]

In 1913, instructions were issued for the demarcation of the boundary between British Columbia and Alberta between the International Boundary and the 120th degree of longitude, and the work was completed by 1916. The instructions issued were very full, and one paragraph is particularly enlightening, for it stated that the parts of the boundary that required first attention were the Crowsnest Pass, owing to the proximity of mining properties; the Vermilion Pass, owing to the construction of the motor road from Banff to Windermere; the Howse Pass, owing to the proximity of timber claims; the Kicking Horse Pass, Simpson Pass, and White Man Pass, owing to their lying within or adjacent to populated areas; the Athabaska Pass, which was a possible railway route; the South Kootenay, the North Kootenay, North Fork, and Kananaskis Passes; the Moose Pass, which had some importance as a possible route to the north via Smoky River, and the Robson Pass, "which is of no importance, except as one of the most striking scenic centres of the entire mountain region."[18]

Settlement east of the Rockies, however, was also spreading northwards, and with it the need for the accurate location of provincial boundaries. In the prairies, the necessity of knowing exactly where the jurisdiction of each province began and ended was needed not only because of the opening up of land for agricultural settlement but also of mineral discoveries in their northern portions. The presence of copper ores straddling the Saskatchewan-Manitoba border has already been mentioned for example, and the southern 500 miles of this boundary, from the U.S. border to Kamuchawie Lake, north of Flin Flon, were therefore marked before 1913.

Further east, in 1906, owing to the activity of prospectors, lumbermen, clay-belt investigators, and trans-continental railway builders in what was then northern Ontario and Quebec, the interprovincial boundary was demarcated for a further 47 miles northward to Okikodisek River, a point in the neighbourhood of the proposed Grand Trunk Pacific Railway. In the following year the boundary was further demarcated for an additional 51 miles.[19]

Presumably for somewhat similar reasons, accentuated by the boundary extensions of 1912, the necessity for further demarcating the boundary between Ontario and Manitoba was discussed by the government of those provinces and the federal government during 1913 and 1914, but owing to the outbreak of World War I the matter was left in abeyance until 1920. In that year the Dominion Land Surveyor who had been surveying mineral claims in the Rice Lake district for several years reported that claims were being staked near the interprovincial boundary, and called attention to the necessity for an early demarcation of the line from Winnipeg River northerly through the mining district. It was realized that the question had now reached a stage where further delay would probably be followed by serious complications, and the work proceeded in 1921 and 1922;[20] the meridian section of the boundary was completed to the 12th Base Line of the Dominion Lands System.

The northward course of settlement had by this time extended well into the Peace River area of northern Alberta and British Columbia. Bisected as this area was by the meridional boundary between these two provinces, which had never been demarcated, jurisdictional overlapping again occurred, as it had earlier in the watershed section of this interprovincial boundary.

As had occurred before 1913, a provisional boundary line had been run by the government of British Columbia, which did not coincide with the surveys made in the area by the federal government. It was also necessary to survey and demarcate the 120th meridian south to its intersection with the "summit of the Rocky Mountains" so as to determine the point at which the interprovincial boundary ceased to follow the "summit". "Finally it was desired to establish the boundary across Peace River – that most noble artery of Northland traffic – and the unsurveyed country to the north of it, with a view to the proper administration by the adjoining Provinces of their respective laws".[21]

The survey of the 120th meridian was carried out from 1922-24, and at the end of their operations the surveyors had reached almost to latitude $57\frac{1}{2}$ degrees north. At this point it was decided to discontinue the survey for the time being as the remaining 174 miles still to be surveyed ran through uninhabited and unproductive country.

The years 1929 and 1930 saw the further demarcation of the Manitoba-Ontario boundary from the 12th Base Line of the Dominion Lands System to Island Lake, and in 1930-31 the remainder of the northern boundary between Quebec and Ontario was demarcated. This became necessary owing to the still further extension northward of the activities of trappers, lumbermen, prospectors, and railway builders, and resulted in the first demarcated interprovincial boundary to reach Canada's northern coasts, at James Bay.

In 1937, the survey of the Ontario-Manitoba boundary was extended to Echoing River, and the following year active development of the mining and fur industries made it appear necessary for administrative purposes to complete the demarcation of that part of the 110th meridian of longitude (the 4th meridian of the Dominion Lands System) that formed an interprovincial boundary. It has already been pointed out that this boundary was not delimited as an interprovincial boundary until 1905, but by 1912 it had been completely demarcated from the International Boundary to the south shore of Lake Athabasca. The great difficulties of measuring a line across so large a body of water made it seem inadvisable to produce it farther at that time.[22]

World War II brought great activity to the Canadian northwest. Among these activities was the construction of the Alaska Military Highway from Dawson Creek, B.C., to Fairbanks, Alaska, in 1942 and 1943. It was known that this highway crossed the northern boundary of British Columbia at several points, but the exact location of the crossings was not known as the boundary had never been surveyed. The matter was brought to the attention of the governments concerned, with the result that Orders in Council were passed by both, stating that "the resulting activity, in the vicinity of the boundary area, makes it necessary that the boundary line be surveyed and marked on the ground for administrative purposes".[23] The work was commenced in 1945 on the west side of Teslin Lake, at a boundary monument established in the survey of 1899, and had been extended eastward to almost 127°30' W. by 1948, those parts of the boundary known to be nearest the highway having been demarcated first. By 1953, the whole of the boundary east of Teslin Lake had been demarcated except for a 66 mile gap between Smith and Beaver rivers. This gap was closed in 1955.

The demarcation of the remaining section of the Ontario-Manitoba boundary between Echoing river and Hudson Bay was completed in 1948 when its terminal point, where the 89th meridian of longitude intersects the shore of Hudson Bay, was reached. The discovery of minerals in the northern part of the province of Alberta led to the beginning of the demarcation of the northern boundary of the province – the 60th parallel of latitude. The demand for mining and oil leases called for precise survey and "accurate ground markings" and the work was begun in January 1951 and completed in 1954. For similar reasons it became necessary to demarcate the boundary between Saskatchewan and the Northwest Territories.

By 1952, uranium had been discovered at Martin Lake, only 25 miles south of the northern boundary of Saskatchewan. Since "further discoveries and stakings could spill over into the Territories, it has become necessary to survey a portion of the boundary. To do so will also delineate the respective interests of the province and the Northwest Territories in regard to administration and management of fish, game and hydro-electric resources".[24] A Saskatchewan-Northwest Territories Boundary Commission was, therefore, established in that year, for this purpose. The work of monumenting this boundary started in the winter of 1954-55. The fifty-two miles extending eastward from the north-west corner of the province were completed in that season, and the remaining portion the following year. The federal Department of Northern Affairs and Northern Resources expressed a desire to see the 60th parallel marked on the ground throughout and hence after the Saskatchewan section had been completed the work began on the Manitoba section. The westernmost 109 miles were completed in 1958-59 and the remaining 146 miles easterly to Hudson Bay in 1959-60.

Thus, by 1960 the interprovincial and provincial-territorial boundaries were to a very large extent demarcated. Where demarcation had not yet occurred, the provinces had generally speaking, found it inexpedient to do so. In 1950, the Controller of Surveys for the province of Saskatchewan said:

The north half of the Manitoba-Saskatchewan boundary

is not yet surveyed. Probably there will not be a need for same until mineral development and increased population in the vicinity of the boundary warrant delineation of the provinces eastern limit.[25]

This had occurred by 1959. Of the 255 miles remaining, the 117 miles from Kamuchawie Lake to Reindeer Lake were demarcated in 1960-61 and the 138 miles from Reindeer Lake to the Northwest Territories in 1961-62.

The longest interprovincial boundary that remains to be demarcated is that between Quebec and Newfoundland. This is mainly because the delimitation was a matter of doubt until the comparatively recent decision of the Imperial Privy Council in 1927. Even the initial point of the land boundary between the two provinces at Ance Sablon has never been marked. As one Member of Parliament described it in 1964

> when I was in Blanc-Sablon [sic] the terminal point of the Quebec Labrador coast, I was quite astonished to see an ordinary rock, having no inscription, thrown there haphazardly, as it were, indicating the frontier between the two provinces.[26]

However, the development of the iron-ore deposits that are intersected by this boundary will undoubtedly call for some demarcation before many years have passed. The lack of precision with regard to the Quebec-Ontario boundary through Lake St. Francis has already been discussed.

For the sake of completeness it should also be mentioned that the boundaries between the territories are not demarcated. The main reason is that demarcation is unnecessary, as territorial boundaries do not separate areas that have different basic administrations. They are all under the control of Ottawa, and any revenue derived from them accrues to the federal government. For similar reasons, so long as the three "Prairie Provinces" did not have control of their natural resources they were not anxious to bear the expense of boundary demarcation.[27]

Methods of Boundary Demarcation

Boundaries today are usually marked by the erection of stones, signs, beacons, pillars, or monuments, particularly if they do not follow prominent natural features.

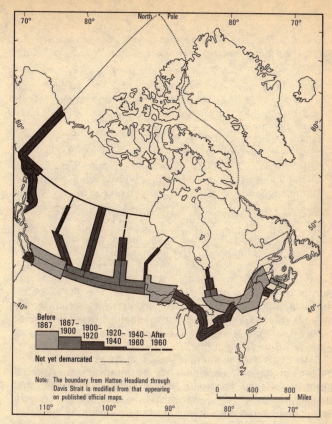

Figure 28: The progress of boundary demarcation in Canada.

Monuments

The type of marker used in Canada has varied considerably. Generally, because of the great distances involved, as well as the fact that demarcation has often taken place in remote regions where transportation is a limiting factor, boundary pillars have been built of whatever materials could be found at hand. For these reasons the earliest boundary monuments were frequently of very similar construction, although if, as time went on, the adjacent areas became settled, the early rudimentary markers were replaced by more permanent ones.

The 1771-74 survey of the 45th parallel was merely a compass line marked by blazes on trees. When re-examined in 1843, these marks were still visible, but iron monuments were erected along the line at every point of deflexion.[28]

David Thompson, who first surveyed and demarcated the part of the boundary between Lake of the Woods and Lake Superior:

> having arrived at the 49th degree of north latitude . . . there placed a heap of large stones with several pickets well driven into the ground, at the first angle of this Lake there being no stones within several miles we erected a square monument of Logs of 12 feet high by 7 feet width, the lower part of Oak, the upper part of Aspin – and nailed to it a Tin Plate marked the North West Corner of the Lake of the Woods No. 1 – proceeding northward at the second Angle of the Lake we erected a Pyramid of stones 7 feet high by 4 feet square at the Base and a Cedar post in its centre nailed a Tin Plate pierced.[29]

The interprovincial demarcation shows the same variety in types of monuments. The original demarcation of the boundary between New Brunswick and Nova Scotia was partly carried out by placing hackmatack (larch) posts one-fourth of a mile apart along the line. On the Alberta-Saskatchewan boundary, some monuments were merely mounds of sand, no stone being available.[30] On the northern part of the Ontario-Quebec boundary, aluminium plaques were nailed to blazed trees.[31]

Later it became common practice to mark parts, at least, of the interprovincial boundaries by means of short metal posts, which are planted in the ground, and mounds and trenches or stone mounds, which are used as markers. In more recent times even these have not been entirely adequate. For example in 1974, new monuments were built for seventy-four points along the 141st meridian between Canada and Alaska. The new marks, made up of copper clad steel rods drilled three to four feet into rock or permafrost with a bronze tablet on top replaced the old stone cairns. Such permanent marks are necessary because the points are used more and more for reference by those doing surveys for re-source developments in the area.

Unless the boundary is clearly marked by a pronounced physical feature, or is in uninhabited or inaccessible country, it is usual to endeavour to make the monuments intervisible. This has usually been interpreted to mean, in Canada, that each monument should be visible from one or more other monuments, though not necessarily from the nearest.[32]

Each monument erected along a Canadian boundary is also

numbered, usually consecutively from one end of the line, and fully described. The description includes all data that might help to relocate the monument if misplaced, destroyed, or obscured.

The Boundary Vista

Where a boundary crosses wooded land, a path or "vista" is normally cut on each side of the line. The width of the vista varies. Along the Canada-United States boundary it is usually sufficient to produce a 20-foot skyline. Along the interprovincial boundaries a 6-foot skyline is the general rule. The width of clearance necessary on the ground to produce a specified width of vista varies. Along the 120th meridian boundary between Alberta and British Columbia the surface clearance necessary for a 6-foot skyline was 10 to 16 feet according to the nature of the timber.[33]

In some places, as on the meridian section of the Alberta-British Columbia boundary, ground is cleared for some distance around each monument, partly to make the monument conspicuous, but mainly to protect it from forest fire.[34]

Water Boundaries

In the case of water boundaries it is not ordinarily possible to erect monuments along them. But it is possible in certain cases to demarcate such boundaries by using alinements made on markers placed on the banks or with the help of floating buoys or fixed beacons.

The International Boundary between Canadian and United States territorial waters has been demarcated in this manner. By the treaty of 1908, the International Boundary Commissioners required these parts of the boundary to be marked by permanent range marks established on land. The two main water boundaries in question were that through Passamaquoddy Bay to the Atlantic Ocean (although the final extension of this boundary to the high seas was not adopted until the boundary treaty of 1925) and that through Georgia, Haro, and Juan de Fuca Straits to the Pacific Ocean. Within the bays and straits the reference points were marked by large, triangular, concrete pyramids, which serve as range marks or cross-range marks for the courses of the boundary. The boundary farther from the shore is referenced to these existing monuments and lighthouses. Some of the lighthouses used as reference marks are frame structures. In order to provide for the recovery of their accurate location should they be destroyed or replaced, concrete witness marks of various designs have been erected, their distances and directions from the lighthouses being accurately determined.

The boundary through the Great Lakes and other waterways between the point of intersection of the 45th parallel and the St. Lawrence River and the mouth of Pigeon River is similarly marked in accordance with the following terms of the Treaty of 1908:

> . . . the said Commissioners shall so far as practicable mark the course of this entire boundary . . . by buoys and monuments in the waterways and by permanent range marks established on the adjacent shores or islands, and by such other boundary marks and at such points as in the judgment of the Commissioners it is desirable that the boundary should be so marked.[35]

With regard to the national boundaries, between the territorial waters of Canada and the high seas, an Order in Council in 1937 not only defined certain of the limits of Canadian territorial waters, but also directed that these limits be mapped. Although it would be almost impracticable to demarcate these boundaries completely, some of the means of demarcation described above might have been used following this Order in Council, but were not. No Canadian territorial waters, therefore, have yet been demarcated, although marking their limits on accurate maps and charts is a step in this direction.

Maintenance and Administration

A demarcated boundary is a man-made structure, and, like other man-made structures, requires maintenance. Without maintenance a demarcated boundary will deteriorate and perhaps disappear.

In Canada monuments suffer deterioration from frost. Freezing in cracks may destroy concrete and stone markers and freezing of the soil often tilts the monument. For example, by 1890, along the boundary between New York and Quebec almost half the monuments were lost, thrown out of place or badly damaged. "These monuments were hollow pillars of cast iron, not well adapted to withstand the rough usage many of them had evidently encountered." In some instances monuments have been destroyed or moved by human agencies. For example, 4 years after the survey of the Vermont-Quebec boundary under the Treaty of 1842, the complaints that Monument 560 in the village of Beebe Plain had been moved from its original position were found to be justified. However to deal with these problems proper records must be kept.

> The lack of the original records of those portions of the boundary which have been defined, not by natural features, but by artificial monuments, is seriously felt when a re-establishment of the line . . . is desired.[36]

The greatest maintenance problems in Canada, however, are concerned with the boundary vistas. These fill in with new growth almost as soon as they are cut and need to be cleared periodically. Such problems were exemplified during the re-tracement of part of the northern boundary between Quebec and Ontario, for in places the line was so completely overgrown that it could not be recognized by the surveyors even when they knew they were actually on it. This was true not only of the 58-year old line but of the 26-year old one as well. Some of the monuments were destroyed and some others were so completely covered that they were located only as a result of the surveyors' measurements.[37]

With some of the earlier boundaries inaccurate or confusing surveys necessitate a re-examination of the whole situation. In 1893 for example, in the Boundary Creek and Grand Prairie regions of the southern British Columbia boundary there was evidence that two lines were surveyed and marked.

> These lines are about one hundred yards apart; both . . . are equally well cut out, and were apparently run about the same time. But the monuments on the northern line are pulled down very completely, while those on the south line are standing in good condition. To the east of Boundary creek the monuments are in ruins on the south line and are standing on the north line, while at Boundary creek there are monuments standing on both lines. At Grand Prairie the land is being farmed by United States citizens up to the north line . . . The condition of affairs is one which may possibly lead to grave trouble, especially in view of the fact that this portion of the boundary is in the immediate neighbourhood of the recently discovered rich mineral deposits of the Kootenay mining region.[38]

To deal with these problems on long or important boundaries a permanent maintenance body was needed. For example, after 1915 it became apparent that on the section of the Canada-United States boundary through the St. Lawrence

River, the Great Lakes, and their connecting waterways, several monuments required moving or repairing. Furthermore, on bridges being built across the connecting waterways, the boundary crossings were not marked, and a new growth of timber had filled in a great deal of the boundary vista. This need for maintaining an effective boundary led to the negotiation of a special treaty in 1925. Under this treaty, boundary commissioners were empowered to

> inspect the various sections of the boundary line between the United States and the Dominion of Canada and between Alaska and the Dominion of Canada at such times as they shall deem necessary; to repair all damaged monuments and buoys; to relocate and rebuild monuments which have been destroyed; to keep the boundary vistas open, to move boundary monuments to new sites and establish such additional monuments and buoys as they shall deem desirable; to maintain at all times an effective boundary line between the United States and the Dominion of Canada and between Alaska and the Dominion of Canada, as defined by the present treaty and treaties heretofore concluded, or hereafter to be concluded; and to determine the location of any point of the boundary line which may become necessary in the settlement of any question that may arise between the two governments.[39]

The commissioners and their staffs are known as the International Boundary Commission. The Commission is divided into two sections, one for Canada and one for the United States.

The Commissioners are required by the treaty of 1925 to submit a joint report to their respective governments at least once in every calendar year. This report must include:

> a statement of inspections made, the monuments and buoys repaired, relocated, rebuilt, moved and established . . . plates and tables certified and signed by the commissioners, giving the locations and geodetic positions of all monuments moved and all additional monuments established within the year, and such other information as may be necessary to keep the boundary maps and records accurately revised.

Even along boundaries which have been surveyed and demarcated for a long time and subsequently re-surveyed and remarked constant inspection and renewal is needed. For example in 1974, the International Boundary Commission inspected 113 monuments along the boundary between Quebec and the United States west of Lake Champlain on the 45th parallel and replaced 27 monuments with permanent markers going five feet into the ground.

The interprovincial boundaries are not maintained and administered in the same manner because they are relatively less important. As problems arise the provinces involved take the necessary action, which as a rule results in a resurvey of the boundary concerned by a properly constituted Boundary Commission. In the case of the British Columbia-Alberta boundary the report of the Commissioners appointed to demarcate the boundary between the two provinces also stated that

> In order to deal with all questions in connection with replacing of all monuments which may be destroyed or disturbed, the re-adjustment of any portions of the Boundary and the dealing with any matters concerning the Boundary, it is recommended that the Surveyor General of Canada, the Director of Surveys of Alberta and the Surveyor General of British Columbia be constituted a standing Committee to which all such matters may be referred.[40]

In 1974 the federal parliament passed the Alberta-British Columbia Boundary Act which provides for the creation of a boundary commission with authority to resurvey the mountain portions of the boundary between the two provinces, to maintain the boundary and deal with any problems relating to the whole boundary.

The Cost of Demarcation and Boundary Administration

The cost of boundary demarcation and maintenance is no small item in a country such as Canada, where such great distances are involved and where boundaries often traverse terrain that is difficult of access. Boundary demarcation not only involves surveying and monumenting, but also the mapping of the boundary areas. Sometimes the cost is too great to permit the necessary demarcation to be carried out. In 1872 and 1874 the government of British Columbia pressed for the demarcation of its boundary with Alaska but although the American government recognized the need when they estimated the cost of the survey, they were unwilling to proceed, a position they maintained until 1892. In 1893 the government of British Columbia complained that its southern boundary

was inadequately monumented. The federal government replied, by means of an Order in Council no less!, that as it
was then spending a considerable sum of money yearly on
the delimitation of the boundary with Alaska, the work in
southern British Columbia would be delayed.[41] In the case
of international boundaries particularly, the surveys have to
be accompanied by accurate maps of high quality, which,
consequently, involve special expenditures. The cost of producing the charts alone for the International Boundary
through the St. Lawrence River and the Great Lakes was
estimated at $60,000 in 1908.

Similarly, the cost of monuments alone is by no means
inconsiderable. The placing of buoys, monuments, and range
marks to mark the Great Lakes-St. Lawrence water boundary
in 1908 was estimated to cost $100,000.[42] When the British
Columbia-Alberta boundary was monumented in 1913-16 each
monument was estimated to cost approximately $35, and
along the 120th meridian section of this boundary there are
232 monuments. In more modern times, aircraft have been
used to an increasing extent in the surveying and demarcating
of boundaries. This was the case with the 168-mile stretch
of the Manitoba-Ontario boundary between Echoing River
and Hudson Bay in 1948 when the total cost of the flying
alone was $16,775.[43] The total cost was $55,000 – an average
of some $327 per mile. Along the 138-mile northern portion
of the Saskatchewan-Manitoba border the boundary vista
had to be cut through woodland and boundary monuments
were erected every 1½ miles. The numerous lakes and mus-
kegs ruled out summer work and it therefore had to be done
in winter with aircraft support. The cost was approximately
$350 per mile (in 1962).

In the case of the provincial boundaries, the federal
government is usually involved in the original survey and
demarcation and shares the costs with the provinces in
varying proportion, but usually equally, so that each government contributes one-third of the total cost. The cost of
demarcating the boundaries between the provinces and the territories is, of course, equally divided between the provincial
government concerned and the federal government. This
was the case with the Saskatchewan-Northwest Territories
boundary for example in 1954. The cost of establishing
ground markers, removing trees from a six-foot strip along
the line, and making a survey of high accuracy was estimated at $190,000 (nearly $700 per mile). Maintenance costs
are usually divided equally between the two provinces concerned. By the 1960's the initial surveys had almost been

TABLE II

International Boundary Commission (Canadian Section)

Expenditures 1945-1969

Period	Average annual expenditure
1945-1950	$ 35,735
1950-1955	55,257
1955-1960	61,902
1960-1965	95,203
1965-1969	111,896

Source: Public Accounts of Canada. After 1969 the federal government changed its method of accounting so that the expenditures for the activities of the Commission are not now available separately.

completed but the federal government's annual expenditure on provincial and territorial boundary surveys averaged $12,530 between 1960 and 1965 and $10,700 between 1965 and 1969. In the case of the International Boundary Commission, the salaries of each Commissioner and his staff and office expenses are paid by the government concerned, but boundary maintenance and other "visible" expenses are shared equally. When it is considered that Canada's international boundaries are marked by 5,463 monuments, a 20-foot vista through 1,353 miles of wooded areas, and an additional 2,522 reference monuments along the water sections, it will be realized that the cost of maintenance is fairly heavy. Some of Canada's expenses in this connection during the last few years are set out in Table II. Occasionally, too, the cost of boundary demarcation has included human lives and suffering as a result of serious accidents to the ground survey personnel. This is particularly true of mountainous country. In 1909, while working on the Canada-Alaska boundary survey, one member of the party broke through the snow cornice of a mountain and fell 2,000 feet to the glacier below, and in 1913 a landslide buried two men at their camp at Cape Muzon in the same boundary area.[44]

The value of adequate boundary demarcation is almost impossible to express in dollars and cents. During the course of demarcation and maintenance operations in Canada, much exploration and map making has been carried out, often in areas that before the boundary work were completely unknown. The foregoing pages are full of the difficulties encountered because accurate surveys of boundary areas were lacking. This often resulted in the language of documents relating to boundaries not being sufficiently clear and, therefore, in lengthy and costly litigation over their correct interpretation. The amounts expended by the province of Ontario alone on the settlement of the northerly and westerly boundaries of the province and the arbitration in reference thereto totalled over $15,000 between 1867 and 1879[45] and this was not an international problem. When one thinks of the results of the errors on the Mitchell map and Vancouver's chart the expense of boundary demarcation and maintenance seems a small price to pay for well-defined boundaries.

CHAPTER IX

BOUNDARY ADJUSTMENT AND ADJUSTMENT TO BOUNDARIES

The preceding chapter was concerned with the process and costs of boundary demarcation and administration, and it makes it clear that this phase of boundary evolution may be very costly and time-consuming.

The earlier chapters of this work showed how boundary delimitation occurred in former times. Each step in the evolution of territorial limits was eventually accompanied by a legal document of some kind, and as Canada emerged as a federal state of ten provinces and two territories, as the need for demarcation grew, and as constitutional processes became more complex, so the legal-geographical ramifications of problems associated with boundaries multiplied.

The Constitutional Processes of Boundary Change and Adjustment

These aspects of boundaries involve the processes through which adjustments and compromises are arrived at before a final boundary is agreed upon, as well as those that are followed if change or adjustment is needed after the recognized legal establishment of a boundary.

International Boundaries

It is a well-known fact, fully substantiated by what has been presented previously, that boundaries between countries are established by treaties made by the sovereign powers concerned. Such boundaries are also adjusted or changed in a similar way. Between 1782 and 1925, the Canada-United States boundary was a subject of negotiation in at least seventeen treaties, conventions, and protocols that have gone into force, as well as others that were not ratified or completed. There have been two arbitrations, and a number of international commissions have been appointed to settle details in dispute relating to the interpretation of treaty provisions.[1] As Canada's international boundaries are also coincident with provincial boundaries, except where they pass through navigable waters and also with the exception of the Yukon-Alaska boundary, any future change in these international boundaries would appear to require at least legal recognition by the province concerned, as was the case with the change in the International Boundary in the Lake of the Woods area in 1925. By this change (a result of the first boundary treaty negotiated and concluded by the government of Canada, rather than the government of the United Kingdom acting on Canada's behalf), Manitoba's boundaries also became altered and the change was legally recognized by that province[2] as well as by the federal parliament.[3]

Interprovincial Boundaries

New provinces may be created by the federal government under the terms of Imperial Acts 34-35, Vict., Ch. 28 (The British North America Act, 1871), which state that

> The Parliament of Canada may from time to time establish new Provinces in any territories forming for the time being part of the Dominion of Canada, but not included in any Province thereof, and may at the time of such establishment, make provision for the constitution and administration of any such Province. . . .

The creation of new provinces out of territories appears to be solely the responsibility of the federal parliament, but when once a province has been created, its boundaries cannot be changed by the federal parliament without the consent of the province concerned, for the 1871 act states that

> The Parliament of Canada may from time to time, with the consent of the Legislature of any Province of the said Dominion, increase, diminish, or otherwise alter the limits of such Province. . . .

Thus a boundary between two provinces of Canada may be changed only by agreement of the legislatures concerned with the federal parliament. In the case of the Ontario-Manitoba dispute, the Judicial Committee of the Privy Council reported that legislation by the province of Ontario as well as by Canada and the province of Manitoba was necessary to give binding effect to the award of August 3, 1878, and as no such legislation had taken place, said award was not binding.

Even after a boundary has been delimited in an official document and agreed to by all parties concerned, further legal action is necessary after the boundary has been demarcated. Thus, after the Alberta-British Columbia boundary had been demarcated "from the 49th parallel up to the point on the 120th meridian of west longitude about latitude north fifty seven degrees, twenty six minutes and forty and twenty-five one hundredth seconds," both provincial governments[4] as well as the federal government[5] passed acts recognizing the boundary as demarcated as the true boundary, whether or not it increased, diminished, or otherwise altered the territory of the respective provinces.[6] Similar legislation was passed by these governments when the remainder of the boundary was demarcated.[7]

Territorial Boundaries

A boundary between a province and a territory is fixed by joint action of the federal parliament and the legislature of the province concerned. When the boundary between Quebec and the District of Ungava had been agreed upon, an Act was passed by the provincial legislature giving effect to the settlement. It was ratified by a federal Order in Council[8] but this appeared to be insufficient and hence the boundary description was embraced in an Act of the federal parliament two years later.[9]

Boundaries between territories are fixed by federal action alone, by an Act of Parliament. So far there has only been one instance of this, namely the Yukon-Northwest Territories boundary.

Boundaries within territories, e.g., district boundaries, are also determined solely by federal authorities, either by an Order in Council or an Act of Parliament. It would appear from Orders in Council of 1882, 1895, 1897, and 1918 that an Order in Council is all that is needed for the creation and delimitation of territorial districts. However, legislation was resorted to in 1906 to define the boundaries of Mackenzie, Yukon, Keewatin, and Ungava in their entirety, and Keewatin, the first district to be created, was the result of an Act of Parliament as early as 1876.

Disputes between provinces regarding boundaries, unless started before December 1958, are now settled by the

Supreme Court of Canada, whose decisions are final. Until 1958, the final Court of Appeal was the Imperial Privy Council, by Imperial Act, 3-4 Wm. IV, Cap. 41.

The above summary re-emphasizes that not only has it cost a great deal to establish the present boundaries of Canada, both with regard to delimitation and demarcation, but it may also be a costly and lengthy process to adjust or change an established boundary. Nevertheless, there have been many advocates of boundary change.

Suggestions Concerning Boundary Changes

Almost all of the suggestions and proposals for boundary changes have concerned those parts of Canada north of the highly developed settled regions. This is due in part to the fact that boundary changes in such areas are easier to implement than in the south and partly due to the greater need for boundary changes in areas where the knowledge of the natural resources has increased rapidly. The following examples illustrate these points.

The Canada-United States Boundary

Attention has already been drawn to the anachronisms in the Canada-United States boundary at Lake of the Woods and Point Roberts and suggestions have been made from time to time that these be eliminated by transferring the "American islands" so created to Canada. But these suggestions have not been pursued with great vigour. The situation with regard to the boundary with Alaska however is a different matter. As was described in Chapter IV the Russian-British Treaty of 1825 permitted free navigation on all the rivers and streams draining into the Pacific. When Russia sold Alaska to the U.S.A., these privileges were abrogated and although by the treaty between the United States and Great Britain of 1871, the navigation of the Yukon, Porcupine and Stikine rivers "was declared free for the purpose of commerce to the citizens of both nations",[10] only the Stikine flows through the panhandle portion of Alaska. Thus the panhandle portion of the boundary effectively cuts off the developing lands of northwestern British Columbia and southwestern Yukon from the shortest and the cheapest methods of getting mineral and timber products to world markets and "the 'fence' created by the panhandle is regarded as one of the most important factors limiting mineral and hydro-electric expansion in the northwestern section"[11] of British Columbia.

In 1914, an American congressman introduced a resolution in Congress calling on the U.S.A. to cede the panhandle to Canada and acquire British Caribbean territory in exchange and in 1918 the Prime Minister of Canada explored the possibility during the Paris Peace Conference. The British Secretary of State for the Colonies told him that "we should get from some authoritative American source an intimation, however informal, that they really would be prepared to give up that strip of coast, or at any rate the bulk of it, in exchange for British Honduras."[12] In a similar vein, a member asked in the Canadian House of Commons in 1965 "whether any consideration was being given to trading access rights through the Panhandle for some portion of the Province of Quebec".[13] Other solutions involving the exchange of territory have also been put forward which would at the same time involve changes in the boundaries of Canada. In the late 1950's the proposal was made that the boundary should be altered so as to run from the 141st meridian south along the Alaska Highway to the N.N.E. of Haines then to Lynn Canal, through its mid-channel and Chatham Strait to the Pacific.[14] Under this proposal about 10,000 square miles of the southwestern corner of Yukon and the northeastern quasi-enclave of British Columbia would be transferred to Alaska while the southern part of the panhandle including the port of Juneau would be transferred to British Columbia. This would be unacceptable to Alaska according to one Alaskan senator who in turn suggested that instead of receiving the southern part of the panhandle in exchange Canada could receive "an equivalent amount of land in northeast Alaska running from just above the Arctic Circle to the Beaufort sea . . . one or more free ports on the Alaska Panhandle, and a corridor from Canadian territory to that port".[15] This would benefit the Americans as they also find the configuration of the boundary awkward. While there is a narrow strip of land connecting southeastern Alaska with western Alaska for purposes of transportation, it is impassable as it is covered with glaciers coming down from the St. Elias mountains to the Pacific coast. A further variation of this suggestion, which appears to have been considered seriously by the British Columbia government, is to change the boundary so as to transfer the Mount Fairweather area of the province to Alaska. In return, Canada would expect to be granted a corridor through the panhandle and a deep sea port.[16]

The idea of "access to the ocean by way of a number of

strips of land or corridors, cutting through the panhandle of Alaska" had been favoured by the executive committee of the British Columbia and Yukon Chamber of Mines in 1953. In 1954 it was raised in a brief to the Royal Commission on Canada's Economic Prospects. In 1956 four such "accessways" were suggested in the Canadian House of Commons: the White Pass and Yukon route to Skagway; the Taku river route to Juneau; the Stikine river route to Wrangell and the Chilkat river route to Haines.[17] These suggestions were considered by the federal government in 1954 and 1956 but the external affairs committee was "quite convinced that we would get nowhere if we suggested some cession of territory for the sake of creating a corridor across the panhandle to the Pacific coast."[18] This was borne out by comments from U.S. officials[19] although proposals which did not involve the relinquishing of U.S. territory had some support. In 1954, one speaker in the U.S. Senate claimed that the U.S. had "a positive obligation to be sympathetic to Canada's need"[20] in the area. At the local level in 1956, the people of Skagway in an unofficial poll, overwhelmingly approved the granting of Canadian accessways to the sea through the southeastern Alaska Panhandle.[21]

In 1964 the matter was revived when it appeared that the glacier in Tarr Inlet had receded at such a rate that the inlet extended ice free into British Columbia thus providing Canada with a corridor to the sea.[22] This did not materialize but the suggestion was made several times in parliament that Canada should be actively negotiating for a corridor[23] and in 1965 the Prime Minister stated that "the possibility of access through the Alaska panhandle is now being studied."[24] One member of parliament made the request that Skagway be made a free port[25] for as the federal Minister of Northern Affairs said "the day when Canada could think in terms of reversing the 1903 boundary settlement has ended. The best prospect appears to be an international port."[26]

Northern Ontario

The recognition that northern Ontario is regionally different from the rest of the province and that it, therefore, has problems that are peculiar to it has manifested itself in many different ways. The Northern Ontario Citizens Planning Conference, for example, passed a resolution in 1950 to the effect that steps be immediately taken to set up an organizing committee for the purpose of forming a Regional Planning Board for Northern Ontario, and at the same conference the case for a separate University of Northern Ontario was also presented.[27] Since then, of course, two universities have been established in northern Ontario-Lakehead and Laurentian. Such actions as these have led to movements to erect part of northern Ontario into a separate province, the idea of which dates back to the 1920's. In 1950 an organization known as "The New Province League", advocated the creation of a separate province, tentatively named "Aurora", because it felt that not only are the characteristics of the people of northern Ontario different from those of the south but also that the development of the natural resources of the region, particularly the forest and minerals, would proceed more effectively if they were under separate provincial administration. This group maintained that:

> The natural eastern boundary of the Province of North Ontario extends north from Sault Ste. Marie, following approximately the route of the Algoma Central Railway to Hearst, and thence to Port Albany. In the event that residents of Algoma and Cochrane preferred to keep their attachment with South Ontario, the boundary line could follow the eastern Boundary of the District of Thunder Bay, taking a general north and south line from Lake Superior through White River to Port Albany. In either case, such a partition would set aside a compact area unbroken by physical barriers and peopled by those with common problems and ambitions. In either case the total area of the new province would be comparable with Manitoba, Saskatchewan and Alberta. The initial population of 200,000 would be just about the same as the population in Alberta and Saskatchewan when they were first created provinces.[28]

In 1973 a Northern Ontario Heritage Party was founded in North Bay which advocated a new province of Northern Ontario and suggested that the capital should be Geraldton "350 miles from the Quebec border and 380 miles from the Manitoba border." However, it also put forward the proposal that there should be a Minister of Northern Development for Northern Ontario. Whether in response to this or not, the legislature of Ontario passed "An Act to establish the Ministry of Northern Affairs" in 1977 "to coordinate the activities of and initiate policies and programs of the Government in Northern Ontario." Its area of jurisdiction embraces that part of the province north of the southern boundary of the Districts of Parry Sound and Nipissing (excluding Algonquin Park).

In 1966, at a zone meeting of the Association of Police
Governing Authorities in Sudbury, a six man committee of
mayors and reeves was set up to study "the feasibility of
Northern Ontario forming an eleventh province of Canada"[29]
and the suggestion for a separate province also came up at
the meeting in Sault Ste. Marie of the Ontario Mayors and
Reeves Association in 1967.[30] In the same year a movement
to merge northern Ontario and northwestern Quebec into a
new Canadian province emerged at a meeting of the Quebec
Provincial Chamber of Commerce. "The proposed province
would have a population of about 500,000 . . . and would take
in all of Northern Ontario and the western half of Northern
Quebec, including La Verendrye Provincial Park."[31]

Northern Manitoba
Somewhat similar ideas have been voiced in northern
Manitoba, where the creation of a province to be known as
"Pre-Cambria" has been suggested. "Roughly, the new province should start at the Ontario-Manitoba boundary, stretch
northerly along a line through the centre of Lake Winnipeg
in Manitoba, shifting west to Grand Rapids on the west
shore of the lake, and thence westerly along the 53rd Parallel
to the Pacific Ocean". The merit of the idea was again, that
northern people would have more say in northern affairs.[32]

The Territories
Provincial extension. In anticipation of the creation of one
or more provinces out of parts of the Northwest Territories,
which ultimately occurred in 1905, it had been suggested that
the new province or provinces would "have no northern
boundary other than the North Pole".[33] The Alberta and
Saskatchewan Acts, however, clearly indicated that this was
not to be so but this has not prevented suggestions being
made with regard to the northward extension of provincial
boundaries.

Since 1900 several proposals have been put forward advocating the unification of the Yukon Territory and the province of British Columbia. The question first arose in 1905
and again in 1914, 1920, 1924, and 1937. In that year the
federal government agreed with the government of British
Columbia upon the terms upon which the Yukon Territory
might be transferred and the terms were announced by the
provincial premier in May.

The supporters of the proposal had one or two main

advantages in mind. The first was the reduction of the relatively high cost of the administration of the Yukon Territory, particularly because serious depopulation had occurred there since the peak of the gold rush days. The second was based on the principle that both British Columbia and the Yukon had the same kind of physical and human resources and both required similar laws for certain activities, such as mining.[34] The first argument lost much of its force when Yukon administration costs were reduced, and, in any case, the citizens of the Yukon at all times were greatly opposed to the suggestion. The probable increase in population that may come with the Yukon power developments and further mining activity might seem to promise more revenue and a better basis for a separate administration.

In January 1938, the premier of British Columbia publicly stated that he had asked the federal government to transfer to the province not only the Yukon but also that part of the Northwest Territories lying to the west of the eastern boundary of British Columbia (120 degs. W.). This prompted Alberta to make a similar request and in March 1939 the Alberta legislature passed a resolution "favouring the inclusion of the Northwest Territories lying west of the 110th Meridian." The following month the premier of the province suggested that no other province could have any claim to that area of the territories lying between Alberta's east and west boundaries. He also suggested that the dividing line might be the Mackenzie river. In 1952, both British Columbia and Alberta "agreed on the desirability" of extending their northern boundaries to 65 degrees north. It was suggested that this would eliminate the difficulties experienced by the companies operating in the northwest, which had their headquarters in British Columbia and Alberta and were, therefore, incorporated under provincial law, but which carried out their development work under federal jurisdiction.[35] In 1956 the premier of British Columbia urged that both the Yukon and "part of the Northwest Territories"[36] join his province but in 1959 he modified this suggestion to embrace only that part of the Northwest Territories between 120 degs. W. and the Yukon border. In fact he emphasized that the Yukon Territory was not involved in his proposal. His objective was to "bring the whole Mackenzie basin into British Columbia. This area is packed with power and petroleum possibilities and has a northern coastline on the Beaufort Sea."[37] But this was rejected by the Council of the Northwest Territories and the premier formally withdrew his suggestion. Manitoba had also considered the possibility of a further northward extension. In 1960 the provincial legislature approved a resolution instructing the Manitoba Development Authority to study all factors involved in taking over part of the territories.[38]

That these ideas had some support in the federal parliament is clear from the remarks made by the Hon. Mr. Aseltine, the Leader of the government in the Senate in 1953[39] and which he substantially repeated in 1958.[40]

> . . . Give the part north of British Columbia, which extends north to the Arctic Ocean, to the province of British Columbia. All the travel out of that country is through British Columbia anyway. Give that part north of the province of Alberta to the province of Alberta. That would take in the Mackenzie river valley, all that territory is adjacent to Edmonton, and all the traffic out of that territory is through the northern part of Alberta. Then, give the part north of Saskatchewan to the province of Saskatchewan, and the part north of Manitoba to the province of Manitoba.

Provincial modification. During 1938 petitions were forwarded to the federal government from parts of northern Alberta and northern British Columbia advocating the formation of a new province out of certain parts of these two provinces and a part of the Northwest Territories – the part that had, since 1905, become more easily accessible and capable of development.[41] It was also the desire of the Alberta government to have the matter placed on the agenda of the 1945 Dominion-Provincial Conference.[42] The idea was revived in 1959 when it was suggested that the Peace River district of British Columbia amalgamate with "cuts" out of northern Alberta and part of the Northwest Territories to form a new province. As a resident of Dawson Creek expressed it "We must cut up the larger provinces. We are 800 miles from the capital [Victoria] here. They barely know we exist."[43]

Provincial Contraction. There have also been advocates of the view that part of the boundary of the Northwest Territories should be moved farther southward on the grounds that it now lies north of the area where effective provincial control and development are being carried on and that it divides an area that forms reasonably coherent territory. For example, the 60th parallel, the present boundary, passes about 1 mile south of Fort Smith, crossing the road that links that settlement to Fitzgerald. Both settlements are part of the same geographical area, which is isolated from the more densely populated parts of Alberta not only by a distance of some 300 miles but also by large intervening areas of swamp and high land. Yet Fort Smith is under the administration of the Northwest Territories and Fitzgerald that of Alberta. "A truck wishing to operate on the 16-mile highway joining them requires a licence secured ultimately from both governments."[44] It has been suggested, though not on a government level, that to overcome such problems those parts of the six larger provinces east of British Columbia that lie north of the 55th parallel should revert to the administration of the Northwest Territories for a limited period of time. Such a boundary would leave most of the well-settled land in the provinces, and would not further complicate the local situation in Alberta by cutting into the area tributary to the road to Alaska. It has further been suggested that the "capital" of the area should be Churchill as "it is more important for the port to be unified administratively with the area it serves to the north" than with any distant lands to the southwest that might be also considered to form a "tributary area" to Churchill.

Whatever the merits or demerits of these suggestions, the question of transferring land within a province to territorial control is worth examining. Something similar occurred in Australia when, in 1863, the state of South Australia was provisionally extended so as to include a large area of semi-arid country to the north of it. This was partly because some good pastoral lands had been found in the area as a result of A. C. Gregory's exploration of 1855-56. South Australia had a particular interest in the area, not only because it was contiguous, but also because of the Stuart expeditions of 1860-62, which were based on Adelaide. But in spite of the valiant efforts on the part of South Australia to develop this northern area, they proved costly and disappointing, and in 1909 the Northern Territory was transferred to the government of Australia.

In Canada, the nearest approach to this kind of arrangement occurred as a result of the terms of union between the Dominion of Canada and British Columbia, when the province agreed to convey to the federal government certain public lands, in trust, in order to further the completion of a railway from the Pacific to the Atlantic Oceans. This arrangement was modified and extended in 1884 by the Legislature of British Columbia, which granted to the federal government "three and a half million acres of land in that portion of the Peace River district of British Columbia lying east of the Rocky Mountains and adjoining the Northwest Territory of Canada, to be located by the Dominion in one

rectangular block". Little was known about the area and
the exact location of the block was not fixed until an exploratory survey had been made, in 1905-06, at the instance of
the then Minister of the Interior.[45] From that time on, however, the Peace River Block was considered as Dominion
Lands and opened for settlement.[46]

It appears likely that the reasons for the choice of an area
in that part of British Columbia east of the Rocky Mountains,
rather than an area in some other part of the province,
were based largely on its remoteness and difficulty of access
in relation to provincial administration. In 1884, even the
southern part of the province had only recently acquired
rail connections with the rest of Canada. No connection
whatever existed with the great tract lying on the eastern
side of the Rocky Mountains.

By 1927, however, the situation had changed materially.
Administration of the Peace River Block had proved to be
very costly, and it was considered that it would be better
"if the lands were in the hands of the provincial authorities
who have all the machinery available for taking care of them,
in as much as the resources of the province with the exception of the lands in question are owned and administered
by the province itself". In 1930, the area was returned to
the government of British Columbia.[47]

Change within the Territories. It has already been indicated that the residents of the Territories resented suggestions
that the Provinces take them over and this was partly borne
out by the deliberations of the Northwest Territories Council
in 1960, which recognized that "factors of political advance,
communications and administrations suggested a change
should be made in the existing Northwest Territories."[48] The
possible development of provinces north of the 60th parallel
would be in accordance with the policy outlined by the
Prime Minister of Canada in 1912, to which reference has
already been made. This statement concluded with the question "Is not that the goal to which we should aspire, that
every inch of Canadian Territory should ultimately be under
provincial organization?"[49] The matter was considered with
respect to the Northwest Territories in 1960 but it was considered unwise to contemplate a province of such a size as
such a province probably would not have the financial resources to develop such a large area, thus slowing down
development drastically.[50]

Consequently the possible division of the Northwest Territories into two Territories – an eastern and a western – was
discussed with the idea that each should eventually be able to

advance to provincial status. There was some minor opposition to this as it would mean the division of the native peoples. In particular it would lead to the separation of the Inuit from the Indians and Metis and this might retard their opportunities for advancement, especially of the Inuit. But it was agreed that Mackenzie is "an economic unit" distinct from the other Districts and hence such a division would recognize the very real differences in the geography of the eastern and western parts of the Northwest Territories as well as the fact that, because they are so different, they could not develop at a uniform rate. Some of the present legislation, which now applies to both the eastern and western parts, is inappropriate to one or the other. Attention was focused on the present District of Mackenzie which because of its greater population density and economic development, might advance more quickly towards responsible government.

> All the arable land in the Northwest Territories (about 2,000,000 acres) is in the Mackenzie area, and good ranching land is available in its south-western portion. It has a better potential for forestry operations than the Yukon Territory and more than half of the total area for freshwater fisheries in Canada. Its mineral potential was already proven, in part as a result of the discoveries of lead and zinc at Pine Point, the gold mining operations at Yellowknife and the oil field at Norman Wells. There is hydroelectric power in abundance, on the Slave River, where it was estimated that nearly three-quarters of a million kilowatts could be developed.[51]

In suggesting possible boundaries for the Territory of Mackenzie the following principles were initially kept in mind:

> 1. The existing boundaries of the Northwest Territories as a whole should not be changed. .
> 2. The Territory should not include any areas where distance and isolation meant that the right to vote could not be made a reality bearing in mind that the area involved would probably be in excess of 500,000 square miles with a population (1961) of some 15,000.
> 3. The Territory should not include any areas which could not readily be administered from a centre within the more settled portion of the unit. This meant that King William Island would not be included in Mackenzie because, although water communication with the island is from the

west, air communication and administration are provided from the east. The 200 people on the island consider themselves part of the east, particularly since many of their dealings are with Spence Bay, on Boothia Peninsula. Furthermore it was expected that most of the children on the island would go east for their education when the facilities were developed.[52] Similarly it was not administratively feasible to include the Queen Elizabeth Islands in Mackenzie since the lines of communication and transportation run east and south from the Queen Elizabeth Islands to Churchill and Frobisher.

4. The Territory should not include areas with special requirements essentially different from those of the Mackenzie Basin itself.

5. Any new boundary should be 'visible on the ground' – that is it should follow a river and/or any other easily identifiable physical feature.

Initially it seemed that a major problem in considering the boundaries of Mackenzie Territory would arise because the pattern of economic development is not yet firmly established. Assumptions about transportation routes, mine locations and similar questions may or may not prove to be correct in future. But the experience in southern Canada has shown that such considerations do not need to play a dominant role in the arguments for any particular new boundary line. There are many places where transportation routes cut across provincial boundaries without causing any insurmountable handicaps. Similarly, mineral deposits lying athwart interprovincial boundaries have been brought into production without the divided jurisdiction creating any insurmountable problems as has been indicated in the case of the Flin Flon base metal deposits which straddle the Saskatchewan-Manitoba boundary or the iron ore which extends across the Quebec-Newfoundland border.

Eight possible boundary lines as well as the existing eastern boundary of Mackenzie District were discussed by the Northwest Territories Council (see Figure 29). Line A was drawn generally northeastwards, following the watersheds as much as possible, from a point on the sixtieth parallel somewhere east of the Alberta-Saskatchewan boundary to the point where the present Mackenzie-Keewatin border intersects the Arctic coast; thence through Queen Maud Gulf, McClintock Channel, Viscount Melville Sound and McClure Strait so as to include Banks and Victoria Islands in the new Territory.

Some members of the council wondered whether a territory

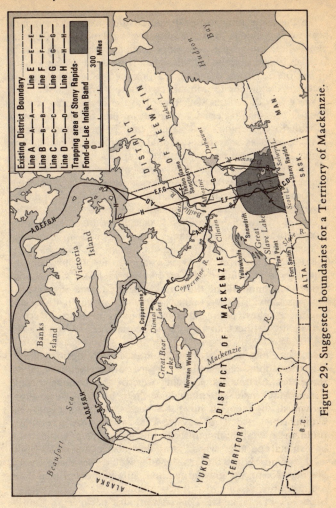

Figure 29. Suggested boundaries for a Territory of Mackenzie.

with this boundary would be a manageable and efficient unit. As the Mackenzie valley is essentially a treed area, would any useful purpose be served if the new administration became involved in the very different problems of the tundra? Inclusion of the area east of the Mackenzie basin and some of the islands might well tend to delay political development in Mackenzie Territory and would certainly impose a heavy financial burden on its relatively small tax potential.

On the other hand, some favoured the proposed boundary because it included Banks and Victoria Islands and Coppermine where the people were more familiar with the Mackenzie area and were already administered from Fort Smith and if, in the future, the area became a province, it would have the necessary resources to administer these outlying islands.

Some saw difficulties with regard to the demarcation of the boundary, as the heights of land in the tundra are very difficult to determine. No 'slashed line' or boundary vista is possible and, as a result, it would be almost impossible for people on the ground, particularly trappers, prospectors and police to know whether they were inside or outside Mackenzie even if the expensive device of erecting boundary monuments were resorted to. This is a point of practical importance in such an environment.

Line B followed the mainland coast from the Yukon Territory eastward to the Hornaday River; thence up the river to the Dismal Lakes following the height of land between Great Bear Lake and the Arctic coast; thence up the Coppermine River and the chain of rivers and lakes which now forms the boundary of the Arctic Islands Game Preserve to approximately 107°W. thence south in approximately this longitude following the lake groupings as much as possible and ending at the 60th parallel at Scott Lake, approximately 106°30′ W.

This line met most of the principles initially decided upon. A territory thus defined should be reasonably economical to administer. All the people living west of this boundary look to the Mackenzie settlements as their base of operations, and most of them could have access to polling stations established there. The government of the new Territory would not have to concern itself with the special problems of the tundra and the islands, and their associated costs. The boundary, for most of its length, would be much more determinable on the ground, without survey monuments, than would Line A.

Line C was, in a sense, a compromise between the other two proposed boundaries. It followed the mainland coast from the Yukon Territory eastward to the mouth of the Coppermine river, thence following the present western boundary of the Arctic Islands Game Preserve southeast to approximately 107°, and thence south on the same course as Line B described above.

Like all compromises, it had clear advantages and disadvantages. About 800 miles of the Arctic coast would be included in the Mackenzie Territory, despite the fact that much of this coast has a different character from the Mackenzie basin. Revenues to be expected from this area are very limited indeed, and there would clearly be some costs in providing necessary government services there. But this boundary would result in a manageable territory with boundaries which look sensible on the map, and which do not give the impression that they have been adjusted to secure the greatest short-term advantage. The boundary would also be easily identifiable on the ground.

The Existing District Boundary. Some members of the Council felt that the existing boundary between the Districts of Mackenzie and Keewatin might suffice as each of the proposed boundaries 'wandered all over the country like a moose'[53] and would be difficult to follow on the ground without very precise survey and demarcation. But the Commissioner for the Territories pointed out[54] that the existing line bore no relation to the physical features of the country and was simply a projection northward of the Saskatchewan-Manitoba boundary. There was no way of following such a line on the ground. Furthermore, if it were retained as the boundary between the proposed new Territories, it would mean that the easternmost point of the Territory of Mackenzie would be almost impossible to reach from the more settled areas of the Territory. Nevertheless, once the new boundary had been set, Mackenzie Territory would develop a new sense of its areal extent and it would then be difficult to reduce its area. The Territory might be made larger in the future but certainly not smaller. He undoubtedly had in mind the experience of the Provinces, none of which have been reduced in area since their establishment, but several of which have been enlarged.

The Council ultimately decided in favour of a boundary following the combined Lines B and C from Scott Lake to Clinton and running thence along Line A (Line D). However, on referring this to legal surveyors for comment, the Council was advised of the many difficult boundary problems which have resulted from descriptions based on physical features. This view was shared by mining engineers at Yellowknife, who pointed out that 'mining regulations call for detailed locations by meridians and the average traveller, especially prospectors, engineers and geologists use this method exclusively to locate'. Therefore two further proposals were put forward so that approximately the same boundary as Line D could be retained, but the descriptions would be more in terms of latitude and longitude.

Line E. Around Banks and Victoria Islands to the point

at which the 103rd meridian W. intersects the ordinary high water mark of the Arctic Ocean; south along the 103rd meridian to the point where it intersects the right bank of the Back river; thence following the right banks of the Back and Baillie rivers and the east shore of Moraine Lake to the 106th meridian; thence following the 106th meridian southwards to the 60th parallel.

Line F. Around Banks and Victoria Islands to the point at which the 103rd meridian intersects the ordinary high water mark of the Arctic Ocean; southwards along the 103rd meridian to its intersection with the 65th parallel; thence west along this parallel to the 106th meridian; thence south along this meridian to the 60th parallel.

But when these proposals came up for discussion, it was pointed out that the boundary cut across the hunting and trapping grounds of the Stony Rapids Band of Indians. The traditional hunting grounds of this Band are in the Scott Lake-Selwyn Lake area of the Territories. Although the Band spends its summers in the settlement of Stony Rapids in Saskatchewan, it would be inconvenient if its hunting and trapping area was subject to the game laws of several governments. There was also some evidence that some Indians from Snowdrift hunted and trapped east of the proposed boundary. The Director of Indian Affairs therefore suggested another boundary.

Line G. From a point on the east shore of Selwyn Lake at 60°N.; thence northerly through Flett Lake to the Dubawnt river thence along the Dubawnt river to the western boundary of the Thelon Game Sanctuary; along this boundary to the Back River; along Back and Perry rivers to the coast; thence around Victoria and Banks Islands to the eastern boundary of Yukon Territory. But ultimately, the Council agreed 'that the eastern boundary of Mackenzie should be the 105th meridian from the 60th parallel north to the Arctic Ocean, extended to include Banks and Victoria Islands. . .' (Line H). Quite clearly some of the initial principles were sacrificed. The fifth principle – that the boundary should be "visible on the ground" was violated even further when the Bill[55] intended to give it legal effect described Mackenzie Territory as follows:

(i) all of that part of Continental Canada north of the Provinces of British Columbia, Alberta and Saskatchewan and west of the one hundred and fifth meridian of west longitude except the portion thereof that is within the Yukon Territory, and (ii) all of the Arctic Islands of Canada that are not part of the Yukon Territory and that lie completely within the area described as follows: commencing at the most southerly intersection of the one hundred and fifth meridian of west longitude and the ordinary high water mark of the Arctic Ocean; thence northerly along the said meridian to the point of intersection of the said meridian and the parallel of north latitude 68°22'; thence easterly along the said parallel to the point of intersection of the said parallel and the meridian of west longitude 101°45'; thence northerly along the shortest line to the point of intersection of the seventieth parallel of north latitude and the one hundredth meridian of west longitude; thence northwesterly along the shortest line to the point of intersection of the seventy-second parallel of north latitude and the one hundred and third meridian of west longitude; thence northerly along the said meridian to the point of intersection of the said meridian and the seventy-fourth parallel of north latitude; thence westerly along the said parallel to the point of intersection of the said parallel and the one hundred and fourteenth meridian of west longitude; thence northwesterly along the shortest line to the point of intersection of the one hundred and twentieth meridian of west longitude and the seventy-fifth parallel of north latitude; thence westerly along the said parallel to the point of intersection of the said parallel and the one hundred and forty-first meridian of west longitude; thence southerly along the said meridian to the point of intersection of the said meridian and the ordinary high water mark of the Arctic Ocean; thence easterly along the said ordinary high water mark to the point of commencement.

The Bill received first reading in the Canadian House of Commons on July 8th, 1963 and was immediately followed by a Bill to create the Nunassiaq Territory which was to consist of all that portion of the existing Northwest Territories "except the part comprising the Mackenzie Territory".[56] However, neither of the Bills went beyond first reading. In 1965, the federal government appointed an Advisory Commission on the Development of Government in the Northwest Territories. It expressed the belief that 'with division there would be a very great risk that the eastern Arctic would become sealed off, would remain dominated by the central (federal) government and might never acquire anything more than a nominal form of self government'. It would be cut off from 'the most populated and articulate part of the

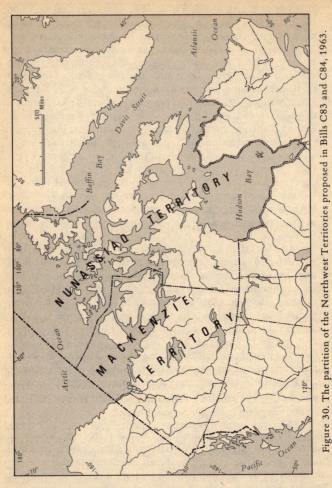

Figure 30. The partition of the Northwest Territories proposed in Bills C83 and C84, 1963.

Territories and from an influence from which the Eskimo has much to benefit'. Secondly, a boundary once established is not easily changed and 'not enough is known about the country to determine with informed confidence where the line should run'. Furthermore 'given the likelihood that the governments would enact divergent laws respecting such matters as game control, a line which must inevitably run through land inhabited by an indigenous race would oblige such peoples, as they move in the normal process of hunting, trapping or fishing, to cope with two sets of laws and

regulations'. For these, and a number of other, less geographical reasons, the Commission recommended against division
at this time.[57]

The concern that had been shown for the traditional ways
of the Inuit and Indians increased as time went on. In 1977,
the Inuit, through the Committee for the Original People's
Entitlement (COPE) proposed a 105,000 square mile separate
territory which extended eastward from the 141st meridian to
110 degs. W. and southward from 80 degs. N. to a strip
along the mainland coast. It thus embraced areas of the
Beaufort Sea in which oil exploration was being carried out.
The federal minister of Northern Affairs saw "no great
obstacle to an Inuit territory as long as it was not based
along racial lines".[58]

Regionalism and Boundary Changes

Provincial boundaries may be said to have been inevitable
in Canada. The geographical, historical, and political factors
involved all pointed to the division of the country into
regions that should be autonomous in matters of purely local
concern, with a federal authority to deal with matters affect-
ing more than one of them. How, then, were the necessary
divisions to be made? As the previous chapters show, geographical considerations have always been to the forefront
in fixing interprovincial boundaries. In fact, regionalism – the
very basis of geographical science today – has always been
an important factor in considering interprovincial boundaries,
even though the resulting legislation has not always delimited
the boundary on a strictly regional basis.

The definitions of a region are multitudinous but its "kernel
characteristic" is that it is "an area within which certain
types of socio-economic adjustments have been made by man
so generally as to provide the reason for separating that area
from adjacent areas which are characterized by different
types of adjustments".[59]

The Canada-United States Boundary

When the familiar statement is made that Canada as a
whole came into being "against geography", what is usually
meant is that the Canada-United States land boundary is not
a good regional boundary. From the Atlantic to the Pacific
this boundary separates the physical regions of Canada from
their United States counterparts by cutting across every

physiographic province it encounters. The 49th Parallel cuts the west coast of Canada from that of the United States; it separates the Canadian Cordillera from the Rocky Mountains in the United States; it divides the interior plains of Canada from those of the United States, and in the east it separates the Canadian Maritimes from their counterparts in New England.

Yet it has been shown that parts of the present Canada-United States boundary were reasonable "natural divides" at the time of their establishment, for they more or less coincided with watersheds between river systems that flowed east-west rather than north-south. "The St. Lawrence waterways system and the network of rivers that fringe the Laurentian plateau (sic) link up with the river systems of the North-West in a manner that has given the northern portion of the continent a peculiar measure of east and west unity which, since the earlier days of white settlement, has stimulated a corresponding separateness and unity in the history of its development".[60] Later, the transcontinental railways followed them, and, in following and leading east-west migration enormously strengthened the latitudinal rather than the longitudinal forces at work. Later still, east-west highways reinforced these effects. Thus, if Canadians think of the political unit "Canada" as a "region", that is, if they think of the State of Canada as embracing a distinct nation, it is essentially based on the geography of the past. But there are signs that the past may be resurrected in a new form in the future. The one physiographic region that is almost entirely included in the Canada of today is the Canadian Shield, once solely the realm of the Hudson's Bay Company. Today millions of Canadians living around its fringes derive their livelihood from its rich mineral resources and forests, which are becoming even more productive as technology advances.

The question whether or not political division between Canada and the United States is desirable, economically or otherwise, is, however, irrelevant to this discussion because of Canada's sense of nationhood. Thus it is the factor of human geography, based on historical development, that outweighs the effects of the economic and physical factors of regionalism and prevents the elimination of the International Boundary, and "inter-regionalism" between the two countries, with the possible exception of the Alaska region, exerts its effect without political boundary adjustment.

The Interprovincial Boundaries

But what of the provincial boundaries? First of all, let us note that the boundaries of New Brunswick, Nova Scotia, Prince Edward Island, and British Columbia, and the Ontario-Quebec boundary from the St. Lawrence to Lake Timiskaming, were established approximately in accordance with regional principles, having regard to the "state of the arts" and the economies of the areas concerned at the time the boundaries were established.

The Ontario-Manitoba boundary would have had a regional basis if the original views of the federal government and Manitoba had prevailed; and the boundaries suggested by such men as Palliser and Premier Haultain had a fundamentally regional basis. But the various boundaries established since 1867 had much less geographical validity when set up. Since then they have acquired more, as a result of the geographical effects they have themselves produced.

The boundaries of the Canadian provinces have, therefore, been established according to two different sets of principles. Before 1867, the trend appeared to be towards making the administrative areas correspond to one or more sets of factors of the life of the area. In the case of British Columbia and Newfoundland it was the distribution of "industry" or the general pattern of economic life. In the case of Ontario and Quebec it was the traditional structure and historical grouping of the population. In the case of the Maritimes it was an effort to equate the areas of administration with the zones of influence of the principal towns in each province.

After 1867, although geographical differences between the western and eastern parts of the prairies were recognized, an effort was made to apply some general quantitative standard to the areas being erected into provinces, with a view to securing areas of approximately similar area or population, as well as to limit the total number of provinces to be created.

Regionalism and Administration

The fact that the provincial and territorial boundaries of Canada have been established according to two different sets of principles raises several problems.

Fundamentally, boundaries are needed to mark off different areas of administration: and it is evident that administrative problems are different in different parts of Canada. The very size and spatial setting that made the federal structure the only workable one embrace such diversity of climate, soil, land form, and vegetation that differing types of administration are inevitable.

As a result, there has been a tendency to put forward the view that administrative areas should be based on regions where resource utilization is similar, i.e., the true "geographic region" – "an area in which the combination of environmental and demographic factors have created a homogeneity of economic and social structure".[61]

Because of the complex factors involved, unanimity as to the specific extent of geographical regions is seldom reached, but thirteen have been suggested for Canada.[62] These are shown in Figure 31. In discussing regionalism and administration, one point is not always made clear, even by those who understand the nature of regionalism best, and that is that regional boundaries generally tend to be zones, rather than sharp lines. Furthermore, all regions are liable to change as technology changes, but are likely to undergo the greatest changes around their fringes. The theory that political boundaries should follow regional lines, therefore, seems unsound, for political boundaries are changed only with great difficulty, and their location in areas where changing conditions may lead to demands for revision seems unwise. No limits can be placed on the rate or the extent of movement of regional boundaries, although these changes usually take place slowly in areas that have been highly developed for a long period. But in the submarginal lands of Canada they may take place in a surprisingly short space of time.

Some of the arguments for boundary change in Canada have been adopted from similar arguments put forward for a more "regional approach" to boundaries in the United States, such as the following:

. . . new boundaries certainly would not coincide with the present ones. In all probability, geographic regions characterised by uniformity of resource use would be employed, for we live, produce and trade regionally. To some extent we also think regionally. Such a division would be reflected in greater homogeneity in the economic and social life of the people.[63]

But neither in its physical nor its political geography is Canada in the same situation as the United States. It has just been pointed out that in the submarginal lands of Canada regional boundaries may change rapidly. Any political bound-

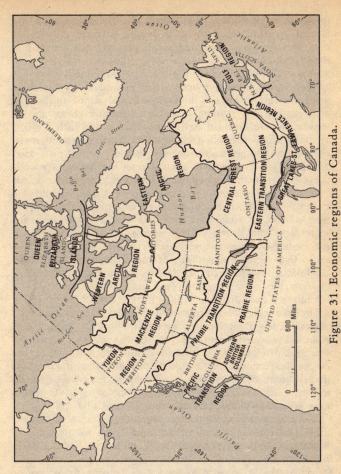

Figure 31. Economic regions of Canada.

ary based on such boundaries would, therefore, soon become unsatisfactory from a practical standpoint. Such a situation does not exist, at least not to the same extent, in the United States. Furthermore, if administrative boundaries did follow the regional lines of Figure 31, they would include vast regions containing very small and widely scattered populations. Either this small number of people would be expected to provide the taxes for the support of their administrative services, or the other provinces (through the federal government) would be expected to subsidize the administration and development of these areas. Generally speaking, the more sparse the population, the greater the dependence on the federal treasury, and the greater the amount of federal revenue from well populated areas that must be devoted to the sparsely populated areas.

If, on the other hand, the sparsely populated lands are divided among the provinces, the provincial governments will have to finance the development and administration of such lands. The average taxpayer is usually closer to the provincial government than he is to Ottawa, and such division of the sparsely populated lands is, therefore, likely to mean a closer and more sustained interest in them, even if provincial control of education and natural resources alone are considered; administrative personnel, also are likely to be drawn from the province, and, of course, will be directly responsible to the provincial capital rather than to Ottawa. Every province as it exists today, except Nova Scotia, Prince Edward Island, and New Brunswick, has some sparsely populated area, and even Nova Scotia and New Brunswick have wilderness areas. One has only to think of the attitude of the people of Ontario toward their provincially-owned Northland Railway, or the pride of the people of Manitoba in the port of Churchill to realize the force of this argument.

The two sides of the question were well stated in 1953. In advocating a province of "Pre-Cambria", to which reference has already been made, it was said "let the mining men look after mining, oilmen look after oil, and the farmers look after farming".[64] "Merge the territories with the same kind of resources, conditions and problems into one province, and they will be better administered".[65] Yet barely a month later Senator Aseltine said "I am informed that the cost of administering the territories is considerable and that there is very little revenue from it, so I am going to suggest . . . that the way to solve this whole problem of looking after the Northwest Territories would be to give them to the provinces that I have mentioned . . . These provinces have local legislatures and governments and the set-up is such that they could handle all this business very easily and relieve the federal government of any difficulties or expense in connection with it".[66] Thus, both the "regional case" and the case for diversity have been stated and "the question is whether areas which have distinct and perhaps conflicting interests, especially of an economic character, should be kept in distinct administrative units or can safely be contained in one unit".[67]

The inclusion of different regions within provinces would lead to a considerable diversification of the economy. The question then arises, should such a diversity of interest within an internal political area be advocated? It might be useful to point out here that there may be a difference between the political geography of an independent state or country and the political geography of the individual members. An independent state or country is usually considered fortunate if it includes within its borders a variety of regions and resources, because it usually results in greater independence and influence internationally. Internally, in a similar way, if a political unit includes a wide variety of regions and resources its independence and power are great. In Canada, it is only necessary to compare the large and small provinces to realize the validity of this statement. One of the most outstanding results of the application of the different sets of principles on which the present provincial boundaries are based, is the unequal influence that the individual provinces exert.

Sectionalism and Administration

It has been said that the section is the political version of the region. Used in this sense 'section' may refer to one administrative unit at the state or provincial level, or to a group of several. The United States National Resources Committee came to the conclusion that, for the purposes of resource conservation, the best achievable administrative units were those aggregations of states that most nearly coincided with divisions based on major regions.[68] It has been suggested that in Canada there is a remarkable agreement between the regional boundaries and the generally recognized provincial groupings (e.g., the Prairie Provinces; the Maritime Provinces) although this is something of a generalization when it is realized that each section includes part of a sub-arctic region and almost every section includes part of an arctic region (Figure 32). Nonetheless in 1964, the premier of British Columbia said "there would be benefits . . . if Canada some day were divided into the five regions . . . British Columbia, the Prairies, Ontario, Quebec and the Atlantic provinces"[69] and one of his successors, thirteen years later said much the same thing – "a confederation of five strong regions – the Atlantic, Quebec, Ontario, the West and the Pacific – is the best system of government for Canada,"[70] a proposal which was repeated some months later in Quebec.[71]

Because such sections have, unofficially, taken shape in Canada in response to the geography of the various parts of the country, and because they have become part of Canadian thinking and organization, it is pertinent to pursue

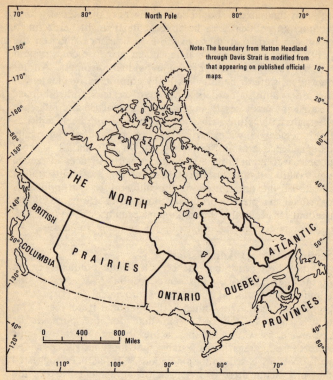

Note: The boundary from Hatton Headland through Davis Strait is modified from that appearing on published official maps.

Figure 32. The "sections" of Canada.

the idea of sections *within* the provinces. The way in which the province of Saskatchewan manifested its recognition that the problems of the northern and southern halves of the province differ materially is instructive. In 1946, the province set up a Northern Administration District in the Department of Natural Resources, in order to bring about a more efficient administration of the province's resources in fish, fur, timber, and minerals in the far north. "A northern administrator to co-ordinate activities of all government departments operating roughly north of Montreal Lake, supervise all activities of the natural resources department, and administer local affairs in the northern area has been appointed . . . who has made his headquarters at Prince Albert".[72] Furthermore, it has been determined as a matter of policy that all departmental personnel in the northern part of the province should be administered by the Prince Albert office, as well as the municipal problems, the work of three separate branches of the Department of Public Health, and that of the Department of Social Welfare.[73]

That the governments of the larger provinces recognize the existence of diverse regions within them is clear from the statement made by the Prime Minister of Ontario in 1965 – "Ontario is simply too big and too diversified for any provincial administration to work out single formula solutions to all our problems."[74] The action of the government of Ontario in establishing a Ministry of Northern Affairs is a further recognition of this situation.

Hence regional and sectional differences in Canada cannot be ignored for administrative purposes. Their existence may be taken into account either by changing the existing internal political boundaries by constitutional processes or by adjusting the internal administrative organization as the geographical situation demands so as to fit the existing boundaries.

CHAPTER X

CONCLUSION

The foregoing chapters have led to four main groups of conclusions. In the first place they have shown the stages by which boundaries have developed in Canada. Secondly, they have demonstrated why the boundaries of Canada have their present geographical location. Thirdly, certain relationships between the evolution of these boundaries and geographical regionalism have become apparent. Finally, they have made it possible to enunciate certain principles upon which attitudes to existing boundaries, as well as to new boundaries that might be established in the future, may be based.

The Stages of Boundary Evolution

It has already been indicated that boundaries are an outgrowth of historical processes supporting the view of Jones that "ideas about boundaries are related to their geographical and historical milieu".[1] Brigham[2] maintains that boundaries undergo a threefold evolution – a primitive or tribal stage; a mixed or transitional stage, in which the boundaries are shifting; and a third stage in which they become in great part fixed: these last two stages have been carried further by Jones. These three stages, as they apply to Canada, may be amplified as follows:

(a) Stage of Loose Delimitation

(i) Tribal stage – The political progress of a group of people has always demanded that the limits of its area of authority be defined. Although such definition was naturally rather vague in the case of Canada's aboriginal inhabitants, such limits none the less existed, although their lack of definition gave them a character more resembling "transitional zones" than "boundaries" as the latter are thought of today by more advanced peoples. To such limits the name "frontier" is best applied, for a frontier is properly a region or zone, having width as well as length.⁴ Any relation of such limits to later boundary evolution was often fortuitous.

(ii) European-originated exploration and discovery – This period usually sets certain latitudinal, and sometimes longitudinal, limits, to the next stage, the limits usually being those within which the explorers operated.

(iii) Claims of sovereignty – These were often made by the explorers; in these circumstances, this sub-stage was coincident with sub-stage (i). On other occasions, claims of sovereignty were made after the explorer returned to the government or organization sponsoring his expedition. The territory over which sovereignty was claimed was, as a rule, simply stated: it was usually defined by lines of latitude and often extended over areas that had not been explored or even, sometimes, discovered.

(b) Transitional State, or Stage of Precise Delimitation

(i) Exploitation and settlement – When exploitation or settlement occurred, the need for boundaries began to be apparent. This need was first recognized in some cases by the people in the areas concerned, in others by the colonial administrators either in Europe or in the colony itself, as the pattern of the economy of the area began to take shape. It may have resulted in a demand for more precise boundaries, or for further political recognition of boundaries, or both.

(ii) Political decisions on the allocation of territory – This sub-stage resulted in the boundaries consequent upon (i), which were then

(iii) Delimited in a state document, which marked the end of the transitional stage.

(c) Final Stage or Stage of Demarcation

(i) Demarcation – Often the state document mentioned above made provision for boundary demarcation and the means or stages by which such demarcation was to be carried out. In some cases, particularly with the inter-provincial boundaries, demarcation was not mentioned in the delimitation document, the matter being left until the need arose. Often, before the techniques of boundary demarcation by means of monuments were well developed, boundary delimitation followed well-known physical features such as rivers or mountain ranges. Such use of physical features, or "natural" boundaries, obviated the need for demarcation of "artificial" boundaries. The adoption of physical features as boundaries was due not so much to a desire for "natural" boundaries as to the wish to avoid the expense of demarcating "artificial" ones. As more modern means of demarcation evolved, however, boundaries delimited by physical features became more difficult to survey and monument than boundaries delimited by lines of latitude and longitude.

(ii) Administration and maintenance – This is really part of the demarcation process, being necessary in order to preserve and keep in good order the various boundary markings.

Not all the boundaries of Canada passed through all these stages. The International Boundary and the older provincial boundaries did, but in the cases of Alberta and Saskatchewan, and to some extent Manitoba and the northern parts of Ontario and Quebec, stage (a) did not occur, and neither did parts of stage (b).

The Pattern of Boundary Evolution

The foregoing chapters have shown that not only did the major boundaries of Canada develop in progressive stages but that they also developed in response to various stimuli. These stimuli were in accordance with a certain pattern in eastern Canada, that is to say in Canada east of the Great Lakes, and a different pattern in western and northern Canada. The two patterns are linked by that of the International Boundary, which shows certain characteristics of both the eastern and western patterns.

In Canada east of the Great Lakes, boundary evolution proceeded hand in hand with settlement and development. It was a comparatively slow evolution not only because it occurred in a period when transportation and communication were much less developed than they are today, but also because of the struggles between French and British over control of the area. If political stability in the northern half of North America was retarded by the alternations of French and British supremacy, these alternations did at least allow the political boundaries to evolve until they met the requirements of the populations involved, as they were affected by the standards of living obtaining before the Industrial Revolution. Perhaps there is no better example of this than the southern part of the Quebec-Newfoundland boundary, which was moved eastwards and westwards until it finally came to rest in a mutually acceptable position. Perhaps this boundary adjustment in eastern Canada was also due to the fact that it occurred under colonial regimes. The "mother-lands" were not particularly concerned with inter-colonial boundaries. Those that resulted in the fewest administrative problems at home were acceptable to them, and as the colonists themselves had relatively little influence on the politics of the home authority, the colonial boundaries were adjusted to suit local conditions as the occasion demanded.

The American Revolution naturally affected the boundary between Canada and the United States of America, and as it can be argued that Canada as a separate political entity dates from the revolution, that event can also be described as the cause of all Canada's provincial boundaries. It certainly had a direct effect on all the interprovincial boundaries east of the Great Lakes. By causing "Loyalists" to settle in blocks in the unsettled areas of what is now southeastern Canada, the American revolution immediately created a need for sharper definition of the existing boundaries and caused the creation of some new ones. Before the revolution, the boundaries in eastern Canada had become adjusted to the predominating economic factors in the various parts of the area. The revolution accentuated these, and also added a further factor, relating to the various patterns of life that the people of the area had inherited from their country of origin. In 1783 many of the inhabitants of eastern Canada were either descended from French settlers or had been born in France; others were descended from settlers who had come to Canada from the British Isles or had themselves come from the British Isles. Still others had come to Canada from the United States, to which they had emigrated from Europe or in which they had been born. The revolution, then, added human factors to the other geographical factors that had played a part in boundary evolution. The southern parts of the Ontario-Quebec and the Quebec-Newfoundland boundaries, the boundaries of Nova Scotia and New Brunswick, and the separate political existence of Prince Edward Island were all due to the desire for different legal systems and different ways of life on the part of people with varied cultural backgrounds as well as varied economic organization. It is, therefore, scarcely an exaggeration to say that the colonial boundaries in eastern Canada were regional boundaries at the time that they became established. It must be stressed, however, that for most practical purposes their evolution was complete before 1840.

The evolution of the International Boundary itself showed a remarkable resemblance to that of the eastern provincial boundaries. There were, of course, some differences in that the evolution of the International Boundary was much more intimately associated with the foreign policies of Great Britain and the United States of America, and that in fixing the eastern part, the idea of defence played a great part in the thinking of both sides. Yet, it was at the time of its establishment a very approximate regional boundary. East of Lake Ontario it separated the heartland of French Canada, as well as certain groups of Loyalists, from the United States. In establishing this division, the boundary ran for the most part through an almost unpopulated region, for the Appalachian Mountains, an obstacle to human intercourse even today, were an even greater barrier in 1783. West of Lake Ontario the boundary recognized the dividing effect of the Great Lakes, as well as the presence of professed anti-republicans along their northern shores. West of Lake Superior, the 49th Parallel, at the time of its establishment as the boundary, left to Britain the major part of the fur trade territory of the Hudson's Bay Company, setting it off from the area to the south, within which agricultural pursuits were more to the fore.

It is notable that west of the Rockies the 49th Parallel took a much longer period to become fixed as an international boundary. One reason for this was that on both sides of it the attitudes and activities of the people were much more alike than anywhere else along the boundary. For this reason, the establishment of that part of the International Boundary was perhaps less geographically sound at the time of its establishment than elsewhere.

Although the boundary between Canada and Alaska developed later, it, too, had a regional basis, dividing, as it did, the controlled land-fur economy of the Hudson's Bay Company from the Russian-controlled sea-fish-fur economy. In this connection, the exclusion of the "panhandle" from Canada showed a remarkable resemblance to the exclusion of the Labrador "fishing shore" from Canada almost a century before.

The provincial boundaries west of the Great Lakes, however, evolved on different bases. In some cases they were the result of factors of economic geography related to the natural resources of the area they enclosed. The boundaries of British Columbia were established to give the west coast colony-province control of gold mining; Manitoba was originally established to give separate administration to an agricultural group surrounded by an area in which the economy was much more primitive, although its dispute with Ontario was basically an economic one, as it was concerned with control of the lakehead ports. But the main common characteristic was that the boundaries developed either before significant settlement had occurred or very soon afterwards. Even by 1867, British Columbia had a population of only 32,000 and most of this small population lived in the extreme southwest of the province. The boundaries in this case were drawn without a thorough knowledge of the country they enclosed or through which they ran. These circumstances were not quite so marked in the case of the other western provinces, where final boundary establishment was slowed down by the establishment of provisional districts in the southern parts of the Northwest Territories. But the retarding effect of the establishment of provisional districts in the west was by no means as great as the retarding effect of the French and British conflicts in the east. Furthermore, in the west, by the time that the Northwest Territories were ready for definitive boundaries, some of the boundary decisions were quite arbitrary. This resulted from the fact that after provinces were established they would have a voice in the politics of the Canadian Confederation, a very different state of affairs from the establishment of colonial boundaries in the east, for these colonies had no voice in the British government.

Boundaries in eastern Canada were, then, based on different principles than those that obtained in western Canada. From a geographical point of view the former were more logical, as they were based on regionalism, which had time to stabilize itself before the political milieu became fixed. The eastern area was also better known by the time the boundaries became established, not as a result of scientific investigation, as understood today, but according to the facts brought to light by the reality of every day living in the area. Later boundary development followed the principle, if such it can be called, of dividing that part of Canada to which it was desired to bring provincial government into approximately equal areas. This was made abundantly clear in the creation of Alberta and Saskatchewan in 1905 and the boundary extensions of Manitoba, Ontario, and Quebec in 1912.

What affected the actual location of the boundary appeared usually to be a compromise between various political and economic forces. Naturally, these forces did not work in a vacuum, but had to take cognizance of the terrain. Geography played a significant role in locating the boundary. However, it is necessary to distinguish between what the people at the time thought to be the geography of the country and its actual geography. In earlier times, boundaries were often drawn on the basis of the imagined geography of the area, because not too much was known and maps were very sketchy and inadequate. In fact, it was partly to get around this difficulty that treaty makers and the makers of provincial boundaries often used parallels of latitude or meridians of longitude. This was convenient, but meant, of course, that later on the boundary concerned may have had little relationship to the economy of the area.

The attempt to draw "natural" rather than "artificial" boundaries was made in places, but again ideas of what a natural boundary was changed. Rivers were thought to be natural boundaries, and, where they were reinforced by ethnic and cultural divisions, were so; otherwise they were seen to become axes of intercourse, not frontiers of division.

It is noteworthy also that the impulses that led to boundary delimitation were not always the same as those that led to boundary demarcation. This was, in some cases, due to the long interval of time between the two processes, during which changes in human values and scientific knowledge had occurred. In the case of every provincial boundary except those that, as pointed out above, were delimited on purely "human" grounds, demarcation was brought about by the administrative problems attendant upon the mining industry, or the need for controlling the resources under the ground, by establishing the location of mining claims. The principle remaining undemarcated interprovincial boundary, that between Newfoundland and Quebec, will also need to be demarcated[5] for similar reasons – a far cry from the fishing problems that led to its earlier delimitation. The administration of mining is, of course, only the main manifestation of the common reason for boundary demarcation, namely, the need for the proper use of all natural resources, jurisdiction over which had passed to every province by 1932.

Boundary Evolution and Regionalism

In spite of the differences in the basic reasons for their establishment, all provincial boundaries today are intended, on paper at least, to serve the same administrative functions. The question as to whether this is satisfactory or not has led us to examine the problem of how fixed boundaries are to be determined in a changing geographical environment. The older boundaries of eastern Canada were good, geographically, at the time of their establishment, but this may not apply with the same force when considered against the total boundary pattern of Canada today, or the present state of the arts. In this sense, they might be considered as unsatisfactory as the boundaries in the west. It is often contended that the increasing complexities of modern life demand regional administration, but the great disadvantage of dividing Canada administratively according to regions is that the sparsely populated regions would be too numerous or too large in extent to be administered effectively. The problem posed can be considered in relationship to boundaries already established in Canada and then to boundaries that may be created in the existing territories in the future.

In the case of provincial boundaries already established, a change to regional boundaries would have to take cognizance of the fact that Canada includes regions that are handicapped by nature, which are in some ways a liability on the national balance sheet, and that the federal government has chosen to divide these, to some extent, among the existing provinces in order that the more fortunately endowed regions might share the responsibility for their administration. A result of this system has been the tendency of some of the provinces that have been given control over some part of the arctic and sub-arctic areas contiguous to them to anticipate expansion farther northward, so as to embrace ever-increasing sections of such areas. Another point to be borne in mind with this system is that if provincial boundaries intersect areas that may, as a result of technological advances, become economic regions, the provinces concerned might not afford the necessary degree of co-operation in their development.

Signs were not lacking that the economy of a region was taken into account and, particularly in Labrador, northwest Ontario, northern Manitoba, and southern Saskatchewan and Alberta, the economic geography of the times had its influence. One of the most interesting questions to arise in these cases was whether a boundary should be drawn to enclose a single-economy area or a multiple-economy one. In northwest Ontario and southern Saskatchewan and Alberta the arguments for making provinces coincide with the lumberman's or with the rancher's domain were pressed quite far. However, events would seem to have favoured the inclusion of several different belts of country, with different climates, and with the possibility of developing different economies, in one political unit. Although such a unit might have many more political problems to deal with than those of one occupation group, it would benefit by greater economic differentiation and stability. The life of the province would, in other words, be enriched by its differences.

That this custom prevailed may have done much towards enriching the life of the country as a whole. Undoubtedly, the kind of boundary drawn has far-reaching effects on the kind of development, social as well as economic, that may evolve. In fact, in the long run, boundaries probably make, rather than are made by, geography. No doubt the geographical factors that are partly responsible for their birth continue to be real. This is especially true of the international boundaries, which are later exaggerated in importance as immigration and tariff boundaries. Nevertheless, once the boundary is drawn, the political use of the space bounded by it leads to an orientation of route-ways, a choice of sites for settlements, policies of resource development, programs of colonization, and so forth, that profoundly affect the human geography of the area.

But if the several present provinces recognize that within their boundaries they have several geographical regions, then they can attempt to devise intraprovincial administrative boundaries that take cognizance of these facts. Such boundaries need not be fixed and certainly not demarcated. In other words, adjustment to the existing boundaries would seem to be the best way out of the regionalism-administrative dilemma in Canada, and in order to evaluate the nature and degree of such adjustment it is necessary to classify the boundaries in some way.

The Classification of Boundaries

Several classifications of boundaries have been proposed in modern times, but they are nearly all concerned with State boundaries. The oldest classification, and the one most widely employed until recent years, is the grouping of all boundaries into two categories – "natural boundaries" and "artificial boundaries". Natural features of the landscape, such as watersheds, rivers, and shorelines of lakes and seas, have long been adopted as "natural" or so-called "geographical" boundaries, whereas boundaries that do not follow natural features of the landscape, and that must, therefore, be marked on the ground by means of stones or monuments placed by man, have likewise been known as "artificial" or "conventional" boundaries. However, in the final analysis, all boundaries are artificial, because they are selected, defined, and marked by man, sometimes in conformity with the physical features of the area, but at other times in complete disregard of them.[6] In the introduction to this book and in Figure 1 another kind of classification was given – one based on the kind or "level" of government each boundary is intended to separate and other systems have been used for other parts of the world.[7] A much more comprehensive classification, based on four major groups was suggested by Boggs.[8] Physical types are those boundaries that follow some features marked by nature; geometrical types those that are straight lines, arcs of circles, and similar boundaries that disregard the physical geography and topography of the country; anthropogeographic types are related to human occupance of the land; and complex or compound boundaries are compromise lines adjusted to a multiplicity of factors. Other geographers, notably Hartshorne, have recognized the limitations of classifications of boundaries that are based upon more physical features such as rivers and mountains, and have advocated classifications that take account of the relationships between boundaries and human society. Thus a boundary that is defined before any settlement whatever takes place in the area through which it runs may be called a pioneer boundary. If a boundary is defined before any very significant settlement has taken place it may be called an antecedent boundary. The term subsequent may be applied to boundaries that were decided upon after the development of the area to which they apply. Such boundaries often conform to major or minor divisions in the cultural landscape. At other times they were established with obvious lack of conformity to such divisions, and to such boundaries as these the term superimposed might be applied, because they have been superimposed on an area with complete disregard for the geographical patterns existing in that area. On still other occasions, boundaries are established on naturally separating physical features such as ranges of mountains. Such boundaries are the result of such outstanding features and may, therefore, be termed consequent.[9]

In the light of the preceding chapters, it is possible to apply Hartshorne's system to Canadian boundaries. It is at once clear that each Canadian boundary as a whole does not fall into a single classification because in many cases different parts of the same political boundary developed in different ways. This again emphasizes the fact that a human-geographical classification depends upon a previous study of the historical-geographical evolution of boundaries. But such a procedure has been followed (Figure 33) with the boundaries of Canada, and the application of the resulting classification can be illustrated with references to the British Columbia-

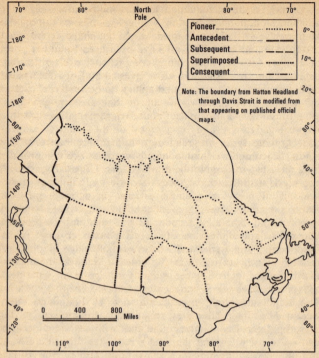

Figure 33. A classification of the major internal boundaries of Canada.

Alberta boundary. The southern part of this boundary, following, as it does a "naturally" separating physical feature – the Rocky Mountains – has been classified as consequent. The northern part was established before significant settlement occurred in the area and hence is an antecedent boundary. Clearly, therefore, the adjustments that might need to be made along the whole boundary in order to lessen any current difficulties in the border region will be much greater in the north than in the south.

The Future

There are indications that such adjustment to existing boundaries is occurring in some provinces, and in others efforts are being made by the citizens themselves to bring about this result. Such an attitude would avoid the other difficulties of changing existing political boundaries to regional boundaries. The chief of these would be the determination of the regional boundaries, which is by no means an easy task because of their inherent characteristics. They are not sharply defined, and are only valid for a given period of time, owing to the dynamic nature of human society. Secondly, a change in established boundaries would be costly, inasmuch as it would involve much new legislation, resurveying and remonumenting.

That diversity of interests is not an insurmountable obstacle at the sub-state level had been demonstrated before 1905 by the legislature of the Northwest Territories. But if regionalism can work within the provinces, it can also function between the provinces. It has been shown, for example, that Prince Edward Island became a separate province as the result of the wishes of its inhabitants; New Brunswick and Nova Scotia became separated because of the settlements of Loyalists in the former. Newfoundland remained politically aloof from its neighbours because, in earlier times, it seemed far removed from them. But are these reasons for marked separation today? The answer is partly demonstrated by the entry of Newfoundland into Confederation in 1949. Just as its interests with Canada ultimately manifested themselves, so the regional interests of Newfoundland with its neighbouring provinces might be recognized. What were the interests of the smaller regions that took shape politically as New Brunswick, Nova Scotia, Prince Edward Island, and the island of Newfoundland have now become the common interests of a larger region best expressed by the French term, "Le pays du Golfe".[10]

Reference was made in Chapter VII to the "thought" of changing the southern part of the boundary between Quebec and Newfoundland so that the entire drainage basins of five rivers would lie in Quebec, and so be capable of development solely by that province. But later discussions discarded this idea in favour of a compromise which would not involve changing the boundary. Newfoundland could grant to Quebec perpetual rights to flood Labrador territory to create reservoirs needed to develop hydro-electricity. In return, Newfoundland could receive part of the power generated together with a corridor through Quebec for the transmission of power from the Churchill Falls development to the island of Newfoundland.[11]

In the case of the creation of new boundaries out of the territories of today, the problems are different. The present boundaries within the territories are not fixed, and it is, therefore, here that there is the opportunity to work out boundaries that might be as geographical as possible in the light of our present knowledge – boundaries not based on ancient, vaguely worded documents or yet on purely political considerations. The fact that human adjustment to existing provincial boundaries appears to be more satisfactory than changing the boundaries themselves does not mean that new boundaries should be considered haphazardly. Sound regional principles should surely prevail in the politico-geographical evolution of the territories, if only by virtue of the fact that no matter what the advances of modern science, the resources of the territories are limited and must, therefore, be used, which means administered, wisely. In establishing any new boundaries there should perhaps, not be so much concern with equal areas as with the benefits that might accrue to all Canadians if new administrative areas were developed on a sound regional basis. The attempts to arrive at a new division of the Northwest Territories which embraces the principles of geographical regionalism and the realities of demarcating a boundary in a tundra environment are an advance on the preliminary considerations which were given to the establishment of provincial and territorial boundaries in the past. At the same time the decisions made in 1963 whether consciously or not, embraced features common to all the major internal political units created within Canada since Confederation. For one thing, an astronomical boundary was selected. A 'natural boundary' appeals most to hunters, trappers, fishermen and those who lead a nomadic existence. It is a feature they can see and recognize and remember easily. But the mining engineer or the forester is more aware of the legal complications that can arise with such boundaries and much prefers to be able to calculate his position accurately with the more sophisticated techniques at his disposal. With an eye to the future, the latter view prevailed. The principle of 'one kind of environment' was also abandoned and if the proposed Territory of Mackenzie ever becomes a province, it will, like Saskatchewan and Ontario, to choose but two examples, have a 'south' and 'north' which will be markedly different from one another. This may give economic variety, and hence strength, to the province, but it will also bring its own set of problems as there is almost always a disparity between the economic growth of two such parts.

Less consideration was given to Nunassiaq Territory. The total population in 1961 was a scant 7,045, of whom 75 per cent were Inuit. More than this, most of the people lived on the west coast of Hudson Bay and Baffin Island, the Island alone supporting about 70 per cent of the total. The Queen Elizabeth Islands and the interior of the present District of Keewatin support very few people. However, it was tentatively predicted that by 1970 the population might be as much as 10,000 which with net immigration could add up to a population at least equal to that of the Yukon Territory. However, the validity of this argument rests on the assumption that the Yukon is a 'viable' Territory with a population of 18,388 (1971). Its population has been as low as 4,157 (1921), which is much less than the present population of Nunassiaq. But its population when it was created a Territory in 1898 was 27,000.

But while access to the area is generally from the east, it is admitted that there is, 'at present stage of development, no natural centre.' Furthermore, Nunassiaq would embrace 772,000 square miles of land – greater than the total area of Ontario and Quebec combined – and would have a north-south extent of more than 2,000 miles – something like the distance from Toronto to Vancouver. But more than this, it would embrace vast areas of water, such as Hudson Bay and James Bay and the many channels and inlets of the far north. Thus it would be essentially a territory of islands. Indonesia, with an area of some 736,470 square miles is the only comparable political entity in this respect. Such a political unit, if it ever became a province, would be a new experience for Canada.

But it would involve Canada and the provinces even more intimately in questions concerning boundaries over and under large water areas. Submarine boundaries become an increasingly pressing issue as minerals are discovered and exploited beneath national waters and on continental shelves; this change is exemplified by provincial suggestions to extend the boundaries of Manitoba, Ontario and Quebec into Hudson Bay.[12]

APPENDIX

Approximate Lengths of Major Canadian Boundaries[1]

Boundary	Length (kilometres)
Canada-Atlantic Ocean-Gulf of St. Lawrence	29,947
Canada-Arctic Ocean-Davis Strait	6,146
Canada-Pacific Ocean	16,244
Canada-United States of America	8,890
Alberta-British Columbia	1,842
Alberta-District of Mackenzie	560
Alberta-Saskatchewan	1,224
Alberta-United States of America	298
British Columbia-District of Mackenzie	207
British Columbia-Pacific Ocean	16,405
British Columbia-United States of America	2,167
British Columbia-Yukon Territory	856
Franklin District-Arctic Ocean-Davis Strait	6,146
Franklin District-District of Mackenzie	4,043
Franklin District-District of Keewatin	3,245
Franklin District-Quebec	4,730
Franklin District-Yukon Territory	343
Keewatin District-District of Mackenzie	817
Keewatin District-Manitoba	1,318
Keewatin District-Ontario	1,210
Keewatin District-Quebec	4,013
Mackenzie District-Saskatchewan	446
Mackenzie District-Yukon Territory	2,005
Manitoba-Ontario	980
Manitoba-Saskatchewan	1,277
Manitoba-United States of America	497
New Brunswick-Bay of Fundy	590
New Brunswick-Gulf of St. Lawrence	933
New Brunswick-Nova Scotia	34
New Brunswick-Quebec	262
New Brunswick-United States of America	557
Newfoundland-Atlantic Ocean-Gulf of St. Lawrence	18,040
Newfoundland-Quebec	4,521
Nova Scotia-Atlantic Ocean-Gulf of St. Lawrence	5,825
Ontario-Quebec	1,313
Ontario-United States of America	2,760

Prince Edward Island-Gulf of St. Lawrence	1,260
Quebec-Gulf of St. Lawrence	3,298
Quebec-United States of America	812
Saskatchewan-United States of America	632
Yukon Territory-United States of America	1,210

[1] Derived from data published by the federal Ministries of Energy, Mines and Resources and the Environment.

Summary by Political Units

| Political unit | *Approximate length of perimeter (kilometres)* | | |
	Land	*Water*	*Total*
Canada	5,062	56,165	61,227
Alberta	3,884	40	3,924
British Columbia	5,072	16,405	21,477
Manitoba	3,155	917	4,072
New Brunswick	853	1,523	2,377
Newfoundland	4,521	18,040	22,561
Nova Scotia	34	5,825	5,859
Ontario	2,295	3,968	6,263
Prince Edward Island	—	1,260	1,260
Quebec	6,908	12,041	18,949
Saskatchewan	3,456	124	3,580
Northwest Territories	3,619	17,000	20,619
District of Franklin	84	18,507	18,423
District of Keewatin	1,302	9,301	10,603
District of Mackenzie	4,035	4,043	8,078
Yukon Territory	4,071	343	4,414

NOTES

Notes to Chapter I

[1] Parts of this Chapter are based on J.W. Watson, "Preface" in N.L. Nicholson, *The Boundaries of Canada, Its Provinces and Territories* (Ottawa: Queen's Printer, 1954), pp. vii-ix.

[2] Stephen B. Jones, *Boundary Making. A Handbook for Statesmen, Treaty Editors and Boundary Commissioners* (Washington: Carnegie Endowment for International Peace 1945), p. 54.

[3] Albert Perry Brigham, "Principles in the Determination of Boundaries", *Geographical Review* (1919), 7, p. 217.

[4] Robert MacGregor Dawson, *The Government of Canada* (Toronto: University of Toronto Press, 1947), p. 91.

[5] Gustav Smedal, *Acquisition of Sovereignty over Polar Areas* (Oslo: Dybwad, 1931), p. 10.

[6] S.W. Boggs, *International Boundaries. A Study of Boundary Functions and Problems* (New York: Columbia University Press, 1940).

[7] Franklin K. Van Zandt, *Boundaries of the United States and the Several States* (Washington: Government Printing Office, 1966).

[8] J.V.R. Prescott, *The geography of frontiers and boundaries* (Chicago: Aldine, 1965).

[9] J.V.R. Prescott, *The evolution of Nigeria's International and Regional boundaries: 1861-1971* (Vancouver: Tantalus, 1971).

[10] James White, "Boundary Disputes and Treaties", *Canada and its Provinces* (Toronto: Publishers Association, 1913), Vol. III, Part III, pp. 751-958.

[11] W.F. Ganong, "A monograph on the evolution of the boundaries of New Brunswick", *Transactions of the Royal Society of Canada 2* (1901), VII, Sec. II. pp. 139-449.

[12] Willard E. Ireland, "The evolution of the boundaries of British Columbia", *British Columbia Historical Quarterly* (1939), 3, pp. 263-282.

[13] Yvon Bériault, *Les problèmes politique du Nord Canadien* (Ottawa: Université d'Ottawa, 1942).

[14] Stephen B. Jones, "The Forty-Ninth Parallel in the Great Plains", *Journal of Geography* (1932), 31, pp. 357-67 and "The Cordilleran Section of the Canada-United States Borderland", *Geographical Journal* (1937), 89, pp. 439-50.

[15] Pierre Dagenais, "Petits conflits d'une grande frontière", *Revue Canadienne de Géographie* (1948), II, p. 3-8.

[16] Julian V. Minghi, "Point Roberts, Washington: The Problem of an American exclave", *Yearbook of the Association of Pacific Coast Geographers* (1962), 24.

[17] Henri Dorion, *La Frontière Québec-Terreneuve* (Québec: Les Presses de l'Université Laval, 1963).

Notes to Chapter II

[1] F. J. Speck, *Family Territories and Social Life of Various Algonkian Bands of the Ottawa Valley* (Ottawa: King's Printer, 1915), p. 2.

[2] Ganong, op. cit., p. 154.

[3] Ellen Churchill Semple, *Influence of Geographic Environment* (New York: Holt, 1911), p. 57.

[4] Samuel Edward Dawson, "Line of Demarcation of Pope Alexander VI in AD 1493", *Transactions of the Royal Society of Canada* (2), V, sec. II, (1899), p. 467.

[5] *Statutes, Documents and Papers Bearing on the Discussion Respecting the Northern and Western Boundaries of the Province of Ontario* etc. (Toronto: Hunter, Rose and Co., 1878) p. 40.

[6] Ganong, op. cit., p. 158.

[7] Otto Klotz, *Boundaries of Canada* (Waterloo: Historical Society, 1914), p. 1.

[8] Lawrence Shaw Mayo, "The Forty-Fifth Parallel: or Detail of the Unguarded Boundary", *Geographical Review* 13 (1923): p. 255.

[9] Ganong, op. cit., p. 165.

[10] Sir James G. Bourinot, *Builders of Nova Scotia* (Toronto: Copp-Clark, 1900), pp. 105-107.

[11] Leo Francis Stock (ed.), *Proceedings and Debates of the British Parliament respecting North America* (Washington: Carnegie Institution, 1924), Vol. 1, p. 436.

[12] Max Savelle, *The Diplomatic History of the Canadian Boundary 1749-1763* (Toronto: Ryerson, 1940), p. x.

[13] *Statutes, Documents . . . Respecting the Northern and Western Boundaries of . . . Ontario,* op. cit., p. 33.

[14] J. N. L. Baker, *A History of Geographical Discovery and Exploration* (London: Harrap, 1931), p. 221.

[15] Privy Council, Great Britain, *In the Matter of the Boundary between the Dominion of Canada and the Colony of Newfoundland in the Labrador Peninsula* (London: William Clowes, 1927), Vol. III, p. 4068.

[16] Savelle, op. cit., p. 4.

[17] J. Mackay Hitsman, "Capture of Saint-Pierre-et-Miquelon, 1793", *Canadian Army Journal,* July 1959, p. 77.

[18] A. Shortt and Arthur G. Doughty, *Documents relating to the Constitutional History of Canada 1759-1791* (Ottawa: King's Printer, 1918), pp. 96, 141, 151-152.

[19] W. P. M. Kennedy, *Documents of the Canadian Constitution 1759-1915* (Toronto: Oxford University Press, 1918), p. 18.

[20] Shortt and Doughty, op. cit., p. 164.

[21] International Boundary Commission, *Joint Report Upon the Survey and Demarcation of the Boundary Between the United States and Canada from the Source of the St. Croix River to the St. Lawrence River* (Washington: Government Printing Office, 1925), p. 275.

[22] W. M. Whitelaw, *The Maritimes and Canada before Confederation* (Toronto: Oxford University Press, 1934), pp. 41, 42.

[23] Shortt and Doughty, op. cit., p. 542.

[24] loc. cit.

[25] Ibid., p. 571.

[26] Andrew Macphail, "The History of Prince Edward Island," *Canada and Its Provinces* (Toronto: The Publishers Association, 1913), Vol. XIII, pp. 343-344.

[27] Whitelaw, op. cit., pp. 43-44.

[28] Hitsman, op. cit., p. 78.

Notes to Chapter III

[1] The present St. Lawrence River.

[2] The present Rainy Lake.

[3] Shortt and Doughty, *op. cit.,* pp. 727-728.

[4] S. W. Boggs, *International Boundaries. A Study of Boundary Functions and Problems* (New York: Columbia University Press, 1940), p. 42.

[5] S. F. Bemis, "Jays Treaty and the Northwest Boundary Gap", *American Historical Review* 27 (1922): p. 477.

[6] John W. Davis, "The Unguarded Boundary", *Geographical Review* 12 (1922): p. 590.

[7] Marion Gilroy, "The Partition of Nova Scotia, 1784", *Canadian Historical Review* 14 (1933): p. 391.

[8] *Cambridge History of the British Empire* (Cambridge: University Press), Vol. VI, p. 272.

[9] J. F. Rogers, *A Historical Geography of the British*

Colonies (Oxford: Clarendon Press, 1911), Vol. V, Part III, p. 129.

[10] E. J. Lajeunesse, *The Windsor Border Region* (Toronto: Champlain Society, 1960).

[11] Shortt and Doughty, op. cit., p. 773.

[12] Ibid., p. 960.

[13] Ibid., p. 1006.

[14] Percy J. Robinson, "Yonge Street and the North West Company", *Canadian Historical Review* 24 (1943), p. 255.

[15] A. G. Doughty and D. A. McArthur, *Documents Relating to the Constitutional History of Canada 1819-1828* (Ottawa: King's Printer, 1935), p. 4.

[16] W. Cousineau, "Historique de la Seigneurie de Treadwell" (M.A. thesis, Université d'Ottawa, 1953).

[17] Which then included the present provinces of Nova Scotia, New Brunswick and Prince Edward Island.

[18] Shortt and Doughty, op. cit., p. 728.

[19] Ibid., p. 1017.

[20] Hitsman, op. cit., p. 81.

[21] Willard E. Ireland, "The Evolution of the Boundaries of British Columbia", *British Columbia Historical Quarterly* 3 (1939), p. 265.

[22] Alexander Mackenzie, *Voyages from Montreal through the Continent of North America to the Frozen and Pacific Oceans in 1789 and 1793* (Toronto: Morang, c. 1901), Vol. II, p. 358.

[23] *Statutes, Documents . . . Respecting the Northern and Western Boundaries of . . . Ontario,* op. cit., p. 28.

[24] International Joint Commission, *Joint Report Upon the Survey and Demarcation of the Boundary Between the United States and Canada from the Gulf of Georgia to the Northwesternmost Point of Lake of the Woods* (Washington: Government Printing Office, 1937), p. 187.

[25] Archer Martin, *The Hudson's Bay Company's Land Tenures and the Occupation of Assiniboia by Lord Selkirk's Settlers* (London: William Clowes, 1898), p. 28.

[26] J. P. Pritchett, *The Red River Valley 1811-1849* (Toronto: Ryerson, 1942), p. 231.

[27] Franklin K. Van Zandt, *Boundaries of the United States and the Several States* (Washington: U.S. Government Printing Office, 1972), p. 21.

[28] Whymper, *Travel and Adventure in the Territory of Alaska* (London: John Murray, 1868), p. 169.

[29] International Boundary Commission, *Joint Report Upon the Survey and Demarcation of the International Boundary*

Between the United States and Canada along the 141st Meridian from the Arctic Ocean to Mount St. Elias (Washington: Government Printing Office, 1918), p. 203.

[30] F. W. Howay, W. N. Sage and H. F. Angus, *British Columbia and the United States* (Toronto: Ryerson, 1942), p. 124.

[31] T. A. Rickard, *Historic Backgrounds of British Columbia* (Vancouver: Wrigley, 1948), p. 283.

[32] F. Merk, "Oregon Pioneers and the Boundary," *American Historical Review* 29 (1924), p. 683.

[33] F. Merk, "British Party Politics and Oregon", *American Historical Review* 37 (1932), pp. 653-677.

[34] Julian V. Minghi, "Teaching Political Geography", *The Journal of Geography* 65 (November 1966): p. 336.

[35] Ibid., p. 367.

[36] Privy Council, Great Britain, . . . *the Boundary between . . . Canada and . . . Newfoundland.*, op. cit., pp. 210-211.

[37] Kennedy, op. cit., p. 246-247.

[38] Doughty and McArthur, op. cit., p. 393.

[39] A. G. Doughty and Norah Story, *Documents Relating to the Constitutional History of Canada 1819-1828* (Ottawa: King's Printer, 1935), p. 138.

[40] H. A. Innis and A. R. M. Lower, *Select Documents in Canadian Economic History 1783-1885* (Toronto: Toronto University Press, 1933), pp. 179-182.

[41] James White, "Boundary Disputes and Treaties", *Canada and its Provinces* (Toronto: The Publishers Association 1913), Vol. VIII, Part III, p. 814.

[42] Rickard, op. cit., p. 302.

[43] Ireland, op. cit., p. 274.

[44] *Statutes of British Columbia,* 1871, Appendix, p. 190.

[45] *Report of the Commission Appointed to Delimit the Boundary Between the Provinces of Alberta and British Columbia, 1913-1916* (Ottawa: Office of the Surveyor General, 1917), p. 1.

[46] Howay, Sage and Angus, op. cit., p. 331.

Notes to Chapter IV

[1] A. E. Millward, *Southern Baffin Island* (Ottawa: Department of the Interior, 1929), p. 11.

[2] W. F. King, *Report upon the Title of Canada to the Islands North of the Mainland of Canada* (Ottawa: Department of the Interior, 1905), p. 10.

[3] Great Britain, *Statutes,* 58-59 Victoria, Cap. 34, 1895.

[4] *Seventeenth Annual Report of the Department of Marine and Fisheries* (Ottawa: Maclean, Roger and Co., 1885), Appendix 30, pp. 189-229.

[5] *Sessional Papers of Canada,* No. 11c, 1886 and No. 15, 1887.

[6] King, op. cit., p. 12.

[7] Ibid., p. 16.

[8] *Report of the Expedition to Hudson Bay and Cumberland Gulf* (Ottawa: Department of Marine and Fisheries, 1898), p. 24.

[9] Howay, Sage and Angus, op. cit., p. 365.

[10] *Joint Report upon the Survey and Demarcation of the Boundary between Canada and the United States from Tongass Passage to Mount St. Elias* (Ottawa: Queen's Printer, 1952), p. 248.

[11] Douglas, op. cit., p. 44.

[12] International Boundary Commission 1918, op. cit., p. 204.

[13] Ibid., p. 211.

[14] *Report of the Second Norwegian Arctic Expedition in the "Fram" 1898-1902* (Kristiania: T. O. Brogger, 1907), Vol. I, p. iv.

[15] Otto Sverdrup, *New Land* (London: Longmans, Green and Co., 1904), Vol. II, pp. 449-450.

[16] A. P. Low, *Report on the Dominion Government Expedition to Hudson Bay and the Arctic Islands 1903-1904* (Ottawa: Government Printing Bureau, 1906), p. 3.

[17] J. E. Bernier, *Report on the Dominion Government Expedition to the Arctic Islands and the Hudson Strait on board the C.G.S. "Arctic" 1906-07* (Ottawa: King's Printer 1909).

[18] *Statutes, Documents and Papers Bearing on . . . the Northern and Western Boundaries . . . of Ontario,* op. cit., pp. 54-55.

[19] Canada, Senate, *Debates,* 1907, p. 276.

[20] *Report on the Dominion of Canada Government Expedition to the Arctic Islands and the Hudson Strait on board the C.G.S. "Arctic"* (Ottawa: King's Printer, 1910), p. 195.

[21] Canada, House of Commons, *Debates,* 1925, pp. 4069, 4085.

[22] Canada, House of Commons, *Debates,* 1953, p. 700.

[23] R. A. MacKay (ed.), *Newfoundland-Economic Diplomatic and Strategic Studies* (Toronto: Oxford University Press, 1946), pp. 329-331.

[24] N. B. Wormwith, "The Fishery Arbitrations" *Canada and Its Provinces* (1913), Vol. VIII, p. 684.

[25] Ibid., p. 716.

[26] International Boundary Commission, *Joint Report Upon the Survey and Demarcation of the Boundary Between the United States and Canada from the Western Terminus of the Land Boundary Along the Forty-Ninth Parallel, on the West Side of Point Roberts, Through Georgia, Haro and Juan de Fuca straits, to the Pacific Ocean* (Washington: Government Printing Office, 1921), p. 716.

[27] Hubert H. Bancroft, *History of British Columbia* (San Francisco, 1887), p. 612.

[28] Douglas, op. cit., p. 22.

[29] *Statutes of Canada,* 1-2 Elizabeth II, Cap. 15, 1952-53.

[30] *Statutes of Canada,* 4 Edward VII, Cap. 13, 1904.

[31] *Halifax Chronicle Herald,* June 29, 1957.

[32] *Vancouver Sun,* January 11, 1962.

[33] *The Province,* August 4, 1956.

[34] See for example Knowlton Nash, "Who Owns How Much of the Arctic"? *Halifax Chronicle Herald,* October 21, 1958.

[35] *Toronto Globe and Mail,* September 18, 1969.

[36] Commander Steele, *Seadragon* (New York: E. P. Dutton, 1962).

[37] Canada, House of Commons, *Debates,* 1957, pp. 3132-3133, 3185-3186.

[38] *Joint Report Upon the Survey and Demarcation of the Boundary Between the United States and Canada from the Northwesternmost Point of Lake of the Woods to Lake Superior* (Washington: Government Printing Office, 1931), p. 11.

[39] Privy Council, Great Britain, . . . *the Boundary between . . . Canada and . . . Newfoundland,* op. cit., Vol. II, p. 754.

[40] Ibid, Vol. II, pp. 347-349.

[41] Ibid, Vol. I, p. 146.

[42] Ibid, Vol. I, p. 129.

[43] Ibid, Vol. XII, p. 1018.

[44] Ibid, Vol. XII, p. 1026.

[45] Deputy Minister of Justice to the Deputy Minister of the Interior, February 17th, 1936.

[46] Raymond Gushue, "The Territorial Waters of Newfoundland", *Canadian Journal of Economics and Political Science,* 15 (1949), pp. 334-352.

[47] *Toronto Globe and Mail,* August 17, 1956.

[48] *Ottawa Journal,* March 6, 1963.

[49] *Statutes of Canada,* 13 Elizabeth II, Cap. 22, 1964.

[50] Order in Council No. 2025, October 26th, 1967.

[51] Order in Council No. 1109, May 29th, 1969.

[52] Order in Council No. 366, February 25th, 1971.

[53] *Statutes of Canada, 1964,* op. cit.

[54] Communique No. 116, (Ottawa, Department of External Affairs, November 2, 1976).

[55] *The Canada Gazette Part I,* Vol. 110, Extra No. 101, November 1, 1976.

Notes to Chapter V

[1] G. Patterson, "Sir William Alexander and the Scottish Attempt to Colonize Acadia", *Transactions of the Royal Society of Canada (2),* 10, X, sec. II (1892), p. 88.

[2] The present Bay of Fundy.

[3] Ganong, op. cit., p. 176.

[4] *Statement of the Evidence Submitted on Behalf of His Majesty . . . in Reference to the Boundary Between the Province of New Brunswick, in the Dominion of Canada, and the State of Maine, One of the United States of America . . . etc. Delivered December 4th, 1908* (London: The Foreign Office), p. 23.

[5] Ganong, op. cit., p. 369.

[6] *Statement . . . in Reference to the Boundary Between . . . New Brunswick . . . and . . . Maine,* op. cit., p. 23.

[7] *Papers Relative to the Settlement of the Disputed Boundaries Between the Provinces of Canada and New Brunswick* (London: William Clowes, 1851), p. 93.

[8] Loc. cit.

[9] *Statutes of the United Kingdom* 14-15 Victoria, 1851.

[10] Ganong, op. cit., p. 407.

[11] *Correspondence, Papers and Documents of Dates from 1856 to 1882 Inclusive, Relating to the Northerly and Westerly Boundaries of the Province of Ontario* (Toronto: C. Blackett Robinson, 1882), p. 185.

[12] White, op. cit., p. 902.

[13] *North Western Ontario: Its Boundaries, Resources and Communications* (Toronto: Hunter, Rose and Co., 1879), p. 2.

[14] *Statutes, Documents . . . Respecting the Northern and Western Boundaries of . . . Ontario,* op. cit., p. 347.

[15] Canada, House of Commons, *Debates,* 1881.

[16] *Correspondence etc. . . . Relating to the Northerly and Westerly Boundaries of . . . Ontario,* op. cit., p. 453.

[17] *Statutes of the United Kingdom* 52-53 Victoria, 1889.

[18] *Statutes of Canada* 14-15 Victoria, Cap. 5, 1851.

[19] *Statutes of Canada* 16 Victoria, Cap. 152, 1853.

[20] R. J. Fraser, *The Lake St. Francis Boundary,* Unpublished manuscript, c. 1960.

[21] *Toronto Globe and Mail,* Wednesday, March 10, 1976, p. 36.

[22] David B. Knight, *A Capital for Canada: Conflict and Compromise in the Nineteenth Century* (Chicago: University of Chicago, Department of Geography, Research Series No. 182, 1977) and Idem, *Choosing Canada's Capital* (Toronto: McClelland and Stewart, Carleton Library Series, No. 105, 1977).

[23] See especially John Hamilton Gray, *Confederation of Canada* (Toronto: Copp Clark, 1872), p. 108.

[24] Douglas H. Fullerton, *The Capital of Canada: How Should it be Governed?* (Ottawa: Information Canada, 1974) Vol. II, p. 11.

[25] Ibid, p. 13.

[26] *Statutes of Canada* 7 Elizabeth II, Cap. 37, 1958. Schedule.

[27] *Rapport de la Commission d'étude sur l'integrité de territoire du Québec: Les problèmes de la région de la capitale canadienne* (Quebec) May 22, 1968.

[28] Fullerton, op. cit., p. 219.

[29] *Statutes of Canada* 61 Victoria, Cap. 3, 1898.

Notes to Chapter VI

[1] *Further Papers Relative to the Exploration by the Expedition under Captain Palliser* (London: Eyre and Spottiswoode 1860), p. 9.

[2] *The Journals, Detailed Reports and Observations Relative to the Exploration, by Captain Palliser . . .* (London: Eyre and Spottiswoode, 1863), p. 16.

[3] Canada, House of Commons, *Debates,* 1883.

[4] *Report of the Department of the Interior* (Ottawa: King's Printer 1875).

[5] *Hudson's Bay Company, A Brief History* (London: Hudson's Bay Company, 1934), pp. 23, 24.

[6] J. A. Denis, "A Short History of the Surveys Performed Under the Dominion Lands System, 1869 to 1889", *Annual Report of the Department of the Interior* (Ottawa: King's Printer, 1891), Part VI, p. 31.

[7] A. S. Morton and Chester Martin, *History of Prairie Settlement and Dominion Lands Policy* (Toronto: Macmillan 1936), p. 209.

[8] *Statutes of Canada,* 33 Victoria, Cap. 3, 1870.

[9] *Statutes of Canada,* 40 Victoria, Cap. 6, 1877.

[10] *Statutes of Canada,* 39 Victoria, Cap. 21, 1876.

[11] N. L. Nicholson, "Some Aspects of the Political Geography of Keewatin", *The Canadian Geographer,* 1, No. 3, 1953, pp. 73-84.

[12] *Report of the Department of the Interior* (Ottawa: King's Printer, 1877), p. viii.

[13] *Report of the Department of the Interior* (Ottawa: King's Printer, 1880), p. iv.

[14] *Report of the Commissioners Appointed to Delimit the Boundary Between the Provinces of Manitoba and Ontario from the Winnipeg River Northerly* (Ottawa: Topographical Survey of Canada, 1925), p. 14.

[15] *Report of the Department of the Interior* (Ottawa: King's Printer, 1881), p. v.

[16] *Sessional Papers of Canada,* 1906-7, No. 64a, pp. 39-40.

[17] W. A. Mackintosh, *Prairie Settlement. The Geographical Setting* (Toronto: Macmillan, 1934), p. 53.

[18] *Sessional Papers of Canada,* 1906-7, No. 64a, p. 39.

[19] Report of the Lieutenant Governor of Keewatin, 1892, *Report of the Department of the Interior* (Ottawa: King's Printer, 1893), Part IV, p. 4.

[20] Report of the Lieutenant Governor of Keewatin, 1895, *Report of the Department of the Interior* (Ottawa: King's Printer, 1896), p. 4.

[21] Actually, the thirty-second correction line of the Dominion Lands System, which was almost 60 degrees north.

[22] *Sessional Papers of Canada, 1901,* No. 25, p. 6.

[23] Report of the Lieutenant Governor of Keewatin, 1893, *Report of the Department of the Interior* (Ottawa: King's Printer, 1894), Part VI, p. 5.

[24] Report of the Lieutenant Governor of Keewatin, 1895, loc. cit.

[25] Canada, House of Commons, *Debates,* 1892.

[26] See Chapter IV.

[27] Lawrence J. Burpee (Ed.), *An Historical Atlas of Canada* (London: Thomas Nelson, 1927), p. 22.

[28] Government of Canada, *Report of the Committee of the Honourable the Privy Council approved by His Excellency on the 2nd October, 1895.*

[29] Government of Canada, *Report of the Committee of the Honourable the Privy Council approved by His Excellency on the 18th December, 1897.*

[30] Canada, Senate, *Debates,* 1898, col. 859.

[31] *Statutes of Canada,* 61 Victoria, Cap. 6, 1898 (Schedule).

[32] *Statutes of Canada,* 1 Edward VII, Cap. 41, 1901 (Schedule).

[33] Canada, House of Commons, *Debates,* 1898, col. 6747.

Notes to Chapter VII

[1] C. C. Lingard, *Territorial Government in Canada* (Toronto: University of Toronto Press, 1946), pp. 8-9.

[2] *Sessional Papers of Canada,* No. 64a, 1906-7, p. 9.

[3] Ibid, p. 10.

[4] *Calgary Herald,* December 2, 1900; March 21, 1901; January 16, 1905; February 18, 1905.

[5] Lingard, op. cit., p. 132.

[6] Ibid, p. 134.

[7] Ibid, p. 72.

[8] See for example *Calgary Herald,* op. cit., *Regina Leader,* December 14, 1904; *Macleod Gazette,* January 10, 1902; *Medicine Hat Times,* February 17, 1905.

[9] *Calgary Herald,* February 7, 1905; February 13, 1905; February 21, 1905.

[10] *Further Papers Relative to . . . the Expedition under Captain Palliser,* op. cit., p. 4.

[11] Lingard, op. cit., p. 74.

[12] *Sessional Papers of Canada,* No. 102, 1905, p. 8.

[13] Canada, House of Commons, *Debates,* 1905, col. 1427.

[14] *Statutes of Canada,* 4-5 Edward VII, Cap. 3, 1905.

[15] *Statutes of Canada,* 4-5 Edward VII, Cap. 42, 1905.

[16] *Calgary Herald,* February 23, 1905; *Medicine Hat Times,* February 17, 1905.

[17] *Report of the Department of the Interior* (Ottawa: Queen's Printer, 1884), pp. 12-13.

[18] *Toronto Financial Post,* September 1965.

[19] *Calgary Herald,* February 23, 1905.

[20] *Sessional Papers of Canada,* No. 97, 1905, p. 5.

[21] Canada, House of Commons, *Debates,* 1905, cols. 1428-31.

[22] *Sessional Papers of Canada,* No. 64a, 1906-7, p. 41.

[23] Canada, House of Commons, *Debates,* 1905, col. 1431.

[24] *Sessional Papers of Canada,* No. 64a, 1906-7, pp. 45-46.

[25] Ibid, p. 27.

[26] Canada, House of Commons, *Debates,* 1907-8, col. 12786.

[27] Canada, House of Commons, *Debates,* 1911-12, col. 4340.

[28] Canada, House of Commons, *Debates,* 1907-8, col. 12779.

[29] Loc. cit.

[30] Ibid, col. 12780.

[31] Ibid, col. 12814.

[32] Ibid, 1912, col. 5270.

[33] *Statutes of Canada,* 2 George V, Cap. 40, 1912.

[34] *Statutes of Canada,* 2 George V, Cap. 45, 1912.

[35] *Statutes of Canada,* 2 George V, Cap. 32, 1912.

[36] *Quebec Le Soleil,* February 2, 1962.

[37] Ibid.

[38] *Winnipeg Free Press,* November 7, 1951.

[39] Government of Canada, Order in Council, March 16, 1918.

[40] *Quebec La Presse,* December 23, 1949.

[41] *Toronto Financial Post,* June 18, 1955.

[42] *Toronto Globe and Mail,* September 2, 1966.

[43] J. Lewis Robison, *Resources of the Canadian Shield* (Toronto: Methuen, 1969), p. 78.

[44] *Toronto Globe and Mail,* April 14, 1964.

[45] Dorion, op. cit.

[46] Canada, House of Commons, *Debates,* 1964, p. 1476.

[47] See, for example, José Mailhot et Andrée Michaud, *North West River Etude Ethnographique* (Quebec: Université Laval, 1965).

Notes to Chapter VIII

[1] Arthur R. Hinks, "Notes on the Technique of Boundary Delimitation," *Geographical Journal* 58 (1921), p. 417.

[2] Shirley King, "The Ontario-Quebec Boundary: Lake Temiskaming to James Bay," *Annual Report of the Association of Ontario Land Surveyors* (1934), p. 143.

[3] *Report . . . [on] . . . the Boundary between . . . Alberta and British Columbia,* op. cit., Part I, p. 2.

[4] Stephen B. Jones, *Boundary Making. A Handbook for Statesmen, Treaty Editors and Boundary Commissioners* (Washington: Carnegie Endowment for International Peace 1945), p. 58.

[5] International Boundary Commission (1925), op. cit., p. 332.

[6] *. . . the Survey from Lake of the Woods to Lake Superior,* op. cit., pp. 217-218.

[7] International Boundary Commission (1937), op. cit., p. xiv.

[8] *Report of the Department of the Interior* (Ottawa: King's Printer 1888).

[9] *Report of the Department of the Interior* (Ottawa: King's Printer 1897), p. xvi.

[10] International Boundary Commission, op. cit., 1918, p. 15 and 1952, p. xiii.

[11] Ganong, op. cit., pp. 368-9.

[12] King (1905), op. cit., p. 144.

[13] Although Manitoba had been erected into a province, control of its natural resources remained vested in the federal government.

[14] *Report of the Department of the Interior* (Ottawa: King's Printer 1897), p. xxvi.

[15] *Report of the Commissioners appointed to Delimit the Boundary between the Provinces of Manitoba and Ontario from the Winnipeg River Northerly* (Ottawa: King's Printer, 1925), p. 6.

[16] A. J. Campbell, "British Columbia-Yukon Boundary Survey", *Report of the Deputy Minister of Land for 1948* (Victoria: King's Printer, 1949), p. 136.

[17] *Report . . . [on] . . . the Boundary between . . . Alberta and British Columbia,* op. cit., Part I, p. 2.

[18] Ibid, p. 8.

[19] King (1934), op. cit., p. 144.

[20] *Report . . . [on] . . . the Boundary between . . . Manitoba and Ontario,* op. cit., p. 8.

[21] Ibid, p. 85.

[22] B. W. Waugh, "Completing the World's Longest Surveyed Straight Line", *Canadian Geographical Journal* 21 (1940), p. 75.

[23] Campbell, op. cit., p. 137.

[24] Government of Saskatchewan, *Annual Report of the Department of Natural Resources for 1952* (Regina: Queen's Printer, 1953), p. 169.

[25] loc. cit.

[26] Canada, House of Commons, *Debates,* 1964, p. 1481.

[27] *Report . . . [on] . . . the Boundary between . . . Manitoba and Ontario,* op. cit., p. 26.

[28] International Boundary Commission (1925), op. cit., p. 310.

[29] International Boundary Commission (1931), op. cit., p. 218.

[30] *Saskatchewan-Alberta Boundary, Report of Survey to North Terminal Point, 1938* (Ottawa: Department of Mines and Technical Surveys), unpublished manuscript.

[31] King (1934), op. cit., p. 150.

[32] International Boundary Commission (1918), op. cit., p. 187.

[33] *Report . . . [on] the Boundary between . . . Alberta and British Columbia,* op. cit., Part I, p. 13.

[34] Ibid, Part III, p. 94.

[35] International Boundary Commission (1921), op. cit., p. 16.

[36] *Report of the Department of the Interior* (Ottawa: Queen's Printer, 1897), p. xx.

[37] King (1934), op. cit., p. 145.

[38] *Report of the Department of the Interior* (Ottawa: Queen's Printer, 1897), p. xx.

[39] "The International Boundary Commission", *External Affairs* 2 (December 1950), p. 449.

[40] *Report . . . [on] . . . the Boundary between . . . Alberta and British Columbia,* op. cit., Part III, p. 91.

[41] *Report of the Department of the Interior* (Ottawa: Queen's Printer, 1897), p. xix.

[42] International Waterways Commission, *Report Upon the International Boundary Between the Dominion of Canada and the United States through the St. Lawrence River and Great Lakes* (Ottawa: Government Printing Bureau, 1916), p. 27.

[43] F. W. Beatty, "Ontario-Manitoba Boundary", *Annual Report of the Association of Ontario Land Surveyors* (1949), p. 139.

[44] International Boundary Commission (1952), op. cit., p. 32.

[45] Canada, House of Commons, *Journals,* 24 (1880), Appendix I, p. 480.

Notes to Chapter IX

[1] Boggs, op. cit., p. 33.

[2] *Statutes of Manitoba* 18 George V, Cap. 3, 1928.

[3] *Statutes of Canada* 20-21 George V, Cap. 28, 1930.

[4] *Statutes of Alberta* 21 George V, Cap. 6, 1931 and *Statutes of British Columbia* 21 George V, Cap. 8, 1931.

[5] *Statutes of Canada* 22-23 George V, Cap. 5, 1932.

[6] Canada, House of Commons, *Debates* (1954), pp. 1935-1936.

[7] *Statutes of Canada,* 3-4 Elizabeth II, Cap. 24, 1955.

[8] Dated July 8th, 1896.

[9] Canada, House of Commons, *Debates* (1898), col. 6746.

[10] Van Zandt, op. cit., p. 51.

[11] *Boston Christian Science Monitor,* March 7, 1956.

[12] Gaddis Smith, "The Alaska Panhandle at the Paris Peace Conference, 1919", *International Journal,* XVII (1961), p. 29.

[13] Canada, House of Commons, *Debates* (1965), p. 13082.

[14] *Toronto Financial Post,* May 16, 1959.

[15] Ibid, June 13, 1959.

[16] Ibid, April 25, 1959.

[17] Canada, House of Commons, *Debates* (1956), p. 2856.

[18] Ibid, p. 6863.

[19] *Toronto Financial Post,* May 5, 1956 and June 13, 1959.

[20] Canada, House of Commons, *Debates* (1956), p. 2855.

[21] *Vancouver Province,* May 24, 1956.

[22] Canada, House of Commons, *Debates* (1964), p. 9130.

[23] Ibid, p. 2046 and 10290.

[24] Ibid, 1965, p. 12400.

[25] Ibid, p. 3768.

[26] *London Free Press,* March 27, 1965.

[27] *Proceedings of Northern Ontario Citizens' Planning Conference* (Toronto: Department of Planning and Development, 1950), pp. 17 and 21.

[28] *The Case for a New Canadian Province. The Province of Northern Ontario* (Fort William: The New Province League, 1950), p. 5. See also *Ottawa Evening Journal,* November 9, 1950.

[29] *London Free Press,* August 22, 1966.

[30] *London Free Press,* August 28, 1967.

[31] *London Free Press,* 1967.

[32] *Toronto Financial Post,* November 14, 1953.

[33] *Calgary Herald,* op. cit.

[34] Canada, House of Commons, *Debates* (1905), cols. 7068-9.

[35] *Winnipeg Free Press,* December 22, 1952.

[36] *Vancouver Province,* April 27, 1956.

[37] *Winnipeg Free Press,* July 20, 1959.

[38] *Edmonton Journal,* May 18, 1960.

[39] Canada, Senate, *Debates* (1953), p. 162.

[40] Ibid, 1958, p. 85.

[41] Canada, House of Commons, *Debates* (1938), cols. 3074-5.

[42] C. A. Dawson (Ed.), *The New Northwest* (Toronto: University of Toronto Press, 1947), p. 33.

[43] *Edmonton Journal,* September 18, 1959.

[44] H. Trevor Lloyd, "The geography and administration of Northern Canada" (D.Sc. dissertation, University of Bristol, 1949).

[45] Canada, Government of, *Sessional Papers of Canada* (1907), No. 178a, p. 1.

[46] *Report of the Royal Commission on the Reconveyance of Land to British Columbia* (Ottawa: King's Printer, 1928), p. 24.

[47] Ibid, p. 27.

[48] Council of the Northwest Territories, *Votes and Proceedings,* July 1961, p. 68.

[49] Canada, House of Commons, *Debates* (1911-12), col. 4340.

[50] Council of the Northwest Territories, *Votes and Proceedings,* July 1961, p. 69.

[51] N. L. Nicholson, "The Further Partition of the Northwest Territories of Canada", in *Essays in Political Geography,* ed. Charles A. Fisher (London: Methuen, 1968), p. 316.

[52] Council of the Northwest Territories, *Votes and Proceedings,* January 1961, pp. 74-76.

[53] Ibid, July 1961, p. 69.

[54] Ibid, January 1962, p. 36.

[55] Canada, House of Commons, *Bill C83,* 12 Elizabeth II, 1963.

[56] Canada, House of Commons, *Bill C84,* 12 Elizabeth II, 1963.

[57] *Report of the Advisory Commission on the Development of Government in the Northwest Territories* (Ottawa: Queen's Printer, 1966), Vol. I, pp. 143-152.

[58] *London Free Press,* May 14, 1977.

[59] George T. Renner, "The Statistical Approach to Regions", *Annals of the Association of American Geographers* XXV (1935), p. 137.

[60] Reginald G. Trotter, "The Canadian Back Fence in Anglo-American Relations", *Queen's Quarterly* 40 (1933), p. 385.

[61] V. D. Lipman, *Local Government Areas, 1834-1945* (Oxford: Blackwell, 1949), p. 404.

[62] N. L. Nicholson, "Economic Regions of Canada", *Canada Year Book 1962* (Ottawa: Queen's Printer, 1962), pp. 17-23.

[63] C. L. White and E. J. Foscue, *Regional Geography of Anglo-America* (New York: Prentice-Hall, 1953), p. 38.

[64] *Winnipeg Free Press,* October 30, 1953.

[65] *Toronto Financial Post,* November 14, 1953.

[66] Canada, Senate, *Debates* (1953), p. 162.

[67] Lipman, op. cit., p. 405.

[68] *Regional Factors in National Planning* (Washington: National Resources Committee, 1935).

[69] *London Free Press*, March 27, 1964.

[70] *London Free Press*, February 14, 1977.

[71] *Toronto Globe and Mail*, May 17, 1977.

[72] *A Survey of Saskatchewan Government Activity, 1944-47* (Regina: Bureau of Publications, 1948), p. 35.

[73] Government of Saskatchewan, *Annual Report of the Department of Natural Resources and Industrial Development for 1949* (Regina: Bureau of Publications, 1949), pp. 153-155.

[74] John Robarts, Remarks at the Niagara Grape and Wine Festival, St. Catharines, Ontario, 17 September 1965. (Mimeographed.)

Notes to Chapter X

[1] Stephen B. Jones, "Boundary Concepts in the Setting of Place and Time", *Annals of the Association of American Geographers* (1959), 49, p. 241.

[2] Albert Perry Brigham, "Principles in the Determination of Boundaries", *Geographical Review* (1919), 7, p. 201.

[3] Jones (1945), op. cit., p. 57.

[4] Ladis K. D. Kristof, "The Nature of Frontiers and Boundaries", *Annals of the Association of American Geographers* (1959), 49, p. 270.

[5] The problems of demarcating this boundary are extensively dealt with in Dorion, op. cit.

[6] A. E. Moodie, *Geography Behind Politics* (London: Hutchison, 1947), p. 74.

[7] W. M. Day, "The relative permanence of former boundaries in India", *Scottish Geographical Magazine* (1949), 65, pp. 113-122.

[8] Boggs, op. cit., p. 25.

[9] Richard Hartshorne, "Suggestions on the Terminology of Political Boundaries", *Annals of the Association of American Geographers* (1936), 26, pp. 56-7.

[10] N. L. Nicholson, "Boundary Adjustments in the Gulf of St. Lawrence Region", *The Newfoundland Quarterly* (1954), LIII, pp. 13-17.

[11] Philip Smith, *Brinco The Story of Churchill Falls* (Toronto: McClelland and Stewart, 1975), p. 223.

[12] *Canada Month* (1964), 4, 12, p. 25.

SELECTED BIBLIOGRAPHY

Alberta Statutes, 21 George V, Cap. 6, 1931.

Baker, J. N. L. *A History of Geographical Discovery and Exploration.* London: George G. Harrap, 1931.

Bancroft, Hubert H. *History of British Columbia.* San Francisco: 1887.

Beatty, F. W. "Ontario-Manitoba Boundary". *Annual Report of the Association of Ontario Land Surveyors* 64 (1949): 138-139.

Begg, Alexander. *Statement of Facts Regarding the Alaska Boundary Question, Compiled for the Government of British Columbia.* Victoria: King's Printer, 1902.

Bemis, Samuel Flagg. "Jay's Treaty and the North-West Boundary Gap." *American Historical Review,* 27 (April 1922): 465-484.

Beriault, Yvon. *Les Problèmes politiques du Nord Canadien.* Ottawa: Université d'Ottawa, 1942.

Bernier, J. E. *Report on the Dominion Government Expedition to the Arctic Islands and the Hudson Strait on board the C.G.S. "Arctic" 1906-07.* Ottawa: King's Printer, 1909.

————. *Report on the Dominion of Canada Government Expedition to the Arctic Islands and Hudson Strait on board the C.G.S. "Arctic" in 1908-1909.* Ottawa: King's Printer, 1910.

Boggs, S. W. "Boundary Functions and the Principles of Boundary-Making". *Annals of the Association of American Geographers* 22 (March 1932): 48-9.

————. "Problems of Water-Boundary Definition: Median Lines and International Boundaries through Territorial Waters". *Geographical Review* 27 (July 1937): 445-47.

————. *International Boundaries. A Study of Boundary Functions and Problems.* New York: Columbia University Press, 1940.

Bourinot, Sir John G. *Builders of Nova Scotia.* Toronto: Copp-Clark, 1900.

Brigham, Albert Perry. "Principles in the Determination of Boundaries". *Geographical Review* 7 (April 1919): 201-219.

British Columbia, Government of. *Report of the Deputy Minister of Lands, Surveys, and Water Rights Branches for 1948.* Victoria: King's Printer, 1949.

British Columbia Statutes, 21 George V, Cap. 8, 1931.

Brown, Richard. *A History of the Island of Cape Breton.* London: 1869.

Burpee, Lawrence, ed. *An Historical Atlas of Canada.* London: Thomas Nelson, 1927.

Calgary Herald. 12 December 1900; 21 March 1901; 16 January 1905; 7, 13, 18, 21, 23 February 1905.

Canada, Government of. *Report of the Advisory Commission on the Development of Government in the Northwest Territories.* Ottawa: Queen's Printer, 1966.

————. *Report of the Commission Appointed to Delimit the Boundary Between the Provinces of Alberta and British Columbia, 1913-16.* Parts I, II, and III. Ottawa: Surveyor General, 1917.

————. *Report of the Commissioners Appointed to Delimit the Boundary Between the Provinces of Manitoba and Ontario from the Winnipeg River Northerly.* Ottawa: Topographical Survey, 1925.

————. *Report of the Department of the Interior.* Ottawa: King's Printer, 1877, 1880, 1881, 1884, 1886, 1887, 1888, 1891, 1897.

————. *Report of the Department of Marine and Fisheries.* Ottawa: Maclean, Roger, 1885, Appendix 30.

————. *Report of the Expedition to Hudson Bay and Cumberland Gulf.* Ottawa: Department of Marine and Fisheries, 1898.

Canada, House of Commons. *Debates.* 1881, 1883, 1892, 1898, 1905, 1906-07, 1907-08, 1911-12, 1925, 1938, 1953, 1954, 1954, 1957, 1964, 1965.

Canada, House of Commons. *Bill C 83,* 12 Elizabeth II, 1963.

————. *Bill C 84,* 12 Elizabeth II, 1963.

Canada, House of Commons. *Journals,* 24 (1880): Appendix 1.

Canada, Parliament of. *Sessional Papers.* 1886 (11c), 1887 (15), 1905 (97, 102), 1906-07 (64a), 1907 (178a), 1912 (94, 110a).

Canada, Senate, *Debates.* 1898, 1906-07, 1953.

Canada, Statutes, 14-15 Victoria, Cap. 5, 1851.

————.   16 Victoria, Cap. 152, 1853.

————.   33 Victoria, Cap. 3, 1870.

————.   39 Victoria, Cap. 21, 1876.

————.   40 Victoria, Cap. 6, 1877.

————.   61 Victoria, Cap. 3, 1898.

————.   4 Edward VII, Cap. 13, 1904.

————.   4-5 Edward VII, Cap. 3, 1905.

————.   4-5 Edward VII, Cap. 42, 1905.

————.   2 George V, Cap. 32, 1912.

————.   2 George V, Cap. 40, 1912.

_____. 2 George V, Cap. 45, 1912.

_____. 20-21 George V, Cap. 28, 1930.

_____. 22-23 George V, Cap. 5, 1932.

_____. 1-2 Elizabeth II, Cap. 15, 1952-53.

_____. 1-2 Elizabeth II, Cap. 53, 1952-53.

_____. 3-4 Elizabeth II, Cap. 24, 1955.

_____. 7 Elizabeth II, Cap. 37, 1958.

_____. 13 Elizabeth II, Cap. 22, 1964.

Canada Month, 4 (December 1964): 25.

"Canada's Sovereignty in the Arctic". *Royal Canadian Mounted Police Quarterly* (1945): 273-74.

Christian Science Monitor (Boston). 22 January 1951; 7 March 1956.

Correspondence Respecting the Alaska Boundary Together with the Award of the Alaska Boundary Tribunal. Ottawa: King's Printer, 1904.

Cousineau, W. "Historique de la Seigneurie de Treadwell." M.A. thesis, Université d'Ottawa, 1943.

Dagenais, Pierre. "Petits Conflits d'une Grande Frontière". *Revue Canadienne de Géographie* 2 (Mars 1948): 3-8.

Davis, John W. "The Unguarded Boundary". *Geographical Review* 12 (October 1922): 585-601.

Dawson, Samuel Edward. "Line of Demarcation of Pope Alexander VI in A.D. 1493". *Proceedings and Transactions of Royal Society of Canada* Second Series Vol. V, Section II (1899): 467.

Dennis, J. S. "A Short History of the Surveys Performed Under the Dominion Lands System 1869 to 1889." *Annual Report of the Department of the Interior for 1891,* Part VI. Ottawa: King's Printer, 1891.

Dorion, Henri. *La Frontière Québec-Terreneuve*. Quebec: Les Presses de l'Université Laval, 1963.

Doughty, A. G. and McArthur, Duncan A. eds. *Documents relating to the Constitutional History of Canada, 1791-1818*. Ottawa: King's Printer, 1914.

Doughty, Arthur G. and Story, Norah eds. *Documents relating to the Constitutional History of Canada, 1819-1828*. Ottawa: King's Printer, 1935.

Edmonton Journal. 18 September 1959; 18 May 1960.

Elton, D. K. ed. *Proceedings of One Prairie Province? A Question for Canada*. Lethbridge: Lethbridge Herald, 1970.

Fremlin, Gerald ed. *The National Atlas of Canada*. Toronto: Macmillan, 1974.

Fullerton, Douglas H. *The Capital of Canada: How Should it be Governed?* Ottawa: Information Canada, 1974.

Ganong, W. F. "A Monograph on the Evolution of the Boundaries of New Brunswick". *Proceedings and Transactions of the Royal Society of Canada* Second Series, Volume VII, Section II (1901): 139-449.

Gardner, Gérard. "La Frontière Canada-Labrador". *Revue Trimestrielle Canadienne* (Septembre 1938): 1-18.

————. "Nouvelles provinces ou rectifications de frontières." *L'Actualité Economique* (Avril-Juin 1959): 137-143.

Gilroy, Marion. "The Partition of Nova Scotia, 1784". *Canadian Historical Review* 14 (December 1933): 375-391.

Great Britain, Government of. *Alaska Boundary Tribunal. Protocols, Oral Arguments, with Index, Award of the Tribunal, and Opinions of Its Members, September 3 to October 20, 1903*. London: The Foreign Office, 1903.

————. *Appendix to the Counter Base of His Majesty's Government before the Alaska Boundary Tribunal*. London: The Foreign Office, 1903.

————. *Boundary between the Dominion of Canada and the Territory of Alaska. Argument presented on the part of the Government of His Britannic Majesty to the Tribunal Constituted under Article 1 of the Convention signed at Washington, January 24, 1903 between his Britannic Majesty and the United States of America*. London: The Foreign Office, 1903.

————. *Boundary between the Dominion of Canada and the Territory of Alaska. Case presented on the part of the Government of His Britannic Majesty to the Tribunal Constituted under Article 1 of the Convention signed at Washington, January 24, 1903 between his Britannic Majesty and the United States of America*. London: The Foreign Office, 1903.

————. *Correspondence Relating to the Boundary Between the British Possessions in North America and the United States of America under the Treaty of 1783*. London: J. Harrison and Son, 1838-42.

————. *Further Papers Relative to the Exploration by the Expedition under Captain Palliser*. London: Eyre and Spottiswoode, 1860.

————. *Papers relative to the Settlement of the Disputed Boundaries between the Provinces of Canada and New Brunswick*. London: William Clowes, 1851.

————. *Statement of the Evidence Submitted on behalf of His Majesty . . . in Reference to the Boundary between the Province of New Brunswick, in the Dominion of*

Canada, and the State of Maine, one of the United States of America . . . etc. delivered December 4th, 1908. London: The Foreign Office.

————. *The Journals . . . relative to the exploration by Captain Palliser . . . during the years 1857, 1858, 1859 and 1860.* London: Eyre and Spottiswoode, 1863.

Great Britain, Privy Council. *In the Matter of the Boundary Between the Dominion of Canada and the Colony of Newfoundland in the Labrador Peninsula.* 12 vols. London: William Clowes, 1927.

————. *In the Matter of the Boundary Between the Provinces of Ontario and Manitoba, in the Dominion of Canada. Joint Appendix of Documents.* Toronto: Queen's Printer, 1884.

Great Britain, Statutes, 14-15 Victoria, 1851.

————. 52-53 Victoria, 1889.

————. 58-59 Victoria, Cap. 34, 1895.

Gushue, Raymond. "The Territorial Waters of Newfoundland". *Canadian Journal of Economics and Political Science* 15 (August 1949): 344-52.

Halifax Chronicle Herald. 29 June 1957; 21 October 1958.

Hartshorne, R. "Suggestions on the Terminology of Political Boundaries". *Annals of the Association of American Geographers* 26 (March 1936): 56-57.

Hinks, Arthur R. "Notes on the Technique of Boundary Delimitation". *Geographical Journal* 58 (December 1921): 417.

Hitsman, J. Mackay. "Capture of Saint Pierre-et-Miquelon 1793". *Canadian Army Journal* (July 1959): 77-81.

Holdich, T. H. "Geographical Problems in Boundary Making". *Geographical Journal* 47 (June 1916): 421-440.

Howay, F. W., Sage, W. N., and Angus, H. F. *British Columbia and the United States.* Toronto: Ryerson, 1942.

Hudson's Bay Company. A Brief History. London: Hudson's Bay Company, 1934.

Innis, H. A. and Lower, A. R. M. *Select Documents in Canadian Economic History, 1783-1885.* Toronto: University of Toronto Press, 1933.

International Boundary Commission. *Joint Report upon the Survey and Demarcation of the International Boundary between the United States and Canada along the 141st Meridian from the Arctic Decan to Mount St. Elias.* Washington: Government Printing Office, 1918.

————. *Joint Report upon the Survey and Demarcation of the Boundary Between the United States and Canada from the Western Terminus of the Land Boundary along the Forty-Ninth Parallel, on the West Side of Point Roberts, through Georgia, Haro and Juan de Fuca Straits, to the Pacific Ocean.* Washington: Government Printing Office, 1921.

————. *Joint Report Upon the Survey and Demarcation of the Boundary Between the United States and Canada from the Source of the St. Croix River and the St. Lawrence River.* Washington: Government Printing Office, 1925.

————. *Joint Report Upon the Survey and Demarcation of the Boundary Between the United States and Canada from the Northwesternmost Point of Lake of the Woods to Lake Superior.* Washington: Government Printing Office, 1931.

————. *Joint Report upon the Survey and Demarcation of the Boundary between the United States and Canada from the Source of the St. Croix River to the Atlantic Ocean.* Washington: Government Printing Office, 1934.

————. *Joint Report Upon the Survey and Demarcation of the Boundary Between the United States and Canada from the Gulf of Georgia to the Northwesternmost Point of Lake of the Woods.* Washington: Government Printing Office, 1937.

————. *Joint Report Upon the Survey and Demarcation of the Boundary Between Canada and the United States from Tongass Passage to Mount St. Elias.* Ottawa: Queen's Printer, 1952.

International Waterways Commission. *Report of the International Waterways Commission Upon the International Boundary Between the Dominion of Canada and the United States through the St. Lawrence River and Great Lakes.* Ottawa: Government Printing Bureau, 1916.

Ireland, Willard E. "The Evolution of the Boundaries of British Columbia". *British Columbia Historical Quarterly* 3 (October 1939): 263-282.

Johnston, W. K. "Canada's Title to the Arctic Islands." *Canadian Historical Review* 14 (March 1933): 22-41.

Jones, Stephen B. "The Cordilleran Section of the Canada-United States Borderland". *Geographical Journal* 89 (May 1937): 439-50.

————. "The Description of International Boundaries". *Annals of the Association of American Geographers* 33 (April 1943): 99-117.

————. "The Forty-Ninth Parallel in the Great Plains". *Journal of Geography* 31 (December 1932): 357-67.

————. *Boundary Making, A Handbook for Statesmen,*

Treaty Editors and Boundary Commissioners. Washington: Carnegie Endowment for International Peace, 1945.

————. "Boundary Concepts in the Setting of Place and Time." *Annals of the Association of American Geographers* 49 (September 1959): 241-255.

Keenleyside, H. L. *Canada and the United States.* New York: Alfred A. Knopf, 1929.

Kennedy, W. P. M. ed. *Documents of the Canadian Constitution 1759-1915.* Toronto: Oxford University Press, 1918.

King, Shirley. "The Ontario-Quebec Boundary: Lake Temiskaming to James Bay". *Annual Report of the Association of Ontario Land Surveyors* (1934): 143-155.

King, W. F. *Report Upon the Title of Canada to the Islands North of the Mainland of Canada.* Ottawa: Government Printing Bureau, 1905.

Klotz, Otto. *Boundaries of Canada.* Waterloo: Waterloo Historical Society, 1914.

————. "The History of the Forty-Ninth Parallel Survey West of the Rocky Mountains". *Geographical Review* 3 (May 1917): 382-87.

Knight, David B. *A Capital for Canada: Conflict and Compromise in the Nineteenth Century.* Chicago: The University of Chicago, Department of Geography, Research Paper No. 182, 1977.

————. *Choosing Canada's Capital.* Toronto: McClelland and Stewart, Carleton Library No. 105, 1977.

Kristof, Ladis K. "The Nature of Frontiers and Boundaries". *Annals of the Association of American Geographers* 49 (September 1959): 269-282.

Lajeunesse, E. J. *The Windsor Border Region.* Toronto: Champlain Society, 1960.

Laxdal, Jon K. "New Iceland, 1875-1950". *The Icelandic Canadian* 9 (Autumn 1950): 17-20, 45-50.

Lingard, C. C. *Territorial Government in Canada, The Autonomy Question in the Old North-West Territories.* Toronto: University of Toronto Press, 1946.

Lloyd, H. Trevor. "The Geography and Administration of Northern Canada." D.Sc. dissertation, University of Bristol, 1949.

Logan, R. M. *Canada, the United States, and the Third Law of the Sea Conference.* Montreal: C. D. Howe Research Institute, 1974.

London Free Press. 27 March 1964; 27 March 1965, 22 August 1966; 28 August 1967; 14 February 1977; 14 May 1977.

Low, A. P. *Report on the Dominion Government Expedition to Hudson Bay and the Arctic Islands on Board the D.G.S. "Neptune" 1903-04.* Ottawa: Government Printing Bureau, 1906.

Lucas, C. P. *Historical Geography of the British Colonies, Volume V, Canada—Part I Historical.* Oxford: Clarendon Press, 1911.

Mackay, R. A. ed. *Newfoundland—Economic, Diplomatic and Strategic Studies.* Toronto: Oxford University Press, 1946.

Mackintosh, W. A. *Prairie Settlement: The Geographical Setting.* Toronto: The Macmillan Co. of Canada, 1938.

Macleod Gazette. 10 January 1902.

MacPhail, Andrew. "The History of Prince Edward Island". *Canada and Its Provinces,* Vol. XIII. Toronto: The Publishers Association, 1913: 305-375.

Manitoba Statutes, 18 George V, Cap. 3, 1928.

Martin, Archer. *The Hudson's Bay Company's Land Tenures and the Occupation of Assiniboia by Lord Selkirk's Settlers.* London: William Clowes, 1898.

Mayo, Lawrence Shaw. "The Forty-Fifth Parallel: A Detail of the Unguarded Boundary." *Geographical Review* 13 (1923): 255-265.

Medicine Hat Times. 17 February 1905.

Merk, F. "Oregon Pioneers and the Boundary." *American Historical Review* 29 (1924).

————. "British Party Politics and Oregon." *American Historical Review* 37 (1932).

Mills, David. *A Report on the Boundaries of Ontario.* Toronto: Hunter, Rose and Co., 1873.

————. *The Canadian View of the Alaskan Boundary Dispute.* Ottawa: Government Printing Bureau, 1899.

Millward, A. E. *Southern Baffin Island.* Ottawa: King's Printer, 1930.

Milton, Viscount. *A History of the San Juan Water Boundary Question.* London: Cassell, Petter and Calpin, 1869.

Minghi, Julian V. "Point Roberts, Washington: The Problem of an American exclave." *Yearbook of the Association of Pacific Coast Geographers* (1962): 24.

————. "Teaching Political Geography." *The Journal of Geography* 65 (November 1966): 362-370.

Montreal La Presse. 23 December 1949.

Morton, A. S. and Martin, Chester. *History of Prairie Settlement and Dominion Lands Policy.* Toronto: Macmillan, 1936.

Nicholson, N. L. "Some Aspects of the Political Geography

of Keewatin." *The Canadian Geographer* 1 (Autumn 1953): 73-84.

_____. "Boundary Adjustments in the Gulf of St. Lawrence Region." *The Newfoundland Quarterly* 53 (1954): 13-17.

_____., ed. *Atlas of Canada 1957*. Ottawa: Queen's Printer, 1958.

_____. "The Further Partition of the Northwest Territories of Canada." In *Essays in Political Geography*, pp. 311-324. Edited by Charles A. Fisher. London: Methuen, 1968.

_____. "The Meaning of our Provincial Boundaries and the 'New Regionalism'." *The Quarterly of Canadian Studies* 1 (Autumn 1971): 67-73.

_____. "The Confederation of Canada". In *The Changing World,* pp. 312-329. Edited by W. Gordon East and A. E. Moodie. New York: World Book Company, 1956.

Northern Ontario Citizen's Planning Conference. *Proceedings.* Toronto: Department of Planning and Development, 1950.

Northern Ontario Heritage Party. North Bay: New Province Committee for Northern Ontario, 1973 (mimeo).

Northwest Territories Council. *Votes and Proceedings*. January 1961, July 1961, January 1962.

Ontario, Government of. *Statutes, Documents and Papers bearing on the Discussion respecting the Northern and Western Boundaries of the Province of Ontario etc.* Toronto: Hunter, Rose and Co., 1878.

_____. *North Western Ontario: Its Boundaries, Resources and Communications.* Toronto: Hunter, Rose and Co., 1879.

_____. *Correspondence, Papers and Documents of Dates from 1856 to 1882 Inclusive, Relating to the Northerly and Westerly Boundaries of the Province of Ontario.* Toronto: C. Blackett Robinson, 1882.

Ontario Statutes, 26 Eliz. II, 1977.

Ottawa Journal. 6 March 1963.

Patterson, G. "Sir William Alexander and the Scottish attempt to colonize Acadia." *Proceedings and Transactions of the Royal Society of Canada* Second Series, Volume X, Section II (1892): 79-107.

Paullin, C. O. "The Early Choice of the 49th Parallel as a Boundary Line". *Canadian Historical Review* 4 (July 1923): 127-31.

Penlington, Norman. *The Alaska Boundary Dispute: A Critical Reappraisal.* Toronto: McGraw-Hill Ryerson, 1972.

Pierce, John G. "On to the Bay." *Annual Report of the Association of Ontario Land Surveyors* (1949): 129-137.

Prescott, J. V. R. *The Geography of Frontiers and Boundaries*. Chicago: Aldine, 1965.

————. *The Evolution of Nigeria's International and Regional Boundaries: 1861-1971*. Vancouver: Tantalus Research, 1971.

Pritchett, J. P. *The Red River Valley 1811-1849*. Toronto: Ryerson, 1942.

Quebec Le Soleil. 2 February 1962.

Rapport de la Commission d'étude sur l'integrité du territoire du Québec. By Henri Dorion, Chairman. Quebec: Government Printer, 1968.

Regina Leader. 14 December 1904.

Renner, George T. "The Statistical Approach to Regions." *Annals of the Association of American Geographers* 25 (1935).

Report of the Royal Commission on Reconveyance of Land to British Columbia. By William Melville Martin, Commissioner. Ottawa: King's Printer, 1928.

Robinson, J. Lewis. *Resources of the Canadian Shield*. Toronto: Methuen, 1969.

Robinson, Percy J. "Yonge Street and the North West Company." *Canadian Historical Review* 24 (1943), 255.

Rogers, J. D. *A Historical Geography of the British Colonies, Vol. V, Canada, Part III Geographical*. Oxford: Clarendon Press, 1911.

Saskatchewan, Government of. *A Survey of Saskatchewan Government Activity, 1944-47*. Regina: Bureau of Publications, 1948.

————. *Annual Report of the Department of Natural Resources and Industrial Development*. Regina: Bureau of Publications, 1949.

————. *Annual Report of the Department of Natural Resources*. Regina: Queen's Printer, 1953.

Savelle, Max. *The Diplomatic History of the Canadian Boundary 1749-1763*. Toronto: Ryerson, 1940.

Semple, Ellen C. *Influences of Geographic Environment*. New York: Holt, 1911.

Shortt, A. and Doughty, A. G. eds. *Documents relating to the Constitutional History of Canada, 1759-1791*. Ottawa: King's Printer, 1907.

Smedal, Gustav. *Acquisition of Sovereignty Over Polar Areas*. Oslo: Dybwad, 1931.

Smith, Gaddis. "The Alaska Panhandle at the Paris Peace Conference, 1919." *International Journal* 17 (1961): 29.

Smith, Philip. *Brinco The Story of Churchill Falls*. Toronto: McClelland and Stewart, 1975.

Speck, F. G. *Family Hunting Territories and Social Life of Various Algonkian Bands of the Ottawa Valley*. Ottawa: King's Printer, 1915.

Stewart, N. C. "British Columbia Provincial Boundaries." *The Canadian Surveyor* 12 (April 1954): 75-96.

Sverdrup, Otto. *New Land*. London: Longmans, Green, 1904.

Taylor, Andrew. *Geographical Discovery and Exploration in the Queen Elizabeth Islands*. Ottawa: Queen's Printer, 1955.

Toronto Daily Star. 14 October 1953.

Toronto Financial Post. 14 November 1953; 18 June 1955; 5 May 1956; 25 April 1959; 16 May 1959; 13 June 1959; September 1965.

Toronto Globe and Mail. 17 August 1956; 14 April 1964; 2 September 1966; 18 September 1969; 10 March 1976; 17 May 1977.

Trotter, Reginald G. "The Canadian Back Fence in Anglo-American Relations." *Queens Quarterly* 40 (August 1933): 383-397.

Van Zandt, Franklin K. *Boundaries of the United States and the Several States*. Washington: United States Government Printing Office, 1966.

Vancouver Province. 27 April 1956; 24 May 1956; 4 August 1956.

Vancouver Sun. 11 January 1962.

Waugh, B. W. "Completing the world's longest surveyed straight line". *Canadian Geographical Journal* 21 (August 1940): 75-88.

White, J. "Boundary Disputes and Treaties". *Canada and Its Provinces,* Vol. VIII, Part III. Toronto: The Publishers Association, 1913.

Whitelaw, W. M. *The Maritimes and Canada before Confederation*. Toronto: Oxford University Press, 1934.

Winnipeg Free Press. 7 November 1951; 22 December 1952; 30 October 1953; 20 July 1959.

Wormwith, N. B. "The Fishery Arbitrations". *Canada and Its Provinces,* Vol. VIII, Part III. Toronto: The Publishers' Association, 1913.

INDEX

DATE DUE

CLEM MAHARAJ

THE DISPOSSESSED

HEINEMANN

Heinemann International Literature and Textbooks
A division of Heinemann Educational Books Ltd
Halley Court, Jordan Hill, Oxford OX2 8EJ

Heinemann Educational Books Inc
361 Hanover Street, Portsmouth, New Hampshire, 03801, USA

Heinemann Educational Books (Nigeria) Ltd
PMB 5205, Ibadan
Heinemann Educational Boleswa
PO Box 10103, Village Post Office, Gaborone, Botswana

LONDON   EDINBURGH   PARIS   MADRID
ATHENS   BOLOGNA   MELBOURNE
SYDNEY   AUCKLAND   SINGAPORE   TOKYO

© Clem Maharaj 1992

First published by Heinemann International Literature
and Textbooks in 1992

Series Editor: Adewale Maja-Pearce

British Library Cataloguing in Publication Data
A catalogue record for this book is available from the British Library.

ISBN 0435 989286

Phototypeset by Wilmaset Ltd, Birkenhead, Wirral
Printed and bound in Great Britain by
Cox & Wyman Ltd, Reading, Berkshire

92 93 94 95 10 9 8 7 6 5 4 3 2 1

Contents

For Shafika and Jan

1 The working man

'Hey, boy, go an get anodder bag ah oats. Dis one nah be enough.' Sankar, who was assisting his overseer, Mr Rooplal, to feed the animals, handed him his nearly empty sack and walked a short distance away to the grain storage area to fetch a new one.

The sacks of oats were piled in heaps of six or a dozen and were stored on a low platform in one corner of the pen. In the opposite corner were stacks of hay also placed on a platform above ground level. The animals – horses, mules, bison and oxen – were kept in individual enclosures in this clean, well organised pen. Sankar, along with fourteen other men, looked after them and prepared them for their work, hauling and carrying freshly cut sugar cane to the area near the railway track on the estate.

As he lifted the sack, its sudden removal surprised a huge rat at the back. For an instant, it appeared paralysed. As Sankar hurled the sack back, it jumped forward to avoid being crushed. Sankar shouted, 'All yuh, look! A rat!'

The men rushed over. The rat, seeing feet coming from the direction it was heading, changed course. The men drew the cutlasses from around their waists and approached the frightened rodent with their sharpened blades, aiming to slice off any part they connected with. The rat veered from one direction to another, looking for a chance to escape. Blades sparked and clanged on the concrete floor as they struck at the rat but failed to connect.

The circle was closing in. The swishing of the cutlasses and the cries of the men rose in a crescendo. Sankar flattened his blade and came down with a mighty force, crushing the head of the rat, which squealed the sound of death. The men, gasping from over-excitement and exertion, stared at its dead body.

'Dey getting fatter all de time,' remarked Rooplal. 'Is hard times we living in. When rat get fat, man belly have less. Yuh kill it, so yuh better bury it, boy. We cyah stand here all day looking at it. Back to work. Sam,' he called one of the men. 'Get a bucket ah water an wash away dis blood.'

Sankar plucked up some straw, walked back to the rat, picked it up by its tail, then walked to the door. Blood still dripped as he walked. The men dispersed and resumed working. Sankar walked through the large courtyard where the empty carts were neatly parked in rows. The sun was low in the west, and for a brief moment its brightness blinded him. White clouds formed a blanket covering parts of the blue sky. The cool, late afternoon breeze gently swayed the canes; birds were flitting between the trees along the ravine. Sankar walked towards the muddy east bank of the ravine. He dropped the rat on the high grazing ground, and, with his cutlass, cleared a small patch to dig a hole. He swore at the creature as he dropped it into the hole, for a moment feeling regret encroach into his mood of conquest.

After the burial, he waded into the fast, clear water of the ravine. His feet sank into its soft bed and sent swirls of muddy water to mingle with the clear patches. He bent over to wash his cutlass and stood for a moment bathing his hot bare feet. He stepped back on to the bank and dried his blade, rubbing it on the grass, and slipped it back to his side, between his belt and trousers. He stood looking up at the undulating hills he had to cross on his way home after work.

Mr Rooplal, the short, fat, balding overseer, appeared through the door of the pen and shouted at him.

'Sankar, hurry up, we eh have all day, yuh know, is soon time to go home.'

Sankar returned to the pen and the feeding and checking of the animals in his charge. From his single cubicle of an office, Mr Rooplal kept on urging the men. 'All yuh, hurry up, nah. It getting late.'

One by one, they replied, 'Ah finish, pusher.'

The day was over. Mr Rooplal inspected the pen and animals and, finding nothing more to be done, finally said, 'All yuh could go now; mek sure all yuh reach early in de morning. Ah doh want no blasted white man telling me off on account ah all yuh reaching late.' As the men walked towards the door, Mr Rooplal shook his head in disgust.

'Yuh see what ah mean? The damn watchman eh reach yet. Is ah what have to wait on he all de time.'

Sankar said his goodbyes to the men as they walked to the nearby

2

village. His home, in the opposite direction, was almost three miles away. He looked at them as they walked away. 'Look at dat, eh, boy,' he thought. 'Dem man an dem does stick togedder real close. Yuh wouldn believe we is Indian alike. Dem brute wouldn even call me for a drink after wok, like ah is some kind ah stranger. To dem, ah is still a Highlands man.'

Until a year ago, he had worked in a pen on the adjoining estate. He had started there as soon as he was big enough to carry a sizeable bundle of grass. Last year that estate had fallen into bankruptcy. Reasons were offered throughout his village and surrounding districts as to why Highlands Estate had failed. However, as Sankar and the rest of the workforce knew, reasons were never going to replace the wages necessary for existence. He was among the lucky few who secured jobs on the neighbouring Good Intent Estate. The remainder were left to eke out a living, cutting cane on a daily basis, or any kind of casual work.

Sankar's new workmates were fortunate: their workplace and houses were nearby. They had known each other from childhood, and knew every inch of ground on this estate. Until a year ago it was the same for Sankar. He understood their closeness, but kept his distance as their tight-knit world held no room for outsiders. Sankar's job in the pen meant he had to arrive before the cane cutters and carter men, and was one of the last to leave. Most of the workforce had long returned home.

On leaving the pen, he walked throught the estate storage yard. The cane cut during the day was stacked in large piles waiting to be loaded on to cane trucks. Adjoining this was a newly built estate bungalow for the white overseer and his family. A strongly built wire fence surrounded the yard, patrolled by a huge Doberman that was allowed to run free after the day's work was over and until the next one began. Whenever a person walked near to the fence, this ferocious animal charged, baring its teeth and attempting to hurl itself through the wire to get at them. Sankar, expecting the charge, fixed his strong brown eyes on the beast and, drawing his shining cutlass, stared at the dog without any sign of fear.

He walked on to the track, well kept and gravelled, unlike those of Highlands Estate which had been allowed to deteriorate and were nothing more than a mud and gravel mix with large ruts, making walking on bare feet very uncomfortable.

The setting sun cast its orange glow over the land. The canes swayed in a gentle breeze; birds nestled in the hedges, chirping their evening song. The soft, cool, late afternoon temperature mixed with the silence, creating an atmosphere to relieve the pressures of the gruelling day. Sankar made his way home. Nearing his village, he could hear cries of mothers calling home their wayward children, and chickens being enticed by calls of 'Chick, chick, chick' and a few grains of rice or corn to come home to roost. A wry smile came across his face, for another day's work was over, and his return was safe.

As he walked past the first ramshackle barracks, he was greeted by a now familiar question. 'Any wok going down dey?'

'Notting, boy, notting,' replied Sankar, as he walked on hurriedly. He tried to avoid the follow-up comments – 'Yuh lucky son-of-a-bitch! Look at me, man wid wife an plenty chirren starving an yuh, yuh getting wok.' He ignored the remarks and hurried on to his barracks, adjoining the old bungalow that once housed the chief overseer of Highlands. The four barrack rooms previously housed the servants. Sankar rented one after the closure of the sugar factory. Two ramshackle verandahs ran at the front and back of his bare room. In the yard at the back was a communal latrine and a broken concrete platform to wash clothes and to bathe on. At the front were the makeshift kitchens.

The village was preparing for the night. Nearly every woman and girl was cooking the one hot meal of the day. The men were either collecting their livestock or cutting grass to feed them. Sankar lived alone. He had never remarried after his wife had run away when his second child was born. His two children were looked after by Suraji, who lived a quarter of a mile away. He visited her every day for his meals, and for other comforts he needed. A tall, thin man with a gaunt face, he looked older than he really was. He kept clean and tidy; Suraji saw to that. Apart from a few cooking utensils and some clothes and a wooden bed, he kept nothing else in his room.

He called out to his neighbours to say he was back. Those who were at home answered him. The warmth of their replies was enough to ensure him of their well-being and their acknowledgement of his presence. He opened his door, entered the bare room and sat on his bed. He felt a bit tired and thirsty. He got up, collecting a change of clothing, and went to his kitchen. Eddie, his immediate neighbour on the left, saw him as he came out.

4

'Wha happen, boy? Ah eh see yuh foh days.'

Sankar shook his head and smiled at Eddie. 'Is yuh who never home, since yuh stop wokking, yuh out chasing ooman all de time.'

'Behave yuhself! A big man like yuh! Is wok ah looking foh night an day but ah cyah conneck at all.'

'Just give it a chance, boy, yuh go be lucky. Wok must turn up, yuh cyah starve.'

'Is so yuh say, but if ah doh try an find a little ting to do here an dey, ah go die from starvation. If wasn foh de card-playing, ah done dead arready.'

'Ah going to bathe now,' said Sankar.

'Go on, boy, it have plenty water in de cistern. Ah going to cook,' said Eddie as he walked into his room.

Sankar collected a bucket and went to the cistern under the overseer's house. He carried his clothes and a piece of cloth to dry himself with. He stripped to his underpants on the concrete floor and scooped out the water from the bucket with an old enamel cup and poured it over him. The sunlight on the water running down his wet skin made him look like a golden statue, the water trickling away like spots of crystal as it passed through the grass. Sankar changed and left his room, on his way to visit Suraji and his children. The night was quickly falling; the sun had now descended below the horizon and only a fleeting remainder of the daylight was left. Kerosene lights and flambeaux were being lit and the hustle of the evening was slowing down. As he walked to Suraji, a few mangy dogs were roaming through the yard. Sankar picked up a stone and pelted it at them. They scuttled among the trees and headed for a gap through the long sweet-lime hedge running along the front of the overseer's house.

2 Suraji

'Gal, me is like a paper flower, yuh know, de kind what does look pretty when it new but does fade an get ugly as de year go on,' said Suraji, a thin, short woman with wrinkled skin, her teeth badly stained. Her hair, in spite of her age, remained jet black. The years of working in the sun had left their mark on her skin, black in the exposed areas and brown where it was covered by clothes. Her neighbour, Savitri, several years younger, was sitting on her back steps talking while Suraji was preparing the evening supper for Sankar and his two children, Dano and Sakina.

'Tell me, gal, why yuh does always cook so late? Is years ah seeing yuh but ah never see yuh cook early.'

'Is de wok, and dat man Sankar, he does finish so late.'

'Why yuh does put up wid it? If was me, ah tell yuh, he eat when I cook, none ah dis late business.'

Suraji replied, 'Yuh is not me. De man does wok late, he does wok hard. Is me an dem chirren is all de family he have. If ah cyah do foh he properly, ah eh doing it at all.'

'Ah know what yuh mean, gal, but yuh does wok so hard an all dem extra tings yuh does do.'

Suraji bent over and picked up a well-used piece of water pipe and blew into the fire. The pipe made a sound as the air passed through. The fire sparked and the wood crackled. It was now dark. Crickets made their noise, children still awake were chasing fire flies and an owl hooted from a nearby tree.

'Yuh see dem chirren?' asked Suraji.

'Dey playing wid my chirren in de yard.'

'Play, play, dat is all dem brute does do, play whole day an night. Dano, Sakina,' Suraji shouted at the top of her loud voice.

A boy answered, 'We over here, Mai.'

'All yuh, is time to come inside,' said Suraji.

'We coming just now,' replied the boy.

'Just now, just now? Is now ah want all yuh, just now will never

6

come, an if me catch all yuh outside playing is plenty trouble foh all yuh.' Suraji picked up the piece of pipe and blew again at the fire. The blaze was steady and the light penetrated the darkness. Dano and Sakina came over from next door. Their feet were muddy and faces grimy with bits of dirt and sugar cane.

'Look how nasty all yuh looking,' said Suraji when she saw them. 'All yuh went to school today?'

'Yes, Mai,' replied Sakina. The tattered home dress looked small on her.

'All yuh go an bathe off an put on some clean clothes,' ordered Suraji.

'Ah, Mai, ah clean,' said the tiny Dano.

'All yuh call dat clean?' said Suraji. She picked up the piece of pipe and raised it as though she was going to strike them. They scampered off into the shack. 'An ah doh want to see all yuh again until all yuh nice and clean.' Suraji smiled as the children ran into the shack. She had kept them from shortly after Dano was born. She turned to Savitri.

'Look at dem! Just nine an ten, ah soon go cyah manage dem.'

The younger woman shifted herself on the step and said, 'Ah doh know how yuh so kind, looking after anodder ooman chirren like if is yours.'

'Dem is mine, is me what pull dem out dey modder womb.'

'Yuh pull out plenty odder chirren but dem eh yours.'

'Ah know dat, gal, but Sankar wife leave he, no one was going to give he a hand, so ah had to take dem on.'

The children came out with two rags. Dano was pulling at Sakina's rag. 'Mai, she tek me towel, ah was using dat one all week.'

'Sakina, give back he towel,' ordered Suraji.

'Is me own, dis boy does lie too much.'

'Give it back, is mine,' Dano screamed.

'Here, tek it back, yuh nastiness.' Sakina threw the piece of rag at him, at the same time pulling the other one from his hand.

'All yuh stop dat fighting an get on cleaning all yuhself,' said Suraji.

Sakina went into the open area behind the kitchen, picked up an enamel cup, walked over to the barrel of water and started to dip into it and wash herself. Dano remained near Suraji.

'When dis food going to finish cooking, Mai? Ah hungry.'

'Soon, me chile, soon as yuh fadder come.'

'Mai, he in de rum shop, we cyah wait foh he,' said Dano, his eyes fixed on the pot of curry standing simmering on the fire.

'But look at me crosses, nah! Stop being so mannish an have some respeck foh yuh fadder, he does buy dis food too,' said Suraji. Dano kept silent but his hungry big eyes never left the simmering pot. Sakina was finished; she dried herself and gave Dano the cup, and went back into the shack to change. Sakina was big for her age, fair-skinned and slightly fat. Dano was the opposite in size, but almost the same colour. His hair was short. 'Always picking up lice,' said Suraji, as she cut it once a month.

The children changed and came to the door. Savitri moved over to the side of the step and said, 'All yuh come an sit near me.' Sakina came and sat next to her. Dano remained standing at the door.

'Mai, when Pa going to come?' he asked.

'Ah doh know, chile. Soon. He have to wok early in de morning.' The dogs in the nearby village kept up their incessant barking. In the nearby house, a woman started to sing a lullaby, off-key and substituting 'la la' for the words she forgot. The dogs barked louder as if to protest at the mutilation of the song.

Savitri stood up. 'Ah tink ah better be going now, gal. Why yuh doh give dem chirren dey food? Yuh know wey Sankar is an he eh go leave dey until de shop door shut.'

Suraji looked at her, wanting to say one thing but ending up saying another.

'Ah tink yuh right, gal, is bout time ah give dem dey food.'

'Ah go see yuh tomorrow.' Savitri looked at Suraji, searching for some sign of approbation, needing an assurance of welcome before planning a return the next day. 'Doh worry, Sankar go come soon. Ah better leave now. Ah gone.'

Suraji shook her head and muttered, 'Ah wish ah had time to hang around.' She felt ambiguous about her friendship with Savitri. She came and sat while Suraji prepared dinner nearly every evening. But she left nothing, a shadow with a voice.

Suraji dished out the children's dinner on two chipped enamel plates, handing it to them with two cups of water. Dano sat next to Sakina; they held their plates with one hand and ate with the other, stopping occasionally to have a sip of water. Suraji sat on a low stool near the fire place, the red embers causing her face to glow with the light. She lit a cigarette and took deep puffs. The dogs barked and growled, a sign that someone was walking down the road. Dano stopped eating.

'It look as if Pa coming,' he said, his huge eyes lighting with hope. The person walked on as the dogs lower down the track were heard growling. Dano took a huge handful of food, stuffing it in his mouth. Suraji puffed on her cigarette and stubbed it on the bare earth of the kitchen, placing the half-smoked butt in her pocket for later on. Dano finished his supper, got up from the step and went to the barrel of water to wash his hands, face and then his plate which he placed on the shelf in the kitchen.

'It eh good to eat so fast, boy,' said Suraji, 'it go mek yuh have belly ache.' The dogs began to growl and bark. Dano rushed inside and ran to the front door, thinking, 'Dis time it must be Pa,' as he opened it.

'Pa!' he shouted.

Sankar entered. Sakina dropped her plate and got up to meet her father. Suraji called her back.

'Come here, gal,' she ordered. 'Wash yuh plate an yuh face.'

Sakina ignored her and rushed to greet her father.

'Pa, why yuh tek so long to come?' she asked as she ran to him. Sankar stopped and lifted each of them in his arms, side by side. He kissed them and quickly put them down and walked through the shack towards the kitchen. Suraji was standing at the foot of the stairs, waiting to be greeted. Sankar stood with a smile and asked, 'How yuh is, gal?'

Suraji answered, 'Ah dey, man, tings just de same. Yuh hungry?'

'Yes, ah ready foh food.'

'Sakina, go an wash yuh plate an cup,' said Suraji. 'Yuh fadder ready to eat.'

Sakina left Sankar's side, picked up her cup and plate from the stair and went to wash it. Sankar sat on the stair; Dano climbed on his back.

'Get off, boy, ah too tired an hungry to play.' Dano jumped off and sat on the floor behind Sankar. He wanted to stay close to his father whom he had not seen since the day before. Sakina brought her plate and handed it to Suraji, who began to dish out Sankar's supper.

'Go an get a cup ah water an give it to yuh fadder.'

Sakina ran to the barrel and brought the water. Sankar took it from her, got up and stepped out in the open and washed his hands with it. He then refilled it and returned to the stair and was handed his supper. Suraji sat down on her little stool and ate hers. Sakina looked at her father, wanting to say a lot but saying nothing. She stood against a pole in the open kitchen and stared at him.

Sankar ate in silence. His fingers moved quickly across the plate, scooping little clumps of roti and curry into his mouth. It was just after eight, and quite dark. The watchman guarding the disused factory rang the bell. His ringing every hour was heard throughout the village, from six at night to six next morning. He had to be heard on guard. Sankar stopped eating as the bell rang.

'Harry feeling strong tonight. Hear how hard he mekking dat bell sound.'

It was a clear night; the stars were high in the sky. In the distance, voices were heard. 'Bodhan and he wife fighting again,' said Sankar.

'Ah doh know why dat man does drink so much. Is right foh he wife to mek quarrel wid he,' said Suraji. 'He cyah tek he drink, dat is de trouble. A petit quart of puncheon rum an he drunk.' Dano laughed. 'All yuh chirren go inside, all yuh doh see big people talking? Who ask all yuh to interfere?' said Suraji.

'Leave dem alone, dey cyah help it if dey jus laughing at two jackass quarrelling so loud as to wake de dead.'

'Yuh does spoil dese chirren. Dey getting outta hand. Sometimes ah cyah manage dem.'

'Dem is jus chirren, and besides, leave dem alone.'

Suraji stopped eating, got up and took her plate into the dark yard. She threw the rest of her meal on the ground and washed her plate. She remained silent, standing near the post in the kitchen, staring at Sankar. Sankar looked up and caught the fierce gaze of her eyes. In the dim light of the lamp, he felt and saw the hostility of the look.

'Ah doh want we quarrel, gal, all ah want is to remain in peace.'

'Whole day yuh does have peace, yuh have any idea what ah have to put up wid?'

'Mind yuhself, gal, watch how yuh talking to me, now shut up an leh me finish eating.'

Suraji fumbled in her dress pocket, searching for the cigarette butt she had put there earlier. She found it and went to the fire, and lit the butt on an ember. She took a deep puff to stifle the feeling of dissatisfaction inside her. It had been gnawing away all day and still

10

she could not identify what was the problem. Sankar was not the bone of contention. He was being made to be the scapegoat. He had finished his supper and handed the plate and cup to Suraji. She leaned back on the step and called the children. They came at once.

'All yuh been to school today?' he asked.

'Yes, Pa,' they answered simultaneously.

'An what all yuh learn?'

'We read from de book,' answered Sakina, 'but we cyah understand it.'

'Ask de teacher, he go show you,' said Sankar.

'Ah does always ask him but he does hardly talk to me.'

'Ah know, me gal, is only because yuh have to send chirren to school ah does send all yuh, odderwise de school police, Mr Mitchell, go get me into trouble. When ah was all yuh age, ah did start wokking, it didn't have no school police den.'

Dano laughed. 'Ah does run away,' he said.

'Doh leh dem catch yuh, odderwise is cut ass foh you,' said Sankar as he passed his hand over Dano's hair and ruffled it.

Sakina fidgeted with her hair, tugging at a strand of it before asking her father for money. 'Pa,' she said, 'yuh couldn give me six cents to buy a new copy book, me own nearly run out.'

'Gal, when Friday come, ah go give yuh. Ah eh have a cent to spare now. Ah living on trust foh dis whole week.'

'Pa, ah sure you have a penny foh me,' said Dano.

'Ah always have a penny foh you, big man, but when Saturday come, you go get it.'

Suraji washed up the remainder of the dishes and started to prepare Sankar's meal for him to take to work the next day. Sankar continued to talk and play with the children. Suraji called out, 'All yuh chirren leave yuh fadder alone, is time to go to sleep.' They ignored her and carried on playing. She entered the shack and this time repeated the call to go to bed. Sankar joined her, adding, 'All yuh mus listen to all yuh stepmodder, is time to go to bed.' Dano tried to protest, but to no avail. Sakina was already spreading a mat made with jute bags in a corner for them to sleep on.

'Good night, all yuh, me go see yuh tomorrow,' said Sankar as he walked out of the shack towards the kitchen.

Suraji followed and handed him a packed lunch wrapped in a piece of old cloth. Sankar took it. He looked at Suraji and left. Suraji sat on the stair and lit a cigarette. She could hear the dogs growling and barking at Sankar as he walked away. She wondered about his behaviour to her. Every day the pattern was the same. He came, ate, played with the children and left. Never a word of affection or concern. He did not seem to care whether she worked or not. He just accepted what was on offer. She felt a need; for years it had been stifled by work and drinking rum, but of late the desire to satisfy it could not be deferred or suffocated by work and alcohol. She wanted contact, not isolation. Sankar was giving nothing. 'What could ah do?' she asked herself, knowing the answer beforehand. Nothing. It was a question she asked herself every night.

She had learned how to practise midwifery and to attend to the needs of other women, to try to displace the unsettled feeling which was her constant companion. Her skills increased her isolation, for people who used her services kept their distance. 'People is funny,' she thought. 'Ah know de body ah nearly every female in dis village an yet ah eh have plenty friend.' She became reconciled to the fact that most were afraid of her betraying secrets or felt she was too crude to be seen with. Yet her services were popular and there was a demand for her attention. Sankar played an important role in her life for he might be neglectful, but at least he depended on her.

She finished her cigarette and washed her face. She could hear the children inside giggling and whispering. She thought, 'Poor chirren, is only a couple more years before dey have to stop sleeping togedder.' Her mind began to race into several areas, a sign she recognised as tiredness. She entered the shack and took out her pillow, mat and sheet from a cardboard box, went into her barred-off corner and spread it out on the floor. She changed into a nightdress and lay down. She wished Sankar was spending the night with her. He stayed only on Saturday nights when he was usually drunk. Nine years of living with a man who only spent one night a week at home. 'Dis me lot in de world, a one-night-a-week husband,' she thought as she shifted her head on the pillow. She constantly wondered why she put up with this situation, why she could not lead the life of other women of her age, who had settled down with their husbands and made their life. It was as though her desires were always distant from reality, wishing for a particular goal and settling for a far from satisfactory compromise.

The children had dropped off to sleep. All around was quiet. The silence of the night was occasionally punctuated by the barking of a dog. She wondered about the next day and whether she would be given a task on piecework payment along with the gang of other women. It was so easy when Highlands Estate was in operation, but now, it was tiring having to get up early and walk so far to get a day's work on a distant estate. She closed her eyes and tried to fall asleep.

3 Highlands

'Boy, ah tell yuh, it have some man what have all de luck. Tek Sankar, he drink rum, he hardly have clothes to cover he bottom an he find wok. Me, ah have to look all over de kiss-me-tail place looking foh a bread to eat.'

'But Eddie, look at de kind ah wok he get. You an me cyah do dat, stick up wid animal whole day,' said Nat.

It was late, just after nine o'clock. The watchman had struck his bell a few minutes ago. Eddie, Sankar's neighbour to the left of the four-room barracks, sat speaking with Nat, the occupant of the room at the other end.

Eddie had spent all his life working in the sugar factory on Highlands Estate. He was short and well-built, with an easy-going personality. He had an appealing round face, always ready to burst into a smile. Nat, on the other hand, was a tall, thin, fair-skinned Indian with a thin moustache which seemed to highlight both his narrow lips and his private nature.

Nat was a bit of a mystery. Never part of the estate, he had only moved in a couple of months ago. No one knew where he came from. People had different stories about him. Some said he was an ex-convict who was too ashamed to return to his own village after a sentence. Others said he was a married man who came to live on the estate, abandoning his wife and children. He got along with people, however, and within a short time of coming to live on the estate became accepted by many of them. He used to sit with Eddie most nights, talking, playing cards and sometimes sharing a meal while doing so.

Eddie sat on a straight-backed wooden chair in his room. Nat sat on the stairs.

'Ah doh envy de man, but tell me, what he want wid money? Man, all he do is drink it as if dey was no tomorrow,' said Eddie, 'an people like we catching we ass to find wok at all.'

14

'Doh worry,' said Nat, 'you is a Creole, it have wok all over de place foh all yuh.'

'Who say so? It have wok foh Creole? Boy, doh mek me laugh,' scoffed Eddie.

'Is we Indian what catching we ass, an yuh know it,' said Nat.

'It mek no difference whedder you is Creole or Indian living on dis estate, we all have one same cross to bear. Ah doh tink we shoulda be left to catch we ass like dis. It eh we fault de estate gone bust, we used to wok hard,' said Eddie, shifting in his chair. The kerosene lamp on the small wooden table flickered. The night was hot. The samaan trees, huge giants with outspread arms, guarded the big house next door. They were there, ever present; on the darkest of nights their outline was still visible.

'Boy, ah doh know dis estate, but to me all estate looks like one anodder,' said Nat.

'Not dis one,' said Eddie, 'dis was one of de prettiest estate in de whole world. We used to be happy here, but when Mr Scott begin hiring de local white people as overseers, dat is when de trouble start. Dey only come here foh one ting, to drink an chase ooman, dat is what make de place go down. Look at Goddard.'

'But what about Scott?' enquired Nat. 'Ah hear he drink out all de profits.'

'Dat eh true, he used to drink, but never in de crop season. Is only in de end when tings start to go from bad to wuss he lose all control.'

'Ah hear more dan dat,' said Nat.

'Doh believe all what yuh hear, it eh so at all, yuh know. He was married once,' said Eddie, springing to the defence of the last owner of the estate. 'He was a good man, it had notting dat man wouldn give.'

'Ah hear so, but yuh know how dis place stop, people does talk,' said Nat.

'People have short memory. Dat man try he best to save dis place, but man, when yuh need such big money, de weight alone does carry yuh down.'

'But why he build dat big house in de middle of de cane if he know he owe so much money?' asked Nat.

◆

15

The house was set some distance away from the estate buildings on top of a hill in the middle of a cane field. From it, Donald Scott could see all he owned: factory, fields, stables, overseers' homes and barrack rooms. The two ponds were the only things hidden from his view, in a valley behind the sugar factory.

◆

'Boy, ah doh know what mek dat man build dat house. Everything inside it come from England. Ah hear is dat what cost de money. Yuh ever been inside it?' asked Eddie.

'Nah, man, ah eh so lucky,' Nat replied.

'Yuh should go an see it, de lights, de bathroom, boy, dat is a palace.'

◆

Scott's house was elegantly furnished before the fall: a large candelabra hung in the hall; downstairs, the sitting room had light cane furniture throughout and wooden deck chairs stood on the verandah. The kitchen had every piece of modern equipment available. The dining room had imported pine furniture and the Welsh dresser was packed with the finest china. Off the kitchen was a well-stocked pantry; beyond it was Miss Bella's quarters, and a toilet and bathroom for the servants.

Upstairs, the six bedrooms each had their own handbasin. The modern bathroom had hot and cold water for a bath tub, a bidet and a shower. It was fully tiled. A living room, a library and another huge verandah completed the upper part of the house. No expense was spared in building and furnishing that great house. Only Donald and his servant Bella had lived there, no one else. The other servants lived in barrack rooms on the estate and were on call whenever needed.

◆

'Boy, if ah had a house like dat, wid all dis land, ah never lose it,' said Nat.

'Dat place jinx from de time it build,' answered Eddie.

Their conversation was cut short by the arrival of Vernon, Nat's room-mate, now working as a barber in the town. He came with his new bicycle and went straight to Eddie's room.

16

'Eh, boy, yuh still up?' he asked as he leaned the bike against the verandah post.

'Yeh, me an Eddie just blagging,' said Nat.

'Wha happening, Vernon boy, how it going?' Eddie asked.

'De same ole story, plenty ah wok, but no money,' said Vernon.

Just as more conversation was about to take place, a figure was seen walking up the driveway towards the barracks. Vernon had a fear of the night; his heart skipped a beat. He whispered to Nat, 'Who is dat?'

'Doh mek me laugh, is only Sankar coming home,' said Nat.

Eddie got off his chair and came to the door. As the person came nearer, he called out, 'Sankar, wha yuh doing so late?'

Sankar replied, 'Ah always come home dis hour every night.' He reached the door and struck a match to light his lamp.

'Yuh lucky bitch, yuh, having a ooman to cook an look after you, an wok on Good Intent an we so, catching we ass,' teased Eddie.

Sankar felt tired. It was late and he had to rise early next morning. 'Yuh all right, ah have to get up early while yuh could lie down an scratch yuh belly,' he replied. 'Ah going to sleep.'

Vernon, Eddie and Nat laughed, and carried on talking and smoking the occasional cigarette.

4 Harry

Harry, the night watchman, struck ten on the factory bell. He felt tired and sleepy. His job was to stand guard over the idle machinery and ring the bell every hour. He had had very little sleep that day and now he kept nodding off. Failure to strike the bell would mean getting the sack. At first the job had seemed easy, but as the months rolled on it began to affect every part of his life. He had no social life at night and the day was usually spent trying to sleep. He made an exception to meet his lover, Sadwine, in the most unusual of places. Their affair had been going on for years, yet Harry was sure no one knew or suspected. His wife, Meera, certainly didn't, nor did Sadwine's husband Sadhu. Sometimes, as now, he wished he could speak to someone about it, but feared breaking the trust Sadwine had in him. In order to stay awake, he switched on his torch and patrolled the silent factory.

From far away, the light could be seen moving in the deserted factory. Only a year ago it had been in full operation, employing dozens of people as engineers, pan boilers and labourers to crush the cane and manufacture sugar. Now it lay dormant with rusting machinery.

Harry was a tall handsome man in his late forties. He had captained the estate cricket team as a young man, and still he retained his youthfulness and popularity. A chain-smoker, he smoked endlessly during his watch. Meera offered to come and spend the nights with him but he turned down her offer, saying his boss, Goddard, wouldn't like it.

Sadwine's husband, Beepat, was the village holy man, Sadhu. To have an affair with his wife was a considerable risk, enough to bring ill fortune to the whole village. Harry feared being made a scapegoat, as the man who had tempted fate and caused the estate to shut down. He constantly vowed to try to stop the relationship but failed each time at the sight of Sadwine, tall and well-built, dark-skinned, with long hair, a round face with a sensual mouth and full, firm breasts; her aura caught the attention of many men. They envied Sadhu but, owing to his status, never made any approaches to his wife.

The estate falling apart meant people were moving on. Harry dreaded the idea of Sadhu and Sadwine leaving. Their affair was based around Sadwine's need for him. Sometimes weeks would pass before she let him know she wished to see him, and on other occasions she saw him daily. She, too, was a popular figure in the village. She was friendly with several women and her home near the village shop always welcomed a visitor or two after work.

He sat down on a rail in the factory and almost dropped off to sleep in his confusion.

'Why today, eh?' he wondered. 'She had to see me today ah all days.'

Sadwine had seemed different, as if she wished to tell him something and at the last moment stopped. Harry continued pacing up and down the factory. He looked at his watch. The time was half-past ten. Some nights he could risk having a snooze and waking on time to strike the hour, but not tonight. He thought of his sons living their seemingly uncomplicated lives. The younger one had taken after him, and was now leading the village cricket team. The older one used to play but now liked drinking and watching rather than playing. When the relationship with Sadwine began, Harry used to urge her to run away with him. His passion for her was strong enough to make him wish to abandon wife, children and home for the sake of her. It was Sadwine, with no children of her own, who refused to leave.

'Tink ah yuh chirren, me cyah do dat, an besides, we managing.'

More and more, he shunned contact with Meera, finding her lacking in every sphere. He felt uneasy whenever she came near him. She worked in the same women's gang as Sadwine, cutting cane. Harry often saw both of them walking with several other women to or from work. He used to greet his wife, calling out to her, but his eyes acknowledged Sadwine with more warmth and affection. Beepat seemed friendly towards him. He always smiled whenever they met, but the sort of smile that was hard to make anything of.

The hours were passing by. The village was asleep. There was nothing to break the silence except the ringing of his bell which penetrated with more resonance the later it became. This night he

19

struck it harder then usual. Sadwine turned in her bed and smiled, as she listened to the loud ringing of his bell.

It began so simply. Sadwine was living with her parents in a village some distance from Highlands. She, being the eldest child of a large, poor family, helped her mother to run the home. Her father, a cane cutter, barely brought home enough money to feed the family of four girls and three boys. He sought to arrange marriages for his children when they had come of age, barely past puberty. The marriages were always with daughters and sons of people wealthier than he was. Not having much to offer, he depended on the matchmaker to sell the good qualities of his children. Sadwine was available for marriage, but no one came to ask for her hand. Perhaps it was her dark skin or quiet nature, but whatever the reason, she remained unmarried. Sadhu, in his capacity as a matchmaker, came to her house to try to set up an arranged marriage for her youngest sister. The talk of the dowry came up, but as usual her father had nothing to offer. Sadhu had nothing to tempt the proposed husband's family with, except the beauty of the child. He was about to end the discussion and leave when he asked for a cup of water. Sadwine's father called out to her to bring the water. She brought it in to this short, squat, greying figure dressed in a clean, white dhoti. He took the cup from her and winked, with a look that was hard to discern. His eyes became fixed on her. He drank slowly and Sadwine, as custom demanded, had to wait until he finished or be sent away by her father. Since she was considered too old for marriage at twenty, her role as a servant of the household became established. Sadhu, instead of leaving, gave Sadwine the cup, a sign for her to leave. He sat down again, and made a proposal to pay the dowry for the youngest sister in exchange for Sadwine as his wife. The father agreed without hesitaiton to the offer, for his youngest and dearest child would be marrying into a wealthy household and Sadwine would at last have a husband.

Sadwine cried when she was told. She did not like the look of Sadhu, when she saw him. He appeared crude, a grown man set in his ways and ugly, with gaps in his teeth. Choice she did not possess; her father decided and his word was to be obeyed. She became Sadhu's wife. He brought her to Highlands. The first sight of their home made her want to escape. With nowhere to run to and no one to help her, she had to accept her fate. She tried, in spite of wanting

20

to run away, to make a go of the marriage. Sadhu, in the role of husband, was not very attractive. He spent much of his time praying and working, and simply expected her to give in to his every demand. He had respect in the village as a holy man; he expected it from her. Their home was an ex-artisan cottage near the village shop; visitors came practically every evening, requesting prayers to be said to alleviate all kinds of difficult situations: unemployment, sickness, or wanting a wife. Gifts from these grateful supplicants and the income from the produce from Sadhu's small plot of land in a corner of the estate, itself a reward for long and dedicated service, made their standard of living higher than the majority who lived on the estate.

Sadwine could not devote herself totally to him and avoided contact whenever possible. Now married for fifteen years, their union produced no children and was a marriage in outward appearances only. They slept in separate beds. This suited both of them. She called him 'Sadhu' and he never addressed her by name. They hardly spoke to one another except when Sadwine informed him his meals were ready. In response, he grunted, and said nothing more. Outwardly they appeared happy enough. It was only when someone came to visit, they mentioned what they observed in each other. 'How yuh do, Sadhu?' 'Ah well, son.' 'And how is Sadwine?' the visitor might ask. 'She fine, too, son, but wokking too hard.'

The cottage where Sadwine lived had a latrine at the back. Harry's household used the one adjoining hers. The partitions were made of planks of wood. It was easy to hear the person in the next cubicle. It was there Sadwine and Harry's relationship developed. He would wait for her to come. He worked first as a cane weigher, and had plenty of time on his hands when the quota of canes for the day was reached. Harry loosened a plank, making it easy to remove and replace, allowing him and Sadwine to enter into the same cubicle, the stench of shit permeating every illicit meeting.

This harmony was about to be broken. On her way to work, Hitler, the leader of the women's gang, had come over to Sadwine in the soft, early sunlight. The rest of the women were making jokes and talking loudly on their way to the agent's bungalow. There they would be told whether work was available. If there was none, they then walked to Good Intent to see if the gang or part of it would be taken on there. A big, strapping woman, Cynthie was nicknamed Hitler by the rest of the women because of her shadowy moustache and because she was shrewd and ambitious. She liked having her independence and would do anything for it. This morning, she had held Sadwine's arm and asked her to walk with her behind the rest of the women.

'Gal, ah have to talk wid yuh, is important.'

Sadwine knew what to expect and was determined to say no to the proposal, but carried on with the pretence. 'What is de matter, gal, yuh in trouble?'

'No, gal, is all ah we in trouble. Man never satisfy an he is de wuss ah de lot.'

'Who you talking bout?' Sadwine asked.

'Dat Goddard, de agent, is he ah mean.'

'You mean me an dat white man? Not me, gal, ah radder suffer.' Sadwine wanted to rejoin the gang of women. Hitler held her back and kept walking by her side.

'Dis eh no joke, we all go suffer if he stop giving we wok.'

'An what de man gang does give him?' Sadwine rejoined.

'Money,' was the short reply.

The morning mist was disappearing in the sunlight. Sadwine looked at the one place where it remained thick, on the pond. Her mind blurred at the unspoken proposal. She felt confused. She knew how many women's wages depended on her acceptance. She looked at the brightening morning sun and the quickly changing night clouds and prayed. Hitler kept her eyes fixed on her. Sadwine, as though appealing for help, called loudly to the rest of the gang for Suraji. 'Suraji, ah have to talk to yuh.'

Suraji shouted back, 'Talk to me later, Hitler is good company, talk to she.'

Hitler realised the pressure she was putting on. 'Tek yuh time, gal, yuh doh have to mek up yuh mind right away. Tink about it an leh me know when yuh ready.'

5 Ripe fig

When the whistle had blown in the factory for the last time, it began around noon and continued blowing for over an hour, mourning the closure. Sampat, a factory hand, looked to the future like many of the other workers, with a certain amount of despair. He lived in a small shack on a rented piece of land on the main road about a mile from the factory. He had his wife, Rosie, and six children to feed. He prayed he would soon find work. Within the first week of looking, he found a job as a night watchman in the town ten miles away. The pay was low but bus travel was cheap and his expenses minimal. He left home around five in the evening and returned the next morning between eight and nine.

Rosie, a tall, well-built woman in her early thirties, was a domineering person and Sampat a tall, thin man with a sharp face who used to be regularly beaten by her during frequent quarrels. Her loud, sharp voice could be heard at a great distance when she became angry, and from fifty yards even in ordinary conversations. Her hair had never been cut and reached almost to her big, broad bottom. Her children were trained as little servants and were kept in constant attendance. Rosie avoided work and could be heard commanding her band of waifs to wash, cook, clean, run errands and look after each other. Rosie was attractive to look at and easy to talk to; she was very generous to some people, but to others she could be mean and hostile.

She took in Ranu, an ex-workmate of her husband, as a lodger. He had found work with the County Council in a road maintenance gang. The family prospered in relation to the rest of the village, but Rosie wanted still more. Ranu became more than a lodger; he began to share Rosie's bed at night when her husband went to work. The children were told to call him Uncle. During her visits to the shop, Rosie would tell anyone who cared to listen that she wanted to get away from the village. 'Ah have two man to keep me an me chirren

23

dem, an by de time ah find somewey to live in de town, ah go move from here.'

Living near the main road with traffic was useful to Rosie. She built a ramshackle shed in her front yard to sell bananas, and placed a big 'For Sale' sign on a piece of cardboard above the stall. The village, already shocked by this woman's behaviour, had a further jolt. Her big selling board was for more than just the sale of bananas. Men became her sole customers. Young children with their pennies and cents were prevented by their parents from purchasing anything from Rosie. During the day the bananas were displayed but she hardly sold any; at nights, men would call out, 'Rosie, yuh have any fig?'

'Yes, boy, ah have plenty, but it all inside. Come, leh me get some foh yuh.' The men would enter and half an hour later would emerge with a bunch of bananas to make their way home. At times, several men would be waiting in her balcony to be sold ripe fig. Schoolboys passing at night from Hindi lessons would point out: 'Look at all dese big men waiting foh ripe fig!'

On the rare nights her husband was at home, no sales took place. The steady stream of men dwindled discreetly, when the sign saying 'No fig today' was placed on her stall. For those who couldn't read, Rosie made sure she sat on her rickety verandah to answer their call, 'Any fig tonight, gal?'

'No, man, ah eh have none at all today. Tomorrow ah expecting some.'

Her children, who were sent to bed early when their father was at work, were encouraged to stay up late and sing for him when he was at home. The community was split over Rosie's behaviour. Some wanted to run her out; others said it was a free country and she was entitled to do whatever she wanted. Some nights Rosie was heard at the top of her voice arguing with men who, having paid, demanded their money back.

'Look, lady, ah spen me money to buy yuh fig but ah didn expect it to smell so stink.'

This was when Ranu came to the forefront; he was her pimp and protector, often having to use his muscle to eject a difficult customer or be seen fending off a person stronger than he was who had become violent. Rosie would then have to end the fight: 'Here, tek yuh stink money an go an doh come back.'

Ranu paid little attention to the younger men in the village who took to teasing Rosie. 'Ripe fig?' they would shout, and when she answered, 'Yes, ah have plenty,' they would reply, 'Keep it, it rotten an stink an nasty.' Rosie, unable to restrain herself, would be heard at the top of her voice, 'It all yuh momma an sister what stink an rotten.' The youngsters, having achieved what they set out to do, would run away laughing.

Rosie spent money every day in the shop, as if to prove she was the only villager capable of making a daily purchase. She became mean and was treated as an outcast by many. A few villagers, however, remained on friendly terms. To them, she loaned money – on interest.

One day she sent her eldest daughter to Suraji, asking her to visit as she wasn't too well. Suraji, on call to anyone who needed her, went as soon as she could over the weekend.

'Gal, is me belly what hurting.' Suraji examined her and diagnosed a strain which required regular massage and rest. Rosie resented not being able to carry on her trade. But this became impossible; the pain increased after a client was served. For days she lay in her bed and no bananas were sold. Then she suddenly reappeared, bedraggled and wailing outside the shop. A hot afternoon, the steam was rising from the asphalt road. Dogs curled up in shady corners trying to remain cool. Even the trees appeared to droop from the effect of the heat. Rosie's wails penetrated sharply through the silence. She was shouting and crying, 'Oh God, he gone, he tief me money an gone. All yuh see him?' she asked anyone who knew her. Her long hair was dishevelled. Her dress hung loosely over her large frame; her big breasts moved freely from side to side as she carried on wailing. 'God! Oh, God! she bawled.

Suraji and her gang were coming home from work. Hitler, hearing from a distance the distressed sound, said, 'All yuh, hush, like somebody bawling in front de shop.'

The women fell silent and quickened their pace.

'What wrong, gal, what happen to you?' asked Suraji.

Rosie repeated, 'He gone! He tief me money an gone, every cent ah mek.'

'Who?' several questioned.

'Dat nastiness, Ranu, dat is who.'

'How much he tek?' enquired Hitler.

25

'Over five hundred dollars, everyting ah save.'

Rosie's daughters attempted to take her away. They tugged at her dress. 'Come, Ma, leh we go home, yuh eh well.'

'Ah cyah go now, ah have to find he an get back me money.'

People who gathered all shared some sympathy for her. The loss of five hundred dollars was indeed a tragedy. But their overall feelings remained divided.

'Is only justice,' said Hitler. 'God punishing you for all de sin an trouble yuh cause here.' Her forthright comment was challenged by Sadwine.

'Hear who talk about sinning! Gal, ah sorry yuh lose so much money. If ah had it, ah would give it back to yuh, ah know yuh wok hard foh it.'

Hitler came up to Sadwine and asked her what she meant. Sadwine took Hitler to one side and said softly, 'What yuh ask me to do dis morning eh no different to what Rosie does do every day.'

'Gal, she do it foh sheself. What ah asking yuh to do is foh all ah we survival. Dat is different. God on we side, he eh go punish we. Leh we not fight, me an yuh is one,' said Hitler, her eyes pleading for agreement. Sadwine turned sharply and left. Suraji was now holding the distressed woman, leading her into the shop.

'Come, gal, come an sit down.' Rosie allowed herself to be led by Suraji and sat down in the shop. The crowd gathered in the entrance discussing where Ranu might have got to. Once inside, Suraji called for a shot of rum. Ramnath, the attendant, asked, 'Who go pay?'

'Doh worry, Ramnath boy,' said the sobbing Rosie, 'ah still have some, ah go pay.' He brought the rum and handed her the glass.

'Now drink it down,' ordered Suraji. Rosie drank it and immediately started to cough. She spat blood.

'Oh God, look, she have consumption,' someone cried. The crowd quickly moved away. Suraji took out a rag from her pocket and wiped Rosie's mouth; she saw her back to her home. The word spread through the village that Rosie carried an infectious disease. The young boys, when they passed, now taunted her. 'Hey, Rosie! Give me two hundred dollars, ah go catch Ranu foh yuh.'

One day she was gone, having kept silent about her plans. A small jitney pulled up outside her shack: she packed her belongings and it moved her out. Some time afterwards, people heard she had moved to the town, living on squatted land.

6 Rum and cards

Tex, the ex-head groom, was sitting on a stool at the bar of the rum shop. It was mid-afternoon. He was having a drink to drown his sorrows, finding it difficult to adjust from a well-paid job to unemployment. 'Is one full year now and still notting come up,' he was telling his drinking partner, Madan, a former groom. 'Remember dem great times we had here on dis estate?' he asked, pouring the last drink from the nip of rum on the counter.

Madan, caught unawares by the pouring of the last drop without being offered, forgot the drift of the conversation. He became very silent and kept staring at the empty bottle. His large frame began to stiffen and his breathing became heavy. He felt deeply hurt by Tex's behaviour, not offering a share of the last few drops. Tex, unaware of what he had done, gulped the drink and reached for the jug on the bar to throw a little water in his glass to wash down the last of the rum. Without thinking, he got off his stool and glanced at Madan. 'Ah go see yuh later, boy, ah have somebody to meet,' he said as he left the shop.

Madan, sitting in his old vest and patched short pants, became angry at the thought of what had happened. His large overhanging stomach leaning against the edge of the bar looked like the inner tube of a car tyre. The grey stubble of his beard showed up in contrast against the dark brown of his face. He needed a drink to calm the hurt he felt. He called the attendant serving in the dry goods section next door. 'Ramnath, ah waiting.'

Ramnath, serving a customer and hearing Madan's voice, answered, 'Madan, yuh know what is de answer, ah cyah trust yuh.'

'How yuh know what ah want? All yuh people like to tink all man is de same.'

Ramnath took the order from the customer and walked over to Madan.

'Wha yuh want?'

'You see wha Tex do me?'

'No, ah eh see notting.'

'Yuh see me an he just sharing a nip ah rum?'

'Yeah, he buy, an all yuh drink, wha wrong wid dat?'

'Well, it come to de las drink an he pour out foh he only an eh bodder to share.'

'So wha wrong wid dat?' Ramnath turned to walk away.

Madan reached over the bar and pulled his shirt. 'Doh go yet, ah eh finish talking to yuh.'

Ramnath waited until he released the shirt, continued walking and went to serve his customer.

'Ah tell yuh, dis world eh have no justice. When ah was wokking, all yuh begging me to buy in dis shop because is a Indian man own it. Man, all yuh doh care if ah here or not, all yuh ungrateful son of a bitch,' screamed Madan, spitting on the floor as he walked out.

◆

Tex was on his way to Eddie, who ran a card school in his room. He had two tables, collecting six cents for three games of rummy per table. The betting was low, but enough to buy a meal from the shop if you won. For Tex this was a meal ticket, one of two he worked at in order to survive. The other was an illegal numbers game, whe-whe, where he collected a commission on the amount of bets received and a percentage of winnings if the punter won. The odds were thirty-six to one: Tex paid out thirty and kept six. He usually made his collection rounds twice a day to accept bets bought on the previous night's dreams. Each dream was translated into a number: a snake in your dream meant you bet on number one; cattle were number nine; number thirty-three was a thatched house.

He walked briskly through the estate to Eddie's barrack room. It was gone three and his collection round was set to begin at five, so he could take the money to the whe-whe den, a secluded spot on the edge of the estate, by half-past six. Time enough to play twelve hands of rummy and, if lucky, win two dollars. He got to Eddie in time to make up the second four men. The early ones were sitting at a table. Tex and his school had to sit on the floor. Eddie sat on his step and only entered the room to collect his commission; otherwise he kept an eye out in case a policeman should ride past on his bicycle.

Occasionally a piece of gossip would enter into the conversation such as who was stealing on the estate, or who Goddard, the receiver's agent, was screwing from the women's gang. Tex, a tall, red-skinned man, was finding it difficult to sit on the floor. He called out to Calvin, his friend sitting at the table, and asked if he wouldn't mind changing places. 'Is de football ah used to play, yuh know, me legs cramping in me old age.'

Calvin declined. 'Ah doing fine here, boy, if ah move, me luck might change.'

Nat got up and changed his seat with Tex. 'Boy, ah doh know how to tank yuh. Ah always say Indian have better manners dan Creole.'

Nat laughed. Tex, paying attention to his cards for a moment, carried on, 'Yuh tink is joke ah mekking? Is someting ah always telling me people. Wen it come to manners, we broke, we eh have none.'

Calvin, thin and half-Spanish, nicknamed Bogart because he often wore a trilby hat and had a cigarette in the corner of his mouth, entered into the conversation. 'Doh talk shit, Tex, coolie people doh know de meaning ah de word.'

'Doh mix up poverty,' said Tex, stopping to pick up a card and drop another, continuing to look at the man on his right, 'wid respeck an manners.'

Calvin, with the cigarette stub in the corner of his lips, mumbled, 'Yuh always making statement yuh cyah back up, ah know wha ah talking about, ah grow up among dem.'

'So what? Dem people have understanding, dat come from manners,' replied Tex.

Eddie called out, 'All yuh, look – Madan, coming up de drive.'

He came to the verandah and said to Eddie, 'Ah want to play on de same table as dat man wha sitting dey. Ah want to teach him he cyah insult coolie people an get away wid it, not in dis day an age.'

Tex looked surprised; he sought a reason for this outburst from Madan. 'Ah eh do yuh notting. Why, ah just share a nip wid yuh.'

'Yes, but yuh finish de last drop, leaving me like a idiot. Yuh doh even treat dog so, yuh only do dat because ah is a coolie.'

'Stop talking shit, Madan, now leh me play me card.

'Ah have money, Eddie, leh me play, ah say.'

'How much yuh have? Let me see.'

'Doh mind what ah have, if ah play, ah go put down me bet like everybody.'

'Madan, look, man, doh waste me time. If yuh want to gamble, den show me yuh money, odderwise leave dis place, ah doh want too much idlers hanging round here.'

Madan pulled out two five-dollar notes from his back pocket, 'Look, money, ah have ten dollars, ah bet all yuh vagabonds eh see so much ah money since de factory close down. Now leh me play, ah go teach dat son of a bitch who is man today.'

The delay, though amusing to some of the card players, began to irritate others. The heat of the afternoon, kept out by the fear of losing or the satisfaction of winning, began to infiltrate. Madan's voice focused the frustration beginning to stir. He was still attempting to come inside and join in the game. Calvin got off his chair and walked towards him. Madan backed away when he saw the anger and determination in his eyes. Up to now, he had hardly met any resistance to his outburst, but what he saw coming he hardly expected.

The huge samaan trees, the sweet-lime hedge and the grass waved in the light wind. Madan fell silent and stood passive. Calvin kicked and head-butted him. He screamed and began to cry out. Another punch to the nose and blood dripped on to the mossy stones that lay at his feet. Tex ran and grabbed hold of Calvin. 'What yuh want to do, kill de man?'

Eddie stood in front of Madan to prevent further attack. Calvin, breathless as he spoke, said, 'No, all ah want is foh people to stop boddering me. Dis is how ah wok an ah doh like no disturbance when ah doing it.'

Eddie called out to Nat to bring over a rag and some water. He began wiping the blood off Madan's face. Everyone was now standing outside, bemused by what had taken place. Calvin, quietened down by Tex's restraining hands, re-entered the room, picked up his hand from where it had fallen on the floor and walked away. 'Ah go see all yuh later.' Some of the others went with him.

'Look what yuh put yuhself in, all over a nip ah rum,' said Tex.

Madan stood silent. Eddie finished wiping the blood off his nose, threw the bloody water over the gravel and returned to the verandah and sat once more on his step. Some of the men were still milling around but the card game for the day was over. Eddie spoke with some anger and regret in his voice. 'Me kiss-me-ass card game break up. Wha make yuh come here, Madan? Yuh have money, wha yuh come here foh, yuh know yuh cyah play card, wha bring yuh here? If yuh have a bone to pick wid a man, do it somewey else, not in me place, especially when ah mekking a few shillings.'

Nat sat on Sankar's steps but said nothing. Vernon's mother, who came out when she heard the commotion, returned inside. Tex was trying to pacify Madan; he felt sorry for him – they had known each other since Tex came to work on the estate many years ago. Madan was one of the earliest friends he had made on the estate. 'Look at what trouble yuh cause foh yuhself, all because ah some misunderstanding over rum! Like all yuh Indian people does lose all yuh head once yuh taste rum. Come an sit down here an catch yuhself.'

He took Madan's hand and tried to get him to come and sit down on Eddie's step. Madan pulled away his hand and walked away. Tex came and sat next to Eddie. 'Boy, some man does turn jackass once rum go to dey head, especially when dey eh have notting to do.'

7 The year of the strike

Donald Scott sat in the back room of the rum shop, drinking with several men. He was attempting to find out more about the planned strike. The national cane workers' union, led by a charismatic figure, was staging strikes in each of the sugar estates, seeking to raise the wages of the workers in each factory. Highlands' turn was next. It was a late December afternoon, just before the harvest of cane began on January 1st. Scott knew the strike would cripple him; he had invested heavily in previous years in new machinery and in his own new mansion. He had borrowed a great deal of money with the expectation that another successful harvest would repay a part of his loan. But a rise in wages would mean foreclosure on his loans. Wages had been controlled all during the war years; now they were over, the demand for higher wages in line with the rising cost of living appealed to the workers.

Donald was a ruddy-faced Scotsman in his early fifties. Well-built and handsome with a full crop of blond hair and doleful blue eyes, he was dressed in his regular uniform of brown shoes, long khaki socks, short khaki trousers and a white, long-sleeved shirt, the sleeves rolled up as far as his thickset arms would allow. His chauffeur, Balgobin, a tall, lean Indian in his thirties, was, as ever, with him. The rest of the men worked as clerks on the estate or were hangers-on who used every opportunity to enjoy a free drink.

'Ah telling yuh, boss,' said Madan, as he refilled his glass, 'we people is too ungrateful, nobody help we as much as yuh an now look wha happen, all de tanks yuh get is dey calling a strike.'

Scott, as usual half-drunk, liking the effect of drink from early in the morning, nodded in agreement and added, 'I know their plans, but no one seems to understand how serious it would be for this estate. No one cares a damn. The entire estate is in serious financial trouble, and to pay extra wages would mean collapse.'

'Dis is serious,' replied one of the men, attempting to show concern but at the same time ensuring his rum glass was kept filled.

Scott continued, 'If these bloody-minded people would only listen to reason, we could save this estate.'

'Is no use, boss, ah keep telling yuh, is bess to sell out, tek what yuh can get, an leave de majority of dem to catch dey ass,' said Balgobin.

'How could yuh advise de boss to do dat. Balgobin?' asked one of the men. 'De boss is one ah we, and besides, dis place is he life. Wha yuh say, boss?'

The man poured another drink as he declaimed his loyalty. The bottle was finished and Donald called out to the bar. 'Ramnath, bring on another bottle.'

'Yes, boss, right away.'

The conversation continued in the dark little room. The walls were painted a bottle green and the galvanised iron roof had been darkened by years of rising smoke.

'Yes, boss,' said Balgobin, 'is ungratefulness what causing all ah we dis trouble.'

'That is not entirely true.' said Donald. 'The trend these days is to amalgamate into larger factories and they can usually afford higher wages; small estates are no longer profitable.'

'Ah know dat, we have dis out every day, but if people tek less money foh just one day in crop time, we bound to mek enough to survive,' said Balgobin.

'Now please, someone, tell me what I can do to avert this strike. If we lose any production, we are in trouble.'

'Boss, to tell de truth, is notting can be done, people mind done mek up,' said another.

Donald wasn't getting the sort of response he wanted. The financial trouble he found himself in was not going to be lifted by the generosity of the workforce. The prosperity that Donald enjoyed during the war had not been shared with the workers. He pleaded for their sympathy, but now they wanted their share.

'All I am asking is time. I cannot afford to pay more wages and pay for the new machinery all at once.'

'Boss, we understand, but why not pay de workers an den foh de machines?' one asked.

Balgobin snapped at the speaker, 'Yuh damn fool, yuh expect business to wait? All yuh coolies only tink ah yuh belly.'

Donald raised his voice. 'Now calm down, Balgobin, it's no use getting heated. Now take me home.' Donald got up. 'Thank you. Gentlemen, please try to get my views across. Let's go, Balgobin.'

One of the men replied. 'We go try, boss, but it going to be hard.'

Donald left, followed by Balgobin. They got into the car parked in front of the shop. The cool evening air had an almost immediate effect on Donald and Balgobin. While inside the shop, they had consumed a great deal of alcohol; the air stimulated their systems and gave the drink a stronger impact. Both were now totally drunk and barely able to walk straight. Balgobin started the car, a black Ford Pilot, and drove off, crunching the gears as he slowly zigzagged down the road.

Bella, Donald's servant, who had looked after him from his birth, was standing at the kitchen door of the mansion. An African woman in her late sixties, she was tall and stout. Out of habit, she waited at the door in case her help was needed. Balgobin stopped the car and slumped over the steering wheel. Bella was not surprised. It had been like this for the past three evenings, since the news of the strike reached Donald. She turned slowly and walked back inside. When she reached the staircase leading to the rooms upstairs, she called out, 'Blue Jean?'

The short, jockey-sized butler, who was checking the rooms for mosquitoes, appeared at the top of the stairs.

'Yes, madam?' he answered.

'What yuh doing?' Bella enquired.

'Ah jus dropping de net.'

'Yuh eh hear? De boss reach.'

'Ah hear, madam, dat is why ah getting de bed ready.'

'Well, come down an give me a hand.'

'Yes, madam,' said Blue Jean, a nickname given to him in school because he was always trying to kill with a slingshot the bird of the same name.

Bella waited at the foot of the stairway for Blue Jean and they went out together to the car where Donald lay slumped across the back seat. Bella opened the door, held Donald's hand and pulled him forward, whispering softly, 'Come on, boss, yuh reach home.'

Donald did not respond. The dusk gave way to night. The lights, powered by a generator, were fully lit. The house, standing by itself, looked like a ship cruising on the cane. Bella coaxed and pulled. The tugging caused Donald to open his eyes.

'What?' he enquired.

Bella whispered, 'Donald, you're home now, get out of the car.'

'Ah, go away and leave me alone. Can't you see I'm resting?' he replied.

'Come on, Donald,' Bella persisted. Donald refused to budge.

Blue Jean said, 'Move aside, Mis Bella, leh me try.'

'Oh, God,' she replied, 'not dat again.'

'Ah doh like it too, but how else we go get he out ah de car?'

'All right, but yuh know what go happen.'

Blue Jean held Donald's hand. Donald called, 'Is that you, Blue Jean?'

'Yes, boss, is me.'

'My love, come here and give me a cuddle.'

'Come inside first, boss, too much ah people go see we out here.'

Donald had a dual approach to Blue Jean. When he was sober, Blue Jean was treated like any worker, but drunk, he longed for him with the passion of a lover. Donald allowed Blue Jean to hoist him out of the car. He embraced Blue Jean as soon as he got out, the tall blond Scotsman engulfing the tiny body of the close-cropped Indian; then Bella moved swiftly to break up this little scene.

'Get away,' Donald ordered. Bella stood still and raised her voice.

'Now break this up, otherwise I'll have to do it.'

'Sour puss,' said Donald as he threw out an arm over Bella and one over Blue Jean and walked into the house. Bella sat him down at the kitchen table. He kept up an incessant appeal to Blue Jean to come to bed with him.

'Come on, my lovely one, let me have you, let us forget the trouble and go to bed.'

'Not tonight, boss, ah have to go home,' said Blue Jean repeatedly.

Bella busied herself getting his dinner. She placed the food in front of him and ordered. 'Now eat, it will make you feel better.'

'I don't want any food, I want my lover, Blue Jean.'

'Now, eat, and shut up,' she said once more, this time with a firmer voice. Donald went silent. He looked at Blue Jean and began to eat the meal placed before him. Bella knew exactly when to be firm with Donald, like a mother taking charge of an ill-behaved child.

Blue Jean asked Bella, 'What about de one still in de car?'

'Leave him right dere. Let him sleep it off, serves him right. Now you get away from here right now, before he start up again.'

'Yuh sure yuh can manage?' he asked.

'Yes, I can. Go.'

Blue Jean left quickly.

'White men an dere dirty habits,' he muttered to himself as he hurried on. Being the boss's pet was no easy existence. Sometimes called by his real name, Hamza, by the rest of the village, he was always at the end of their jokes. They all knew of the relationship he had with Donald. However, the fun stopped short whenever one of them wanted employment or a loan off Donald. Instead of being teased with, 'Short man, long prick!' it became, 'How yuh do, Hamza, long time no see.'

8 Blue Jean

Blue Jean's role in the village had changed almost overnight. As a butler who had daily access to Donald, he was looked upon as a man of some influence. Now, with the demise of the estate, the villagers talked more openly of his relationship to Donald. Some of them also began to confront him about his sexual preferences. He was in the village shop one afternoon making a purchase. Madan, an *habitué* at the bar, saw him, walked over to the dry goods section, crept silently up behind him and grabbed his collar. This huge man with large hairy arms got hold of the short, boyish Blue Jean. He addressed him by his proper name.

'Ah get yuh, Hamza, yuh lil bugger. When yuh was living wid white man, yuh behaving like boss.'

'Leh me go, yuh drunken fool, who yuh tink ah is?' Blue Jean countered.

Madan held on to Hamza's collar but with his other hand grabbed him by the seat of his trousers and lifted him up on to the counter, spreading him out. Blue Jean made desperate efforts to get away but the force used by Madan was too strong. The other customers in the shop laughed and Ramnath, the assistant, joined in the fun by holding on to Blue Jean's head, saying: 'Hold still, we just want to see what kind ah man yuh is.' Blue Jean, realising that his strength was not enough to budge, lay still waiting to see what was about to happen next.

'Leh me see what kind ah man yuh is. What dat white man want from yuh? Ah hear short man does have long toti,' said Madan, at the same time fumbling with the buttons on Hamza's crutch, trying to undo them.

'Tek off he pants,' shouted an excited customer.

Suraji came in just as this bit of excitement was taking place and tried to stop it. 'Leave he alone, all yuh see all yuh too big, why all yuh doh pick on somebody big?'

'Haul yuh ass from here, old ooman, dis boy doh even like ooman,' said Madan. Hamza remained still, long enough to take a deep breath and gather his senses. He felt Madan's hand slacken its tight grip on his body while he was preoccupied with the removal of the trousers. With a mighty leap, Blue Jean sprang up, pushed Madan aside and ran from the shop. Madan attempted to grab hold of him but after three attempts gave up and quickly disguised his failure with a loud raucous laugh.

What began in jest had a serious intent about it. The idea of two men having sex with each other awakened his curiosity as well as that of many other villagers. He leaned against a pile of bags of flour, exhausted, not caring whether white dust stuck to his clothing, so preoccupied was he with his thoughts.

'He get away,' he called out to Ramnath.

'Yes, boy, we miss we chance,' said Ramnath. Madan remained silent while Ramnath busied himself serving Suraji. She felt relieved that Blue Jean had escaped, as whatever form his loving took, his body ought not to be inspected publicly, accompanied with ridicule. She left the shop with her foodstuff. Madan wished for another drink but, having no money left, he went and sat by himself under the young cassia tree nearby.

It was late afternoon; the sun was sinking and people were hurrying to their homes. Voices were heard in the distance calling in the wayward children and chickens. A feeling of unease began to occupy Madan's mind as he tried to stifle the fear that he too might discover that the sort of sex Blue Jean practised might appeal to him. He tried to hide that by conjuring up revulsion, the traditional method of dealing with that sort of sexuality. Love and respect were absent in his world; love and care were shown only to children. For Madan, love was haste and punishment: pain followed by pleasure, followed by silence and departure.

Blue Jean ran all the way back to his shack. He locked the door as soon as he entered and sat in the corner, expecting to feel guilty and ashamed. Instead, his mind drifted to the time he spent with Donald. There was no feeling of guilt or regret. Madan wanted to see the size of his penis. He could not understand the pleasure of someone offering love to another who was pleading for it. Blue Jean had first given in to Donald's request out of a sense of duty, but as months passed by, their love-making became more intimate, strong enough to overcome the loathing and disgust many felt towards him. He also knew that it was not meant to last. He began to enjoy its moments without expecting it to continue. Now that Donald was leaving, he simply accepted the end and was looking for an existence without him.

Hamza unlocked his door and stared at the passers-by returning home from work, tired but with enough energy left to follow the evening routine before going to bed. He, too, was accustomed to feeling weary at this time of day. Now he woke up late in the day and, with little physical work to do, his daily pattern was disturbed. Hamza felt he had to make the most of the time Donald had remaining on the estate. After considerable thought, he had turned down Donald's request for him to come and live with him and Bella. He knew that, while it may have been possible to live comfortably, that sort of life was not the kind he had mapped out. He wanted a wife and family. In spite of its rapid decline, Highlands was his home and every emotion and growth had to stem from here, this land.

Suraji sat in her kitchen, looking at the meal cooking on her fireplace. The pieces of wood were burning with an even flame, casting shadows on the rusty galvanised iron roof. 'Ah must do someting to help dat boy, Hamza,' she thought. She more than understood the pain caused when someone close moves away. He might appear nonchalant about Donald but his leaving was going to affect him more than most. She wanted to save Hamza from the familiar quest of finding someone to replace a loved one. 'Ah must get a gal to marry he,' she thought. She dreamed of overcoming the conditioning which only allowed the exploration of certain kinds of loving.

9 The barracks

'Ah hate coolie people, yuh know, boy,' said Vernon, as he sat with Eddie on the steps of the barracks.

'Yuh mustn say dat. My modder was a coolie ooman, just like yours,' Eddie replied.

'Sometimes ah does feel so shame foh dem, coming in de town an mekking ass of demself, dressing in funny clothes an getting drunk.'

'Creole people does do de same,' said Eddie. 'What it is troubling yuh?'

'Boy, is me momma. Like today, Sunday, she eh home, she gone to some wedding house an mek a fool ah sheself.'

'Wha yuh going to do? She eh right in she head, yuh know dat. What is it really got she so?' asked Eddie. Vernon hesitated.

The bright midday sun shone over the whole village. The disused factory roof glistened in the light, the tall chimney now without smoke, the dark lines of the brick showing. Heat vapours rose from the pond. The dry yellow gravel road was clear enough to see every bump and ridge. Chickens were scratching under the shade of the tall samaan trees, whose leaves were wilting in the intense heat. Vernon, in long white flannel trousers and white shirt, was dressed for the afternoon cricket match. Eddie was wearing a cotton vest, once white but now greying, and short pants. No gambling school had been arranged until late afternoon, after the cricket match was over.

'Boy, ah believe somebody put a light on she. Dat is what mek she go crazy.'

'Doh talk shit. Who go put a light on yuh momma?' asked Eddie.

'It have all kind ah jealous people in dis world. My modder was a pretty ooman, now look at she. An every time de moon full, she gone mad.'

'She doh trouble nobody; leh she be. Ah know what yuh mean; was de same foh me old lady.'

40

'Come to tink ah it, ah never hear yuh one day telling about yuh momma. She still living?'

'Yeah, she around, but ah doh like to talk about she. Since me fadder dead she gone back to live like a Indian an she doh have much to do wid me.'

'Ah know she?'

'Ah doh know,' said Eddie as he got up and walked to the little platform in the kitchen and picked up a cup.

'Say, dis wedder does mek me feel thirsty.'

Evading the question further, he dipped the cup into a bucket of drinking water and drank from it slowly. Nat, who was still half asleep, came out of the barracks dressed in a clean set of pyjamas and a pair of rubber slippers.

'Boy, how yuh could sleep so late?' asked Eddie. Vernon shifted on the step to allow him to pass.

'Ah went out last night, ah come home late.' Nat stood and smiled, wanting to say something, but hesitating. 'Ah hear all yuh talking about Vernon momma. Where she gone?' asked Nat as he passed a hand round his eyes to remove the sleep, his long fingers picking at the corners.

'Ah doh know. Ah hear she going early dis morning,' Vernon replied.

A car filled with passengers was passing. The dust from the road flew up as Vernon waved back at someone waving in it.

'Who was dat?' asked Eddie.

'Ah doh know but he know me.'

The car stopped and a man no one had seen before came out. His jet black hair shining in the sunlight, he was well dressed in a bright red shirt and long black trousers, with a clean pair of brown shoes. Nat hurried back into the barrack room.

'Ah going to bathe, all yuh,' he announced as he left. The man with his dark brown skin and watery eyes walked slowly towards Vernon and Eddie.

'Good morning. Ah looking foh a man call Sonny Boy. Where he does live?'

Eddie looked at Vernon and the man, a bit unwilling to give Sonny Boy's address.

'Doh worry, he is me family,' he added, as he noticed the hesitation in the faces of the two young men.

41

'Is over dey, in de house right in front ah where yuh park.'

The man looked at the newly erected shack at the side of the barracks and said, 'It eh look like he home.'

Vernon looked towards Sonny Boy's shack. A goat tied to a post was feeding on a bunch of grass.

'It look like he gone out, man. When he home he does tie de goat in de fields.'

The man nodded. 'My name is Nadir. When yuh see Sonny Boy, tell him ah did come.'

'All right,' said Vernon as the man walked towards the car, then turned and asked a final question. He covered his eyes to shade them from the glare of the sunlight.

'It have a man called Sankar. All yuh know who he is? Ah doh know he, but dis business concern he too.'

Eddie looked at Sankar's door; it was shut. 'He does live here, but he hardly does stay home in de day.'

'Well, never mind, we will come again,' said the man as he quickened his steps and returned to the car. Eddie and Vernon watched it driving off to turn back to the main road.

'Ah wonder what dat was all about,' said Vernon.

'Doh ask me, boy, but dat Sonny Boy does get up to all sorts ah tings. Ah sure it must have someting to do wid ooman,' said Eddie.

'It look like Sankar in it too. Leh him play fast, Suraji go cut he ass good an proper,' said Vernon.

'Boy, whatever it is, dem two men too happy,' said Eddie as he got up once again and started to light a little Primus stove. 'Ah going to mek someting to eat, ah hungry foh so. Yuh eat?'

Vernon said, 'Ah going to play cricket. De las ting ah want to do is eat. Yuh cyah run on a full stomach.'

Nat, now fully dressed in brown gabardine trousers, a cream shirt and black shoes, came to the front of the building. His hair was well combed, his clear-complexioned face looking slightly red after a vigorous rub.

'Look at de saga boy!' said Eddie.

'Ah eh no saga boy,' said Nat.

'Boy, it look like de two ah all yuh going out. Sankar and yuh momma not home. Is me alone remaining in dis barrack till evening.'

'Is time yuh get a ooman to keep yuh company,' joked Nat.

'Ooman at dis time?' Man, de day come ah hardly have nuff to feed meself, much less foh a wife.'

'Well, ah go see yuh later,' said Nat as he left.

'Well, well, look at dat, eh? De man doh wok no way but he does dress like a king,' said Eddie.

'Boy, to tell de trut, de man does stay here wid me, but ah doh know how he does do it,' said Vernon.

'Where he really does come from?' asked Eddie.

'Ah doh know,' said Vernon. 'He jus come and hang round de barber shop an den he ask me to leh him stay wid me, dat is all ah know bout de man.'

10 The navel string

It had been a hot, hard and at times gruelling day. Suraji was longing to sleep. She took a large drink of strong rum as a sedative, hoping to induce sleep almost at once. The night was starry and calm. The chorus of insects chirping their nightly song was interrupted by the barking of dogs; that was all there was to be heard. She laid out her mat on the floor and closed her eyes. As sleep was just about to overcome her and take her on the journey into the subconscious, she heard a knocking on her front door. She woke in a stupor and took some time to gather herself.

'Oy,' she called out in answer to her name. She got up from the floor and by instinct headed to the corner of the room where a lamp and matches were kept. Lighting the lamp, she went towards the door and called out before opening it. 'Who is dat?'

'Is me, Suraji, me wife going to have a baby, me modder send me to call yuh.'

She failed to recognise the voice but, realising it was male, said, 'Wait a minute, leh me put on some clothes.'

She returned to her corner and got an old dress and put it over the flimsy one she used for sleeping, hurried back and opened the door. The light shone on the caller, who placed a hand over his eyes to protect them from the sudden glare. Suraji moved to one side and saw it was Bato, the son-in-law of an acquaintance. She knew his wife was expecting and the visit ceased to be a surprise.

'How long de pains start?'

'Around six o'clock dis evening,' he replied anxiously, the concern on his face conveying the urgency of the situation. It was their first child; they had been married for just over a year.

Suraji saw the look on his face and said, 'Wait, leh me get meself ready, ah woh tek long.' She closed the door and went to the children. She stooped over and checked; they were fast asleep.

'Sakina,' she called out softly, trying not to rouse the younger

44

child. The girl turned away from the disturbing hand in an effort to avoid waking.

Suraji shook her once more and called, 'Sakina, Sakina.'

Sakina, realising she was being shaken, responded: 'Yes, Mai?'

Suraji whispered, 'Look, Bato wife, Choti, going to have a baby, ah have to go by she. If yuh want me, yuh know where ah is.'

'Yes, Mai,' came the response as Sakina turned once again to resume sleeping. Suraji, satisfied the message had got through, stood up and got herself ready to accompany the worried Bato back to his house. She moved quickly and in silence, dressing and getting together a few bits and pieces of clothing she might need, and placed them in an old basket. She went out of the back door into the kitchen and picked up a half bottle of rum and placed it in the basket. She returned the lamp to its usual position and blew it out, walking in darkness to the front door, closing it gently as she left. Bato moved away as he saw her and stood in the road. The gravel felt unusually hard as she walked towards him, her bare feet feeling the sharp edges of the stones pressing against them.

'Leh we go,' she said. They walked in silence, the tall line of trees and the intermittent hibiscus hedging, familiar to her eyes, marking their hurried passage. The few dogs still awake barked lazily at the two figures moving through the village. Bato's home was less than a quarter of a mile away, a little shack hastily erected in the wake of the chaos which followed after the estate collapsed. A light borrowed from someone shone brightly in the dark. Suraji saw it from a distance, after they turned the corner. They walked down the small path to the shack. A few women were gathered on the floor of the seating area. In another area, barred off, Choti lay on the floor, sweating and writhing from the labour pains. Bato stood in the semi-open kitchen. Choti's mother was squatting on the floor next to her, a bottle of toilet lotion in one hand, a soaked rag in the other, wiping her daughter's head, trying to soothe the strong pains. Sadwine was among the women. None were strangers; all knew Suraji and her reputation as a midwife and most had used her services themselves.

Suraji wasted no time in her work. Sadwine got up as she entered the room and asked, 'Can ah get yuh anyting, gal?'

'Yes, mek me some boiling water. Ah go need plenty.'

Suraji stood over the prostrate Choti and her mother. She asked the mother about the pain and was given an up-to-date report.

45

'Get me some cloth,' she ordered.

'Ah have some arready. Ah send Bato over to de shop as soon as he come to tell me about Choti,' replied the mother, who got up and handed Suraji a few yards of clean cotton wrapped in brown paper which had been standing on a window sill. Suraji stepped out and handed it to one of the other women sitting in the other room. 'Tear dis up for me in strips, some big an some small. De way dis chile looking, it look like if ah go need plenty.'

She returned and stooped over Choti, removing the sheet which covered her body. Underneath, she was naked. The stretched skin shone under the bright light. Sweat was pouring down from her face and arms; she needed mopping constantly. The sheet underneath her was soaked. The woman returned with the strips of cloth and handed them to Suraji.

'Tell Sadwine to hurry wid de water, dis chile water done buss.'

The woman turned and hurried to Sadwine. Suraji rested the cloth on a dry part of the sheet and moved closer to Choti. She wiped her brow and raised her head and plumped up the pillow.

'Doh worry, chile, it soon be all over, doh worry, ah go tek care ah yuh,' said Suraji.

◆

The pains were becoming more frequent and Choti's cries were piercing the silence. Saraji had taken charge of everything to do with the delivery of the baby. Some of the women began to leave, realising there was nothing further to be done except wait. Sadwine stayed behind, assisting Suraji and Choti's mother. She made coffee and tried to calm Bato, who was becoming anxious and restless. He kept on wanting a boy, saying, 'Notting else will do.'

About four o'clock, just as the stars began to fade and thin streaks of daylight were beginning to replace the intense darkness, the baby was born. Soft cries brought the half-asleep father chasing into the room. He was blocked at the door by Choti's mother.

'Wait, yuh cyah go in yet, leh Suraji finish.'

'What she mek?' he asked, his voice full of anticipation and anxiety.

'Wait,' repeated Choti's mother, 'Suraji still have a few more tings to do, boy; give she five more minutes.'

Sadwine brought in more warm water and an empty bowl and

handed it to Suraji. Choti, drenched with sweat, lay completely still, released from pain and in a stupor. The baby was placed by her side, wrapped in clean white cotton. Suraji lifted it up and handed it to Sadwine. She washed Choti, cleaning the blood from around her vagina. She shifted her to one side of the mat where she lay and spoke to her mother.

'Gal, get a clean pillow, a sheet an a new pall foh Choti.' Choti's mother turned to Bato, still waiting anxiously in the other room, and asked, 'Yuh hear dat? Wey she does keep it?'

'Dat is all we have, Mai,' he said, apologetically.

'Go an borrow some. Ask anybody. Go an ask . . .'

Before she could finish, Sadwine stepped out.

'Is a girl, look at she, look how much hair she born wid! Now, go to me house an wake up Sadhu an tell he what yuh want, tell he ah send yuh. Now go fast before yuh wife catch cold.'

Bato left in a hurry. He had one glimpse of his baby before speeding off to Sadhu to get the things his wife required. Suraji shifted Choti to the drier part of the jute mat pall. She placed the placenta and the umbilical cord in the bowl, and poured some water over it.

'Sadwine, gal,' she said, 'go out an bury dis.' Sadwine handed the baby to Choti's mother and took the bowl from Suraji. She went about two hundred yards from the shack in an abandoned cane field and buried the contents, reciting a little prayer in the early dawn. The birds were now waking, singing their morning chorus to greet the day. A rooster crowed, starting off a chain reaction among every rooster within hearing distance. The grey light of early dawn was turning to blue. She looked up and saw Bato running towards the shack with a bundle in his hands. 'Me clean sheet an pall – what ah go do in a emergency? Ah eh have much to replace dem,' she thought.

Bato entered the shack and handed the sheet and pall to Suraji. Choti's mother said, 'Here, hold yuh baby.' The panting Bato took the child gently from Choti's mother and stared at its closed eyes. He looked intensely at the nose, the only distinguishable feature on the otherwise wrinkled face. His warm breath blew over the child. Without taking his eyes from the child, he asked, 'How is Choti, she all right?'

'Yes, she all right, just sleeping after de pain,' said Choti's mother.

'Come in now, but keep quiet, she still resting,' said Suraji.

Bato tiptoed into the room to look at Choti. Suraji got up and handed the soaking bedclothes to Choti's mother. She stepped outside and saw Sadwine gazing at the sun rising. She wanted to be alone, a habit she had developed after a delivery. She walked to the far side of the hut, leaned against the wall, supporting her thoroughly exhausted body, lit a cigarette and gazed expressionless into the distance. Thoughts flashed through her mind, but in her tiredness she felt unable to retain any. Sadwine walked wearily towards her and said, 'Suraji, ah tired, gal. Ah going home now.'

Suraji stared blankly at the sunrise and said, 'Yes, go home, yuh need some rest.'

11 Sankar

Sankar sat on his step staring idly at the track of ants hurrying to and fro on the ground beneath him. It was Sunday, and he had just come outside after spending the entire morning resting in bed. Earlier he had heard a man asking for him or Sonny Boy. He refused to get out of bed because he knew what it was about and wished to avoid meeting the man. He had committed himself to an arranged marriage some months ago. The decision was taken during a drinking session with Sonny Boy and others in the village shop.

'Yuh sure yuh serious?' Sonny Boy had repeated.

'Yes, man, ah serious, yuh doh play round when it come to dat kinda business,' said Sankar.

'Den as soon as tomorrow break, ah going ahead wid it,' said Sonny Boy. Whenever Sonny Boy saw him, he reported on the finding and possible acceptance of brides for both of them. Sankar felt unable to say, 'Ah sorry, boy, ah change me mind.' He kept on giving the appearance of encouraging his friend, but wished somewhere along the line the exercise would falter and the plans would be dropped.

Today, luckily for Sankar, neither Sonny Boy nor his children were at home, for if they had been, he felt that once confronted, he would have agreed, and would have to face the consequences of telling Suraji. He got up from the step, dressed quickly and left his barrack room. He headed to Suraji for his breakfast, wanting to feel secure in her friendship to him.

Suraji and the children were not at home. She was attending to someone in the village, but had left his meal for him. He sat down on the kitchen steps and ate, gazing at the landscape and fending off the buzzing flies. A feeling of restlessness had overcome him and he felt he needed a drink to restore calm. The thought of taking a wife and leaving Suraji was causing an upheaval within him. He watched a fowl that wandered up to where he sat, scratching at the earth

49

hoping to find a morsel or perhaps expecting to be thrown a scrap of food.

His past experiences with women were not happy ones. He remembered his wife, the mother of his children, who had run away, never to be seen again, shortly after the birth of their son, Dano. The memories of her, up to now tightly shut away in the bottom of his mind, began to seep through to the surface. He got up almost immediately with the rising of the thought, dropping his empty plate, and rushed into the yard, breaking off a piece of sugar cane growing in a small clump in the garden. He ripped off the trash with his hands, hoping that the memories would disappear. Standing still, he cried out, 'Oh God!' as he felt the anguish within him rise. Peeling the stump of cane with his teeth, standing under the blazing sun, he sucked the sweet, sticky juice from the pulp. He broke out into a sweat. The fear of being left alone again was too much to face.

His mind felt it couldn't cope with the confusion and he left the house seeking refuge, wherever it was to be found. He walked to the cricket ground not far away. He saw from a distance a match was on. Figures dressed in white were on the field and sitting under the samaan trees at the edge of the sloping ground. He hurried towards them as though he were late for the match. He knew what to expect when he got there, but was prepared to put up with anything to escape from the feelings he had stirred up within; perhaps someone might have a bottle of rum and share a drink.

The village team was fielding and he sat with a group of older men. They all knew each other and any latecomer was greeted with neither welcome nor rebuke, but accepted as of right. A soft afternoon breeze was blowing; the sky was bright blue. The ground was on a hill overlooking the pond. Occasionally someone would shout, 'Hit de ball, nah, man,' as the batsman took a swipe and missed, indicating he was a visiting supporter. His exhortation to the batsman would not be taken up by the home crowd, but encouragement shouted to the bowler: 'Bowl him, Vernon!'

Eddie came and sat near Sankar. 'A man in a car came looking foh yuh today, boy,' he said.

'Ah hear him,' Sankar replied.

'Boy, yuh is a son of a bitch! Yuh mean yuh was dey an wouldn come out to see who it is or wha he want?'

'It eh me he come to see, is Sonny Boy he really want, not me.'

'Wey he gone, Sonny Boy?'

'He be somewey, yuh know he arready, always mekking big plan an wasting odder people time.' Sankar, now feeling part of the supporting home crowd, called out to some of them. He felt particularly pleased to see Tex, his foreman until the estate ceased to operate. He was sitting at the front of the small group taken up with the play going on in the field.

'Tex,' Sankar called. Tex turned to see who was calling.

'Sankar, yuh old scamp, when yuh get here?' His gold tooth glinted in the sunlight as he greeted him. He stood up and dusted the dried grass and specks of earth from the seat of his trousers and came and sat next to Sankar.

'So wha happening, pardner, long time no see,'' he said in a loud voice.

Someone in the crowd replied, 'All yuh shut up behind dey, yuh cyah see ah man concentrating on de cricket?'

'Why yuh doh go an concentrate somewey else? Ah eh see me pardner Sankar foh a long time, wha wrong wid yuh,' said Tex, who, however, lowered his voice when he next spoke.

'Boy, ah dey, but de wok too hard, said Sankar.

'Is only man what wokking does talk like dat. It have any Creole wokking on dat estate yet?' asked Eddie as he joined the conversation, checking on Good Intent Estate's policy of not employing people of African descent.

'Nah, boy, dey eh want all yuh,' said Sankar, 'not one Creole does get wok dey.'

'De white man know how to divide an keep we apart so one go feel he better dan de odder when all de time none ah we eh really worth a fart,' said Tex.

Another wicket fell. Someone shouted, 'Come on, Highlands, give it to dem, show who is boss.'

'Boss me ass, boss doh feel hungry,' said Eddie.

'Ah hear de main estate in St Madeline tekking people on,' said Sankar. 'Ah hear Mr Rooplal talking in de pen.'

'De las ting ah want is to wok anodder sugar estate,' said Tex. 'Ah had enough ah dat, an dis time ah looking foh a wok what cyah finish, wey de boss have so much ah money, is no way he go bankrupt.'

Calvin, who was sitting in the front keeping the scorecard,

51

overheard Tex and asked, 'Wey yuh going to find wok like dat? Always talking shit.'

Someone called his attention to register a run. 'Why yuh doh mind yuh business? De batsman make a run. Yuh see it?'

'Here, Bone, score foh a while,' said Calvin, rising from his seat, and at the same time thrusting the score book and pencil to a fat Indian, a former cane-weighing clerk in Highlands. Bone accepted and Calvin came and sat nearer to Tex. The sun was now shining through the tall bamboo patch near the pond. Calvin felt cheated on finding himself unemployed and having to depend on gambling to feed himself.

'Boy, all yuh shoulda listen to some ah de men. De estate was closing down, we coulda tek it over an run it weself,' he said, feeling dissatisfied by the lack of resistance shown by the workforce when the news broke.

'De same ole story,' said Eddie. 'Why yuh cyah leave dat alone?'

'What is to be must be. Look at Sankar here, is like notting happen, all he have to do is walk a little further to get to wok.'

'Is not de same, and de people different,' said Sankar, tugging at a blade of grass and placing it in his mouth as he spoke.

'Yuh tell dem,' said Calvin, finding support for his long-held point of view.

'Ah always have to listen to yuh, boy, but yuh wouldn listen,' said Tex, looking at Calvin. 'Dat cyah wok in dis country, de government wouldn never allow dat to happen.'

'Why, yuh tink dey prefer to see me go hungry?' asked Calvin.

'In de fuss place, even if we tek de place over, we couldn manage it, everybody go want to be big boss an . . .

Calvin attempted to intervene.

'No, leh me finish. Yuh had yuh say,' said Tex. 'Even if we get over dat, nobody wouldn buy we cane.'

'We could plant someting else, we doh have to plant cane. Dis land could grow anyting.'

'Yes, but den de question is, can we plant it to mek money?' asked Tex.

'Yuh doh know what yuh saying. We could plant anyting,' said Eddie.

'Like what?' said Tex in a more forceful manner.

'Corn, pepper an dem tings,' said Eddie.

'Boy, dat is not enough foh a big area ah land like dis. Yuh have to plant big. Yuh talking bout small market garden and ah talking ah how to mek a big estate feed an clothe all ah we.'

'Ah sure we woulda get help,' said Calvin.

'Help, me ass. Ah know what yuh saying but de problem is we doh know how to do anyting except how to grow cane an wok in de factory. Dat is what dey brought our parents foh. We need to know more dan cane. Ah sit down an tink about dese tings. It eh so simple,' said Tex.

'If we never try, how else we would know wha we can or cyah do?' said Calvin. 'Look at Scott, tell me what qualification he did have?'

'Money,' said Sankar.

'Yuh tell him, Sankar, boy,' urged Tex. 'Money! If yuh have dat, yuh could be what yuh want to be, but me, all me have from de time me born is to know how to wok in one place, no odder skill, notting to depend on. We is cane people and notting else and when de cane is done, we finish. Scott haul he ass. He skin white, he eh go starve, he people go see he all right, but me . . .' Tex's voice broke off as he looked at the play going on in the field. The interest in the conversation faded and the cricket attracted the attention of everyone. Sankar got up and left.

He walked slowly towards Suraji's place, hoping by now she had returned. He still felt uneasy. His mind was occupied with the thought of contracting into a marriage he was not prepared for. Now, however, a little more relaxed, he felt able to think about it. He walked up to a young cassia tree on the way and picked a flower. He looked at it and continued on his meandering walk, separating the petals and dropping them as he went. 'If only Sonny Boy didn go so far,' he kept repeating in his mind, thinking of the turmoil it would cause and the hurt to Suraji. The memories of his earlier marriage and the thought of the same thing happening again increased his doubts. He did not blame his wife for running away; the life on an estate was a hard one and few outsiders felt able to endure it. But for her to run away with a person of a different race, that was the bit he could hardly face. He felt totally ashamed and humiliated. His wife not only let him down but his whole race. She had broken the ultimate taboo and he took on the burden of guilt and remorse for what she had done.

Sonny Boy had been so convincing, putting forward the argument that he needed a real woman, not someone like Suraji who had lived with several other men in the past. He could hear his voice as if the conversation was right now. 'Boy, is two ah we in dis business, an ah hear de woman an dem pretty an know how to wok hard.' The thought of beauty lured Sankar into accepting. He hoped that an attractive, hard-working woman would absolve him and remove the cloud hanging over him for allowing his former wife to run away. He reached the hut. Suraji was not at home. He entered and lay down on the floor and fell asleep.

12 Vernon

The mist hanging over the pond was disappearing as the sun came up over the valley. The dew drops began to run off the leaves and blades of grass and were quickly soaked up by the parched dry earth. It was just after six and the time when the church bells in the distance pealed simultaneously with Harry's final ringing of the bell on the night watch in the disused factory. Vernon was up and getting ready to go to work. He stood in front of his room, brushing his teeth and holding a cup of water. The gang of women were standing outside Goddard's house, talking and laughing in their usual loud manner, waiting to see if any work was available before moving on to Good Intent to look there. One of them bawled out, 'Boy, mind yuh doh clean out yuh teeth.'

'Nah, gal,' Vernon replied, 'dey strong like me,' and raised the cup of water to rinse and spit into the sweet-lime hedge. He waved and returned to his room to change, a tall, thin man with a worried look shading over a pleasant face. His wavy hair, although well cut and groomed, seemed long; his moustache, though cared for, from a distance looked dishevelled and his clothes, neat and styled to the latest fashion, too big: a neat man when next to you but clumsy in appearance from afar. Now in his late twenties, he remained a bachelor, caring for his mother. He started off his working life as a cane cutter but learned the art of cutting hair during the idle months of the rainy season. The discovery that he had talent led him to seek employment in the nearby town and, two years before the estate folded up, he found work in a small barbershop sharing cramped premises with a shoemaker. He continued to live at Highlands, leaving early in the morning and returning late in the evening. Now dressed, and checking that his mother had sufficient food and money to get through the day, he wheeled out his bicycle and rode slowly over the bumpy road to work.

Shortly afterwards, his mother got up and began moving about,

55

waking up Eddie and Nat, the two remaining dwellers in the barracks. She sang in a flat, discordant voice, stopping to clap and dance as she moved about. Eddie turned in his bed, swearing at her for disturbing his sleep. Nat could no longer close his eyes as his partition was no barrier to her incessant sound and noisy movement. It was not possible to continue sleeping after Vernon's mother began her day. The noise and rising heat and a day with nothing to expect made Eddie swear at Vernon's mother. Nat joined him in the yard.

'Dis blasted ooman, eh? Every morning is de same ting. As soon as Vernon gone, she begin she madness. She getting wuss dese days.'

The two men stood idly, dressed in shorts and sleeveless vests, discussing the ravings of a mad woman on an early sunny morning against the backdrop of a closed-down factory on a deteriorating estate.

Vernon arrived in the small town and opened the shop, sharpening his scissors and razors and waiting for customers to arrive. One by one, men showed up to play draughts and prepared to argue on any topic while waiting their turn. The clatter of the draught pieces, the clicking of the scissors and the constant chattering created the impression that this ramshackle old building contained activity that was an essential part of the old town. Years ago, the town was the centre of the cocoa trade, but since the decline of that crop its existence depended on several other sources and as a transport terminus. Taxis and buses were everywhere; cane trucks and carts hurried through and private cars of nearly every description were either parked haphazardly or weaving through the chaos. People, old and young, went about their business. Indians dressed in their traditional dhotis and saris, ohrinis covering the heads of the women and turbans wrapped round the heads of the men, mingled with the various western styles worn by people of African descent. Idlers stood in groups on selected corners, calling out to attractive women or showing each other the latest dance craze. This was a busy place with more than its share of people with little to do.

Around midday, at the height of the busiest period, Vernon heard a voice he recognised. The one thing he dreaded had happened. His singing and dancing mother was directly in front of the barbershop. A crowd was gathering around her as she sang and danced. One of the draught players looked up from the draught board and said, 'All yuh, look at dat mad coolie ooman.'

Vernon stiffened and carried on cutting the customer's hair. Apart from the other barber, Rudy, who owned the shop, no one associated him with the crazy dancing woman outside. The crowd began to obstruct the traffic; a policeman arrived and moved them to the side of the road. Vernon's mother, taking advantage of the extra space, began to make more sweeping movements and sing louder. Her eyes seemed filled with pain, while a broad smile appeared on her mouth. Her slender brown body and long black hair, swinging from side to side, moved in a rhythm. The policeman attempted to grab her.

'Mind she bite yuh, if she draw blood yuh go turn crazy too.'

The policeman hesitated as more advice came his way from the crowd.

'Send foh de dog-catcher to hold she.' Laughter trickled through at this suggestion. A tear fell on Vernon's cheek; he wiped it off with the back of his hand and carried on cutting. He tried to make conversation from the thoughts summoned up from the depths of his mind, but the distance from brain to mouth was too great and only the will to concentrate on the job before him acted as a barrier to what was going on outside.

'Doh do dat,' someone called out to another, as he threw a pebble at Vernon's mother. When Vernon saw what had happened, he walked briskly to the shelf, dropped his scissors and went to ask Rudy to continue cutting his customer's hair. He rushed outside and grabbed hold of his mother by the arm and pulled her away.

'Come on, Mai, we going home.'

She was reluctant to move, as if she wanted to change the torment and the jeering of the audience into pity and understanding.

'Look, is Vernon modder,' someone pointed out. Some people laughed, but no one moved. Vernon pulled harder and his mother offered no more resistance. He approached a few empty taxis to take them home. Some drivers refused in a polite manner while others reacted and simply said, 'Ah doh tek mad people in me car.' Eventually, one of his customers said, 'Here, boy, ah go tek all yuh. Get in de car.'

Vernon's mother sang all the way home. Nat was around when they arrived.

'Get inside an stay dey,' said Vernon as they got out. Vernon's

57

mother obeyed without question. Vernon sat down on the step next to Nat.

'Boy, ah doh know what to do, de ooman come quite in de town to show me up in front ah all dem people. Ah doh know if ah have de courage to show me face dey again.'

'Doh be a fool,' said Nat. 'Dere eh notting to feel shame bout. People does forget quick an beside, it better to help yuh modder.'

'Ah doh know what have she so. One minute she calm an good, de odder time she gone completely out she head. Somebody musta put a light on she.'

'Yuh eh see? Somebody put a light on she. Yuh have to do someting about it,' said Nat.

'Ah agree, but who?' asked Vernon, hoping it was so, so that his mother's malady could be cured. He continued by quickly repeating his question to Nat. 'Who yuh know in dis village good at getting she better?'

Nat thought before answering and then said, 'Ah doh know really, doh forget ah is a stranger here. But ah know someone who might be able to help.'

'Who is dat?' asked Vernon.

Nat replied, 'Suraji. If anyone in de whole place know, is she.'

Vernon's mother continued with her singing and shouting but, in the relative quiet and safety of Highlands, this went largely unnoticed or ignored. Vernon began to think of his mother in the early years of his life, before she developed this illness. She was pretty and worked extremely hard along with his father cutting cane. He died when Vernon was still a boy, and she, overcome with grief, used to go into long spells of silence. She cut herself off from everyone and thought only of providing for her son. At first her illness was not noticeable, for the singing and dancing were camouflaged by a broad smile and friendly face. Only by noticing the distant look in her eyes were you able to tell that something was wrong. Over the years, this behaviour became more pronounced. Vernon blamed himself for his mother's condition, feeling that had he not been away, he might have been able to do something about it. Perhaps if he had sought help from other villagers his mother might have been saved from this living death. Secretly he feared it was too late, but the idea that someone might have cast an evil spirit over his mother's mind was a convenient excuse. He got up and said, 'Leh we go find Suraji.'

'Nah, boy, she eh home at dis time, she mus be wokking. Leh we wait till later,' said Nat.

The realisation of the time made Vernon remember his bicycle.

'Oh, shit, ah leave me bike in de town an dat shop eh safe. Ah have to go foh it.' It was around two in the afternoon. 'Oh, God, to face dem people, ah feeling shame.'

'Doh worry,' said Nat, 'Ah go bring it home foh yuh. Ah have to do someting in de town.'

Vernon felt relieved. 'Boy, Nat,' was all he managed to say. He walked to the corner of the barracks near Eddie's room, took up a cup from his kitchen and drank from the barrel of rain water.

'Ah suddenly feeling hungry. Yuh eh have notting to eat?' he asked.

'Nah, boy,' said Nat. 'Dat is why ah going in de town to find someting to cook.'

Vernon went and stood in the yard and saw smoke coming from his mother's kitchen which, unlike the three others, was situated at the back of the barracks.

'Yuh see what ah cyah understand? She might be mad, but when is time to eat, she damn well know how to cook.'

'Yuh right, is light somebody put on she. De sooner we get somebody to lift it, de better,' said Nat.

13 The christening

It was a happy occasion, the blessing and dinner given by Choti and
Bato to celebrate the birth of their child. The pundit said the prayers
around mid-morning. The previous day Bato, with the help of other
villagers, had erected a tent from bamboo, covered with coconut
leaves, adjoining his shack. The men congregated there; while some
were cooking pots of food, others sang, played cards or just talked. It
was rumoured that Donald financed the gathering; no one knew for
sure as he was always discreet about his gifts of money, and Bato
refused to divulge where he got it from. Almost everyone in the
village was there. The preparation began the previous afternoon, for
there was plenty to do. Bato, between drinks, was boasting of his
dreams for his daughter to anyone who cared to listen. Choti
remained in the shack, speaking to the women about her child's
qualities, and singing praise to Suraji for her attendance during the
birth and organising the after-care. Because it was a Sunday, many
found time to attend and even those who worked got off early enough
to do so. On the whole their preoccupation with the adverse effects of
the closure of the factory were temporarily shoved aside by having
something to celebrate. Tomorrow or the day after the hurt would
resume.

The feeding of the guests began around midday on this hot
afternoon in February. The air was still and the noise travelled far.
The shack rocked as dancing women swayed to the beat of the drum
from outside. A few of them passed around, surreptitiously, little
nips of rum kept hidden in the pockets of their dresses. Suraji sat in a
corner, clapping her hands, her body aching with tiredness, relaxing
with the alcohol. Sadwine kept making excuses to Hitler, who was
asking that they go outside to have a woman-to-woman talk. She
threw herself into the party and in the exhilarated mood she was in,
her excuses came across not as hostile or unfriendly, but as if this was
not the time to have such a talk.

People wore their best clothes; women wore white ohrinis covering their heads, and long coloured dresses, a change from the tattered and faded ones used for work or staying home, their bare legs and feet gleaming with coconut oil. The men wore shoes, long trousers and clean shirts. Some were already drunk, either singing too loudly, sleeping in the tent or vomiting at the edge of the came field. Eddie and his gang of card players sat in a clearing near the tent. Tex was as usual holding forth.

'Dis place had so much ah happiness going foh it,' was among the many comments he made while concentrating on the cards he received. The one woman to break the strict divide between men and women was Vernon's mother, who danced inside the tent, much to the amusement of some. Vernon, playing cards with Eddie and the others, ignored her, knowing that in this environment no harm would come to her. This was Highlands at play.

A car pulled up and Donald, Balgobin, Blue Jean and Bella came to join the party. Donald was dressed in a clean khaki outfit and was almost sober. Balgobin and Blue Jean stuck close to him. He greeted everyone and was kindly received.

'How she going, boss, any chance ah de estate starting up again?' was a frequent question to him.

'Not a chance in hell,' was his reply, but he was in no mood to talk about the future. He came to enjoy himself and to mix with his former employees. He had begun to do this when the opportunity arose. Like every other guest, he ate from a banana leaf with his hands. He enjoyed the curried vegatables, pumpkin, dhal and rice, calling for more.

Around four o'clock, people started to drift away. Sankar and Sonny Boy were sitting on the side of the road.

'Boy, ah tell yuh, is a good move. Look at Suraji,' said Sonny Boy, 'go inside de house, yuh go find she drunk. What yuh want is a nice wife, who know how to behave sheself.'

'Nah, boy, it go cause trouble, ah done tink about it,' said Sankar.

Sonny Boy, lean and dark, in his late forties, was not prepared to give up. 'Look, boy, is like dis. De one who promise to married me wouldn come to live here by sheself, she want company. She is a big ooman, she doh mek new friend dat easy. She say if she friend could find a husband, only den she would come. Ah go tek care ah yuh, yuh go see is no trouble when it done. Here, have anodder drink.' He passed a bottle over to Sankar, who took a long drink and passed it back.

◆

At last, Hitler persuaded Sadwine to have the long-awaited talk. They walked back slowly to Sadwine's home.

'Is like dis, gal. De man an dem does give he money foh he to give dem wok. He doh want money from a ooman, he want more dan dat.'

'But why me?' asked Sadwine. 'Ah too shame to do dis kinda ting.'

'It eh no different from wokking, in fact, in some ways it easier, but ah know how yuh feel. Ah feel de same way, but he doh want me.'

'Gal, ah doh know,' said Sadwine.

Hitler sensed she was wavering and paused in her attempt to get Sadwine's agreement. 'Look, ah know it hard, yuh doh have to do it,' she said, trying to force Sadwine to agree without seeming to do so. She held Sadwine's hand and their bare feet brushed the still warm grass at the side of the road. Sadwine looked up and stared at the trees as they walked.

'Is really notting to it. When yuh tink, nobody go talk. Plenty women done it arready, it easy, yuh go inside de house foh half an hour an yuh get pay like if yuh cut a task ah cane. Yuh could go home early an beside, he doh stay wid one woman foh long, de most is one week.'

The thought of spending most of the day at home attracted Sadwine for obvious reasons. Harry spent a great part of each day sleeping after work; she smiled as the thought entered her mind. They passed by a mango tree whose flowers were turning into fruit. The afternoon sun was bright, but its heat was already on the wane.

'So what yuh say, gal, yuh go do it?' enquired Hitler. Sadwine remained silent and continued to look at the mango tree.

14 Hitler

The dawn was cool and misty. Hitler was under the gallery of the village shop, waiting for her gang of women to congregate. She was usually the first to get there. She was tall and broad-shouldered; her face had strong features and always had a stern look about it. She was never seen without her head fully covered with a headscarf and a hat over it. She worked extremely hard, to earn every penny she could. There was also a benign, caring side to her and at times she was full of fun. On some mornings her laughter could be heard throughout the estate. This morning, dressed in her long tattered work dress, stained with the ash from the burnt canes, her bag filled with water and food for the day, and holding a cutlass, she appeared to be worried. One of the men who had begun to gather asked her, 'Ah yuh expecting any wok here today, gal?'

'Ah doh know, boy, it depend on Mr Goddard. All yuh have?' she asked.

'Yes, he give me some tasks since last week. What happen, he eh do de same foh all yuh?'

'Nah, boy, dis man does give me wok from day to day, me eh lucky like all yuh,' she replied, slightly disconcerted that none of the other women had turned up as yet. She lit a cigarette and blew the smoke into the remaining mist.

The sun was beginning to rise, its golden glow slowly shifting away the dark blue early morning cloud. All round, cocks were crowing. The trees, hidden by the darkness of the night, began to show themselves, and the rest of the vegetation began to take shape. The factory bell rang five times. In the distance, men and women were seen walking to the shop. In the silence of the early morning, their voices carried. Hitler was becoming more anxious as the women started to arrive, wondering whether Mr Goddard would give them work. Suraji arrived, walking slowly to the shop.

In the olden days, work was guaranteed but now work depended on a favour granted by white men. Goddard woke up as the bell struck five, a strong, hardy man whose job it was to ensure the remaining cane crop was cut and the money paid to the receivers. Brought to the estate by Donald from Barbados to be an overseer, he remained in charge after the collapse. After this crop was cut, he would be moving on, but for now he wanted to make more money on top of his salary and to enjoy himself while doing so. He lived in the bachelor quarters above the newly built office and weighing house. He was a man in his early fifties, and nothing delighted him more than his present circumstances. He hired a servant, a young girl called Marie. He expected his gangs any moment now. After his shower, he got himself ready to receive them.

He looked at the daily requirements, having already given out work to the men, and found that there was work for the women, provided Hitler was prepared to pay his price. Marie brought him a cup of coffee as he sat in his office and waited. The fifteen women who were led by Hitler had arrived at the shop; it was time to leave. She, as she had been doing since Goddard asked her for Sadwine, walked at the back with her, trying to persuade her to do it. This morning was supposed to be the day when it all happened.

'It so easy, gal, yuh go laugh when it all over. Jus imagine, yuh clothes wouldn get dirty nor yuh foot an dem stained wid de black ash from de burn cane.'

Sadwine felt crowded and walked in silence, her bare feet brushing against the wet grass. Dew dripped slowly off the leaves. Hitler swiped her cutlass at a young fly-bush weed. She was attempting to hide her true feelings and appear to be nonchalant about getting Sadwine into Goddard's bed. As they neared the bachelor quarters, Sadwine whispered timidly, 'Ah fraid, gal, suppose Sadhu find out?'

Hitler held her hand and said, 'Wait here.' They stood under the huge overhanging branches of a samaan tree. Ferns covered most of its trunk and branches; a few wild orchids grew on its upper branches, while on the lower ones, some birds had made their nests. Hitler called out to the rest of the women, 'All yuh go on past de factory an wait foh me behind Donald Scott's house. Dis morning we mus get wok.'

The women understood what she meant, as they knew what Goddard wanted in exchange for work.

After they walked off, Hitler turned to Sadwine and said, 'Look, yuh is not a little gal, yuh know as de rest ah we, some ooman had to give sheself to him so dat de rest ah we could get wok. Now is your turn, dat is all, is notting to fear. Is either dat or we starve.' She spoke with a strong, firm voice as though she were issuing a command that had to be obeyed. Sadwine's fear turned into confusion. Up to now she had thought it would be an easy thing to refuse, but now it seemed so difficult. Hitler held her hand once more and said, 'Come, leh we go.'

Sadwine looked at her eyes; they appeared strong and full of conviction, without a hint of remorse or hesitancy. She surrendered meekly as Hitler led her to the stairs of the bachelor quarters. They walked slowly up. The factory bell struck six. Sadwine remembered Harry. She pulled her hand away from Hitler and almost ran up the stairs when she heard the bell. She was afraid he might see her and it was too late to turn back. Hitler felt relieved, for today she knew work was available. Sadwine waited for her at the top of the stairs, trembling with fear.

They both entered Goddard's office at the end of the veradah. He looked at Sadwine for a full minute before saying anything, then he examined his books, took out a pencil from his shirt pocket and wrote a note and handed it to Hitler.

'Here, give this to the driver working with the men, he will tell you what to do.' Goddard's eyes again rested on Sadwine, examining her firm, well-built body and innocent face. 'This is one conquest I will enjoy,' he thought. Hitler stayed put.

'Well, what are you waiting for?' he asked in a slightly angry tone.

'Ah jus want to know how long dis piece ah wok go last,' Hitler replied.

'Why, it is for one day at a time.'

'Den ah taking she away from here. Dis is at least a week ah wok.'

One of Goddard's weaknesses was his lack of patience; sometimes he expressed it with a show of bad temper. Now, however, he was eager and did not wish to put up a fight or even barter.

'All right, you have work for a week. Now go before I change my mind.' Hitler looked reassuringly at Sadwine, winked one eye at her and left.

Harry, whose cubicle was situated in such a way that Goddard could keep an eye on him, except when he was walking around, had seen two women going up, one of whom was Sadwine. Now, as he prepared to leave for home, he saw Hitler coming down alone.

15   Donald Scott

The time came when Donald was forced to leave Highlands. No longer the ruler, he had found poverty and inactivity hard to take. Instead of cooking what Donald liked, Bella cooked what she could afford. He became a pathetic figure, drinking most of the time. Bella was now in charge of the household. She wore neat clothes and always kept her hair covered. She had a kind face which was hardly seen beyond the estate. On her days off, she stayed in her room and prayed. A mysterious person to most people, she had no family and cared only for herself and Donald. She was always paid a weekly wage, but no one knew what she did with the money, and no one dared ask.

Donald had inherited Highlands while in his early twenties. His family had owned it for three generations. His mother and father, having had enough of the tropics, retired to Scotland, only to die of pneumonia during their first winter. As a condition attached to the inheritance, Donald had to marry. He underwent a marriage ceremony with a landowner's daughter, who left him after nine months.

At first he was successful in running the estate. When he inherited it, the sugar market was flourishing, labour was cheap and living costs low. Then came the Second World War and sugar was in great demand. The old factory was turning out many tons, for both export and home consumption. He bought racehorses and gave large parties entertaining the visiting troops; many soldiers and sailors on leave spent time with him on the estate. He was doing his bit for the country. Then came the post-war decline. The surplus money made during the war was used towards the purchase of a new mill and the building of his palace in the cane field, just when most sugar estate owners found running their own factories too expensive and were closing down operations, selling out to larger companies.

Donald was in debt and couldn't sell; the estate was valued at less than what he owed. He had to swim against the tide and try to make some money. Two years later, the receivers moved in and declared him bankrupt. 'Stabbed in the back by my friends', he often said while drinking in the village shop. He resorted to drinking and love-making to ease the pain of failure. Any man who wanted a free drink or a couple of dollars sought his company. Donald spent freely whatever money he made, drinking and buying sex.

Bella looked on with despair at his decline. He found time when sober to visit her in the kitchen where she spent most of the day. She sat in a comfortable armchair, reading a Bible, and Donald like the boy he once was, occasionally fell on to her lap weeping bitterly and seeking solace. She stroked his blond hair with her dark hand gently and never attempted to stop him.

'What can I do? What can I do, dear Bella?' She sat in silence, saying nothing. At first, in order to make ends meet, she grew a kitchen garden with the help of Blue Jean. But Donald in his drinking bouts would take his hangers-on to visit it, to convince them that he could have made the estate prosperous by growing veg-etables instead of cane. Some picked the crops to take home to their wives: 'Look what come from de boss garden!'

Donald became unmanageable. Strangers were invited and some-times stayed for days, using up the last bit of cash he had. Some nights, Bella and Blue Jean had to search the house and throw them out.

'Is de boss wha ask me to stay, yuh cyah trow me out.'

'Get out right now,' came the stern reply from Bella.

One day Goddard, the receiver's agent, visited the mansion. It was a clear, bright morning. He came to the kitchen door and knocked. Bella answered.

'Good morning, Miss Bella. Is the boss home?'

'No, Mr Goddard,' said Bella, 'these days with nothing to do he leaves quite early.'

'I know. It's sad to see this happening to him, he is such a nice man,' said Goddard.

'What can I do for you?' asked Bella.

'I might as well tell you. I wanted to say this to him personally to avoid you hearing the bad news from someone else, but I suppose he no longer cares,' said Goddard.

67

'What bad news? Nothing could be worse,' said Bella.

'I'm afraid so. I've been told by the receiver to get Donald off the estate,' said Goddard.

'Where can he go?' asked Bella.

'Back to Scotland? Or one of his friends might have him?' said Goddard.

'What about me? I will never leave him,' said Bella.

Goddard hesitated before answering. He was sad at having to do this. Donald was his former friend and employer, whom he still held in high regard, and Bella was never unkind to him.

'Please, Miss Bella, I know how much you care for him, but he is beyond helping at this stage. Stay with us on the estate. I'll get you a room at a cheap rent,' said Goddard.

'No, thank you,' said Bella, 'we are not fininshed yet. How long have we got?'

'Another month, that is all,' said Goddard.

'All right,' said Bella, 'I'll see that we are out of here before that.'

'Thanks, Miss Bella,' said Goddard. 'I'll have to go now, so many things to get done. Goodbye.'

As he turned and walked away quickly down the drive, Bella stood at the doorway looking at him go. She was thinking, 'What a strange man.' She had heard of his carrying on with the women since being placed in temporary charge of the estate, about his accepting bribes from the men, but in spite of the power he wielded, he was still afraid of Donald. He chose a time when Donald was out to come and tell him to leave.

She closed the kitchen door and returned to her chair. It was a silent time of day. No dogs barked, no birds whistled, nobody moved about. It was a time to concentrate without distraction. After a while, she stood up and went to her room, packed some clothes in a suitcase and changed. She returned to her kitchen and called loudly for Blue Jean who was sleeping on one of the beds upstairs. When Blue Jean heard her powerful voice echoing through the house and into the cane, 'Yes, Mis Bella, ah coming,' was his equally loud reply. He quickly got out of bed and hurried down the stairs towards her.

'Yes, Mis Bella, what yuh want?' he asked. She remained silent and looked at him. He found her silence difficult to understand and in his mind pleaded guilty to every indiscretion he had committed since coming to work for Donald. Even now, when his payment was an occasional handout and he could, if he wished, be at home or working for someone else, he still felt in awe of Miss Bella.

He looked at her once more and this time noticed that she was dressed and wearing a hat. Before he had time to comment, she placed her hand gently on his shoulder and said, 'Sit down, ah have something to tell.'

The guilty feeling turned into deep concern as he sat at the kitchen table. She remained standing.

'Now, ah want yuh to promise not to tell a soul about what ah am about to tell yuh, yuh understand?' she said.

'Yes, Mis Bella,' came his reply, his voice soft and almost a whisper. Her eyes glanced at her old suitcase near the door; noticing it for the first time, he feared the worst.

'Ah am leaving . . .'

He interrupted before she could finish. 'Yuh cyah do dat, not now!'

'Leh me finish,' she said in a strong, assertive tone. 'Mr Goddard was just here. It is time for Donald and me to leave dis estate and ah am going to find somewey foh us to live.'

'But where, Mis Bella?' he asked, his small brown face creased at the brow, indicating that this was a matter which caused great concern. She remained calm but assertive. He could detect no signs of uncertainty when she spoke.

'Ah have some plans, ah have been thinking about dis for some time. But ah want yuh to promise to look after Donald while ah am away. Here is some money.' She took up a handbag resting on the table, opened it and gave him a wad of notes.

'Ah might be gone for some days. Now, only spend what yuh need and if Donald ask yuh, tell him is credit from de shop, doh give him dis money.'

'Doh worry, Mis Bella, ah could take care ah dat.'

'Please, ah am begging yuh, doh tell anyone, including Donald, about me going to look foh somewey to live, it will spoil everyting. Now, ah trusting yuh, yuh hear?'

'Ah hear, Mis Bella, ah hear.'

She bent down and gave him a kiss on his forehead and left before he had time to question her plans or the meaning of the kiss.

◆

Later that afternoon when the villagers returned, rumours began to spread. The village shop was busier than usual; people came there to buy items which they could have done without in order to hear the gossip. The younger men sat around the clearing under the young cassia tree. Madan sat in his usual place on a stool at the bar.

'Two ting happen today, boys,' he was telling a group of men as he gulped down the drink of rum someone had bought. The women in the dry goods section strained their ears to hear the news. 'Well, dis place finish now, ah tell yuh, we is real hungry dog from now on. Mis Bella leave de estate, she leave Scott an gone. Ah hear she eh coming back.'

'Who tell yuh dat?' asked one of the men.

'Ah watch she go,' he said as he scratched his fat stomach through his dirty vest.

'An wha else happen?' asked one of the men.

'Bodhan an he wife fight right here in de shop. She catch he drinking an she put some good lash on he ass. Ask Ramnath, it happen right here.' He called out to the attendant, 'Ramnath, come here and tell dese men wha happen here today.'

Ramnath, busier than usual, selling candles, small quantities of butter and biscuits to several customers, replied, 'Ah eh have time, all yuh, ah busy right now.'

'Come here, boy, a man want a drink, dat eh right?' Madan asked of the group at large.

'Yes,' came the reply, 'ah will buy anodder.'

Madan called Ramnath again. 'Ramnath, come, boy, dis man here say he want a nip ah puncheon.'

'All right, ah coming,' said Ramnath as he walked over to the group. As he was pouring the rum from the large bottle into a quarter-size bottle, Madan said, 'Tell dem, boy, how Bodhan get he ass beat.'

'Boy, I get used to dat now. Dem two always fighting in dis shop. It eh serious,' he said.

'Not serious?' said Madan. He became slightly agitated. He was about to get another free drink on the basis of what he knew and Ramnath was lessening the importance of it.

'Ah tell yuh, coolie man will tek any excuse to beat up he wife, but not Bodhan. He only mouth an trousers. Dat ooman bussin lash on he ass from de day dey get married,' he said, trying to increase the

70

seriousness of the news he was about to divulge. Ramnath placed the rum on the counter and checked the water jug. Madan waited anxiously to be offered the bottle. The men hesitated, waiting for Gavin, the purchaser of the rum, to take his drink and offer the bottle. He poured out a larger than usual drink and passed over the bottle to another who emptied the remainder into his glass. Gavin drank quickly, wiping his mouth with the back of his hand.

'If Ramnath say is a joke, den is a joke. Ah going home.' The men left. Madan sat stunned. He could not believe what had just happened to him.

'Well, look at me crosses, eh?' he called out to no one in particular. 'An dey was more, too! Dese modder-ass people treating me like if ah is shit in dis place.'

◆

Harry walked into the shop to buy his evening drink before going to work. His face was glum and serious. He stared at Madan, who left to go and join the younger men sitting idly under the trees. They were discussing the departure of Miss Bella. Madan came and sat next to Tex who was talking.

'All ah know is, she never set foot outta dis place since ah know she. Ah telling yuh, African ooman have strange ways.'

A well-kept Chevrolet taxi passed, its green paint shining brightly in the sunlight. Eddie said, 'Look at how Shah does keep dat car, eh, boy? So clean an inside it does smell nice.'

'Dat is why he does get so much passenger. Dat is what cause de downfall ah dis estate. People stop caring enough foh it. Look at Madan here. Yuh tink anybody in dey right mind go give him wok?'

Madan, still peeved at being refused rum, walked away; this lot was certainly not buying him any rum and he was not prepared to be the butt of their jokes without reward. He heard as he walked on, 'Man doh know what dey have until dey lose it.'

'Is all right for dem to talk dat way, all ah want is a drink, not ole talk.'

16 Sadwine

Today she returned home frightened and excited rather than tired and bedraggled. Hitler had said it was easy, less tiring then cutting cane, and so it was, for on entering Goddard's room the overwhelming shyness caused her to behave in what appeared to be a perfectly normal way. There was almost a mechanical air to the whole situation. He undressed and got into the well-made bed. Sadwine took off her clothes and felt more disturbed by the dirt from them soiling his neat and tidy room than by her nakedness. She placed them in a bundle on the floor. Goddard became impatient when he saw her brown body standing at the foot of the bed. Sadwine hesitated, wanting time to assert herself and clear up the confusion she felt within and to find some meaning to the situation. He reached up and grabbed her and in spite of her protest of, 'Wait, wait,' he paid no attention and carried on, treating her hesitation as meaningless. It was over as quickly as it began. Goddard got up and wiped himself with a towel, then passed it to her. He lit a cigarette and took a drink from a bottle kept on his bedside table. He seemed cold and dejected. Sadwine, for a moment, felt she was a complete disappointment to him and wanted to extend her arms to invite him back, but as soon as he replaced the cork on the bottle, he turned and said, 'Get up, I have a lot of work to do today, just make sure you return tomorrow.'

She got out of bed, wiped herself with the soiled towel, keeping her eyes fixed to the ground, the feeling of pity turning to embarrassment. She got dressed and, looking straight into his face, said, 'Yes, ah go come back tomorrow,' and left.

As she walked home she imagined she could feel the fingers of everyone in the village calling her a harlot and a woman without shame, a betrayer of her race and religion. Her sin was that she had slept with an outsider. She condemned herself and invited everyone else to do the same. But no one appeared to do so. Everyone she met greeted her in their usual friendly fashion: 'Sadwine, yuh home early, gal.'

She replied, 'Yes, me eh feeling to wok today,' and carried on homewards.

She went to her room and changed into a cotton dress she used for bathing. Her bathroom was a rusty, galvanised iron enclosure in her small yard. A bucket and full barrel of water remained there as her husband had to have a bath every morning before praying, and he filled it up afterwards before his breakfast. She took a cake of scented soap from the kitchen, a towel and an enamel mug, draping the towel over the galvanise and placing the soap on the concrete floor of the bathroom. She filled the bucket and poured water from the mug over her. The soaked dress clung to her body, leaving rising patterns along her skin. The water washed away the feeling of guilt and reinforced the idea that what she did was more of a sacrifice than a sin. Women would get work, she knew, and laughed at the attempt of men like Goddard to exercise their power.

She compared the performances of the three men in her life. Sadhu demanded subservience from a wife and when that was not forthcoming expected secrecy and an outward show of harmony. Harry, her lover, in spite of being confined to a cramped, smelly latrine over the years, performed entirely to her satisfaction. And now, Goddard, whose only impact was to make her take a bath at an unusual hour. The soap travelled all over her body. She inhaled the sweet perfume of the soap and looked up at the clear blue sky, the white froth on her hair shining under the glare of the hot sun. She poured several buckets of water over her to wash away the stain of the morning, thinking how correct Hitler was when she said it would be easier than cutting cane.

She wiped herself and got dressed after rubbing herself all over with coconut oil. She began to look forward to meeting Harry. She summoned him by opening a window which normally remained closed. She sat near it waiting for his tall, lumbering frame to appear and head down the track to the latrine. He failed to appear. Perhaps he had forgotten that she had told him she might be home early. She got up and began to talk to herself in a loud voice, hoping he would hear and see the sign indicating that she was at home and prepared to meet him. She prayed silently but intensely, urging him to respond. Still no sign of any movement. She began to get angry and searched her mind for an explanation for his behaviour. 'He doh know about Goddard, so dat cyah have anyting to do wid it. He doh

73

mind about Sadhu, what we have is different. It doh matter who I go wid as long as we togedder afterwards, he know is he I like.' She was beginning to feel disappointed in Harry and closed her window. 'If dat is de way he want to play it, den two ah we could play dat game,' she thought as she walked slowly over to her bed and lay down. Before she had time to close her eyes, she heard his window opening. His sign of calling! She rushed out of bed and saw his heavy frame walking to the latrine. Today, she had thought of inviting him to her home, but when she saw the look on his face she thought otherwise; he appeared to be stern and angry. She waited for a little while before going to the latrine to meet him.

'Ah see yuh, ooman, going up to Goddard, yuh of all people giving yuhself to dat nasty kind ah man.'

'Was either dat or no ooman in de village get wok, all yuh man all right,' said Sadwine in a loud voice.

'Keep yuh voice down,' he said, 'yuh want de whole village to hear we?'

'Ah doh care, is time de whole village wake up an face de truth. Ah had to go wid he, odderwise some people woulda starve,' she said, facing him in this tiny, stinking cubicle with white maggots circling the pit underneath their feet. He slapped her with a great deal of force; the crack from his palm on making contact with her face echoed through the trees and bushes around. She stared unbelievingly at him and spat blood through the latrine hole on to the maggots feeding on the shit below. 'Dis is dreadful,' she thought and remained silent, staring at his angry contorted face. Getting no response to his slap, he increased his attack, punching uncontrollably at her body. She stared at him and began to cry, not from the effects of the pain, but from the devastation he had caused to a perfect set-up. Rain clouds gathered overhead, the light became dim as she opened the latrine door and ran back to her home, leaving him punching the wooden walls. 'Ah finish wid he,' she thought as she flung herself on to her bed.

17 Eddie

A tropical storm broke quite suddenly. One minute the sky was bright and cloudless and the next, lightning followed by heavy winds and rain covered Highlands. It was unusual for this time of year, but in a climate where there are only two seasons, wet and dry, rain sometimes falls in the dry, and long periods of sunshine occur during the wet. It was around two o'clock when the rain started. People who were working in the fields got soaked and, with the lightning flashing, those with cutlasses had to put them away. Some animals drawing the carts began to panic at the sound of the thunder. Their drivers had to hold on to them to prevent them from bolting.

Eddie sat in his room, the front door open, watching the rain. Looking directly upwards, he saw the dark body of threatening clouds but, in the distance where the sun still shone, their grey was overlaid with bright orange as though they had been set alight. Highlands took on a dismal appearance during the rain, the water cascading along the edge of the gravel road, the heavy raindrops resounding as they struck the earth. Drops of water began to drip through the old galvanised roof of his barrack room. He went into his wet kitchen to get a pot to collect the water. He placed it under a leak. He moved the bed from under another; water was everywhere. Eddie took out every receptacle he could find to collect water from the leaks but there were not enough. The sound of the rain pouring on the roof drowned out the sounds of the dripping water collecting in pots, pans, cups and a bucket.

People were hurrying home, soaked and cold. He looked at the clock. It was only just after two, but the darkness made it feel like six o'clock. He was alone in the barracks. He wished there were company, but it was too early for his card school to congregate and none of his neighbours had braved the rain to come home. The storm made him feel scared; its ferocity and volume seemed greater than he had experienced before. It was a long time since he had felt frightened; that was when someone who was bigger than him

75

wanted to fight. Now, with the heavy rain and dark atmosphere, it was hard for him to understand that what he felt was fear.

He belonged to both the races who occupied Highlands, his mother Indian and his father African. His mother had brought him up and taught him a lot of Indian practices but, although he hardly knew his father, he adopted Creole practices because he assumed them to be stronger and it was more fashionable to do so. He was taught one set of values and copied another. He had covered the walls of his room with old newspapers and cinema posters. Water seeping down disturbed the paper and some began to slide off. He sat looking at the pouring rain and the damage it was causing to his room, accepting the inevitable.

His mind began to recollect the wild days of his youth when his mother had tried to correct his errant behaviour and failed. She spoke to him in Hindustani, which he understood and could speak enough so that others were able to make sense of what he was saying. When he reached the age of fourteen he had run away and found work in the town. The life there was different from what he imagined it to be and, after drifting from place to place and from one menial job to another, he returned to the estate bringing with him some city ways and a few cinema posters which reminded him and others of where he had been.

He found steady work in the factory, and this barrack room. His mother was glad to see him, but she had settled down to a new life and contact between them was limited. He longed for the days when she had loved and cared for him. Perhaps it was due time that another person showed him some affection. Now, in spite of having visitors almost every day, he felt lonely. He wanted to be close to someone but felt unable to do anything about it. Every Friday night he went to the pictures, but apart from that, every day was the same. He had some savings, but they were running out. 'Ah mus get a job,' he thought, as he did almost every day.

The rain began to ease off, but the darkness remained. He lit a lamp, hoping the light would change the desolate feeling of his room. Uneasiness persisted within him, a mixture of belonging and unbelonging. He felt like a prisoner, trapped by walls of water, contained in this semi-soaked cell. Highlands was his home and his prison. What the future held was difficult to imagine. To be able to exist was all that mattered. After the factory ceased to operate, he

76

had planted a few strips of corn on a disused piece of land. He now wondered whether the rain had caused any damage, washing away the soil. The restlessness was now coming in waves; a feeling of wanting to brave the rain and head for the village shop became a compulsion. As fast as he pacified that thought it returned again, stronger each time. It was the thought of getting soaked that prevented the attempt he might have made to leave.

The pond began to overflow its banks. As Eddie stood up, he could see the muddy water covering areas far beyond the bamboo patch which bordered it. As a young boy, he had spent many happy days swimming and playing around the pond. Highlands was at its height then. Donald Scott had money to invest in thoroughbred racehorses. One, a champion imported from England, was the pride of the estate. Eddie longed to ride it, but was never given the opportunity nor found an occasion to take one. The decline had been coming for a long time. Eddie knew the racehorses, fancy cars, the new mansion and new machinery for the factory were costing too much money. He noticed this profligacy, but felt as long as he received wages it had nothing to do with him. He joined the strike for better wages, not believing it would be the last straw for the estate.

In the card school, his one regular means of earning, they talked constantly of the excessive spending by Donald, his team of overseers and the dishonesty of some of the men in supervisory positions. Eddie envied their power and their ability to ensure against whatever happened; they had sufficient money stashed away to ensure the continuance of a comfortable life. He wished he had the power to do the same.

He longed for Nat or Vernon to return. At least their company would break the isolation he felt. Even Sankar, he thought, even if it was to tease him as he usually did. His mind raced continuously from past to present. 'Ah should get up an cook some food,' he thought, 'since ah eh have notting else to do.' Just as he began to clean the rice, picking out weevils and odd bits of dirt, he saw a soaked and bedraggled Sankar returning home. At last, company.

18 Vernon's mother

The faint voice of a woman was heard calling Vernon late one night. With her was a wizened old man with a long white beard, both of them scarcely visible in the darkness. Vernon was not in his room but was next door gambling. Eddie, the first one to hear her voice, said to the rest of the group, 'All yuh, shut up. Ah hearing someone calling.'

The room fell silent and the voice was heard again. 'Vernon, Vernon.'

He got up and shouted, 'Oy,' acknowledging the call. He turned to Eddie and said, 'Lend me yuh torch, boy, ah cyah mek out dat voice.' Eddie picked up a bicycle light from the corner near his bed and gave it to Vernon. Nat stood up at the same time and both of them went to the door. Vernon flashed the light in the direction of the voice and called out, 'Who is dat?'

'Is me, Suraji,' came the reply. 'Ah bringing somebody to see yuh.'

'What de ass is dis?' said Vernon in a low voice to Nat, then he called to her, 'Come, nah, it a bit late but ah eh sleeping.'

A voice from the card school said, 'Wha happen to dis game den?'

Vernon replied as Suraji and the old man approached, 'All yuh have to go on widout me. Nat, go pick up me money. Ah tink ah know why she want to see me.' He left Eddie's room and went to his, two doors away. He opened his door and said, 'All yuh come inside, it eh so comfortable, but at least we can talk in private.' Suraji and the old man followed him in. He searched his pocket for a box of matches. The old man took out a box and handed it to him.

'Tanks,' said Vernon, as he lit the lamp he kept near his bed. The two beds, a table and bench was all the furniture in his tiny room. Vernon placed the lamp on the table and said, 'All yuh sit down.'

Suraji sat down and introduced the old man to Vernon. 'Dis is Syne,' she said. 'Ah bring him to look after yuh momma.'

Vernon looked at the man. He was a short, slender man with a slight stoop. His face, from what he could make out behind the long,

78

unkempt beard, looked serious, the wrinkles of his forehead and above his cheek bones highlighting his sharp eyes. Vernon shook Syne's hand which was soft, indicating he was not a manual worker. 'Sit down, Mr Syne,' he said. Syne sat down on the edge of Nat's bed and Vernon sat on his. The light cast a shadow on the papered walls, while small flying insects danced near the flame.

'Ah sorry to come so late, boy, but Syne came from far,' said Suraji. Vernon noticed Syne was carrying a cloth bundle attached to a long stick which he threw over his shoulder to make carrying easier. He wondered what was inside the cloth.

'So what is dis?' asked Vernon.

'Well, since yuh an Nat did ask if ah know somebody who could see to yuh modder, well, ah was looking an dis is yuh man.'

Syne nodded. The shadow of his beard moved up and down with the movement of his head like a silent broom sweeping the partitions.

'How he going to do dat?' asked Vernon.

'Dat is me secret,' said Syne. 'Ah cure plenty people, but what ah do is a gift from Allah.'

Suraji lit a cigarette and inhaled deeply. Vernon seemed baffled by this response, and Syne's method seemed to demand a great degree of trust and, as he did not know the man, he found himself in a tricky position.

Suraji, sensing his uncertainty, spoke: 'Ah wouldn bring a man here if ah didn tink he could help in dis kinda sickness. Yuh have to try everyting.'

'Is me momma all yuh talking bout. If someting happen to she, ah go get really mad.'

'Doh worry, son,' said Syne. 'Ah does look at de person, try to talk to dem an see wha wrong, before doing me best foh dem.'

'Dat is all right den. Ah want me momma to get better, dat is de firs priority,' said Vernon.

'Syne come from far, ah tell yuh. He need somewhere to stay until morning, den he go look at yuh momma,' said Suraji.

'Oh, God,' said Vernon, 'dis place so small, it hardly have room here, but besides dat, ah have to work in de morning, it is not a convenient time.'

'Dis is de right time, son, de moon jus right. Odderwise we have to wait anodder four weeks before is time again,' said Syne.

The voices in Eddie's room echoed in the silence of the night. The stars shone brightly and dogs began to bark as the factory bell rang ten times. 'Is late,' said Suraji, 'ah have to go soon. Mek up yuh mind what yuh going to do.'

Vernon remained silent, passing a hand through his greased curly hair. 'Yuh could sleep on de floor between me an Nat, but yuh go have to get up early,' he said.

Syne stared with his strong eyes directly into Vernon's and said without blinking, 'Ah is a old man, ah come here to do yuh a favour, ah leave a soft bed wey ah does live an yuh want to put me on de floor.'

'How much yuh charging to look at me modder?' asked Vernon.

'Ah doh charge foh using me gift, son. If yuh feel to mek me a gift afterwards, is all ah is allowed to tek. If ah ask foh money, den de power go disappear,' said Syne.

'In dat case, ah go sleep on de floor an give yuh me bed,' said Vernon.

'Anodder ting,' said Syne, 'ah have to get anodder person to be here when ah seeing bout yuh momma. Ah cyah wok alone.'

Vernon turned to look at Suraji. Before he could ask, she said, 'Ah cyah come, boy, dat is why ah bring Syne tonight.'

'Den ah go get Nat to stay, he eh wokking,' said Vernon.

Suraji got up, cupping the ash and cigarette stub in one hand, went to the door and said, 'Ah going home now. It getting late.'

'Tanks,' said Vernon. Nat came as Suraji was leaving. He stood under the canopy waiting for her to step out of the doorway.

'Well, ah go pass tomorrow to see how yuh get on,' she was saying to Syne, before hurrying down and walking quickly through the dark night. Vernon, who had been standing behind her, said to Nat, 'Suraji just bring a man to look at me modder. Ah wondering if yuh could stay here tomorrow an help him.'

Nat entered the room and looked at the stranger sitting on his bed. Vernon introduced him to Syne, who nodded and remained silent.

'He sleeping on me bed,' said Vernon.

'An wey yuh go to sleep?' asked Nat.

'On de floor,' said Vernon. 'We go manage, dis is de best time to look after me momma, he say.'

'Well, ah better get some sleep, tomorrow me have a busy day,' said Syne. Nat and Vernon left the room and went outside, allowing Syne to get undressed and get into bed. He came out after them and was shown to the latrine. He preferred to piss in the hedge in front of the barracks. He washed his hands and face and, when Vernon and Nat re-entered the room, he was already fast asleep, snoring loudly.

◆

On waking next morning, Vernon noticed that Nat and Syne were already up and out of the room. For Nat, this was unusual as he was a late riser, getting out of bed only when the heat of the day made it impossible for him to remain asleep. Vernon got dressed and went outside. It was early; the sun was rising and dew drops slid off the leaves and blades of grass. Some of them caught the early morning light, like beads of silver resting on the green. He looked for Nat and Syne but saw his mother, who was preparing breakfast. Thick smoke emanated from her fireplace as she tried to get a blaze going. Her hair was long and untidy, loose around her shoulders, and she was wearing a satin dress which glistened when it caught the sun. She was singing her usual unmelodic, guttural song, and occasionally burst out in a spontaneous dance, clapping her hands above her head, causing her silver bangles to jangle. Vernon sensed that someone else was looking at her, for she seemed more agitated than normal. He looked around, and some distance away he saw the squatting figure of Syne, observing her with a great deal of concentration. He was dressed in white, his beard merging into his shirt, leaving only the brown blob of his face discernible.

The sound of someone wielding a cutlass in the nearby hibiscus fence made Vernon look towards it. He saw the familiar figure of Nat. He walked over and called out, 'Wha yuh doing dey, boy?'

Nat, continuing to hack away, answered: 'De man say to cut plenty whip, someting to do wid how he planning to deal wid yuh momma madness.'

'Once he doh kill she, he could do anyting,' said Vernon, who walked back to his room to prepare himself for work.

Syne stayed squatting and staring at Vernon's mother. He was beginning to look like a piece of sculpture made out of chalk and bronze. A strong wind began to blow, but it failed to move him. Vernon got on his bike, raising his hand to wave goodbye as he coasted past Syne. Syne took no notice, but continued with his observations, allowing nothing to distract him. Nat, as instructed, placed the whips on the step at the back of the barrack directly in the

81

path of the sunlight. Having completed his task, he went to the kitchen to make some coffee and to see if he could find something to eat. He sweetened the coffee with condensed milk and sat on his step. Eddie woke, and on seeing Nat sitting on the step, called out, 'Wha yuh doin, boy? How come yuh get up so early?'

Nat, reminded about sleep, passed a hand over his face before answering: 'Ah helping dat man over dey,' pointing towards Syne. 'He come to cure Vernon modder madness.'

'An wey Vernon?' asked Eddie, as he stepped outside.

'He gone to wok,' said Nat.

'An leave yuh wid a stranger an he modder? Boy, he mad, like she,' said Eddie. 'Who is he anyway?'

'A man Suraji bring, called Syne. Dat man strange! He only drink water since he come, notting else, an he hardly say a word,' Nat answered.

'Boy, all yuh happy, yes? Why all yuh doh leave de ooman alone, she eh troubling nobody,' said Eddie, pumping his small Primus stove and lighting it to boil a pot of water for his coffee.

Noon. The sun was directly overhead. Shadows walked underfoot when Syne rose from his position and walked slowly to the back of the barracks and collected the clump of whips. The news of Syne's coming to cure Vernon's mother had travelled through the village and those at home gathered in a small group in the yard to look at the ceremony. Children played and ran after each other. Occasionally, an adult would call out to them, 'All yuh, dis is no place to be. Run away from here before dat man hold one ah yuh.' Some pretended to take heed and went behind the sweet-lime hedge to continue their play, but still watched what was going on through the gaps. Syne returned, carrying the bundle, and looked at Nat; by extending his arm and moving his finger, he indicated Nat was needed. He rose; the crowd became silent as he went over to Syne who whispered in his ear. Nat called Eddie over and Syne spoke to them in a soft, gentle voice.

'All yuh, ah want complete control in all ah have to do, so dis is what ah want. She notice me looking at she whole morning so she gone quite inside. She know someting wrong, so when ah go in, she go try to run away. Ah want all yuh to lock up de door after me and whatever happen, doh matter how much yuh hear screaming from she or me, doh leh me out until yuh hear me hit de door tree times wid a stick.'

Eddie looked at Nat; he wanted to burst out laughing, but managed to keep a serious face. Nat called out for two more men standing in the crowd, Tex and Madan, and told them what Syne wanted. They were placed at the back door while Nat and Eddie stood guard outside the front. The crowd came closer once Syne was locked in.

Vernon's mother screamed when this strange man entered her room. Syne looked at her; the intensity of his stare caused her to cower initially, then she sought to escape. She ran to both doors, only to find them locked. She dived under the bed to seek refuge. Her room was well furnished with a small table and two ladderback chairs, a single bed and a wardrobe. A couple of religious pictures hung on the walls and on the shelf near the window stood a vase of fading paper roses. A new curtain was stretched across her window. In spite of the confusion of her mind, she lived an organised life. People often wondered about her, how she managed to cope. Vernon gave her money every week, she cooked regular meals, washed her clothes and ironed them. Except for her unmelodic singing and dancing in public places, she lived an ordinary life.

Syne started to pray in a loud voice. The crowd became silent, the footsteps running from door to door were heard no longer. Then Vernon's mother shouted as he moved the bed to get at her. The distinctive cry of 'Devil!' came from Syne, followed by the sound of the whip striking her body. She screamed for help. 'Devil! Devil!' Syne was shouting, as he used his whips on the helpless weeping woman. She stood up to try to overpower him but he grabbed her by her dress and pushed her off, ripping the garment from her body. She stood only in her bodice and panties, embarrassed to be seen by a man. She tried to cover herself with her hands as he continued to shout and bawl. She ran to the bed to get under the sheet; he pulled it away. Then as she placed her hands over her breasts and face, he ripped off her panties. Removing her hands from her face, she tried to cover her naked bottom. He then ripped off the bodice and she lay naked and panting for breath before him.

The crowd outside, on hearing that it was the devil that possessed her, showed no sympathy or wish to intervene. They were pleased that someone was prepared to tackle this devil which had entered her soul and to drive him out. Someone said that Syne's method was the only way to deal with Satan, to beat him. Syne took a breather and stared at Vernon's mother lying naked before him. Red marks covered her bottom and she was bruised all over. He found himself drawn by her beauty and the tender look she gave him, pleading for the beating to stop. Both were sweating. Syne took off his clothes down to his underwear and started to beat her. The blows became softer as he got tired. He got into the bed and their two sweating bodies embraced each other. The crowd burst out laughing as the sounds of a couple making love came from the room. Vernon's mother was never the same after that, as Syne, who came to expel the devil, stayed with her to ensure he never returned. Another tenant had moved into the barracks.

19 Sankar's wedding

The population of the village was rapidly declining. People who were fortunate to find jobs and accommodation moved out every week, except in the barracks where Sankar lived. For shortly after Syne moved in with Vernon's mother, Sankar brought home a wife. The secrecy and suddenness of her arrival were a shock to everyone and, as the news spread, it was taken for a joke, coupled with the expectation of trouble with Suraji. Sankar came home early one Saturday and did something unusual: he cleaned his room and prepared and stocked his kitchen, transforming the entire appearance of his dwelling from its makeshift look to something more permanent. He brought back all of his clothes from Suraji, telling her he wished to be more in control of himself.

Eddie, noticing what he was doing, kept teasing him, but was pleased at his effort for Sankar's room had looked gloomy and in need of attention. The cleaning and preparation were done in an efficient and concentrated manner. Nothing was allowed to distract Sankar as he carried out the operation. He paid no attention to Eddie. That evening he went as accustomed to have his meal from Suraji, and next day he was married.

That Sunday he was awake, dressed and was seen preparing his own breakfast for the first time. Then he went across to Sonny Boy's shack, returning that evening with his wife. Two cars were seen in front of Sonny Boy's shack. Inside the shack, a party was in full swing; there was lots to eat and drink. Sankar sat in a corner, looking at the woman he had wed in a short unofficial ceremony. His mind was filled with doubts but he was determined to allow events to take their own course as far as explaining to Suraji his reasons for abandoning her. In this mood, filled with uncertainty about his own behaviour, he tried to make himself believe that he was doing the right thing, but, with the memory of his first wife still in his mind, and the need to fend off Suraji, plus the fact that at no time had he declared that he had children, this was an uncomfortable period. He

85

ate and drank a lot amid Sonny Boy's constant reminders – 'We have real ooman in de place, we go show dese people we is real man' – increasing the uncertainties which hung over him. He danced, ate and drank, trying to overcome his fears, but inwardly felt increasingly wary and filled with doubts. He looked at Sonny Boy, whose circumstances were different. He had fathered three children who lived with him. Their mother had died several years ago and he needed someone to assist in caring for them and to be a wife. For Sankar, this was a fresh start, without consideration of his responsibilities or current commitments.

Sankar knew nothing of his new wife's origins. Some said she came from another estate while others said she hung around in the Indian cinema in a nearby town and was prepared to go with any man provided he paid her entrance fee to see the movie. Both had an element of the truth. Two dominating thoughts raged in his mind all through the celebrations and caused a great deal of confusion: the eagerness to experience a fresh start at married life, and how to deal with Suraji.

The real moment of truth arrived. It was time to go home; the food and drink had run out and the guests were beginning to leave. Sankar looked at his bride, Latchmin. She too was shy and all evening she kept close to her friend, Mona, the bride of Sonny Boy. Latchmin had had more than enough to drink and, when it was time to go, was unable to show any reluctance to leave. Sankar was dreading this moment, which had come too quickly. More than the question of Suraji, he had to think about many other problems such as whether his room was sufficient for her, and whether she would be faithful during the day while he was at work. The greatest doubt was whether he would be able to satisfy her as a man. His past failure at marriage shot to his mind as he extended his hand and said, 'Come, gal, leh me tek yuh to wey we go live.'

Latchmin tried to stand up but was unable to rise from the bench where she sat. Sankar moved close and held her hand and pulled her up. She got up but couldn't stand without assistance. Mona, who was less drunk, came over and tried to speak to her.

'Latchmin, Latchmin, is all right. Is time to go home wid yuh nice new husband.'

Latchmin stared blankly; spittle ran down the side of her mouth. She was too far gone to hear anyone or to do anything. Sankar decided to use whatever strength he had remaining and placed his arm under her shoulder, took her weight and went on his way. As he was leaving, he said to Mona, 'Keep she tings here, gal, she bound to come for dem tomorrow.'

'Dat is all right, boy, she go feel better in de morning, is de strangeness what have she so,' said Mona.

Sonny Boy, who was standing next to her, placed an arm around her waist and whispered, 'De chirren gone to sleep long time now, leh we lie down.' Mona, the less shy of the two women, held his hand tightly as he turned quickly and closed their door.

On the way home, the movement and fresh air began to have an effect on Latchmin. About half-way between Sonny Boy's shack and the barracks, she stopped and pulled away from Sankar's grasp, went towards the grass and began to vomit. Sankar walked on a few steps and looked at her. She was wearing a long, brightly coloured dress, barely distinguishable under the light of the moon. Their skin colours were almost the same but now she looked pale and withdrawn, lacking confidence, the sort of person who rarely spoke. Doubts re-entered Sankar's mind as he stood and looked at her retching out her stomach over the long grass. When he was certain that she had finished, Sankar walked back towards her and escorted her home without any effort.

'Yuh feeling better now?' Sankar asked.

'Yes, boy, is de food an heat,' said Latchmin as she took a handkerchief from her pocket and wiped the remains of the vomit from her lips. When they reached the room, Sankar walked quietly ahead and opened the door and lit the lamp. Its brightness shone over the dark yard. The card school in Eddie's room went quiet on hearing the door open. Eddie placed a finger over his lips as he whispered 'Is Sankar an he new ooman, leh we hear how dey get on!'

'Since when he tek one?' asked Tex.

'Shush,' whispered Eddie, 'Ah go tell yuh bout it later.'

'Is dis wey we sleep?' asked Latchmin, looking at the mat spread out.

'Ah was waiting foh yuh to come, gal, before ah get plenty tings,' said Sankar. That was all that was heard until the sounds of two people snoring were heard coming through the wooden partition. Eddie and his friends burst out laughing and carried on making raucous comment, causing Sankar and Latchmin to wake. Sankar shouted out to them, 'All yuh better keep quiet from now on. Is two ah we all yuh have to deal wid now.' This caused even more laughter and comments which carried on long into the night.

Sankar sat up in the darkness wondering what to do or say. Latchmin curled herself in a corner, the white cotton sheet tightly wrapped around her body. Sankar tugged at her in a gentle, rather indecisive manner, but she pulled away even further. He pulled again, using a little more force, and she rolled towards him. He unwrapped the sheet from around her and embraced her. The smell of the vomit on her breath caused him to pull away, but then she took him in her arms and this time, without any resistance, they kissed. Their love-making was short and quick. She wanted it to continue for much longer, but Sankar, feeling all the guilt and doubts about his capability, said, 'Behave yuhself, ooman, ah have to save me strengt for wok,' turning away and closing his eyes, forcing himself to sleep.

20 Sankar's dilemma

Conflict and regret churned over in Sankar's mind as he woke the morning after his marriage. The fears he harboured as to whether he was capable as a man to sustain a marriage returned repeatedly, with the added fear of what Suraji would do once she found out. He woke early and went outside, leaving his new bride sleeping soundly on the mat. On the spur of the moment he decided to take time off work and spend the day at home. In order to avoid seeing those he knew, he went to the back of his barrack and stood on the concrete platform.

The sun was rising; black, dark blue and golden clouds were rolling away before it as its rays cleared the darkness. The dawn chorus, of cocks crowing, birds chirping and cows bellowing in the distance, was in full voice as he tried to sort himself out. Perhaps it was the rum which was making him feel uncomfortable. The images of Suraji and his sleeping wife, Latchmin, returned with more strength. He wondered what would happen to his children. His room was too small to accommodate them along with Latchmin. This feeling of uneasiness caused him to walk on and try to find something to divert his attention.

He returned to the room for his cutlass and went to gather firewood, a task men seldom did unless they lived alone. He walked to the back of the old overseer's house to the fruit orchard and began to hack away at dead branches. The sunlight glistened on the shining steel blade as he struck with more force than was necessary. He returned with a huge bundle, enough for all the occupants of the barracks for a week. His trousers were soaked up to his knees from the morning dew on the bushes.

Sweating and slightly tired, he sat on the step at the front of his barrack with his cutlass in his hand and began to bury the blunt point idly into the bare earth, spinning it around. One by one, the others began to wake. First it was Syne who came out fully dressed to pray. He nodded to Sankar as he went out to the back to face the east.

Shortly afterwards, Vernon's mother came out, still dressed in her night clothes, and with a chamber pot in her hand headed for the latrine. She smiled broadly, slightly embarrassed, at Sankar as she quickened her step. He sat defiantly looking at nothing in particular as he kept flicking his cutlass from side to side.

Hitler and her gang were on their way to work; he could hear their chattering voices in the distance and felt in two minds: to stay and face them, or to return inside and remain until they went past. The first was only an idle thought, as almost by instinct he returned quickly to his room. The voices grew louder.

'Come on, gal,' someone was shouting.

'Leave me alone.' It was Suraji's voice.

Sankar took off his trousers and lay down next to the sleeping Latchmin. He began to sweat with fright. He got up as the voices of the women came from just outside. Then he heard Suraji.

'Is me an he today. He want wife, de bitch!'

Dressed only in his underpants, he took up his cutlass and opened his front door. Latchmin stirred and asked, 'Wha wrong, boy?'

'Go back to sleep, it have notting to do wid yuh,' he said as he went out to face Suraji.

She stood with her arms akimbo, a cigarette between her lips, the sunlight shining in her face, staring angrily at him. He ran towards her holding his cutlass above his head as though he was about to cut off her head. The other women screamed, but Suraji stood still as if she did not care. He stopped just short of her and dropped his arm. Suraji said nothing. The women, breathing a sigh of relief, began to urge Suraji to come away. The others rushed out from their rooms.

'Get away from here, yuh nasty old bitch,' shouted Sankar, trying to reassert himself. Eddie walked up behind Sankar and grabbed the cutlass away from his hand.

'Give me back dat,' he shouted.

'No, yuh could talk to she widout it,' said Eddie, as he stared back at him.

The women jeered. One said, 'Leh we see who is more man now.'

Latchmin, who was standing at the door, was noticed. Hitler saw her and called out, 'He is man foh dat ting.'

Latchmin quickly closed the door and bolted it.

'Go home an tek yuh chirren. When ah come back, ah doh want to see dem dey,' said Suraji. Sankar, hurt and bemused by this incident, grabbed at Suraji's cutlass; she quickly stepped aside. Hitler moved between them to face Sankar. She was taller than him and twice his size.

'Try to hit me if yuh call yuhself man, Suraji too small.'

Sankar looked at this big, angry woman and wished he was any place else. He had expected confrontation but not on this scale. Eddie took pity on him, and Vernon's mother, whether intentionally or not, no one knew, began to clap her hands and sing and dance. Syne grabbed hold of her and hustled her inside. This caused some laughter.

'All yuh leave de man alone,' said Eddie. 'He done do what he want, notting cyah change dat. All yuh go to yuh work.'

'De nasty ungrateful dog,' cried Suraji. 'All dese years ah mind he an his chirren an now he tek wife.'

Sankar tried to smother all his feeling, standing numb, making believe this was not happening. One of the women called out, 'Look at he, yuh call dat man? Leh we go to wok, it better dan standing here looking at dis dry-ass man.'

The crowd dispersed. Suraji, shaking her head from side to side, went with them. Sankar returned to sit on his step. Eddie began to pump his Primus stove to light it. Vernon and Nat looked on with a big grin on their faces as Eddie said, 'Wey yuh wife, worried man? Bring she out here, leh we see she.'

Vernon laughed loudest and Sankar turned to him.

'Look at yuh momma, she tek husband.' This increased their laughter.

'Is someting yuh doh know, if yuh did cut she head off, den ah would ah chop yuh up like meat,' said Eddie.

'What dat have to do wid yuh?' asked Sankar.

'What it have to do wid me, it have plenty more dan yuh know,' said Eddie, as he dipped a saucepan into the water barrel.

'Yuh better watch yuh ass from now on,' said Sankar.

'Yuh cyah do notting to me,' said Eddie as he lit his stove and began to boil water.

'We go see,' said Sankar as he scratched at his bare stomach. He got up and turned to go back into his room. Eddie called him back.

'Listen, leh me tell someting, is bess yuh know now. Suraji is me modder family. If yuh touch she, yuh is a dead man, yuh hear what ah telling yuh?'

'Ah doh want to hear notting from yuh,' said Sankar, as he returned to his room. Latchmin was sitting in a corner staring at him. The room was dark with the door closed. The mat for sleeping was still on the floor. He looked at her and a wry smile crept across his face. He could hear the voices of Nat, Vernon and Eddie laughing at his predicament. Eddie kept repeating, 'He want wife!' while they analysed the confrontation. Sankar felt numbed and hopeless. He dropped to the floor and lay down on the mat, ashamed and troubled. Latchmin reached out to touch him but he pushed her hand away. She tried again, coming to lie next to him. He got up and started to get dressed.

'Stay away from me foh now,' he said, 'ah have tings to do. It have plenty food in de kitchen.'

'Wey yuh going?' she asked, still lying on the floor.

'Ah going to do some business, it wouldn tek long,' he said, as he quickly stepped out and closed the door behind him. He walked past the three men, still grouped together talking, without saying anything. One of them called out, 'It have ants in yuh bed, Sankar, leaving yuh wife on yuh honeymoon so?'

He did not respond, as his bare feet stepped firmly on the ground, going away from them as quickly as possible. His children saw him as he approached Suraji's home. They were playing with some others on the road.

'Pa, Pa!' they shouted, surprised at seeing him at this time of the day. He stopped and hugged both of them, bringing them together on his chest.

'We have to go out, all yuh,' he said as he stood up.

'Wey we going, Pa?' asked Dano.

'All yuh pack up everything, we going far away, is far wey we going.'

'When we coming back?' asked Sankina.

'Ah doh know as yet,' said Sankar. 'Leh we go. Plenty tings happen an ah decide to tek all yuh away foh a while, so go an pack now.' The children looked puzzled; their friends playing with them overheard Sankar's conversation and one of them shouted at the top of his voice, 'Dano an Sakina going away.'

Sankar turned to him and snapped, 'Shut up yuh mouth.' The stress and uncertainty began to take effect; the children went quiet and slowly dispersed. Dano and Sankina whispered to each other about where he was taking them.

They left the estate and walked the three miles to the nearest town. On arrival, he took them to a small triangular open space in the centre.

'All yuh wait here, an doh go a place, ah going to look foh somebody.' Looking at the people, the buses and the cars, the two children came closer together; this was their first visit to the town and they were frightened. Sankar was away, gone for what seemed a long time. They became hungry and sweaty, unaccustomed to the heat and noise, and overcome with fear. Passers-by stopped to enquire whether they were lost, but Sakina, the braver of the two, said they were waiting for their father. Sankar returned. He brought them a bag of sweets and off they went to a nearby grocery. The owner and his wife were waiting at the side entrance of the building. Sakina and Dano looked at this strange couple who greeted them.

'Dis is de two ah dem,' said Sankar.

'Come in,' said the man, his sharp nose jutting out of his somewhat podgy face. The woman standing behind him was tall and fair-skinned; both looked healthy and well fed. Sankar remained at the entrance.

'Well, dem is good chirren, dey go work hard,' he said. 'Ah go come back an see dem from time to time.'

He turned to leave. Dano and Sakina tried to go after him but the man held them back with a strong firm grip on their small hands. Despite the cries and pleas of the children, Sankar kept going.

21 The watchman's error

Harry was no longer his usual jovial self. He had become withdrawn and gloomy since he saw Sadwine visiting Goddard in the scale house. He tried on several occasions to speak with her but she refused to answer his questions and simply avoided him, saying she was busy and would talk some other time. She was polite with him, in a rather defensive sort of way. Harry wanted to confront her again, to hear the reason why she had behaved as she did. In his head, he knew what made her visit Goddard, but in his heart, where it hurt the most, he felt she had betrayed not only him, but all men of East Indian origin. She was now stained for life and her status in the village would be destroyed. An Indian woman in appearance only was fair game for anyone of any race.

He sat in the rumshop during the day, at times when he ought to have been at home sleeping. His work as a night watchman became sloppy. Sometimes he would miss ringing the bell at the hour or miscount his strokes, throwing the whole village into confusion. One night he missed ringing the bell at eleven, and at twelve he rang twenty-three. Insomniacs were bewildered but laughed at the bungle. Next morning everyone he met sought an explanation but he was in no mood to offer one or joke about it in the normal way.

Madan, standing outside the rumshop, spotted a pair of feet resting on a stool underneath the swing doors of the bar. He entered and saw Harry drinking from a half bottle of rum which was almost full. In a flash, without waiting to be invited, Madan pulled up a stool and sat next to him.

'Wha happen, boy, how yuh get so serious?' he asked.

Harry took a drink, passed the palm of his hand across his handlebar moustache to wipe away the remains of the liquid and stared at him.

'Wha yuh want from me?' he replied.

'Notting,' said Madan, his eyes fixed on the bottle. 'Ah see yuh here, looking so serious like if someting wrong an ah thought ah better ask to see if dey was anyting ah could do.'

Harry softened towards him; he knew that Madan was after the drink and would adopt any role to try to get him to offer it. He called out to Ramnath, the shop assistant, to bring another glass, and offered the bottle to Madan. Madan took it, his hands shaking from excitement, and poured himself a drink almost to the brim of his rum glass. He drank it in one gulp and slammed the glass down on the table and cleared his throat very loudly. He turned to Harry and said, 'Boy, yuh should be home sleeping. Watchman mus never see de daytime and if yuh do dat, yuh in trouble wid yuh wok.'

Harry poured himself a drink and passed the bottle. Madan could not believe his luck. One drink was all he expected, but two meant he ought to stick around more. As he drank the second, he again asked Harry, sensing that all was not well, 'Is everyting all right?'

Harry's tight control on his emotions was now loosened by the alcohol and he began to speak in an incoherent and confused manner, in contrast to his customary direct approach. It was as if he was transformed into a different person, the opposite of himself.

'Boy, is dat ooman, ah didn tink she was so.'

'Which ooman?' asked Madan. 'Yuh wife?'

'Not me wife, if was she, ah woulda tek me cutlass an cut she neck off, is dat bitch who everyone in de village does feel is so great.'

'Who is she?' asked Madan. Just as Harry was about to divulge the name of the woman who was causing him problems, Bodhan, who quarrelled with his wife every day, burst into the bar and began to pound the counter shouting for Ramnath.

'Shit,' said Madan, below his breath, 'look at de time dis man go come mekking noise in dis place.'

Harry left Madan and went across to Bodhan. 'Who trouble yuh, boy?' he asked, as he stumbled towards him.

'Is today ah go show she! In me ass every day, a man cyah get no peace, ah go show dat bitch. Ramnath!' he called again. The assistant hurried towards Bodhan. 'Ramnath, ah want a bottle ah rum, a pound ah rope an a sof candle. Ah go show dat bitch today.'

Ramnath hesitated. It was an unusual request but with a clear purpose. The rope and soft candle were to make a noose, and the rum obvious. He remained still. Bodhan again shouted out his order, saying, 'Ah hurry, doh jus stan dey, ah paying yuh foh it.'

'Give de man what he want,' said Madan.

'Cool down, no ooman eh worth hanging yuhself foh,' said Harry, momentarily forgetting his own troubles and attempting to pacify his friend. As Ramnath reached towards the shelf to get the soft candle, Bodhan's wife, Rookmin, entered the dry goods section of the shop and continued the quarrel with her husband. She was a fat, fair-skinned woman in her late fifties with a shrill tone in her voice. Bodhan, small, dark-skinned and wizened, with a large grey moustache covering his lip, whose voice was equally grating, gave no quarter. The shop echoed with their loud shouting and swearing match. Ramnath stopped serving and tried to pacify them, but it was futile. In this mood, nothing could restore peace between them. A crowd gathered, but they continued as if they were alone. Then Bodhan tried to ignore her and called out to Ramnath to hurry up with his request.

'Go on,' said Rookmin, 'give de bitch de rope, leh him hang heself, de jackass, he better dead.' Ramnath laughed out loud.

'Is notting to laugh bout,' said Bodhan, 'ah sick ah dis ooman. Ah going wey ah cyah hear dat stinking voice no more.'

'Go on, give it to he,' said Rookmin. Ramnath brought out the rope, soft candle and rum to Bodhan who took out a five-dollar note to pay for it. Ramnath took the money and brought back the change. Rookmin went silent and Madan, seeing Ramnath handing Bodhan the change, said, 'Give me dat money, boy. Wey yuh going, yuh cyah use it.'

Bodhan, seeing an opportunity to convince his wife of the seriousness of his intention, said, 'Yes, boy, yuh right,' and handed Madan the money. Before he had time to put it in his pocket, Rookmin rushed across to the bar and grabbed it from his hand.

'Dat is me money,' she said. 'Leh de jackass kill heself but me and me chirren have to eat.'

Bodhan pushed her out of the bar and she turned and left. He opened the bottle of rum and shared it with Harry and Madan and a few others. He continued speaking of the troubles he was having at home, the state of the village, how he had no future and wished to end it all. In this mood and with the fact it was his rum, he dominated the conversation, allowing no one else much room to speak. He then took up the rope, greased it with soft candle, made a noose, tied it round his neck and walked home.

The crowd followed him. He went into the house, but was quickly out again, chased out by his wife with a saucepan in her hand, attempting to hit him. The crowd doubled up laughing. He ran into the cane field and, tying a knot at the root of a cane plant, lay down on the ground and tried to pull the rope. Harry, unable to stand by and see his friend make a complete ass of himself, went and got a bucket of water and threw it over him, took away the rope and tossed it into the cane field. Bodhan insisted he was being serious and said, 'If only ah could climb a tree, ah would show she.'

Harry paid him no attention, held his arm firmly and escorted him back into the house, and shouted at both of them. 'Stop mekking a laughing stock ah all yuhself.' He walked out and ordered the crowd to disperse, which they did, but with some reluctance.

Madan waited and, as Harry walked towards his home, accompanied him. 'Boy, yuh eh finish tell me which ooman causing yuh so much trouble.'

Harry, without thinking, told Madan of his affair with Sadwine and her visits to Goddard. He could feel as he spoke he was betraying a trust and it would harm Sadwine, but it was an unguarded moment and he had lost the power to restrain himself.

22 Donald's departure

Searching the abandoned barrack rooms for money, jewellery, items of furniture, clothing or bits of food was done quite openly by some of the villagers who remained in Highlands. Faced with large arrears of rent, no more credit at the shop and owing the shopkeeper, many families left. The barracks had been lived in for over a hundred years, first as the home of African slaves and following them the indentured Indians and their descendants.

Every dwelling was searched, hoping for the big find, over and over again. This included Donald's mansion. Apart from the household fittings which could not be moved, he had left nothing behind. The search became more of a tour, looking at bare rooms which only the privileged had seen in occupation.

While the majority moved away in silence to face an uncertain future, Donald's move, though inevitable, was not done in this manner. Bella organised help and made the arrangements. She was in charge and Donald remained sober. He now kept away from his drinking friends, and from drink. Whether it was from the feeling of disgrace at the loss of power and wealth or from the thought of leaving the estate where he was born and had grown to love the land and people, no one knew. At first, he hardly spoke to anyone, keeping his thoughts and feelings to himself. He was seen sitting on his upper verandah, staring at the cane fields in the direction of the bamboo patch about a mile away, a former burial ground of indentured labourers. No gravestones or tombs or mounds marked the graves, for the burial was a compromise when the right to burn was denied by the authorities. Many who had worked for Donald's father were buried there.

Bella's initiative in finding a place to live brought about a radical change in Donald. It was this transformation rather than his departure from the estate which had everyone talking about him. He changed almost overnight from a drunken, belligerent estate owner, to being a silent, soft-spoken and, at times, curious person. A victim himself, he began to enquire about his former workers' welfare and show concern for those whose predicament after the closure of the estate was worse than his. He took to visiting nearly everyone he knew who remained on the estate, stopping to speak with those whom in the past he acknowledged by name only.

Bella organised Suraji and a group of other women to help with the packing and dismantling of the household. Donald, freed of responsibilities, returned to being the boy who grew up on the estate. He still felt bitter about the loss of the estate, but it was easier to bury reality than to face it.

Sometimes he would visit the card school in Eddie's room to speak with Tex who had shared, as head groom, in his past glories as a racehorse owner. At first, these visits were uncomfortable as those who were playing cards were too shy to carry out a conversation with him. Overnight, those barriers came down and conversation began to flow. It was a simple incident which brought them together. Vernon's mother was carrying on in her usual entertaining manner and Tex related how Syne was brought to drive away the devil and remained to expel him every day. Donald laughed and laughed; he clearly enjoyed listening to the tale, and he began to tell stories he had heard during his time as the estate owner.

The men were amazed at how he helped to nurture the myth that the ghosts of two Indian women occupied the two large steel coppers, used for boiling the cane syrup in the olden days, now overturned and embedded in the earth at the entrance to the estate. 'Those two women helped enormously in keeping discipline on the estate. People were too scared to travel late at night,' were his words as he sat on a chair in Eddie's room.

The conversation gradually turned to why he lost the estate.

'I'll tell you,' he said. 'In this business, it's no longer possible to operate on a small scale. I borrowed money to expand, and I couldn't meet my debts.'

'But what about me?' asked Eddie.

'I did my best but, like the factory, you all had to go, it is that simple,' said Donald, quickly adding, 'I lost my home and money, and you, your means of earning a living.' He won the confidence of the men and they began to feel sorry for him.

'But ah sure yuh miss de days when yuh was boss ah everyting,' said Eddie.

'Of course I miss it; who wouldn't? But what can I do? Things have come to an end, and so it is.' They reminisced over old times and discussed the dismal prospects for the future. Donald felt as if he had found a group of friends and sometimes stayed for hours talking with them as they played cards.

He began to take notice of the landscape, noting little details to take away with him. He walked through the fields, occasionally picking bunches of wild flowers, looking at trees, or, when the mood took him, running and shouting over the lonely paths just as he had done with he was a boy. On most days after lunch, he fell into the practice of taking a long nap. In the late afternoon he went visiting. He seemed constantly amazed by the lives of the people he met. With the older ones, he listened to the stories of India, how they had come to the island and of their experiences. One of the men translated whenever someone spoke in Hindustani. Their stories were of the hardship and disappointment in life, of reincarnation and interpretation of the Bhagavad Gita. They were not hindered by this newcomer in their circle: they had known him since he was a child, had worked for his father and were pleased that he visited. Later at night when almost everyone else was asleep they brought a large pipe, filled with ganja, and slowly brought an end to the session. Donald left as the pipe was brought out.

The more he came into contact with those whose lives he had controlled, the more he realised the enormity of his loss. He was once in total control and knew no one except as workers, and now, no longer in control, he found that the workers existed as people. He discovered their secrets, like the well-kept lettuce garden at the side of the pond. The soft black earth was ideal for that sort of crop. Next to the lettuce was a whole field of pineapples. In the space of just under a year, people were planting in the abandoned land crops which might have been profitable. He felt that, in spite of his education and wealth, workers were better able to utilise the land. If only he had consulted them, he thought, perhaps the whole estate might have been saved. This land was his home, not Scotland or anywhere else.

Near the pond was a savannah where he kept the animals during the idle months of the rainy season. He stood on the grassy slope and remembered his champion racehorse which won many prizes. The memories flooded in as the days before his leaving became fewer. 'So much to remember,' he thought as he stood and looked at the reflection of the setting sun on the dark water in the pond. His main regret was the role he played in the strike, the one opportunity he had had to face the truth and perhaps save the estate, but he chose to take sides with the other planters and factory owners to withstand the demands of the strikers. He thought now of their dependency on him and he on them. Together they might have solved some of his problems, but it was too late; all was lost.

◆

Bella completed her purchase of their new home, using her life savings which she had secretly accumulated, and was ready to move. Donald wept openly when she told him what she had done. He spent the last days with Blue Jean, who turned to him in one of their more intimate moments and said in a sad tone, 'Yuh never coming back.'

He replied in a reassuring manner, 'Oh, yes, I will, I'll often come back,' but never said when.

23 'Is ooman business'

Although she kept on visiting people and attending to the women of the village, Suraji began to feel desperate. She began to blame herself for the loss of the children and Sankar. So used to having them around, their sudden departure, and Sankar having taken up with a new woman, was hard to bear. She became increasingly dependent on rum to ease the suffering. Where before she was an outgoing and jolly person, in the space of two weeks she became a silent recluse. Women had to come and call her out and plead with her to attend to them.

The days were long and hard; sleep and rum were her only relief. She saw Sankar from time to time in the village. He seemed to be having a new lease of life. One day, about a month after they left, the children returned. They had run away from the grocery, complaining of being made to work all day and sometimes at night. Before, their faces were rounded and showed no sign of restraint or worry; now they looked slightly older and paler. At first, Suraji thought of taking them to their father, who had so casually given them away, but on second thoughts she decided to let them stay. It was good to have them back, but so much had taken place while they were gone it was no longer the same. Dano reminded her so much of his father that it was difficult for her to stop thinking of him. This was slightly unfortunate for the child as she attacked him for minor misdemeanours and at times almost without reason.

The village gossip reached her ears about Sankar's new wife. According to Hitler, Sankar's wife was married once before and was a part-time prostitute along with Sonny Boy's wife. Suraji believed what Hitler had said to her; she felt even more hurt and rejected. Afraid to face her friends, she took to drinking away the pain. The children noticed the change and took charge. Sakina started to prepare meals. Dano waited for her after work to ensure that she did not get drunk on the way home. Sometimes he would be distracted by other little boys playing outside the shop and afterwards had the unenviable task of taking home a drunken, singing stepmother. Those who understood her suffering took pity on her, while the rest of the village began to tease her and call her names. Some men gave her drink in order to encourage her to have sexual intercourse with them. Now Suraji was working less, the children sometimes went hungry, depending on mangoes and other seasonal foods to fill their starving stomachs.

The rum flowed, and the men came and went. Some even stayed for two days. At times when the hunger and thirst for rum was acute, she would hang around the shop to beg for money, with very little success. It was a period of immeasurable suffering and a less hardy person would have become ill, and perhaps even died. She was not the first in the village to find herself in this position but, unlike the others who chose to leave, she remained, to care for those who still needed her and to look after the children. Her skin became even more wrinkled and her teeth darker. Her voice sounded deep and gruff, deeper than a man's.

◆

Slowly, she began to pull herself together. Nothing in particular caused the change. Perhaps it was a desire to overthrow the gloom and self-pity which enveloped her after Sankar's leaving. Her friends rallied around, giving her old dresses and other clothing. They invited her to their houses and as quickly as their doors had been shut, they opened to welcome her. She never gave up drinking altogether, but returned to having just an occasional drink in the evening, as she was accustomed to. To supplement her meagre income as a cutter, she had begun to plant quick-growing vegetables. Late one evening, while she was watering a bed of spinach, she heard the throaty voice of Sadwine calling her.

'Suraji, Suraji,' the voice called, sounding as if Sadwine was in some distress and needed help. Suraji left her bucket and cup where she stood and went to meet Sadwine. Dano and Sakina were hovering around. Sadwine looked worried.

'All yuh, go an finish water de bhagee,' she ordered the children, who paid little attention and stuck around to see why Sadwine had come to visit.

'Wha wrong, gal?' asked Suraji. Sadwine whispered something to

103

her. She shouted at the children, 'All yuh leave we big people alone an go an water de garden.'

This time they left and Sadwine was able to say why she had come.

'Ah have someting wrong wid me, gal, ah so shame. It so nasty an smelly!'

'What it is?' asked Suraji.

'Ah really doh know, gal, ah want yuh to come home wid me an have a look.'

'Just a minute, gal. Yuh wait here, ah going to wash dis dirt off me an ah go come.'

'Yuh better bring a razor too, ah believe ah have dat an all.'

Suraji went to the barrel of water and began to wash her feet, face and hands. She dried herself on an old piece of cloth hanging in the kitchen and went to her room to change her dress and pick up her razor. She sharpened it on a strap and placed it in her pocket.

Sadwine's husband was sitting on an old rocking chair in the gallery of their home. He smiled at them. He continued sitting and took no further notice. Sadwine was afraid to speak about what was troubling her. All she said was, 'Sit down, gal, ah have one or two tings to do before we talk.'

She lit two lamps and placed them in position to give maximum light. Suraji sat and looked at the still smiling Sadhu, who continued to rock and say nothing. After Sadwine had busied herself in the house, she went to Sadhu and said, 'Ah wonder if yuh would go out de house foh a while? Ah have someting wrong wid me an ah doh want yuh to see Suraji examining me.'

'Wha wrong?' asked Sadhu.

'Is ooman business, not too serious, but ah doh want yuh here.'

Sadhu got up and left.

104

24 Madan

There were no farewells or long goodbyes as the villagers left their homes. The main barracks near the idle factory were almost vacant; forty empty rooms, once a hive of activity with children seemingly everywhere. No more flea-ridden dogs or Christians trying to convert the heathen workers while they rested on a Sunday afternoon. Highlands was abandoned. Flies and mosquitoes returned to the manure heaps and to the stagnant pools of water, their parasitical life off humans severely curtailed. The hardest hit was Ramnath the shopkeeper. His business declined; hardly anyone paid their bills when they left. He chased after those who owed large amounts, following them to the far flung villages and towns they moved to. The majority, for so long dependent on his goodwill in the rainy season and used to his urging and threats during crop time, left, having to pay him no longer.

Madan kept him informed of who left or was planning to leave and at the same time giving him an assurance that he intended to stay, come what may.

'Ah is one coolie man who eh running,' he used to say, while sipping a drink bought for him by another person or given by Ramnath in return for information. 'Ah born an grow here, wey ah is going? Dis is me place.' Madan, like the others who took that line, left shortly afterwards.

The shop was no longer the same place. His last bit of gossip about Sadwine's promiscuity had its effects, however, and she never recovered from his malicious rumour-spreading tongue. After Harry had told him of his affair with Sadwine and the disappointment he felt when she was with Goddard, Madan's imagination, fired by his thirst for rum, ran riot. In his mind, any woman who had three men sharing her body wouldn't be too particular about having a fourth. One afternoon, he saw Hitler in the shop. He went and stood outside on the pavement to wait for her. As she came out, he called her.

'Hitler, wait, gal, ah want to ask yuh someting.'

Hitler, who hardly ever spoke to the man, looked at him without saying anything.

'Is like dis, gal, ah hear someting an ah was wondering if yuh could put me right, so much ah gossip does spread in dis place ah was wondering . . .' Before he could finish, she stopped him.

'Ah doh know what yuh on about but yuh come to de wrong ooman. Now say what yuh have to say. Ah busy, ah have plenty tings to do.'

Madan, unsettled by this approach, looking for a way out, attempted to evoke some sympathy and kindness from Hitler.

'Ah is a lonely man, ah tired from drinking. Ah wanted to settle down an ah thought . . .' He hesitated. Hitler was bored and impatient with this conversation.

'Ah doh know what yuh on about, man, but ah have to go. Leh we talk some odder time.' Hitler walked away.

Madan hurried after her and said, 'All ah asking yuh to do is to help me find a ooman. Yuh could find plenty foh white man, what about helping yuh own kind?'

Hitler turned while still in stride and swung a punch at him, making contact with his cheek, knocking him over. A few people saw the incident and began to laugh. Hitler walked on, angered by the suggestion. For days afterwards it preyed on her mind and she, although not leaving the estate, began to think about another job.

Madan picked himself up and announced, 'Ah is one man who never fight back ooman. Ah was only putting she straight on de nastiness she was up to, de ole bitch.'

He returned to the shop, hoping to find someone to buy him a drink so he could tell of his experience. No one wanted to know. They all kept to themselves except for the small group of boys playing outside who at once started to tease him.

Later that evening he went to Eddie's room, not to gamble but to spread his news. Eddie and the others began to humour and tease him. As the cards were dealt, he sat on a chair giving whatever reason he could put together for his behaviour.

'Is like dis, she is a pretty ooman, ah cyah stan up like a man an let she go to a drunken white overseer, juss because he have money.'

'As man, yuh intend to do anyting about it?' asked Tex.

'Ah doh know, but ah sure ah one ting, if is a good prick she after, ah could give she all she want.'

106

'Leh me see what yuh have,' said Calvin, as he jokingly grabbed at Madan's crutch. Madan pulled away and fell off his chair, his fat body hitting the floor, shaking the whole barracks.

'Mind yuh break down me room,' Eddie shouted, as the rest of the room broke out in laughter.

'Why yuh doh behave like a big man?' Calvin asked Madan, who was dusting his already dirty vest and ragged short trousers. 'Ah only wanted to see what yuh got. Ah hear yuh hardly have anyting up yuh pants.'

'Go an ask yuh momma,' said Madan.

'Leave me momma outta dis. Say what yuh have to say, but keep away from mekking dem kind ah joke,' said Calvin.

'Go on telling me,' said Tex. Madan sat down once more.

'Well, first she have she husband, den is Harry an now Goddard. Ah tell yuh, de ooman cyah keep away from men.'

'Who tell yuh so?' asked Eddie.

'Who else but Harry, he is me friend,' said Madan. 'Ah doh mind if is one ah we, after all, Creole an Indian juss de same, but a white man, dat stick in me craw.'

Tex stood up and dropped his cards to the floor. He went up to Madan and held him by the back of his neck. His gold tooth glistened in the light as he opened his mouth to speak.

'Leh me tell yuh someting. It have a name foh man like all yuh,' his hands gripping Madan's nape till it hurt. 'Yuh is a mamapool man, neider man nor ooman, now haul yuh ass from here and doh come back.' He lifted Madan up and pushed him out of the door, dusting his hands afterwards and shutting the door. 'Is people like dat what does mek me vex. De man doh have no respeck foh heself or dis place.'

Madan walked home in tears. The card session was conducted with few words spoken, just the occasional voice saying, 'Deal!' or 'Rummy', and the sound of the winner collecting the coins he won, until Tex calmed down and began to carry on with the conversation. 'Slackness does trow man head,' he said. 'Look at Donald Scott. Is slackness an idleness what caused him to lose dis place an now Madan, he used to wok hard an good, now he turn stupid. Ah too better get out before ah come like dem.'

'Wey it have foh yuh to go?' asked Eddie.

'Ah doh know, but ah going. Man mus live,' said Tex. 'Ah luckier

107

dan most, me wife is Indian, she used to putting up wid hard times. We could mek ends meet until ah find someting to do, and we eh have no chirren.'

'Boy, me eh tekking dat chance,' said Nat. 'Ah go stay here until someting else come along, tings cyah remain hard for ever.'

'Is all right foh yuh to say so, yuh juss come to live here, but ah going too,' said Calvin. 'Dis place dead. It eh have no future.'

One by one, the card school left for the night. Next morning, the shop was more silent than usual. At first it was hard to pinpoint the reason for this, but as the day wore on it became evident. Madan was not around. Ramnath asked a few people who knew Madan whether they had seen him; no one had. A day passed; his door was closed, his goats left unattended. Ramnath became concerned, and told Sadhu, Sadwine's husband, about his fear that something might have happened to him. Sadhu suggested that they go and have a look. The two of them went and broke into the decaying artisan's cottage where he lived. On entering, they saw his hanging body with flies buzzing around, swinging from the rafters.

25 The burial

Ramnath and some older villagers contributed towards paying for Madan's funeral. The doctor brought in by the police examined the body and ordered the burial. Suraji came and made all the preparations, dressing and shaving the corpse. Tex felt guilty for abusing Madan and took charge of the wake; Sadhu said the prayers. Nearly everyone had mixed feelings about Madan. Ramnath, who was closest to him, was most affected, wishing he had listened to him and offered guidance instead of just the odd drink, hoping he would cease to be such a pain in the ass. Death being the final chapter, people tended to be more broadminded when speaking of the departed. The small cottage was packed with women indoors and men outside, telling stories about his life, and moving on to other things, playing cards, eating biscuits and drinking coffee. Occasionally someone would sing a few chants from the Bhagavad Gita to emphasise the sacred aspect of paying homage to the dead. Arguments frequently broke out among the card players but were quickly hushed up and the game continued.

Sankar and Sonny Boy brought their wives, who joined the rest of the women inside. The two of them sat with a small group of men under a large tree near the entrance to Madan's cottage. The men were speaking of reincarnation and suicide. In Madan's case, it was said because he took his own life he would return as a beast of burden, destined to work hard for the rest of eternity. Sankar joined in with the old proverb, 'So yuh sow, is so yuh going to get.' The talk petered out and the men turned to Sankar and Sonny Boy, making enquiries about their married life.

'My wife is a champion ooman, boy,' said Sonny Boy. 'She does wok too hard, when de day come ah cyah get she to stop. Ah glad ah togedder wid she.'

Sankar was reluctant to speak of Latchmin, although she was causing him a great deal of concern and expense. He was deeply

109

moved about what Madan had managed to do, and quickly shut out of his mind the wish to die.

A week after the marriage, she had introduced him to her cousin, a man who came almost every day to visit her. On his return from work, whenever the cousin was visiting, dinner was prepared and the evening was spent eating and drinking and having a good time. On the days when the cousin was not there, no dinner was cooked and Latchmin seemed depressed and distanced herself from him. A wake was certainly no place to speak of such troubles and all Sankar could do was to smile and say, 'She OK, boy, we getting along.'

The funeral took place the following day. As customary, no women were allowed to accompany the procession to the cemetery. The men, dressed in their everyday clothes, some of them barefoot, placed the cheap, unvarnished coffin on a bier made of bamboo and carried it, stopping from time to time for a rest and a change of bearers. As they passed through the town, some onlookers laughed and scoffed at them, calling out to others, 'All yuh, come an see a cheap coolie funeral.' To some in the procession, it felt like running a gauntlet of hostility during this part of the journey. Their heads remained bowed and the bearers sought no rest. The non-Indians were called out: 'Wha all yuh doing dey? Since when all yuh turn coolie?' Tex, Eddie and Calvin just stared back at the caller, disgusted by his attitude. Some others in the town joined in with the procession, not because they knew Madan, but in respect for the dead, and possibly to share a drink after the funeral.

When Sankar reached home, he found Latchmin's cousin there. Food was being prepared and a bottle of drink opened; before he had time to gather himself, the cousin stood up and placed an arm round his shoulder and said, 'Eh, Sankar boy, yuh come back arready, ah so glad to see yuh, leh we have ah drink.' He poured out a large shot of rum in a chipped enamel mug and handed it to him. Sankar drank it and was quickly handed another. He was given no time to settle down, and by the time he did, the alcohol had taken effect and it was time to join the party.

At times, Sonny Boy and his wife came to join them. The cousin was friendly towards both women. Sankar's cash was beginning to run out but whenever he tried to get Latchmin to spend less and save for the hard months of the rainy season, she would brush aside his concern with, 'Is all right, boy, we go manage, doh let dat worry yuh, ah go find someting.'

She was referring to the practice where those who remained in the village would search the old abandoned barracks and nearby ground for items of value left behind or buried by previous owners. The favourite place was under the zinnia beds, the sweet-smelling yellow flowers used for making garlands and in religious ceremonies. There were several small clusters planted at the front or back of these dwellings. They were all dug up, the dead flowers fading, still attached to decaying branches, flung aside, leaving a hole in the dark earth where they once stood. All round and underneath the barracks was searched; whether there were any finds, no one knew for sure. Those who looked usually left the village, never disclosing the results of their search.

One of those who searched and left was Sonny Boy's wife. Her departure was unexpected and came as a blow to Sonny Boy. On his return home one afternoon, his children told him she had gone but her clothes and other possessions were left behind as though she intended to return. That evening Sonny Boy waited and the next, but she failed to appear. He managed to gather a few men on the third day and they searched the entire estate without any success. The cousin was questioned, but he too was as shocked by her disappearance as Sonny Boy. Rumours of her sighting began to filter back to Sonny Boy. 'She ran away with a taxi driver', 'She was seen with a next man', but these led nowhere. The pond was searched, divers looking under the murky water for signs of her. About a month later, Vernon brought news that she had been seen in the town drinking in a rum shop.

'Ah wouldn tek she back if ah was yuh,' he advised Sonny Boy. 'Why mek up wid she? She drinking wid a set ah men, she like she lost all respeck.'

Sonny Boy refused to believe him and rushed to the shop. He found her just where Vernon said he would and tried to pull her out.

'Leh me go,' she said as he grabbed her arm.

'No, yuh is me wife an ah come to tek yuh home.'

'No,' she screamed, and one of the men got up and held on to Sonny Boy.

'Leave she alone, yuh don't own she.'

He looked at the man, who was powerfully built, and decided that

111

it was better to adopt a tactful approach to try to persuade Mona to return home. 'Ah give yuh a good house, we had food, come go home, gal, is all right, we go mek a good life togedder.'

This infuriated Mona even more; she was determined to remain and have nothing more to do with him. She replied, 'Look, ah never like yuh, ah leave everyting behind. Yuh buy me? Now leave me behind an go.'

Sonny Boy refused to budge and tried again, looking for words to persuade her. This time he tried to bring out the racial difference.

'Look, gal, Creole people is no good foh Indian, dey doh know how to wok, or earn money, dey always have hungry belly.'

One of the men who was with Mona shouted, 'Look, get yuh coolie ass out ah here an leave dis ooman alone.'

'Yes, get he ass outta here, ah tired living in shit an hard wok. Dis is me people, yuh hear, Sonny Boy? Ah turn Creole now, no more slaving an sweating foh me, ah tired being a coolie ooman, ah want to enjoy meself,' said Mona, as she kissed the tall, strong-looking man nearest to her. The man placed his arm around her waist and said in a strong, firm voice, 'Ah is a police, now get yuh little coolie ass from dis town before ah lock yuh up.'

Sonny Boy dropped his head, held back his tears and left. With no money even to buy a drink, he walked back the three miles to Highlands as if in a dream, afraid to face the weakness he felt inside. He could not bring himself to talk about this incident afterwards, but quickly closed it behind him and joined the daily party at Sankar's.

112

26 'It will pass'

Once the news spread of Sadwine's supposed inability to refuse an offer of a man, all types of men, rich, poor, tall, small, young and old, made approaches to her. Wherever she went, she was looked at either out of curiosity or desire. Some men were crude in their attempts to have her; others came to her home under the pretext of wanting to see her husband, especially at a time when he wasn't expected to be there.

'Is a long time ah looking at yuh, gal, give me a little business, nah?'

She took Suraji's advice and saw a doctor about the venereal disease passed on from Goddard, and stopped seeing him. Harry nailed up the loose boards in the latrine and Sadhu was beginning to behave as if he didn't want her around. He smiled more than ever. People were puzzled by this strange side of his personality; he smiled when he was angry and looked serious when he was not. Now his face had a broad grin most of the time. He was also becoming more remote; hardly a word passed between them for days, except for her telling him who came to call. She tried speaking to Hitler to try to seek a solution to the problem. All Hitler had to offer was, 'Doh worry, gal, it will pass. When dog tired looking foh bone, it does go away when it eh find none. Keep to yuhself.'

The other women all said more or less the same thing. One morning on her way to work she came across Harry and out of desperation did something she had been reluctant to do over the years they had known each other: she approached him in public.

'Ah want to see yuh,' she said, as the gang of women walked on.

He was so surprised at her stopping him that he waited for her to speak, but it still took a little time for him to find his voice.

'Ah cyah tek dis any longer,' she said. 'We have to talk. Go home an open we place, we go talk tomorrow.' His anger towards her had disappeared as soon as she had stopped him, the sun striking her dark brown face as he gazed at her in a stupor.

'OK,' he said, as she hurried to catch up with the gang.

She worked hard, cutting the burnt canes during that day, holding the cane and swinging it with more force than was required, failing to look for the still burning cinders left over from when the cane field was fired two days before. The women begged her to slow down as it was becoming difficult to keep up with her, but she paid them no mind. At a small ravine she found a mongoose, injured, trying to escape from the blaze. She stepped into the muddy water, cut off its neck and carried straight on. Her legs were now coated up to her knees in black, sooty mud, the sweat pouring out from her body making little channels as it ran down.

After cutting their allocated task, the women had to assist in loading up the carts. Sadwine's impatience with herself and every-thing around her came to the fore. She grew tired of waiting for the empty carts to pull up for loading. She saw Hitler with a group of women sitting in a dusty mound joking and laughing while they ate. She called out to her, 'Hey, gal, ah want to talk to yuh, come over here.'

Hitler shouted back, 'It eh have notting in private in dis field, yuh come here. Leh we talk. If yuh eh tired, ah is.'

Sadwine walked over and began to reproach Hitler.

'When yuh wanted me to give me body to dat stinking man, it was private, yuh used to shush, shush wid me. Now ah paying for it an all yuh eh doing notting to help me.'

'Wha yuh talking bout, gal?' asked Hitler. 'How we could help if man chasing after yuh? Ah done tell yuh arready to keep to yuhself, but, nah! Dis morning, as bold as brass, yuh stop to talk to yuh odder man, Harry.'

Sadwine threw herself at Hitler but the tall strong woman was too powerful; she held Sadwine's wrists and tried to calm her. Suraji came and placed an arm around the now weeping Sadwine and took her away to a far corner of the field and tried to comfort her.

'Is all right, gal, ah go come an stay wid yuh, doh worry, it go pass.'

Sadwine began to tell Suraji her troubles, feeling relieved that someone had made an offer of help. The long stretch of burnt brown fields were now beginning to turn green as the young canes began to sprout from the old roots. Suraji, searching for words of comfort, lit a cigarette and stared blankly at them.

'Doh worry so much, gal. De crop soon over, man would have less money, dey go stop troubling yuh.'

Hitler came over to join them and offered an apology for mentioning Harry. Sadwine looked at her, her tears mixed with sweat marks covering her face. Hitler took out a piece of cloth from her pocket and bent down and began to clean Sadwine's face. Suraji got up and went for the water she took to the fields in a calabash and brought it over. Hitler soaked her cloth, and wiped all the dirt away. The other women drew nearer and one of them drew out a comb and handed it to Hitler.

'Look how pretty she is now, no wonder all de man dem in de estate after she.' Sadwine smiled and began to feel better. This idyll was quickly broken up by the sound of the carts returning, with their drivers shouting 'Jooi, jooi,' and whipping the already running animals, urging more speed out of them.

On her way to work the following morning, Harry stopped her.

'Sadwine, ah have someting to tell yuh,' he called out as she walked with the gang. She stopped and he waited until the rest of the women had walked on.

'What it is? Yuh know ah arranged foh we to meet,' she said, expecting that he had a change of heart and wished to postpone the meeting.

'Is yuh what remove de nail from de board?'

'What yuh talking bout?' asked Sadwine.

'Is somebody done it. Ah nail up de board in de latrine an when yuh tell me yuh want to talk to me, ah went to move dem out. Dey no longer dey.'

'Yuh mean yuh didn notice dat before? Yuh sure yuh nail dem up?'

'Ah sure as day, gal, is someting wrong. We better doh meet dey foh a few days but look to see who find out about we. Ah have a feeling who it is.'

Sadwine agreed and walked on. The field where she was working was near Sankar's pen. She called out to him sitting on a rail carving a bit of wood.

'Is dat you, gal?' he answered.

'Yes, we wokking on dat field,' she pointed out. 'Suraji dey too.'

Sankar replied, 'Leh she haul she ass. Ah mekking someting here dat all ooman after.' He showed her the shape he was carving from a lump of guava wood. Even from that distance, it looked like a huge penis.

Sadwine joked, 'Wha happen, yours eh good enough?'

Sankar, taken aback, replied, 'Man eh enough foh some ah all yuh ooman, is dis size some ah all yuh want.'

Sadwine said, 'All right, boy, keep on,' as she returned to work.

The mystery of who removed the nails in the latrine was easy to solve. She knew it was her husband Sadhu, but why was hard to fathom. She long suspected he knew of her seeing Harry, but thought he accepted it as long as it was kept secret. Now she saw him in a different light. That evening and whenever she was at home, she kept a close eye on him. He moved about in silence, busying himself with little things she hadn't previously noticed. She discovered under the house little stacks of dried green mango which he never brought upstairs into the house. He gathered tools for mending small household items, although he did little repairing at home. This aroused her curiosity, making her determined to find out more.

It did not take long. She saw him standing at the back porch overlooking the latrine, and a little while later he disappeared when she was not looking. She crept silently up to the cubicle and flattened her ear against the dry, rot-ridden wood. The shock of hearing another person in there with him made her understand the reasons for the years of coolness and lack of interest in her affair with Harry. She walked around to the door; the stench of the latrine and the flies caused her more bother than usual as she pulled at the door. Sadhu called out, 'Ah in here, ah coming out juss now.' She tried Harry's section: it was locked. She called out to Harry or to his wife Meera. She called out again to Harry, who looked out of his window and came charging down the hill.

'Wha wrong, gal?'

'Is Sadhu an somebody in dey! Break down de door, ah want to see who it is.' As he was about to charge at the door, it opened and a smiling Sadhu and a frightened Meera emerged.

27 Sankar's regret

The crop was almost over. The light brown trash from the cut canes now covered the rolling hills, a slight mist of green sprouting up among them. Fiery red cane lilies grew in cool damp areas, a sure sign, according to some, that the rainy season was about to begin. This ought to have been a comfortable time of year for Sankar, a period when he should have saved enough money to tide him over the long wet idle months of the rainy season. With only a few more weeks of regular work in the offing, he found he had to borrow money to take him through the week.

Latchmin was spending more than he earned. Sankar had mixed feelings about his wife's behaviour. Reluctant to challenge her, instead he blamed the people she entertained: her cousin, Sonny Boy and his children, but all along he knew it was her and not them to blame. For she could, if she wanted, stop them from coming to the room. They were always around, Sonny Boy's children playing in and out of the room and the cousin and Sonny Boy sitting about and chatting. In the mornings before he left for work, there was always the unsightly mess from the night before, and in the evenings on returning home the chatter of the men and the sound of noisy children playing about the yard. At times he longed for the days when he, Suraji, Dano and Sakina were together but knew that circumstances had altered so drastically that it was impossible for him to seek a return to them. He could not bear the thought of facing his children after months of neglect. Latchmin was his wife now, and at least she was prettier than Suraji. If those people would just go away, their marriage might work.

Sex with Latchmin seemed impossible. Even when the cousin was not there, she usually made excuses and if they did make love at night, she always seemed to end up saying, 'A big man like yuh doh know how to control yuhself.' It was a skirmish which neither of them enjoyed. There were more peaceful moments, early in the morning when the tension between them eased and he would wake

117

and sit beside her, looking at her long black hair loose about her, his eyes travelling in the dim light of early dawn slowly up and down her sleeping form before gently placing his rough hand on her smooth thighs, moving it slowly upwards waiting for her to respond. Those were rare moments, short and swift, when although she kept her eyes closed, she turned and pressed her flesh against him and only turned away when the factory bell and the dawn chorus reminded him it was time to get up. He left for work, not wholly satisfied, uncertain as to when next she would respond, and continually asking himself whether these few moments were worth the trouble he could foresee when his wages dried up in the months of the rainy season and he could no longer afford the entertaining Latchmin appeared to enjoy.

The spending continued. His fortnightly pay was insufficient to cover the credit she ran up in the shop. Ramnath was beginning to worry; Sankar, instead of paying off the entire debt as he used to do, was now paying on account. Whenever Sankar tried to voice his concerns to Latchmin, she would dismiss them saying, 'Boy, stop worrying, is only one life yuh have to live. Which one more important, friend an family, or money in yuh pocket? Tomorrow will look after itself. Yuh lucky, yuh wokking; yuh want people to tink yuh mean?'

While working, he thought of many ways to try to stop the spree he was supporting. Sonny Boy was his friend; he would speak with him. They went back a long way, knowing each other since childhood; perhaps they could come to an agreement where his visits would be less frequent without upsetting anyone. He valued the friendship and would not have liked to stop seeing Sonny Boy altogether. However, when he returned home, Sonny Boy was already there enjoying all that was put before him. One look was sufficient to make Sankar feel it was useless to broach the subject. She had them all eating out of her hand. Sankar knew talking to her cousin was entirely out of the question; 'blood thicker than water'. He too was becoming more bold, demanding food whenever he felt hungry, asking Sankar for money to buy rum while repeating what a good husband he turned out to be. 'Boy, yuh is de bess family a man could have. Latchmin really lucky to find a husband like yuh. Ah know ting hard, but everyting will work out all right in de end, doh worry.' Sankar found this all strange, for this man knew and somehow understood what he was doing to him. He continued, 'Boy, never mind, yuh is a better man dan Sonny Boy any day. Yuh prove it. He wife run away but yours still wid yuh.'

Sankar was almost reassured, and resigned himself to the spending to make this show of a marriage appear successful. Latchmin's extravagance extended to offering Eddie, Nat and Vernon food if any was left over. Once a week, Latchmin took to going to the cinema accompanied by her cousin and, at times, when he could afford it, Sonny Boy. For the rest of the week Sankar had to put up with tales of the exploits of an Indian movie star or endless retellings of the story and discussions about the motives of the star boy and the head crook.

The reality of married life was entirely different from the way he had imagined it to be. Work in the pen was at its toughest nearing the end of the crop. Nurturing tired lame animals to carry on working, stocking up supplies and mending broken carts, the pen bustled with activity in order to meet the deadline of cropover. It was no time to have to put up with personal problems. His only hope, if he was to manage for the rest of the year, was to be taken on as part of the skeleton staff retained to look after the animals in the rainy months. Coming from another estate, his chances of being asked looked rather slim.

One Saturday night, after a meal, before drinking themselves into a stupor, he steeled himself to take action. 'Come, Sonny Boy,' he said, 'leh we tek a walk, we have a lil business to talk.'

'What kinda business, man? Is plenty drink we have here to finish tonight, leh we talk some odder time,' said Sonny Boy, sitting down on the step, about to pour himself a drink. The kerosene lamps in the four rooms of the barracks lit up four patches of ground in an otherwise dark night.

'Leh we go, man, it eh go take long. Latchmin, all yuh go easy on de drink, me an Sonny Boy have a few tings to talk about,' said Sankar, as he walked across and gently took hold of Sonny Boy's wrist. Sonny Boy looked at him in the dim light and could sense a degree of urgency in his request.

As they walked in the dark, Sankar turned to Sonny Boy and said, 'Listen, boy, is time yuh stop coming to me place all de time, ah hardly have money to keep feeding an buying drink foh all ah all yuh.'

As he said it, he knew it was the wrong approach, for Sonny Boy appeared to take it as an insult. 'Wha wrong wid yuh, boy? Indian doh refuse food to nobody. If me wife didn run off wid dat Creole man, all ah all yuh could come to me place. Wha happen? A lil bit ah money in yuh pocket an yuh want to turn miser! If yuh wasn me friend from long time, ah turn me back an go home an never once more darken yuh door. Look, man, count yuhself lucky to have a ooman like dat an behave yuhself.' A dog barked in the distance. As they turned and headed back to the room, Sonny Boy continued, 'If yuh call yuhself a man, den a little ting like dis wouldn upset yuh. If yuh have anyting to say, den tell Latchmin, doh tell me.' Sankar, defeated, fell silent.

◆

When he allowed the truth to surface, he became despairing and sought refuge in carving the large wooden penis, a symbol of what he thought was required to subjugate a woman, making her subservient to his every wish and command. He saw no quality in himself to make another human being like him. Who in their right mind would take a simple pen-worker who drank too much and only knew how to care for animals? Even Sonny Boy, with his latest fondness for Indian movies, had more to talk about with Latchmin. In the evenings after supper Sankar would sit on his step sharpening his cutlass and listening to the conversations between Latchmin, Sonny Boy and her cousin. Leaving them as the night wore on, he would say, 'All yuh all right? Ah going to sleep.' He had hoped the sight of the cutlass with its razor-sharp blade would act as a deterrent to anyone should they develop an interest in Latchmin. But they carried on, not taking a blind bit of notice.

Eddie began to tease him whenever they met, constantly reminding him of the number of times he heard Syne expelling the devil from Vernon's mother, and how he, Sankar, went for weeks without shaking the barrack walls. Sankar smiled and could only retort, when he was in a more friendly mood, 'Is not how much times, boy, but how good it is.'

'Well, ah still waiting to hear she bawl from pressure,' Eddie would reply. Sonny Boy, too, was beginning to bore him with the repeated accusations he made about Mona.

'Ah telling yuh, boy, no ooman who call sheself Indian would go wid a Creole of her own free will,' or 'Dat ungrateful wretch! All

120

ooman is de same. No matter what you give dem, if yuh doh have a big prick to go wid it, dey go leave yuh.'

This he repeated to Sankar daily. No respite, no let-up. Every day the pressure seemed to grow. Sankar longed to return to Suraji as a way of solving his problems, but she had taken to sleeping around with different men and doubts about his ability to control her as he once did crept into his mind. To live alone was out of the question: he was not prepared to face the emptiness. There was nothing to stop him from becoming a total drunkard to dull the effect of that pain.

Eddie kept up the teasing as though he wanted to tell him something, but he did not know how to broach the subject. He kept dropping little hints about, 'Yuh spending yuh money but yuh eh getting notting in return,' or ending up a crack with, 'Ah have no news to give yuh. Open yuh eyes.'

This increased Sankar's uncertainty even more. If Latchmin was unfaithful, then the fact that Eddie knew meant that eventually the whole village would be aware of the disaster of his marriage. He challenged her one pay day.

'Look, gal, ah giving yuh money, but ah hope notting going on behind me back, because ah swear ah killing yuh an whoever it is.'

Latchmin replied, 'Look, man, ah having notting to hide, ah is a big ooman, not any lil gal. If ah doh like a man, ah eh going to stay wid he.'

The fact that she was still there convinced him that she was at least faithful to the marriage. He began to arrive home at different hours, sometimes coming earlier than normal, or later. Latchmin was always there when he returned, either sitting talking with her cousin or busy preparing a meal. He could not find a suspect, least of all the cousin who always looked docile and in need of nourishment, and in Sankar's eyes was no match for him. Latchmin appeared to dislike Eddie at most times and, with her cousin always around, had little opportunity to develop anything with him or Nat. To his relief and, at first, his utter disappointment, one afternoon he returned from work and found her gone. His scream at finding his room empty of her things echoed throughout the estate, causing people to run to his room to enquire what was the matter. They saw a weeping man in a great deal of distress whose sobs were interjected with, 'She gone, she gone.'

Eddie wanted to break the news, but waited until later in the night when he had his friends over to assist should there be need to contain and comfort Sankar. He went across to fill in the details of her leaving.

'Ah wanted to come over an tell yuh, boy, but doh get vex.'

'Who she gone wid? Ah sure is dat blasted cousin.'

'No, boy, was Sonny Boy.'

Sankar screamed.

28 Sadwine

Harry's reaction to finding his wife, Meera, in the latrine with Sadhu was not what Sadwine had envisaged. She had been led to believe his marriage was a failure and she was the most important person in his life. His behaviour that afternoon was a total contradiction to all that he had said to her. He swore and shouted at the top of his voice, almost going berserk with anger. People who heard the shouting and realised what had happened broke out in uncontrollable laughter.

Sadhu said nothing; he stood outside the latrine, smiling in his usual angry way, the muscles around his bull neck swollen, betraying the rage he tried so hard to contain. Angry at the exposure of his closely guarded secret, now his reputation as a holy man was tarnished. Harry, the elegant and self-assured night watchman, had been cuckolded by the unsophisticated little Sadhu whom he had laughed at for many years.

Sadwine moved out of her house and went to stay with Suraji the same evening. Harry went to work after soundly thrashing Meera. That night he struck the bell with a great deal of force. The village was reminded of the afternoon's episode, and laughed again.

The scandal at this time of unemployment and the end of the estate broke into the droning feeling of uncertainty about what lay ahead. This night, when the bell struck, the sound brought humour into many dour households. It was the main topic in the rumshop earlier on. Comments began: 'If she was me ooman, dat could never happen,' or, to the men, 'You see, man must never believe he too strong.' In the home, the common silent acknowledgement of hard times, the unexpectedness of Sadhu and Meera raised hope – 'You see, anyting could happen.' The following morning there was even more talk. After the beating, Meera packed up her belongings and moved in with Sadhu.

Opinions were divided. Some believed Harry got what he deserved, that Sadhu was the most cunning of the lot. Some questioned his morality as a holy man, but the majority wondered about when it all began. It was agreed that Meera had to have someone to look after her. 'She will do all right wid Sadhu, since he have money, a plot ah land an somewey to live.' Some believed that Harry got what he deserved for fooling around with another man's wife. Others thought it was perfectly natural for the couples to change partners for the sake of harmony but, on further consideration, thought Harry received the raw end of the deal because he ended up with Sadwine.

'He have a big man to fight against: Goddard. He eh finished wid Sadwine yet. Harry never like to share. Look what he do Meera.'

'Boy, dat Sadwine, ah doh know how she could put up wid three man. Who woulda believe a woman like dat could be man-crazy?'

Days passed and the situation became more entangled. Women in Sadwine's gang, under strict instructions from their husbands, refused to speak with her. Suraji and Hitler were the only ones who carried out any conversation, encouraging her to continue working and to ignore the women's attitudes. Harry was heard during the night but it was his custom wherever he was to hide away in the disused factory and avoid any contact.

One night Sadwine was still awake, tossing on the floor of Suraji's hut, when the bell struck nine. The children and Suraji were already fast asleep; Sadwine could hear restful breathing coming from their corner of the darkened room. She crept over and searched the darkness for Suraji, careful not to wake the children; she shook her gently and, as she woke, whispered 'Ah cyah sleep, gal. Come outside, ah want you to help me do someting.'

The two women crept slowly outside and went and sat in the kitchen. Embers were still glowing in the fire. 'Ah have a plan to talk to Harry, gal, ah want you to go wid me,' said Sadwine.

'Yuh must be crazy, gal, me cyah go to de factory at dis time, he might get vex.'

'Ah cyah go on, de rest ah de ooman stop talking to me, every man eider pretending to hate me or odderwise trying to put demself to me. Ah jus cyah let dat happen widout trying to do someting about he an me. Ah telling yuh de truth, is Harry alone ah was wid all dis time.'

'Ah know dat, gal,' said Suraji as she lit a cigarette.

The village was very silent. Stars shone brightly in the heavens. Highlands, Sanwine's home since marriage many years ago, that she had grown to love, had turned against her. She looked at her last remaining friend, making out her features as the glow from the cigarette flickered on her face. Highlands, where she found love, made sacrifices, and gave help to those in need, was now forcing her to confront a man hiding in a disused factory.

'OK,' said Suraji, 'leh me go an find a dress, we going.'

'Bring out mine foh me too, it hanging on de wall next to wey ah does sleep,' said Sadwine.

The two women went to meet Harry. Walking swiftly through the darkness, ignoring the threats of barking dogs, they reached the factory. Sadwine called out at the entrance, 'Harry!' Her voice echoed through the silence.

'Who is dat?' a voice replied, a torch flashing to where the two women stood.

'Is me, Sadwine.' The light grew closer and the tall, solemn figure emerged from the depths of the building.

'Wha yuh doing here so late?' he asked, surprised by her coming to see him.

'Why yuh never try to see me after de trouble, boy?' asked Sadwine.

Harry looked at the time on his pocket watch, and switched off the torch. The darkness was almost frightening in the dismal old building.

'Ah doh have notting to say,' said Harry. Suraji stepped out into the open yard, leaving the two of them to sort out their affair in private. She could hear heated exchanges coming from where they stood. Suddenly she heard Sadwine screaming and rushed into the factory, where she saw Harry beating her with the stick he carried. Grabbing it from him, she screamed at him to stop it. The fast-breathing Harry swore at them. 'Get dat fucking ooman away from here, she done ruin me life,' he shouted as he walked back into the darkness. Suraji picked up Sadwine, who was bleeding from a crack on her skull; the blood pouring out mingled with the tears flowing uncontrollably from her friend's eyes. Suraji dressed the wound when they returned home, never once saying anything which might cause further upset. Sadwine urged her to go to bed after a while, saying she needed to be alone to try and sort things out.

The following morning, Goddard stood on his balcony, giving out the tasks for the day. He made an announcement before he set out to distribute the work.

'I need a new night watchman. Harry gave in his notice and left.'

Some of the men rushed forward to volunteer. He chose Nat, the youngest and fittest. Then, as usual, the men were dealt with first. They were given the bulk of the work while the women stood around under his balcony, waiting to see whether there was work for them or not. His pink face and brown eyes stared down at them. The gang understood his intention; it was always like this whenever he wanted a reward for giving out work.

They walked off. Only Hitler remained and went up to see him.

'I heard noises in the factory last night. When I looked out, I saw the three of them, my watchman, the little short one, and Sadwine. I want Sadwine today.'

Hitler came down the stairs and walked over to the gang. It was only two weeks before the work would end. Everyone was trying to earn whatever they could get. Without Sadwine, the men would get it all. The women were standing under a young samaan tree next to the scale house. She walked straight over to Sadwine.

'Gal, we know how yuh feel.'

Sadwine immediately excused herself. 'Not dis morning, gal, ah sick.'

Some women protested immediately. 'Leave she alone, if she doh want to go with dat stinking man, den we jus will not wok. Leh him give it all to de man dem.'

Suraji stood next to Sadwine, and said to Hitler, 'She eh able today, gal, Goddard's bad luck. Leh we go home.'

Sadwine looked at the gang of women. Some of their husbands worked in the men's gang. Their earnings were barely enough to feed the family. Those without husbands had it even harder. Two weeks of work not guaranteed, and then they had to find somewhere to live in the rainy season. The future looked bleak. She remembered the events of the last few weeks, giving up her comfortable home, sleeping on Suraji's floor, of last night's beating by Harry. She turned and walked towards the steps. As she was about to climb them, she turned to the women and said, 'Ah is a whore foh all ah we. All yuh going to get wok.'

She climbed the stairs and walked bravely into Goddard's flat. He looked slightly puzzled when he saw the tall, dark-skinned Indian woman, her head tied with a band, and her dress stained by the burnt cane she worked in. She went and stood next to his books. She pointed to the section where work was entered and said, 'Put dem down. Mek sure we have plenty wok until cropover.'

Goddard turned and looked over the gallery; he called Hitler. 'Next to the men, see their driver and start working on Field 16.'

He walked back inside the flat, past Sadwine, heading into the kitchen, and returned with a bottle of rum and two glasses.

The following morning, Sadwine went to Suraji's shack and collected her things and returned. All she was now interested in was earning money. Their affair came out in the open. They drank, made love, hardly ate during those final weeks. The maid had been dismissed, and Goddard in his more sober moments would say, 'We're going to have a good winding-up party, you and me.'

No one who depended on the estate for work said anything about Sadwine. The village gossipped, but never challanged. The one person to do so was Sankar. He called out, when he returned from work one day, 'What yuh doing up dey, gal, yuh turn white lady?'

Sadwine, who was drunk and leaning wearily against the bannister, cried, 'Yes, boy, ah turn white ooman. Coolie ooman does wok too hard.'

Sankar stood back and looked at the unkempt Sadwine.

'Wha happen, coolie man not good enough foh yuh?'

'Nah, boy, all yuh cyah do notting. All yuh good foh is drinking rum an all yuh never have money.'

'Wait, yuh go see. When ever ah catch yuh, ah have someting in me back pocket just foh yuh.'

Sadwine said, 'Whatever yuh have, boy, keep it. Go an look foh yuh wife and give it to she.'

Sankar put his hand slowly towards his back pocket and pulled out the large wooden penis he had carved so patiently. His eyes filled with rage, he held it out like an Olympic runner.

'One day, ah go give yuh dis an den yuh go understand why she run away. Is dis she did fraid.'

Sadwine scoffed, 'Yuh could keep dat make-up ting, boy, ah have de real ting up here.'

29   The closedown

The estate finally closed. Goddard's employment was over. Sadwine behaved as if nothing had happened, having lived with Goddard for the past two weeks. He gave her several hundred dollars when he left, to find somewhere decent to live. She moved back with Suraji, intending to leave in a couple of days, but the time stretched on, especially as she had a more likeable drinking partner in Suraji. She still intended to leave Highlands.

Sankar came around once or twice, but was chased away. He openly showed her the wooden penis, which he took with him everywhere. In the rum shop he showed it around to the other drinkers, stating it was the right size for a woman. Some men laughed; others just turned away. He had used this particular party piece ever since his wife ran off. He continued to occupy his barrack room, though space was now available in Good Intent. Some of the seasonal workers had left, and he was kept on at the pen at a reduced rate of pay. His drinking became worse. Sakina and Dano were left to do as they liked. Both of them stopped attending school, spending their days roaming the estate or in Sankar's room when he was at work. Eddie and Nat sometimes gave them food. They tried to talk to him about the children but he paid them no mind. It was now August. It was raining heavily, mud was everywhere. The days were hot and humid. The barracks were beginning to fall apart. Many were gutted to build shacks off the estate on nearby rented land.

The card school began to drift away. Tex, Calvin and the others left for the town. Vernon and Nat were looking for somewhere to move to. Vernon's mother was the problem. Eddie encouraged him to leave her behind, saying, 'Boy, yuh modder will be all right, she have a man to look after she.'

◆

Bracken grew in the cane fields and the pond was covered with vine. Sankar drank and brooded over his prick. He sat one afternoon, looking at the rain falling from the darkened skies. It was leaking throughout the barracks and everywhere was wet. He longed for a drink. It was pay-day; he had money enough for a bottle if he wanted. The children were playing quietly at the back of the room. He decided to brave the weather, placed a sugar bag on his head and ran to the shop. He called for a nip and drank it in three gulps. His courage rose. For weeks, he wanted to do what he now set out to do, but had always managed to restrain himself. Today he decided it had to be done. He blamed the length and size of his penis for all the unsatisfactory relationships he had had with women. He could think of no other reason to sustain a satisfactory relationship with a woman other than to dominate her with the size of his penis. He had developed a strong desire for Sadwine, fuelled by the reputation she now had as a woman who could not say no to a man. But at the thought of his inadequacy, he decided to insult and threaten her rather than let her know how he felt. Today, he was going to show both women how he felt, and since the children were in his room, he knew they were alone and he could do as he liked.

He left the shop and headed for Suraji's shack. He kicked open the door, brandishing his cutlass. Suraji and Sadwine were on the floor, asleep. They jumped up when they heard him enter. He was soaked from head to toe, his shirt sticking to his skin.

'Today, ah go show all yuh who is man.'

Suraji was quick to respond and shouted at him to leave. She felt dull and tired as both women were sleeping off the effects of the last bout of drinking. Sankar struck menacing blows in the air with his cutlass. The air swished as the blade swung in different directions. Sadwine appeared cool and tried not to panic. Suraji bawled for help at the top of her voice, but the falling rain was too heavy for anyone to hear. Sankar hit her with the flat part of the blade on her shoulder. She fell against the wall of her shack and collapsed in a heap. Sadwine bawled and begged him to stop. He pushed her to the floor and, holding the blade across her neck with one hand, lay down beside her. He took out the wooden penis from his back pocket and tried to insert it into Sadwine with her bloomers still on. She was too frightened to call out. He had already killed Suraji, so she thought, and he might kill her. The bruising and pain were almost unbearable

129

while Sankar, breathing heavily kept repeating, 'Yuh bitch! Yuh like man? Take prick!'

He began to tire as he tried to increase the pressure on Sadwine. When he thought she was sufficiently subdued, he dropped the cutlass. With one hand now free he started to rip her cotton dress off her. She screamed. He punched her face. She forgot all fear and pushed him off her with all her might. Sankar fell back. She quickly got up and grabbed the cutlass. He looked up and saw the weapon in her hand, poised to come down over him. 'Doh do it, doh do it,' he pleaded, as this time it was Sadwine who was threatening to cut. From the floor, he saw the anger on her face. She kept pushing back her dishevelled hair from her face and resting her hand where she was punched.

'Boy, ah could cut yuh down like a piece ah cane.'

Sankar drew back and sat against the wall. He glanced at Suraji lying on the floor, and for the first time wondered whether he had killed her. He knew she was struck with the side of the cutlass but nevertheless looked to see if there was blood. Sadwine kept her eyes firmly fixed on him as she considered what her next move ought to be. She shook with anger but seeing the shivering, wet Sankar crouched before her, she began to feel pity. 'Look at de trouble he put heself in if Suraji dead.'

Then her eyes rested on the wooden penis lying on the floor and pity disappeared. She struck out with the side of the blade as he had done. She caught him on his shoulder, knocking him sideways. She kept swearing as the blows connected with his body. The house shook, and an enamel cup fell from the table. She raised to strike him this time with the sharp edge of the cutlass but Suraji came to just as Sadwine was about to come down on his cowering body, and shouted, 'Stop!'

Sadwine's arm froze in mid air. Sankar screamed, 'Oh God! Oh Ram!' curling his body away from her. Sadwine turned her head. The cutlass dropped to the floor as she rushed to Suraji. Sankar uncurled but remained crouched against the old wooden wall.

'God, yuh lucky she eh dead,' said Sadwine as she helped Suraji sit up.

'Go an get me some water. Ah go be all right.'

Sankar kept his head bowed. He was now completely sober. He thought of grabbing the cutlass and making a run for it. No one would believe two women who were often drunk. Before he could move, Suraji picked up the cutlass, her face swollen on one side. Their eyes met, hers cold, dark, grey, sending a clear message to his, deep brown, and frightened: 'Doh try to run.' Sadwine came hurrying back with the water. Suraji drank most of it before speaking. The heavy rain turned to drizzle.

It was now dusk. Dogs began their evening chorus from underneath the houses. Sankar crouched, wet and shivering, before the two women.

Suraji's neighbour, Savitri, had been sitting in her front gallery, looking at the rain, when she saw Sankar with his cutlass in his hand staggering down the muddy track towards Suraji's shack. She called out to him, but he didn't hear her. Her eyes followed him to the back of Suraji's shack where she saw him kick the door and enter. The rain was pouring down; lightning flashed, thunder rolled. Savitri was not on speaking terms with Suraji, forbidden by her husband to go across while this drinking spree carried on with Sadwine. Nevertheless, when she saw Sankar enter in this manner, she felt something was bound to happen. She became afraid at the thought that he was going to harm the two women. She felt she had to do something to stop it from happening. Through the rain she ran to the shop to get help. People were sure to be there drinking or just sheltering.

The rain had eased by the time she arrived. Eddie and Nat followed her back to Suraji's, but, on reaching there, they found the drama had already taken place. A few more people came afterwards. Some were in favour of calling the police, to arrest Sankar for attempted murder. He sat in a corner, listening to their threats without saying a word. He hid his head between his knees. Sadwine and Suraji insisted that it be taken no further, except that Sankar move out of the area.

'He could go wey he wok,' someone suggested. Another said, 'He can go where he like, once he doh show his face here again.' Someone asked about the children. 'No,' replied Suraji, 'de chirren remaining wid me.'

Eddie, who up till now had restricted his involvement to a condemnation of Sankar, backed her up. 'De chirren have to stay wid Suraji. Of de two drinkers, he is de worse. Is better if he live near wey he wok. Dey have more people down dey to look after he.'

The attention then turned to Sadwine. Some began to blame her

131

for all this trouble, saying, 'Is all she fault, drinking an carrying on wid every kinda man in de place. Look at poor Sankar, she even have he head crazy. She should go too, if yuh ask me.' She looked into the crowd, pleading for some understanding, but no one came forward. Suraji tried to say something. She was shouted down. 'Yuh better keep yuh ass quiet, before yuh too get chase away.'

Eddie spoke out. 'All yuh, one person leaving here is enough. All yuh eh satisfy wid Sankar? All yuh want more?'

Next day, Sadwine left by bus.

30 'Let her rest'

Sadwine got off the bus near the shanty town. It was a ramshackle collection of huts made from old pieces of tin, disused boards and cardboard, covered over with rusty galvanised iron. Indian-owned shacks had prayer flags on poles outside their entrances to show they had held a prayer ceremony before squatting. There were no drains, running water or sanitation. The toilets were holes dug in the ground, scarcely made private by even more flimsy building materials.

A railway track bordered the shanty town on one side, separating it from the mangrove growing in the sea. On the other side was the fence dividing the neatly trimmed hospital grounds from this derelict land where the shanty town stood. People had to walk far to collect water from the standpipe in the fish market beyond the hospital.

Sadwine found sleeping space in an Indian-owned shack. The man and his family were also displaced cane workers who now ran a roti-stall and allowed her to remain in exchange for working in their tiny hovel of a kitchen. She made vegetable curry and the dough for the roti. Before Sadwine came, the wife did all the cooking. Now she helped sell in the stall. Her husband wasted little time in making approaches to Sadwine. She tried to keep out of his way, but one day he burst in and grabbed her.

She foolishly took the advice of a neighbour, and went to the police to report the rape. When she revealed where it happened, the policeman laughed and said, 'I wish all you people would stop coming here to bodder we. I tired hearing of rape and thieving and fighting down dere. Get out dis station!'

She had nowhere to go, and no one to turn to. She stumbled down the hill and when she reached the edge of the shanty town, she dried her face and went into the rum shop. She headed straight in, something she had never done before, and called for a petit quart of strong rum. She drank it in one shot and rested her face on the counter. A man sitting on a stool nearby put his arm around her and

133

said, 'Come here, mai. Come an sit wey it more quiet.' She did not resist as he led her to a table near the wall. She looked up and saw a smiling face; whether it was the effect of the alcohol or the soft look in his eyes was hard to say, but she felt a certain tenderness towards him, something she hadn't felt since leaving Highlands. The man called for more rum. Sadwine drank more than she had ever done before. Her head felt light and her troubles seemed to pass away. Several other men gathered round the table. She began singing and dancing to make them laugh and when she felt too tired and weary, she rested her head on the man's shoulder.

She came to in a disused railway shed. Several men were still waiting to have their turn with her. An old tramp found her later that night, bruised and battered, blood trickling from her mouth. He covered her with a sugar bag and rested her head on an old rag. He lit a flambeau and wiped the blood from her mouth. He called for help and several other tramps came over. They tried to take her to the hospital, lifting her up by her arms, but she was too weak to walk. Several of them suggested remedies, like 'Give her sugar water,' and 'Let her rest.' They seemed easier options, and that was what they did.

When Sadwine recovered she remained with the tramps, sleeping under the shed near the sea until the railway authorities drove them out. It was a small group of men and women who went through the town begging for money and food. Each one looked out first for themselves, and then for the others. What they shared was the begging and a desire to forget their past. It was only the present that mattered, the next drink or the next bite of food.

Once they were driven away from the shed, they went to sleep under the verandah of the nearby rumshop. Each night they would creep back with their dirty old sugar bags, spread them on the concrete floor and sleep for a few hours before they were woken up by the shopkeeper. He opened the side door of his shop and shouted a warning.

'Eh, all yuh get up an go from here. Ah going to open de shop just now.'

The old hands knew that he was going to wash down the verandah with disinfectant before opening the shop. Those who failed to move got soaked. One rainy morning, Sadwine failed to move. She had drunk heavily the night before, and slept through the warning. She was soaked, and stiff and shaking. The tree where she sought shelter gave her little protection.

She developed a fever. The next night she went back under the shop, still wet and shivering. A few tramps offered her meagre bits of food but she was too weak to eat. The following morning, as he was about to throw the water, the shopkeeper stopped when he saw this emaciated ghost-like figure lying shivering on the concrete floor. The tramps huddled around her begged him to stop.

'Boss, don trow de water! Dis ooman sick, she need a doctor.'

He sent word to the hospital, and an ambulance came and picked her up, but they were too late to save her. The hospital informed the shopkeeper of her death, and asked whom to notify. He found out that all they knew was her name, Sadwine, and some said she came from a sugar estate. No one claimed her body, and she was buried as a pauper.

31 Finale

Windows slammed open or shut, depending on the direction of the wind. No more care, concern, laughter or heartbreaks in the cottages and barracks. The end of the final crop had come, and with it, after Sankar left, the trickle of departures turned into a rush. Highlands was no more. Goddard left to be replaced by a caretaker, Hamza. It was Goddard who recommended him. The machinery in the factory was sold off bit by bit. The tall bamboo encircling the pond swayed and danced in the strong winds. Birds, now left undisturbed, whistled and flitted from branch to branch, and tall bushes grew wild.

Some said the estate was founded during the days of slavery; others insisted that it originated with indentured labourers who were brought after 1850. Some had remained on the island, while others took up their return passage to India. In 1917, the last boat brought its passengers, coolies bound for estates everywhere, Highlands getting its quota. These people, the passengers of the last boat, remained; there were no return passages. Whatever this estate had taken to build in terms of pain, suffering and displacement was of no account when the end came. The children of the last boat were adrift again.

The voices at the end fell silent, like Harry's bell; the card school, whose voices had been heard arguing or laughing long into the night, was no more. Eddie was left alone in his room to find new ways to survive.

Sankar remained working at Good Intent. Alone in his room there, he took to drinking and, with no one to cook and take care of him, he died a most tragic death, kicked by a mule when he tried to apply medication to the animal's sore leg. Mr Rooplal said his resistance to withstand injury was low, but he was also slow to move away from the kicking animal. Some compensation was paid to his children, Dano and Sakina. Suraji used it to buy a plot of land just outside the estate where she built a new shack, almost a carbon copy of the old, on stilts which allowed her chickens to roost underneath.

The silence spread from the centre outwards to the boundaries. The shop closed. The only remaining sounds on the once noisy compound were of Syne trying to chase the devil from Vernon's mother, who continued to sing and dance. Hamza's instructions were to allow no one to remain. Syne and Vernon's mother simply refused to leave, and failed to take heed of his notice to quit. Where they all went was difficult to record. Tex and most of the card school moved to the town. Vernon slept in a makeshift room underneath his barber's shop. Nat simply moved on. Hitler and her gang left with their husbands to look for employment wherever they could find it. Sadhu and Meera had left together. Suraji allowed Eddie to erect a shack on her land. Hamza, the caretaker, moved in to Donald's house to keep watch over the abandoned Highlands.